Election Commission of India

Election Commission
of India

Institutionalising Democratic Uncertainties

Ujjwal Kumar Singh and Anupama Roy

OXFORD
UNIVERSITY PRESS

OXFORD
UNIVERSITY PRESS

Oxford University Press is a department of the University of Oxford.
It furthers the University's objective of excellence in research, scholarship,
and education by publishing worldwide. Oxford is a registered trademark of
Oxford University Press in the UK and in certain other countries.

Published in India by
Oxford University Press
22 Workspace, 2nd Floor, 1/22 Asaf Ali Road, New Delhi 110 002

ISBN-13 (print edition): 978-0-19-949425-5
ISBN-10 (print edition): 0-19-949425-8

ISBN-13 (eBook): 978-0-19-909696-1
ISBN-10 (eBook): 0-19-909696-1

Typeset in ScalaPro 10/13
by Tranistics Data Technologies, Kolkata 700 091
Printed in India by Replika Press Pvt. Ltd

Contents

Figures and Tables

Figures

Tables

Acknowledgements

We would like to acknowledge, jointly and individually, the support, help, and assistance received from persons and institutions in the course of writing this book. Research for this work began and remained in its incipient stages while we were based at the Nehru Memorial Museum and Library (NMML), New Delhi, as a fellow (Ujjwal), and in the Centre for Women's Development Studies, New Delhi, as a senior fellow (Anupama). We acknowledge the support that we received from both these institutions.

We are grateful for the feedback received on the papers presented on different aspects of the Election Commission of India at conferences at the following universities: North Carolina State University, Raleigh, USA; University of Michigan, Ann Arbor, Michigan, USA; University of Delhi (Department of Political Science), India; Sun Yat-sen University, Guangzhou, China; the University of Macau, China; and Sungkyunkwan University, Seoul, South Korea. We are grateful to David Gilmartin, Robert Moog, E. Sridharan, Daniel Tokaji, M.P. Singh, Milan Vaishnav, and K.K. Kailash for their comments and suggestions which helped us sharpen the arguments. We are beholden to Wendy Singer for sharing with us a poster issued by the Ministry of Information and Broadcasting, most likely in 1991, and for providing us a digital copy of the same. We thank Yamuna Shankar for permitting us to reproduce three cartoons by Shankar in the first chapter of this book.

Our fieldwork in India was supported by the University Grants Commission Department of Special Assistance (UGC DSA) programme of Centre for Political Studies, Jawaharlal Nehru University (JNU), New Delhi, India, and the Faculty Research Fund, University of Delhi, India. We are grateful to Ajay Naik, Sanjiv Kumar, Vivek Kumar Dewangan, Priyanka Sinha, Sanjay Kumar Agrawal, and Shahid Iqbal for sparing time to talk to us about their experiences in conducting elections at the district and state levels.

Subarta Singh's help in going through the microfilm collection at the NMML, New Delhi, for newspaper sources pertaining to the first general election in India, is acknowledged with deep gratitude. We appreciate the help provided to us by Shipra and Aditya with the preparation of the images for publication. We would also like to thank the editors at Oxford University Press for steering this manuscript at all stages.

We thank our family, in particular, Anatya, our son, for his encouragement and love. This book, as always, is for him and for our parents—Lalita Sinha, Usha Roy, Krishna Ballabh Sinha, and Siddheshwari Narayan Roy.

Abbreviations

AASU	All Assam Students Union
ACLU	American Civil Liberties Union
ADR	Association for Democratic Reforms
AIMIM	All-India Majlis-e-Ittehad-ul Muslimeen
BDO	Block Development Officer
BEL	Bharat Electronics Limited
BJP	Bharatiya Janata Party
BLO	Booth-Level Officer
BSP	Bahujan Samaj Party
CAG	Comptroller and Auditor General of India
CAO	Chief Agricultural Officer
CBDT	Central Board for Direct Taxes
CEC	Chief Election Commissioner
CEO	Chief Electoral Officer
CIC	Central Information Commission
CII	Confederation of Indian Industry
CPI(M)	Communist Party of India (Marxist)
CRPF	Central Reserve Police Force
CSDS	Centre for the Study of Developing Societies
CWC	Congress Working Committee
DBT	Direct Benefit Transfer
DC	District Collector

DEO District Electoral Officer
DEW Delhi Election Watch
DGP Director General of Police
DSDV DBT Seeding Data Viewer
ECI Election Commission of India
ECIL Electronics Corporation of India Limited
EIC Economic Intelligence Council
EMB Electoral Management Body
EPIC Electronic Photo Identity Card
ERO Electoral Registration Officer
EVM Electronic Voting Machine
FIU Financial Intelligence Unity
HAVA Help America Vote Act
IEC Information, Education and Communication
IMDT Illegal Migrants Determination by Tribunal
IPC Indian Penal Code
IPS Indian Police Service
JD(U) Janata Dal (United)
LWE Left-Wing Extremism
MLA Member of Legislative Assembly
MP Member of Parliament
NBW Non-bailable Warrant
NCRWC National Commission to Review the Working of the Constitution
NERPAP National Electoral Roll Purification and Authentication Programme
NOTA None of the Above
NRI Non-resident Indian
NSA National Security Act
NVD National Voters Day
OBC Other Backward Class
PIB Press Information Bureau
PURE Proper Urban Electoral List
RJD Rashtriya Janata Dal
RPA Representation of the People Act
RTI Right to Information
RWA Resident Welfare Association

SC	Scheduled Caste
ST	Scheduled Tribe
SVEEP	Systematic Voters' Education and Electoral Participation
UIDAI	Unique Identification Authority of India
UPA	United Progressive Alliance
VVPAT	Voter-Verified Paper Audit Trail

Introduction

On 23 October 1951, a couple of days before polling began for the first general election in India, *The Hindu* carried a brief editorial comment titled 'The Ensuing Elections', with two subtitles—'Great Experiment in Democracy' and 'The Working of Adult Franchise'. The editorial claimed that the election 'should be a simple affair to most of its voters'. All that the voters had to do was 'to walk a short distance up to the polling booth on the polling day', which would be a holiday, and vote twice, first for the State Legislative Assembly and then for Parliament. The only difficulty that the voters could face, as the editorial saw it, was in deciding whom to vote for, especially in places where canvassing by political parties and contesting candidates had been carried out vigorously enough.[1]

On 25 October 1951, Shyam Saran Negi of Kalpa village in Kinnaur district of Himachal Pradesh became the first person to cast a vote in independent India. Polling for Chini and Pangi constituencies in Himachal Pradesh took place two months before the rest of India due to the snowbound conditions and inaccessibility of these regions in the winter months. Then a school teacher in a primary school run by the government and part of the polling party,

---

[1] 'The Ensuing Elections,' *The Hindu*, 23 October 1951, p. 4.

Negi recalled several years later that ballot boxes had to be transported on mules on the difficult mountainous terrain. The polling booth was set up at a height of close to 10,000 feet above sea level inside a primary school building in the village. The *Times of India*, on 26 October 1951, reported the first polls in independent India on its front page, alongside the news of 'Britons flocking to the ballot box'. The outcome of the polls in England would have decided whether Attlee's Labour Party government continued for another term or was replaced with Churchill's Conservative Party. Precise figures of the record-breaking turnout in the United Kingdom were available to the newspaper from London. The same was, however, not the case for the Indian state of Himachal Pradesh. The details of how the polling fared in the two tehsils of Chini and Pangi on the northern borders of India would be known much later. The means of communicating with the tehsils were almost none. There was one wireless link, and that was used for official purposes only.[2]

The first general election earned the epithet of having been 'an act of faith',[3] not simply because a newly independent country embarked on the unfamiliar course of *universal* adult franchise, but also for putting in place an electoral machinery to make the exercise of franchise possible for one-and-a-half-million voters spread across a vast country, most of whom had never voted before. Sukumar Sen, the chief election commissioner of India (henceforth, CEC) who steered India's first general elections, recounted the challenges faced by the Election Commission of India (ECI) in transporting ballot boxes and other polling material in the hilly areas of Manipur and Tripura. Sen had to secure the support of the hill chiefs for obtaining a supply of porters to help negotiate the tough and unfamiliar terrain. In return, the CEC promised those who helped, by way of reward, a red blanket and a gun license. While elephants were used to carry the polling material in some parts of Tripura, in most cases, the polling parties reached their polling stations on foot, walking a distance of about 40 miles in

---

[2] 'Polling in Himachal,' *The Times of India*, 26 October 1951.

[3] Referred to as such by Sukumar Sen, the first CEC, in Election Commission of India, *Report of the First General Election of India 1951–52*, Vol. I. New Delhi: Election Commission of India, 1955, p. 16.

a day.[4] In Rajasthan, on the other hand, the vast stretches of desert areas without road, telegraph, and telephone connections compelled the ECI to arrange high-powered army vehicles for the Barmer and Jalore districts in particular, to help the polling parties commute from one place to another. The army vehicles, however, often got stuck in the sand, putting the poll schedule at risk. As a result, all the jeeps of the state government were procured, pooled together, and sent to the two districts to enable the completion of the polling programme according to schedule. In districts like Jaisalmer and Jodhpur, the polling party moved on camels. A large number of camels were hired for the purpose and each polling party moved like a caravan carrying polling parties and equipment.[5] Almost 2,500,000 steel ballot boxes were used, in addition to the 111,095, wooden boxes that had to be made subsequently because the number of steel boxes fell short. All of this cost the Government of India Rs 12,287,349.[6]

Since the first general election held in 1951–2, the electorate in India has increased manifold. The electoral data for 2014, released by the ECI on 14 February 2014, showed more than 4.7 times increase in the size of the electorate, which grew from 173,212,343 million electors in 1951–2 to 834,101,479 million in the 16th general election held in 2014.[7] Apart from the magnitude of the elections, their nature has also changed, alongside changes in the political field and innovations in electoral strategies and campaigns of political parties. The multiple ballot boxes used in the first general election have given way to electronic voting machines (EVMs) and election campaigns have transformed through the use of technology by political parties, aided by campaign managers and computer professionals. The door-to-door contacts by political parties have been supplemented by 'informed' and 'mediated' campaigns through print and electronic

---

[4] Election Commission of India, *Report of the First General Election of India*, pp. 127–8.

[5] Election Commission of India, *Report of the First General Election of India*, pp. 127–8.

[6] Election Commission of India, *Report of the First General Election of India*, p. 98.

[7] Press Information Bureau, 'Comparison of the Indian Electorate from 1951–1952 to 2014'. ECI, Government of India, 23 February 2014.

media. Innovations in campaigns, which give the illusion of direct personal contact, have abounded. One such experience of a journalist is narrated below:

> I was rushing to attend Govinda's press conference; the Bollywood star had joined the Congress party and was going to take on BJP stalwart Ram Naik.
>
> I just about managed to climb onto an Andheri-bound local train when my cell phone rang. It was an STD call. When I answered, the first word I heard was a polite '*Namaskar*'.
>
> '*Namaskar*', I replied, pleasantly surprised.
>
> '*Main* Atal Bihari Vajpayee *bol raha hoon* [This is Atal Bihari Vajpayee speaking]', said the voice again. I almost dropped my phone. The voice, however, continued without a pause. '*Aap ko tatha aapke parivar ko meri subkamnayein* [My best wishes to you and your family]. *Paanch saal pehle aapne mujhe seva karne ka mauka diya tha, uske liye dhanyavad* [I would like to thank you for the opportunity you gave me five years ago]'.
>
> I listened intently.
>
> Even as he talked about national development and his plans for the future, my mind began to churn with questions I had always wanted to ask the prime minister.
>
> Then he said, '*Dhanyavad* [Thanks]', and, before I could say a word, disconnected. I grinned at myself; I had been fooled by the BJP's latest campaign innovation—a recorded message from the Prime Minister.[8]

The 2004 elections witnessed a flood of voice messages from the then prime minister, Atal Bihari Vajpayee, seeking the voters' cooperation in 'taking India to greater heights'. The *Business Standard* reported the 'shock' of scores of persons who answered a call on their cell phone or the landline service provided by Bharat Sanchar Nigam to hear the unmistakably recognisable voice of the prime minister greeting them.[9] Ten years later, the electoral victories of

[8] Vijay Singh, 'Main Atal Bihari Vajpayee Bol Raha Hoon,' *Rediff.com*, 29 March 2004. Available at http://www.rediff.com/news/2004/mar/29diary.htm; accessed on 11 June 2013.

[9] Meghdoot Sharon. 2004. 'Namaskaar, Mein Vajpayee Bol Raha...,' *Business Standard*, 3 April. Available at http://www.business-standard.com/article/economy-policy/namaskaar-mein-vajpayee-bol-raha-104040301085_1.html; accessed on 11 June 2013.

the Bharatiya Janata Party (BJP) in the parliamentary elections of 2014, and the *mahagathbandhan* of the Rashtriya Janata Dal (RJD), the Janata Dal (United) (JD(U)), and the Congress in the Bihar State Assembly election in 2015, were attributed to the innovative use of technology. The 3D hologram rallies of Narendra Modi in 2014 and an active media cell that planned campaign strategies for Nitish Kumar in 2015—responding swiftly and cleverly to all the moves in the BJP's electoral campaign—generated an altogether new mode of political communication and electoral competition. These and other changes generated demands and precipitated new challenges for efficient and effective electoral governance, commensurate with electoral integrity and democracy.

A Trusted Institution

When the framers of the Indian Constitution provided for an institution to 'superintend, direct and control' the conduct of elections, they had envisaged a body that would be sufficiently empowered to discharge the responsibility of making the exercise of franchise free and fair. The ECI has since emerged as a significant public institution within the shared space of democracy in India. Surveys carried out from time to time have revealed the steadily increasing credibility of the ECI as a *trusted* institution. The increase in credibility owes to the ways in which electoral governance has unfolded over the years, and the manner in which the electoral system has been constituted through enduring rules and structures ensuring procedural certainty. The nature and magnitude of the task that the ECI has been performing may be seen as having contributed substantially to the consolidation of the electoral system. As an institution primarily responsible for administering and regulating the electoral space, between and through each electoral trial, the ECI has enhanced this faith over the years. The general election in 1977, for example, in which the ECI exhorted the voters to 'vote without fear', brought it into the public arena as an institution entrusted with carrying out the constitutional mandate of 'fair and free' elections.

A myriad of other commissions that exist in the institutional space of democracy in India, including the National Commission for Minorities, the National Commission for Scheduled Castes, the

National Human Rights Commission, and the National Commission for Women, to name a few, are statutory bodies. They owe their origins to specific laws of Parliament and have as their objectives the protection of the rights of particular groups. The ECI, on the other hand, quite like the Comptroller and Auditor General of India (CAG), has a different *pedigree*, which generates a different set of rules of recognition and source of validation of its authority.[10] Provided for by the Constitution of India (Article 324), the ECI does not owe its existence to an Act of Parliament. Moreover, as the Constituent Assembly Debates discussed later would show, the ECI is an institution that captures the essence of the foundational moment of the *transformative* in which the Constitution of India was being framed.[11] Unlike other administrative institutions of the state such as the police, the bureaucracy, and the army, which embodied the structural logic of 'rule and authority'—as residuum of the colonial state, considered essential for the expansion of the ruling apparatus of the state and the sustenance of its structural field of 'power-effects' (Scott 1995)—the ECI signified the fundamental rupture that independence from colonial rule was to bring in its wake. While a number of innovations in the Indian Constitution emulated or borrowed from other constitutional cultures, there was no existing precedent for an election commission of the kind envisaged by the makers of the Indian Constitution. Indeed,

---

[10] Ronald Dworkin (1967: 17) refers to the 'pedigree' of rules, that is, the manner in which they were adopted or developed as distinct from their content. The pedigree of rules constitute the standards by which they may be distinguished from spurious legal rules, which lawyers and litigants wrongly argue are rules of law, and also from other social rules, which are generally clubbed together as moral rules, that the community follows, but which are not enforceable through public power.

[11] The camaraderie of equal citizenship was at the heart of the constitutive moment, of the transformative that characterised the new constitution. A central motif of this transformative moment was conscious and meticulous sequestering from the past and the refiguration of this relationship. In order for the present to transform itself into a constituent moment, a remarkable capacity for being autochthonous in the domain of law and government, and liberation from domestication and subjection—which characterised colonial rule—had to be displayed (Baxi 2008b; P.B. Mehta 2010; Roy 2010; U. Mehta 2010).

as an expression of the transformative in the republican constitution, the ECI embodied 'the desire to have a democratic process that was institutionally entrenched, and yet at an arms-length [sic] from party-political or governmental interference' (McMillan 2012: 187).

For some time now, especially since the 1990s, the ECI has come to be seen as a *regulatory* body (Rudolph and Rudolph 2001), which performs a set of rule enforcement functions pertaining to the conduct of elections, sustaining, thereby, the vitality of the electoral system. The ECI is often also seen as an institution that reflects the sagacity of the Constituent Assembly in providing a constitutional body that would guard against self-destructive tendencies within democracies, by performing an oversight function over the conduct of elections (Thiruvengadam 2017: 138). Devesh Kapur and Pratap Bhanu Mehta (2005) have referred to the ECI as a 'referee institution', while James Lyngdoh (2004), former CEC, sees the ECI performing the role of a 'pitcher'. The expansion and entrenchment of the ECI's powers of administering elections have, however, been considered a case of administrative overreach and the 'stretching' of its 'regulatory powers' (McMillan 2012; Katju 2009). Questions pertaining to the limits of the ECI's powers and its relationship with other institutions, especially Parliament and the Supreme Court, have subsequently been posed.

In this work, we argue that the ECI can be seen as performing a range of overlapping functions, not all of which are regulatory. The *pedigree* of the ECI's powers, which can be traced to Article 324 in the constitutional architecture, has paved the way for the Article becoming, through authoritative judicial interpretations, a repository of the ECI's powers. These powers buttress the autonomy of the ECI, making it also a site of contestation between the ECI and different political regimes. The roots of this contestation lie in the paradoxical location of the ECI in the institutional space of democracy in India, whereby it is located in the domain of the state, but is driven by the logic of democracy. The logic of democracy specific to the ECI can be seen in the various strands of the debate in the Constituent Assembly, which were concerned with the objective of achieving democratic citizenship. Yet, this logic was also animated by an enduring quest for *procedural certainty* to ensure the *democratic uncertainty of electoral outcome*, and *electoral integrity* to assure the *deliberative content* of election.

The Paradox

The ECI adopted a practice of preparing a narrative report of every general election from 1951–2 to 1983, after which it presented annual reports to Parliament. Neither of the two practices was a requirement in the Constitution of India or the election law. Sukumar Sen considered this a desirable exercise even when there was no constitutional or statutory requirement, so that an exhaustive record of the ECI's experiences in administering elections could be prepared and preserved for later reference, especially for the purposes of suggesting reforms in election law and procedure.[12] The narrative reports of the ECI present a documentation of the bureaucratic practices that accumulated within the legal and institutional frameworks of electoral governance. These documents may well be read as comprising a record of the activities of the ECI, expressing the ways in which institutions acquire an identity through a replication of bureaucratic practices associated with the processes of structuration within the state. At the same time, however, in its narrative reports, the ECI may also be seen as invoking a *distinctive* identity, wherein it stands apart from the political apparatus of the state—as an institution of a different kind—as the custodian of the right of the citizens to vote and an enabler of informed political choice among citizens.

It is this paradox of its location in the bureaucratic apparatus of the state, while simultaneously entrusted with the responsibility of enabling regime change through a democratic exercise of political choice by the people, that makes the ECI an institution difficult to study. The ECI is at one level indistinguishable from the logic of the state. As part of the institutional ensemble of the state, it exhibits the characteristics of a governmental institution wearing the 'masks' of secrecy, inaccessibility, and authority. As an integrated and hierarchically organised bureaucratic structure, it shares with the state the pursuit of legitimacy through the electoral domain. Yet, the ECI is part of the logic of democracy—the quest to build and consolidate a democratic polity and buttress it against collapse—by providing the institutional mechanisms through which consent can be mobilised

---

[12] Election Commission of India, *Report on the First General Election of India 1951–52*, Vol. I.

democratically, and dissent leading to regime change, registered peacefully.

The difficulty of studying the ECI emerges precisely from its ambivalent location in the public domain where it contributes to the 'structuration' of the state but does not form part of what Abrams (1988: 58) calls the 'palpable nexus of practice and institutional structure centred in government'. All public institutions represent aspects of state power—procedural and formal, as well as ideological, hegemonic, and regulatory—to different degrees, in their structure and functions. They also reflect the conflict that lies at the heart of modern politics between 'universal ideals' such as, civic nationalism, individual freedoms, and equal rights, and 'particular demands' of cultural identity, which call for group-differentiated treatment on grounds of vulnerability, backwardness, or historical injustice (Chatterjee 2004: 4). This conflict, according to Chatterjee (2004: 5–6), represents the transition that occurred in modern politics in the course of the twentieth century 'from a conception of democratic politics grounded in the idea of popular sovereignty to one in which democratic politics is shaped by governmentality'. In the introduction to their anthology on public institutions in India, Devesh Kapur and Pratap Bhanu Mehta (2005) argue that institutions and institutional processes are committed to procedures as well as the formal and informal incentives within state institutions. It is through procedural effects that the state is 'constituted and enabled to act on the one hand and constrained in its powers and capacities on the other' (Kapur and Mehta 2005: 2). While all three—Chatterjee, Kapur, and Mehta—concur that contestations in the domain of the state shape institutional forms and practices, they differ on their emphasis on the modalities through which state power is exercised in institutional practices. If Chatterjee makes a distinction between the exercise of sovereign power and governmentality, Kapur and Mehta emphasise the way in which institutions act rationally and weigh their choices by taking into consideration the consequences of adopting a particular course of action for the durability of the institution.

While institutional functions contribute to state formation and accumulation of state power, institutions themselves acquire distinctive attributes corresponding to their functions through an amalgamation of clusters of rules and practices that endure over a period of time. The identity and effectiveness of institutions may be drawn entirely from these rules irrespective of who interprets and executes them, but they may also be dependent on particular individuals who are in charge of deciding how the rules are to be interpreted and implemented. The larger political field, its composition, and nature of social and political contests that constitute it—in other words, the complex set of inter-relationships in which an institution is located—also have an impact on an institution's identity and character. The ECI as an institution may be seen as functioning in a field where a range of institutions 'interlock' in a constellation, within which they function with 'a broad-based ideological vision', but also 'compete with each other, set bounds on what other institutions can do [and] interpret directives in their own way' (Kapur and Mehta 2005: 1).

It may be argued that the ECI has emerged as a significant institution within the common political space of democracy in India. In no small measure, this is a consequence of the institutionalisation of procedural certainties embodied in the functioning of the ECI. The statutory framework and institutional structures of electoral governance are entrenched in specific socio-historical contexts and substantive notions of democracy, with philosophical underpinnings of self-determination, freedom, and equality, all of which make for democratic participation and the generation of a democratic public space. These statutory and institutional arrangements provide enduring frameworks of democratic governance that unfold in the institutional space of modern democracies. In order for rules and procedures of electoral governance to be conducive to democracy, they should generate 'a radical uncertainty about authority', through certainty of procedures. Such procedures give momentum to participation and release processes of critique that 'question and subvert all certainties of social life', 'lead to mobilisation of new groups', 'unsettle existing power relations', and 'produce new openings'.[13]

Procedural Certainties and Democratic Uncertainties

The electoral process involves much more than periodic acts of voting and competition among political parties for forming the

---

[13] Pratap Bhanu Mehta (2003: 11) writes about the transformations in the meaning of social existence that the right to vote brings.

government. It involves some enduring rules and institutional structures that must ensure procedural certainty. Procedural certainty may be regarded as the principal task of electoral governance, helping to ensure the democratic principle of uncertainty of electoral outcome. The constitutional provisions and legislative enactments that govern the conduct of elections in India along with the institutional structures, it may be argued, have been designed to achieve this democratic principle. Electoral governance, comprising a set of related activities, including the making, implementation, and adjudication of rules, determines the framework within which the substantive uncertainty of democratic elections unfold.[14] Mozaffar and Schedler (2002) consider the principle of procedural certainty an essential principle of electoral governance in societies which are 'democratising' as well as for long-sustaining democracies where elections have become 'routine', in order to make them 'credible'.

Apart from laying down the rules of the electoral game and organising them for procedural certainty, questions concerning whether the procedures designed to conduct elections are appropriate and can achieve the objective of democratic uncertainty of elections are also important. The evaluative frameworks for assessing the appropriateness of procedures concern themselves largely with the question, whether or not and to what degree, the integrity of the electoral system is maintained. Comparative studies of 'electoral integrity' have identified certain standards to evaluate the degree of integrity

---

[14] Shaheen Mozaffar and Andreas Schedler (2002: 8) elaborate on these functions as follows:

Rule making: 'choosing and defining the basic rules of the electoral game', namely, rules of electoral competition including the delimitation of constituencies, choosing one system of election over the other, electoral time table, rules governing franchise, voter registration etc.;

Rule application: 'organising the electoral game' including the registration of voters, candidates, parties etc., registration of election observers, voter education, voting, counting and reporting;

Rule adjudication: 'certifying election results and resolving disputes' including admission of complaints, processing of cases, and publication of implementation of rulings.

achieved by electoral management bodies (EMBs).[15] Electoral integrity scholars have emphasised 'standard of procedural performance' as an important index for studying electoral practices in what they call 'electoral authoritarian' (Schedler 2006) regimes as well as established democratic regimes (Birch 2011; Elklit and Reynolds 2005; Kelly 2012; Norris 2004, 2014; Norris, Frank, and Coma 2014). While arguing that electoral malpractices, voter fraud, poll violence, and voter intimidation characterise electoral authoritarian regimes (for example, in Cambodia, Thailand, and Afghanistan, among others) and sustain the control of the ruling incumbent on elections despite the establishment of democratic institutions, these studies draw attention to the fact that malpractices may occur at different stages of the election cycle and may also emerge from non-electoral political processes in specific regimes. Even among established democracies, there may be a range of challenges to electoral management despite the existence of 'good rules'.[16] Pippa Norris (2015: 3), for example, argues that lack of integrity may have 'serious consequences', including diminishing legitimacy for political authorities and erosion of people's satisfaction with democracy and confidence in political parties and Parliament itself—all of which accumulate and result in 'weaker electoral turnouts'.

The evolution of a democratic public sphere in India involved multilayered struggles, not merely for rolling back colonial rule but also for a civil society founded on principles of horizontal *camaraderie* rather than ascriptive hierarchies. Apart from the bewildering complexity of society, to which the electoral process adapted itself, it was the deep-rooted hierarchies that denied large sections of people access to the political process, which had to be dismantled by electoral democracy.

---

[15] These standards include an assessment of whether or not they are able to achieve: legitimacy, independence, impartiality and fairness, integrity and honesty, transparency and openness, efficiency and effectiveness, professionalism, and public service. See the trilogy of books by Pippa Norris (2014, 2015, 2017) on the theme.

[16] As set out in the agenda for research on 'the hidden challenges of electoral integrity' by Margarita Zavitskaya and Holly Ann Grant, for the European Consortium for Political Research. Available at https://ecpr.eu/Events/SectionDetails.aspx?SectionID=403&EventID=94; accessed on 20 December 2017.

Elections, however, are not by themselves exhaustive of the democratic imaginary of a people, nor can democracy be reduced solely to elections. Yet elections and electoral processes generate expanding circles of participation and unleash potent forces of democratisation that realise, simultaneously, the ideological and cultural plurality of a democratic polity and the egalitarian potential of democratic citizenship. Thus, when one talks of elections, one is alluding not merely to the periodic act of consent that the people express at the polls, but the entire gamut of historically emergent political and socio-economic configurations in which elections are embedded, and also the new upsurges and churnings they produce. In different historical periods, struggles by different sections of people have brought about a progressive universalisation of franchise, mobilising and politicising large sections of people who were excluded from the political community on account of their race and sex or for being workers and colonised subjects.[17] The issue of franchise became important in the context of

[17] Representative government was not the proclaimed aim of the British until the First World War (1914–18) when it became imperative to seek the support of educated and politically articulate sections of Indian opinion. Mahesh Rangarajan (2001) argues that before the First World War, Lord Ripon's Minute in 1883 laid down the foundations of a limited system of franchise in the municipalities and cities. In many cases, though not in all, all these were first initiated in the 'white town' or the Civil Lines where the British military and civilian officials lived. Over time, a measure of self-government was introduced, through the various reforms Acts in 1909 and 1919, and then under the Government of India Act of 1935. With each legislation, more Indians were allowed political participation, though in a diluted form. Even in 1946, only one-third of the people in British India had the right to vote in the provincial elections. The vote was an even more restricted privilege in the polls to the central legislative body, with 90 per cent of the people having no rights at all. Schedule Six of the Government of India Act 1935 laid down the qualifications for electors based on property, taxation, and literacy criteria. Under the Act of 1935, the right to vote was extended to more women. Earlier, the proportion was 1 woman to 20 men. After the Act of 1935, the proportion became 1 woman to 5 men in an electorate of 35 million voters. Women over 21 years of age could vote, provided they fulfilled one of the following requirements: they were literate, were property owners, or were wives and widows of men having property. Thus, only literate and married women of 21 years of age and above were eligible to vote, provided they had the same

the promise for constitutional reforms made by the British government towards the close of the First World War. Montagu's announcement in the House of Commons on 20 August 1917, promising the gradual development of 'self-governing institutions' and the 'progressive realisation of responsible government', was instrumental in shaping demands for broadening the existing contours of franchise. Organised activism by women for the right to vote and for representation in the promised self-governing bodies emerged in this context.[18]

The end of colonial rule in India involved putting in place rules and procedures, including those of political participation, which were consonant with the democratic imaginary of a sovereign people. These rules and procedures, in order to be democratic and to be seen as such, had to be universal. The framework of rules and procedures of elections, along with the principle of universal franchise, may be seen as constituting a system of just and fair elections, by incorporating a principle of formal equality. The unfolding of the electoral system and electoral processes in India has thrown up debates over the institutional forms and processes of elections. The questions—who votes and who represents whom—have been fraught with contests and have become significant not only for understanding electoral democracy but also democracy as a system of the government and a value system of which equality and freedom are foundational principles.[19]

---

property and taxation qualifications as men. In the absence of ownership rights and widespread illiteracy, only a minuscule percentage of women constituted the electorate. The Act enfranchised 6 million women and 29 million men. See Kaur (n.d.: 372). See also Enskat, Mitra, and Singh (2001: 561).

[18] See for details of women's struggles around franchise and the meaning of the vote in the colonial context, 'The Womanly Vote and Women Citizens in Late Colonial India', Roy (2005: Chapter 4).

[19] In a paper presented at the international symposium on Global Dimension of Electoral Democracy, ECI golden jubilee celebrations, E. Sridharan (2001b) suggested that for electoral democracy to be truly a liberal democracy in which all, including the poor and ethnic and regional minorities, are able to effectively compete in elections with non-trivial chances of getting elected, several other conditions have to be met. These include, the rule of law, constitutional constraints on executive power, an independent judiciary, independent media, civic pluralism, and strong commitment to

In this context, the phenomenon of the 'second democratic upsurge' has become a significant counterpoint to proceduralism and 'design fallacy', directing attention at the *processes* whereby the democratic will of the people *is able* to make itself effectively manifest, breaking free from the historically entrenched hierarchies that inhibited political participation by large sections of people. The significance of the democratic upsurge lies in the possibilities of participation that the electoral process offers, irrespective and independent of the design of the electoral system, transcending thereby, what has been called 'simple minded belief in the magic of design'.[20] On the other hand, the churning process or the democratic upsurge through the electoral process has also shown that the universal body of voters envisaged in the Constitution makes itself effective in practice through a multiplicity of identities, as groups struggle to construct political (ruling) majorities.[21]

The principles and rules for electoral governance and the frameworks of inclusion in the institutional design of elections were deliberated upon and finalised in the Constituent Assembly. The various subcommittees of the Constituent Assembly engaged in discussing different aspects of the draft Constitution were concerned that the act of voting, as well as the statutes and institutions which enabled it, should manifest these fundamental premises of democracy. The Fundamental Rights Subcommittee unanimously accepted the principle of universal adult franchise, bolstering the right to vote by the

---

fundamental freedoms entrenched as basic rights. These basic rights are equality before the law, the right to freedom (of belief, faith, opinion, assembly, association, movement, residence, occupation, speech, publication, demonstration, and petition) and rights of religious, racial, ethnic, linguistic, cultural and other minorities.

[20] The belief in the magic of design has been explained by Yadav (2000: 298) as the belief that 'all we need to do in order to solve any problem is to change the law. Once we have the right design, the desired set of consequences will follow as a matter of course'.

[21] What is again important to note here, as Sunil Khilnani (2004: 59) points out, is that 'such identities were less significant for four decades after independence, and then surged into national politics, showing how much they are creations of modern politics, and not residues from the past'.

principle of equality.[22] While endorsing the principle of equality, debates within the Constituent Assembly also showed a concern for building institutional and statutory safeguards within the constitution for the protection of the weaker sections of society. It is not surprising, therefore, that it was the Minority Rights Subcommittee that insisted upon *a neutral and autonomous election commission* implementing *unified rules* to conduct 'fair and free' elections (Shiva Rao 1968: Vol. II, 251).

The concern for inscribing institutional safeguards for promoting equality and protection against discrimination prompted B.R. Ambedkar to move an amendment in the Constituent Assembly envisaging 'a radical change' in the proposed system. The amendment moved by Ambedkar on 15 June 1949 preferred an *integrated* election commission instead of separate commissions for the Union and the states. The members of such a commission were to be appointed by the president, *to centralise* the election machinery in the hands of *a single commission* to be assisted by regional commissioners, not working under the provincial government, but under the central government. For Ambedkar, a centralised and integrated election machinery was necessary because of the 'mixed nature of population' in some provinces and the fear that 'racial or linguistic minorities' may be excluded from the political process.

Reports of certain provincial governments that were 'managing things in a way' that excluded from the electoral rolls 'those people who did not belong to them either racially or linguistically' had been brought to the notice of the drafting committee and the central government, corroborating Ambedkar's fears.[23] A 'Note on Election Commission' prepared by the secretariat of the Constituent Assembly had already underscored the need to *consider carefully* 'what machinery should be employed to implement the direction of the Constituent Assembly':

---

[22] Provisions for elections formed Part XIII of the Draft Constitution, but the right to franchise was not mentioned in it. On 16 June 1949, the Constituent Assembly adopted the principle of universal adult franchise in the form of an amendment (Article 289B). By an earlier amendment (289A), voting right was granted irrespective of religion, race, caste, sex, or any of them (*Constituent Assembly Debates*, 1949. Vol. III, pp. 438–9).

[23] *Constituent Assembly Debates*. 1949. Vol. VIII, pp. 904–6.

This is a matter which requires careful consideration.... Without going into the question of the correctness or otherwise of these allegations, it may be readily conceded that the machinery to be set up to direct and control the elections under the new Constitution should be an impartial and independent body, above party politics, so as to avoid giving ground for any suspicion of the nature mentioned.[24]

The decision to adopt a centralised and integrated authority rather than a decentralised body was unlike the 'federalist tendencies' that the Constituent Assembly had shown otherwise (Sridharan and Vaishnav 2017: 421). The decision was clearly to buttress the institution against local structures of power and biases, while also preserving the democratic principle of diversity. The Constituent Assembly hoped to do so through an election machinery that was *not only integrated* but would also *implement unified and universally applicable rules*. If elections were to be universal, free, and secret, they should be controlled by an *independent* commission. Freedom from control by the Executive was, therefore, as the 'Note on the Election Commission' demonstrates, a primary concern:

As a matter of fact, this matter was dealt with by the Fundamental Rights Committee. The Fundamental Rights Committee came to the conclusion that no guarantee regarding minorities or regarding elections could be given if the elections were left in the hands of the executive of the day. Many people felt that if the elections were conducted under the auspices of the executive authority and if the executive authority did have power, as it must have, of transferring officers from one area to another with the object of gaining support for a particular candidate who was a favourite with the party in office or with the Government of the day, that will certainly vitiate the free elections which we all wanted. It was therefore unanimously resolved by the members of the Fundamental Rights Committee that the greatest safeguard for purity of elections, for fairness in election, was to take away the matter from the hands of the executive authority and to hand it over to some independent authority.[25]

[24] Shiva Rao, B. 1968. 'Note on Election Commission by the Secretariat of the Constituent Assembly', 14 May 1949, Vol. IV, p. 538.

[25] Shiva Rao, 'Note on Election Commission by the Secretariat of the Constituent Assembly', p. 539.

The Advisory Committee recommended to the Constituent Assembly that the granting of voting rights to all citizens at the age of 21, the conduct of voting by secret ballot, and the superintendence and control of elections be left under an election commission (Chaube 1973: 102–6). To guarantee this, a separate chapter dealing with elections was included in the Constitution of India (Part XV, Article 324–9). On the basis of this endorsement, the draft Constitution of February 1948 provided in Article 289 for a Union Election Commission, whose personnel would be appointed by the president, and an election commission for each state, whose personnel would be appointed by the governor, *to superintend, control, and direct the elections*. The decision to include the right to vote in the chapter on Elections, rather than in the chapter on Fundamental Rights in the Constitution, has remained a 'puzzle' on which the Constituent Assembly Debates throw scant light (Thiruvengadam 2017: 139–40). In addition, the decision on the manner in which the CEC was to be appointed continues to linger as another puzzle, having ramifications for the autonomy of the ECI. Within the Constituent Assembly, questions were raised on the power of the president to appoint the CEC, raising the concerns that the power could be used in future by a prime minister to appoint a 'party man' as the CEC. Shibban Lal Saxena sought to 'entrench the position of the Chief Election Commissioner' and Ambedkar conceded by moving an amendment that laid down that the president's power to appoint the CEC would be subject to a law of Parliament (Thiruvengadam 2017: 150–1). The Constituent Assembly felt that if elections were to be universal, free, and secret, they should be controlled by an independent commission that would implement certain unified principles and, at the same time, remain autonomous of the political power structure.[26] An important principle that emerged from the entire gamut of debates surrounding the nature of electoral institution was the principle of independence of the ECI in carrying out its duties. The fact that the ECI derives its authority directly from the Constitution and not from any elected government gives it considerable autonomy of action.

---

[26] *Constituent Assembly Debates*. 1949. Vol. III, pp. 438–9.

Article 324: Superintendence, Direction, Control of Elections

Articles 324–9 of Part XV of the Constitution provide the legal–constitutional framework for conducting elections. In keeping with the dominant sentiments of the Constituent Assembly, a single centralised body, the ECI, has been entrusted with the task of 'superintendence, direction and control of elections'. Article 324(1) of the Constitution provides that the ECI shall superintendent, direct, and control the preparation of the electoral rolls, and conduct of elections to Parliament, to the legislature of every state, and of elections to the offices of president and vice-president.[27] As far as the officers of the commission are concerned, the Constitution lays down that the commission shall consist of the CEC and other election commissioners, their numbers being fixed by the president from time to time. The appointment of the CEC and other election commissioners is made by the president, subject to the provisions of any law made by Parliament [324(2)]. In case any other election commissioner is appointed, the CEC acts as the chairman of the ECI [324(3)].

To assist the CEC in the discharge of his responsibilities before each general election to the Lok Sabha (House of People) and elections to the legislative assembly of each state, the president may, after consultation with the ECI, appoint regional commissioners [324(4)]. The president, or the governor[28] of a state, when requested by the election commissioner, makes available to the election commissioner or to a regional commissioner the staff necessary for the discharge of the functions conferred on the ECI by clause (1) [324(6)]. The conditions of service and tenure of the election commissioners and regional commissioners are determined by the rules made by the president, subject to the provisions of any law of Parliament [324(5)]. The Constitution also provides that the CEC

[27] The words 'including the appointment of election tribunals for the decision of doubts and disputes arising out of or in connection with elections to Parliament and to the Legislatures of States' were omitted by the Constitution (Nineteenth Amendment) Act, 1966, Section 2.

[28] The words 'or the Rajpramukh' were omitted by the Constitution (Seventh Amendment) Act, 1956, Section 29 and Schedule.

shall not be removed from office except in the manner laid down for Supreme Court judges. The conditions of service of the CEC, it lays down, 'shall not be varied to his disadvantage after his appointment'. An election commissioner or a regional commissioner cannot be removed from office except on the recommendation of the CEC [324(5)].

Of the six articles in Part XV, Article 324 may be seen as providing the framework for the composition and functioning of the ECI. The six clauses in the article assure the independence of the commission and, at the same time, leave room for a degree of political control by Parliament. As discussed in the earlier section, the decision to centralise the election machinery under a single central election commission was taken after protracted discussions in the Constituent Assembly in the committees and subcommittees. When the draft articles came up for discussion in the Constituent Assembly on 15 June 1949, however, there was opposition to the appointment of election commissioners by the president. Apprehensive that appointment by the president would, for all practical purposes, mean appointment by the prime minister and the ruling regime, Shibban Lal Saxena proposed an amendment saying that the appointment of the CEC should be subject to confirmation by a two-thirds majority in a joint session of both Houses of Parliament.[29]

Ambedkar agreed:

With regard to the question of appointment, I must confess that there is a great deal of force in what my friend, Professor Saksena, has stated that there is no use of making the tenure of the Election Commissioner as fixed and secure one if there is no provision in the Constitution to prevent either a fool or knave or a person who is likely to be under the thumb of the Executive [sic]. My provision—I must admit—does not do anything to provide against nomination of an unfit person to the post of Chief Election Commissioner or the other Election Commissioners.[30]

Ambedkar proposed an amendment, whereby the appointment of the CEC and the ECI was to be made by the president 'subject to any

[29] *Constituent Assembly Debates.* 1949. CAD, Vol. VIII, pp. 907–8.
[30] *Constituent Assembly Debates.* 1949, Vol. VIII, p. 928.

law made in that behalf by Parliament'. Article 324(2) contains this decision of the Constituent Assembly.[31]

The powers of the ECI relating to direction and control of elections are limited by the fact that all its orders must be traceable to some existing law,[32] and cannot violate the provisions of any law including state acts.[33] Article 324(1) has, however, been interpreted liberally, and the ECI is seen as having residual powers relating to the electoral process, in areas unoccupied by legislation,[34] empowering the commission to issue all directions necessary for the purpose of conducting smooth, free, and fair elections for this purpose.[35] Article 325 is seen as crucial in so far as it gives direction regarding the nature of the electoral rolls to be prepared by the ECI in the discharge of its function under Article 324 of preparation of the electoral rolls. Article 325 gives effect to the constitutional principle of equality of the citizen-voter, stating that no person can be excluded from the electoral roll on grounds 'only of religion, race, caste, or sex'. Accordingly, there is a single general electoral roll for every territorial constituency for election to the Lok Sabha and the Legislative Assemblies of states and no person is ineligible for inclusion in any such roll or can lay claim to be included in any special electoral roll for any such constituency on grounds only of religion, race, caste, sex, or any of them.[36] Article 326 lays down the principles of voter eligibility, stating that elections to the House of the People and to the legislative assemblies of states are to be on the basis of adult suffrage. Every citizen of India who is not less than 18 years[37] of age on a date fixed by a law made by Parliament,

---

[31] There has been no attempt by successive governments to make a law as per Article 324(2) on the manner of the appointment of election commissioners. But there have been several reports and recommendations by committees and political parties on electoral reforms, including the appointment of election commissioners.

[32] *Kanhiya v. Trivedi*, AIR 1986 S.C.111 (para 16).

[33] *Dasappa v. Election Commission*, AIR 1992 Kant.230 (para 10).

[34] *Kanhiya v. Trivedi*, AIR 1986 S.C. 111 (paras 13, 16).

[35] See D.D. Basu (1996: 1061–2), especially for judgments pertaining to the limits on the powers of the ECI.

[36] *Poudyal v. Union of India*, (1994) Suppl.(1) S.C.C. 324 (para 206) C.B.

[37] Substituted by the Constitution (Sixty-First Amendment) Act, 1988, Section 2, for 'twenty-one years'.

and is not otherwise disqualified under the Constitution or any law made by Parliament on the ground of non-residence, unsoundness of mind, crime or corrupt or illegal practice, shall be entitled to be registered as a voter at any such election. Article 327 gives Parliament the power to make provision with respect to elections to legislatures.[38] It is significant that the power of Parliament has been made subject to 'provisions of [the] Constitution'. This would imply that the legislative powers of Parliament over elections are circumscribed by other provisions of the Constitution, including Article 324, which makes the 'superintendence, direction and control' of elections, the primary, and also primarily the responsibility of the ECI.[39]

Article 328 similarly gives the legislature of a state the power to make provision with respect to elections to the state legislature.[40] Article 329 puts important bars to interference by courts in electoral matters relating to (a) the validity of any law relating to the delimitation of constituencies or the allotment of seats to such constituencies, made or purporting to be made under Article 327 or 328, and (b) election to either House of Parliament or a state legislature. Only an election petition presented to an authority in the way provided by law by the concerned legislature can question the latter. Under the Representation of the People Act (RPA), 1951, the power to decide election disputes vests in the high courts with a right of appeal to the Supreme Court. Disputes relating to the election of the president or vice president are, however, to be settled by the Supreme Court. It may not be incorrect to say that Articles 324 and 329 are the sources of

[38] Parliament may, from time to time, by law make provisions with respect to all matters relating to, or in connection with, election to either House of Parliament or to the House or either House of the Legislatures of a state including the preparation of electoral rolls, the delimitation of constituencies, and all other matters necessary for securing the due constitution of such House or Houses.

[39] *Sadiq v. Election Commission*, AIR 1972 S.C.187.

[40] Subject to the provisions of the Constitution the legislature of a state may, if a law by Parliament on these provisions does not already exist, from time to time, enact laws with respect to all matters relating to, or in connection with, the elections to the House or either House of the Legislature of the State including the preparation of electoral rolls and all other matters necessary for securing the due constitution of such House or Houses.

the ECI's autonomy, giving it superiority over Parliament in matters concerning the administration of the electoral domain at all times (through Article 324), and over the judiciary in election time (through Article 329).

Subsequently, numerous court decisions have had their impact on determining the scope of the ECI's powers. A 1978 judgment by the Supreme Court interpreted the expression 'superintendence, direction and control' as empowering the ECI to act in contingencies not provided for by law and to pass necessary orders for the conduct of the election, for example, whether a repoll should be held or not at a particular polling station,[41] to decide disputes relating to the allotment of symbols to political parties,[42] to recognise such parties or to derecognise them for such purpose,[43] to determine the status of rival groups within the same party, and to determine the effect of merger or separation of parties for this purpose.[44] While the determination of citizenship is outside the jurisdiction of the ECI, when revising an electoral roll according to the procedure prescribed by the RPA, 1950, the electoral authorities have the power to decide individual cases raising questions of citizenship.[45] Also, if the ECI is of the opinion that having regard to the disturbed conditions of a state or a part of it, free or fair elections cannot be held, it may postpone the elections.[46]

The last-mentioned function of the ECI drew attention in the latter half of 2002, throwing up a situation of conflict between the ECI and the National Democratic Alliance (NDA) government, especially its primary constituent, the BJP. The event in question was the dissolution of the Gujarat Vidhan Sabha on 19 July 2002, and the appointment of the erstwhile Chief Minister Narendra Modi as the caretaker chief minister till the time fresh elections could be held. The BJP hoped that under Article 174 of the Indian Constitution, which required that six months should not lapse between the last sitting of the Legislative

---

[41] *Mohinder* v. *Chief Election Commissioner*, AIR 1978 S.C. 851 (paras 91, 114–15, 121). For details, see Basu (1996: 1061).

[42] *Sadiq* v. *Election Commissioner*, AIR 1972 S.C. 187.

[43] *S.S.P.* v. *Election Commissioner*, AIR 1967 S.C. 898.

[44] *S.S.P.* v. *Election Commissioner*, AIR 1967 S.C. 898.

[45] *Inderjit* v. *Election Commission*, AIR 1984 S.C. 1911 (para 4).

[46] *Digvijaya* v. *Union of India*, (1993) 4 S.C.C. 175 (paras 12, 14).

Assembly in one session and the date appointed for the first sitting in the next session, and given that the last sitting of the last session of the Gujarat Assembly was on 3 April 2002, election for the new assembly should be held before 3 October 2002. It is to be noted that at the time of this dissolution, the state of Gujarat was still recovering from the communal violence that left thousands of Muslims dead and homeless. While Narendra Modi survived the demand for his resignation, the attempt to dissolve the Vidhan Sabha was being seen as a bid to draw political benefit from the sensitive political situation. The BJP asked for early elections, but the opposition parties, as well as some other parties that were part of the ruling combine, feared that elections in Gujarat could provoke further violence and demanded president's rule in the state. Between 31 July and 4 August 2002, the ECI sent a team of officials to Gujarat followed by a visit from the entire three-member commission to decide on a possible time frame for elections in Gujarat. Contrary to the Gujarat government's argument that only 12 out of its 25 districts were affected, the ECI observed that almost 80 per cent of the state's administration remained unstable, and 154 of the 182 constituencies in the state were affected by riots, which included 151 towns and 993 villages.[47] Of the 121 relief camps, only 8 camps were still functioning, but the inmates of the camps that had been shut down had not returned to their homes. On 3 August 2002, the State's Secretary, administration, informed the ECI that 'neither the Revenue Department nor the Collectorate have any system to track down the inmates of the camps once they have left without returning to their home'.[48] The large numbers of riot-affected persons who were displaced or missing made the task of preparing the electoral rolls that was underway impossible to accomplish at an early date. In a detailed order dated 16 August 2002, the ECI accepted that under Article 174, elections should normally be held before the expiry of six months. This, however, was not possible in Gujarat because the state was still in turmoil, the electoral rolls were not ready, and the electoral machinery needed reinforcements.[49] The ECI concluded that in the

[47] See, for details, Rajeev Dhavan, 'The Supreme Court Reference,' *The Hindu*, 23 August 2002.

[48] Dhavan, 'The Supreme Court Reference'.

[49] Rajeev Dhavan, 'The Gujarat Reference,' *The Hindu*, 1 November 2002.

context of incomplete rolls and missing electorates, elections could not be held before the end of November 2002. The ECI officials were quite firm on the question that even if a state assembly is dissolved, or comes to the end of its term, the opportune time of the polls can be decided by the ECI only.[50]

The central government construed that the position taken by the ECI was a matter under Article 143, where the president was empowered to refer to the Supreme Court a question of law and facts. The presidential reference that was subsequently sent for the opinion of the Supreme Court raised suspicion over the constitutional validity of the ECI's order, arguing that it amounted to 'non-compliance with the mandatory requirement envisaged under Article 174(1) of the Constitution'.[51] The Supreme Court's opinion on the presidential reference rejected the arguments made by the central and Gujarat governments regarding the ECI's decision. Arguing that Article 174(1) did not apply to a *dissolved* assembly, the Supreme Court further elaborated that the Article 'neither relates to elections nor does it provide any outer limit for holding elections for constituting the Legislative Assembly'.[52] While denying that Article 174 put any kind of limits on the ECI's powers under Article 324, the Supreme Court held that the holding of elections 'is the exclusive domain of the Election Commission under Article 324 of the Constitution'.[53]

Constitutional provisions for conducting elections have been supplemented by laws made by Parliament, filling in the details of the statutory framework of electoral governance in accordance with

[50] Commenting on the speculation that the government may hold elections in Gujarat, the former election commissioner, C.V.G. Krishnamurthy, emphasised that it was not for the prime minister or the chief minister to announce elections, but the prerogative of the ECI. The ECI decides the time of the polls only after taking stock of the ground reality and whether or not they are conducive to free and fair elections. ('Polls in Gujarat are for the EC to Announce,' *Hindustan Times*, 19 April 2002.)

[51] 'Text of Presidential Reference,' *The Hindu*, 22 August 2002.

[52] 'Six-Month Rule Won't Apply to Dissolved Assemblies: EC,' *The Hindu*, 29 October 2002, p. 1.

[53] 'Six-Month Rule Won't Apply to Dissolved Assemblies: EC,' *The Hindu*, 29 October 2002, p. 1.

the meta-rules laid down in the constitution.[54] The two major laws in this respect are the RPA, 1950, that deals primarily with the preparation and revision of electoral rolls, the delimitation of constituencies, prescribing additional qualification for voters, and so on, and the RPA, 1951, that deals in detail with all other aspects of conduct of elections and post-election disputes.[55] The 1950 Act provides for a state-wise distribution of seats, which means that a constituency of the Lok Sabha cannot traverse two or more states. The constituencies of the legislative council of states are determined by the president and the various electoral officers in the state and in the districts, namely, the chief electoral officer for each state, and the district electoral officer (DEO), electoral registration officer (ERO), and assistant ERO for each district, are considered to be on deputation to the ECI. The Act also lays down that a person who is not less than 18 years of age on the qualifying date and who is ordinarily resident in a constituency and is not otherwise disqualified is entitled to be registered as a voter in the constituency. The electoral rolls are revised and updated regularly by the EROs. Before every general election to the Lok Sabha or the state legislature, or before a by-election, an intensive revision of the roll is to be carried out.

[54] Apart from the provisions of the Constitution of India (with subsequent amendments, especially Articles 84, 101–4, 172–4, 193, Part XV, Article 324–4, 341–2), Tenth Schedule (Articles 102(2) and 191 (2) [Provision as to disqualification on ground of defection]), RPA (1950, 1951), The Presidential and Vice-Presidential Elections Act (1952), Representation of the People (Conduct of Elections and Elections Petitions) Rules (1956), Representation of the People (Miscellaneous Provisions) Act (1956), The Registration of Electors Rules (1960), The Conduct of Elections Rules (1961), Election Symbols (Reservation and Allotment) Order (1968), Criminal and Election Laws Amendment Act (1969), The Delimitation Act (1972), Election Laws (Extension to Sikkim) Act (1976), Disputed Elections (Prime Minister and Speaker) Act (1977), Representation of the People (Amendment) Act 1989, Cancellation of General Elections in Punjab Act (1991), Conduct of Elections (Amendment) Rules (1998), The Representation of People (Amendment) Act (1998), and the like, and various sections of the Indian Penal Code (IPC), form the statutory framework of elections in India.

[55] See the official website of the ECI. Available at https://www.eci.gov.in/infoeci.

The RPA, 1951, deals with all aspects of conduct of elections and post-election disputes. It lays down the nut-and-bolt aspects of an election: detailed provisions regarding qualifications and disqualifications for candidates; time schedule for elections; administrative machinery for conducting elections; power to requisition premises, vehicles, and so on by a government for the elections; role and functions of candidates and their agents; manner of voting, counting of votes, and declaration of results; disposal of election petitions; specification of corrupt practices and electoral offences;[56] suspension of poll or countermanding of election; registration of political parties; deposits for contesting elections; prevention of impersonation and limits on election expenditure, and so on (Gadkari 1996: 10). As mentioned in the previous section, the Supreme Court has held that where the enacted laws are silent or make insufficient provisions to deal with a given situation in the conduct of elections, the ECI has the residuary powers under the Constitution to act in an appropriate manner.

As far as the institutional design is concerned, the ECI consists of the CEC and other election commissioners, who are by convention

---

[56] The main difference between an electoral offence and corrupt practice is that an electoral offence attracts penalty in a criminal code, whereas a corrupt practice disqualifies a candidate whose election can be set aside. The IPC, 1860, has declared certain actions in connection with elections as offences. These are promoting enmity, and so on, between different groups on grounds of religion, race, place of birth, residence, language, and the like. (Section 153 A); imputations and assertions prejudicial to national integration (153 B); bribery (171 B); use of undue influence to interfere with the free exercise of any electoral rights (171 C); personification at an election (171 D); making false statements (171 G); illegal payments (171 H); failure to keep election accounts (171); and making or circulating statements conducive to public mischief, enmity, or hatred and so on between different classes. While most of these provisions were part of the IPC before Independence, 153 A and B were added in 1969 and 1972, respectively. Some of these offences like bribery, undue influence, promoting enmity, and the like, on the ground of religion, race, and so on, have also been declared corrupt practices under the RPA, 1951 (Section 123), which also identifies several other electoral offences such as holding a public meeting during 48 hours before polling begins (Section 126), creating disturbances at election meetings (Section 127) and so on.

drawn from the Indian Administrative Service (IAS).[57] The CEC is appointed by the president and acts as the chairperson of the ECI. The CEC enjoys security of tenure and cannot be removed from office except in the manner specified in the Constitution (that is, through a process of impeachment) and the conditions of his service cannot be changed to his disadvantage during his tenure. While Article 324(a) provides for 'Election Commissioners' besides the 'Chief Election Commissioner',[58] till October 1993, the ECI functioned as a 'one-man Commission', except for a short period between 16 October 1989 and 1 January 1990, when, for the first time, two additional commissioners were appointed. It was in this period that the question of the number of election commissioners to be appointed and the associated question of their relative powers became a matter of debate and judicial arbitration. In October 1989, in what has been seen as a move to curb the powers of CEC R.V.S. Peri Sastri, a month before the general

---

[57] As far as the integrated structure of electoral administration is concerned, the ECI has a secretariat in Delhi. The ECI is supported by chief electoral officers (CEOs) in each state, a position that received statutory backing through an amendment in the RPA in 1956. Like the election commissioners, the CEOs are also drawn from the IAS and are appointed by the ECI in consultation with the state governments. The CEOs head the 'field machinery' and are the 'eyes and ears' of the ECI in the states. Below the CEOs are the DEOs in each district, who are the district collectors (DCs) of the district, and serve as the returning officer for the district. The EROs are below the DEOs in the hierarchy and it is their job to oversee voter registration and revision of electoral rolls for the 4,120 state assemblies and 543 parliamentary constituencies. Lowest in the hierarchy are the booth level officers (BLOs), in charge of each polling booth. In addition, observers—general (drawn from the IAS) and expenditure (drawn from the Indian Revenue Service), monitor election proceedings. The expenditure of the ECI, unlike other constitutional bodies, is not charged on the Consolidated Fund of India, and is voted in Parliament (Sridharan and Vaishnav 2017: 423–34).

[58] Article 324 states that 'the Election Commission shall consist of the Chief Election Commissioner and such number of other Election Commissioners, if any, as the President may from time to time fix and the appointment of the Chief Election Commissioner and other Election Commissioners shall, subject to the provisions of any law made in that behalf by the Parliament, be made by the President'.

election, the president notified that besides the CEC, two other election commissioners with coordinate powers would comprise the ECI.[59] On 1 January 1990, however, the president revoked his 1989 notification with the result that the two election commissioners who had been appointed lost their office as election commissioners. One of them, S.S. Dhanoa, challenged the revocation of the notification, which was subsequently rejected by the Supreme Court.[60] In the process, however, the Supreme Court laid down the following principles that came to determine the composition and functions of the ECI in subsequent years:

1. It was desirable that more than one individual should exercise the highly vital functions of the ECI.
2. The creation and abolition of posts was a prerogative of the executive, and under Article 324(2), the president could fix and appoint such number of election commissioners as he may, from time to time, determine.
3. While it was obligatory to appoint the CEC, the appointment of other election commissioners [Cl.(2)] or regional commissioners [Cl.(4)] was left, by the Constitution, to the discretion of the president.

With the articulation of the principle that it was 'desirable' for the ECI to have more than one person to exercise its 'highly vital functions', the question of the relative powers of the members became a festering issue. In the *S.S. Dhanoa v. Union of India* case (1991) discussed earlier, a division bench of the Supreme Court had observed that the other election commissioners were placed in an inferior position. This inferiority, according to the Supreme Court, was implicit in the constitutional provisions pertaining to their removal from office. While the CEC could not be removed from office except by a

---

[59] The appointment of S.S. Dhanoa and V.S. Saigal as election commissioners by Rajiv Gandhi's government was seen as a ploy to limit the powers of the CEC and was resisted by the opposition. V.P. Singh's government, which subsequently came to power, removed them by abolishing the posts through another notification from the president amending the previous one. For details, see Sridharan and Vaishnav (2017: 432)

[60] *S.S. Dhanoa v. Union of India*, AIR 1991 S.C. 1745.

process of impeachment [Article 325(5), Prov.1], the other commissioners could be removed by the president on the recommendation of the CEC (Article 325(5), Prov.2). 'Hence', concluded the Supreme Court, 'the status of the other Election Commissioners has not been placed by the Constitution *at par* with that of the Chief Election Commissioner'. On the other hand, the provisions of Article 325(3) lay down that when any other election commissioner is appointed, the CEC shall act as the chairperson of the ECI. The provision was interpreted as implying that the CEC could not issue any order of the Commission without calling a meeting or consulting with other commissioners.

The question whether the election commissioners would hold coordinate powers with the CEC, or a relatively subordinate one, remained unresolved. Since the Constitution itself seemed to be ambivalent on the issue, the division bench suggested that the issue could be resolved through legislation or by amending the Constitution itself. The government subsequently promulgated an ordinance, replaced later by the Chief Election Commissioner and other Election Commissioners (Conditions of Service) Amendment Act, 1993, with retrospective effect from 1 October 1993. The ordinance gave coordinate powers to the election commissioners as envisaged in Article 325(3). The appointment of M.S. Gill and G.V.G. Krishnamurthy as election commissioners in 1993 by Narasimha Rao's government was largely interpreted as an attempt to 'check Seshan's power, as he was seen as a loose canon' (Sridharan and Vaishnav 2017: 433). The appointment was challenged by the then CEC, T.N. Seshan, in the Supreme Court.[61] A constitution bench of the Supreme Court rejected T.N. Seshan's petition and, overriding the Court's decision in the Dhanoa case, affirmed the multi-member nature of the ECI, and the relative powers of the election commissioners as laid down in the ordinance. According to Basu (1996: 1064), the constitution bench lay down that:

1. The notification of the president appointing Gill and Krishnamurthy as election commissioners was valid and that under Article 324, the Constitution had made the ECI a *multi-member* commission.

---

[61] *T.N. Seshan v. Union of India, Judgement Today,* 1995 (5) S.C. 337.

2. As far as possible, all business of the commission shall be transacted unanimously, and in case of difference of opinion, according to the opinion of the *majority*.

The practice of appointing two additional election commissioners that was resumed on 1 October 1993, with the appointment of M.S. Gill and T.S. Krishnamurthy, has since been followed. While the CEC remains pre-eminent as the head of the machinery, the powers of the election commissioners are coordinate and coequal since all decisions, in principle and in practice, are to be taken by consensus or majority vote. This guiding principle of the working of the ECI was affirmed by CEC T.S. Krishnamurthy, who proposed to remove the 'larger than life' image of the CEC by asserting in an interview that the ECI was an institution that functioned as a team:

> I realise that as the CEC I have a lot of responsibility. Yes. But it is a collective body though for every deficiency pointed out, I must find an answer to meet that deficiency.... One thing I am particular about is that the Election Commission is recognised as a team.... We have only 300 people. But we try and run the elections with the help of so many unknown faces.[62]

About two years later, however, in the context of BJP's objecting to the appointment of Navin Chawla as an election commissioner alleging that he was close to Congress leaders, CEC Gopalaswami informed the Supreme Court in an affidavit that if he received complaints or petitions against election commissioners, he could take suo motu action against them by virtue of powers vested in him by the Constitution.[63] A petition from senior BJP leader Jaswant Singh questioning Chawla's neutrality as an election commissioner and his appointment had earlier been made before the Supreme Court. Chief Election Commissioner Gopalaswami's statement before the court was a departure from the position taken by his predecessor B.B. Tandon

---

[62] 'Q & A: T.S. Krishnamurthy: The Commission Should be Recognised as a Team', *The Hindu*, 16 March 2004, p.13.

[63] 'Can Take Suo Motu Action against ECs, CEC tells SC,' *The Indian Express*, 7 August 2007, p. 3.

who, in June 2006, told the court that he could not act on Jaswant Singh's memorandum unless he received a reference from the president.[64] Gopalaswami, on the other hand, seemed to have understood the powers of the CEC vis-à-vis other commissioners differently. In his affidavit to the Supreme Court, before a bench headed by Justice Ashok Bhan, Gopalaswami opined that the primary concern of the CEC was 'to preserve and uphold the independence, impartiality, neutrality, integrity and dignity of the Election Commission'. In order to do this, he had the powers vested in him 'under the second provision of Article 324(5) of the Constitution', which allowed him to act independently on information received in two conditions—when information was received in the course of the ECI's functioning or on 'receiving information or petition filed before him by a political party or by any other person or body'.[65] Under this provision, according to Gopalaswami, the powers of the CEC could be seen as including recommendation of action against an erring election commissioner. Chief Election Commissioner Gopalaswami's statement was largely seen as inconsistent with the earlier positions of the ECI[66] and was met with

[64] The former CEC B.B. Tandon took the legal position that he did not have suo motu jurisdiction over his colleagues and must wait for the president to forward the petition to him, referring the matter to him. In other words, the CEC, according to Tandon, had no powers of initiating an inquiry on his/ her own. Tandon had inferred this after 205 members of Parliament (MPs), most of them affiliated with the NDA, had approached the president with a petition against Navin Chawla, a copy of which was handed over to him by the BJP leader V.K. Malhotra. Pankaj Vohra, 'Commission vs. Commission,' *Hindustan Times*, 13 August 2007, p. 10 (editorial page).

[65] Vohra, 'Commission vs. Commission,' p. 10. BJP leader Jaswant Singh later withdrew the petition that he had filed in the Supreme Court against Navin Chawla. While allowing the withdrawal of the petition, the court made it clear that it was not expressing any opinion on the CEC's power vis-à-vis his or her fellow election commissioners.

[66] The newspaper *The Hindu*, on 11 August 2007, printed statements of 'senior members of the Election Commission' who were of the view that the CEC's position as stated in the affidavit was a 'personal' one and did not reflect that of the ECI. They argued, moreover, that the stand taken by CEC Gopalaswami was inconsistent with the position the ECI had taken earlier before the government and the Law Commission of India on the question

opposition from the Congress-led United Progressive Alliance (UPA) government, notably the then prime minister Manmohan Singh and his law minister H.R. Bhardwaj, who believed that the position would erode the independence and equality of the election commissioners.[67] Bhardwaj reverted to the position taken by B.B. Tandon earlier that the CEC had no independent powers in the matter. Indeed, any suo motu action by the CEC could be construed as a breach of what was construed as the sole prerogative of the president. Even as the CEC's position had the potential of precipitating a constitutional crisis, Gopalaswami responded to the report on his affidavit published in the *Hindu*, claiming that an 'assertion had been attributed to him' that he had never actually made. He clarified that while he had stated that the powers of the CEC extended to recommending action against an EC, in his affidavit, he had 'nowhere talked of removal' of the election commissioner. He claimed in addition that the question of 'inconsistency' with the past position did not arise because the Supreme Court had asked for the CEC's position and not the election commissioner's position on the matter. Gopalaswami emphasised:

> However, until Article 324(5) of the Constitution is amended, the legal position is that in regard to the removal, the CEC and the EC are placed on different footing. It may perhaps be of interest to your newspaper to note that in his written statement before the Supreme Court, Shri Ram Jethmalani, the counsel for Shri Navin Chawla, clearly conceded the point in para 10 that 'A Chief Election Commissioner knowing from his personal knowledge that an Election Commissioner is unfit

---

of removal of election commissioners, which was one of parity between the CEC and other ECs. In the Chief Election Commissioner and other Election Commissioners (Conditions of Service) Act, 1991, the CEC was deemed to have the same protection and privileges as that of a judge of the Supreme Court and the ECs were to be on a par with the High Court judge. An amendment to the act in 1993 brought parity between the CEC and the ECs in matter of salary, perks, warrant of precedence, and voting rights, and stipulated that the commission's decisions would be by consensus or, if necessary, by a majority vote. As late as June 2002, the ECI wrote to the government to correct what was seen as an ambiguity, that is, the disparity in the matter of removal of the EC. Vohra, 'Commission vs. Commission,' p. 10.

[67] 'Gopalaswami's Stand Opposed,' *The Hindu*, 11 August 2007, p. 1.

to hold that office must be thoroughly incompetent or corrupt himself *if he takes no action at all.* The Supreme Court had the following to say in the case of T.N. Seshan, Chief Election Commissioner of India vs. Union of India (1995) 4SCC 811 'the Scheme of Article 324 is that after insulating the CEC by the first proviso to Clause (5), the ECs and RCs have been assured independence of functioning by providing that they cannot be removed except on the recommendation of the CEC. Of course, the recommendation for removal must be based on intelligible and cogent considerations which would have relation to efficient functioning of the Election Commission.... It is, therefore, needless to emphasise that the CEC must exercise this power only when there exists [sic] valid reasons which are conducive to efficient functioning of the Election Commission. This briefly stated, indicates the status of the various functionaries constituting the Election Commission (emphasis added).[68]

The question regarding the number of election commissioners and their relative powers remains unresolved. As Sridharan and Vaishnav (2017: 444–5) have pointed out, this is not only a question of the stability of the current configuration of the ECI, but also one that has the potential of eroding the autonomy of the institution through political interference. The possibility of 'stacking' the commission, the insecurity of the tenure of the election commissioners, and the absence of a law which lays down in precise terms that the senior-most election commissioner would take over as the CEC, keep alive the possibility of political control on the composition of the ECI.[69]

[68] 'Gopalaswami Clarifies on Supreme Court Affidavit,' *The Hindu*, 12 August 2007, p. 11.

[69] Since M.S. Gill's appointment as CEC, the convention of a three-member commission and the seniority principle in the appointment of the CEC has been followed. There were, however, phases in between when the convention stood the danger of interruption. Before the retirement of James Lyngdoh in 2004, the BJP government under Atal Bihari Vajpayee, which was unhappy with Lyngdoh over the manner in which the ECI resisted the government over the issue of elections in Gujarat after the Godhra riots, contemplated appointing retired cabinet secretary T.R. Prasad as the CEC, superseding the two ECs T.S. Krishnamurthy and B.B. Tandon. The two ECs threatened to resign, and the BJP government gave up its move. CEC S.Y. Quraishi and other CECs have suggested that the convention should be given the force of law. See Sridharan and Vaishnav (2017: 433).

The Institutional Space of Democracy: The Thematic and the Problematic

Despite the constitutional entrenchment of autonomy, the ECI is seen to have come into its own only in the 1990s. The explanation for this appears to lie in two interrelated developments that altered the nature of electoral politics in this period. In what may be seen as a second phase of the dismantling of the 'Congress system'—the first having occurred in the late 1960s—in the late 1990s, the party system in India reconfigured into a competitive multi-party system, with regional parties emerging as strong contenders for power at the state level and laying claims to sharing power at the central level as well. This was accompanied by the 'second democratic upsurge',[70] which reflected the churning that was occurring in the Indian electorate, with large sections of people, who had hitherto been pacified into the practice of 'deference legitimation' (Kaviraj 2003) imposed by the upper-caste dominated state, coming out in large numbers to vote. The two developments opened up spaces for marginal political parties and intensified electoral contests. In such a context, where the political field or the ideological 'constellation' was no longer homogeneous and increasingly more plural and competitive, non-elected and non-political institutions like the ECI and the Supreme Court came to play significant roles. Significantly, the 1990s is seen as having initiated an 'activist' phase of the ECI (McMillan 2010: 100), marked by the presence of strong CECs, including T.N. Seshan (1990–6), M.S. Gill (1996–2001), and James Lyngdoh (2001–4), who used constitutional provisions to assert the ECI's autonomy.[71]

[70] The *second* democratic upsurge is the term given by Yogendra Yadav (1997, 1999) to refer to the 'new phase of democratic politics' in India in the 1990s, particularly in the state assembly elections during the period 1993–5. The expression refers especially to the dynamism that the electoral process witnessed in the period, characterised by a hitherto unprecedented upsurge in political participation, particularly by the lower classes of the Indian electorate.

[71] Arun Thiruvengadam (2017: 155) argues that the coalition era gave T.N. Seshan the opportunity to 'flex the institutional muscle power' of the ECI. Seshan took a series of initiatives pertaining to voter registration, candidate fraud, and electoral corruption, which were 'not always successful'.

It may also be recalled that the 1990s is often presented as a period when the state recast itself from an 'interventionist' to a 'regulatory' state. The institutional matrix in such a state presented a new configuration of power, in which the earlier contests among institutions (for example, between Parliament and the Supreme Court) gave way to new ones. In the regulatory state, the executive and the legislature are diminished even as institutions like the Supreme Court and the ECI, which perform roles that are 'more procedural than substantive, more rule-making and enforcing than law-making and policy-making', acquire more scope (Rudolph and Rudolph 2001: 129–30). In their work, *In Pursuit of Lakshmi* (1987), Susanne and Lloyd Rudolph had problematised the relationship between the judiciary and Parliament as an aspect of the 'struggle over stateness'—the institutional rivalry between the two manifesting the contests inherent in state power, and the functional differentiation among different parts of the government. If 'state issues' in the 1980s were largely about institutional rivalry, with the outcome of aggregation of state power, by the 1990s, the move towards 'market competition festered by the regulatory state' saw a corresponding shift, which was experienced in the 'conduct of politics'. The political field changed, becoming decentralised and heterogeneous, with implications for the arrangement and distribution of political power. Indeed, the Rudolphs explain the new 'regulatory roles' of existing institutions as providing stability to the system through a 'renegotiation of balance of power'. This involved filling in the political space by playing their 'constitutional roles as the regulatory mechanisms of democratic politics', but in ways which were more 'procedural than substantive', ensuring procedural fairness in the 'operation of a multiparty system and the formation and conduct of coalition governments in a federal framework' (Rudolph and Rudolph 2001: 129–30).

---

on the ground. While they helped propel Seshan to national prominence, they somewhat undermined the perception of the ECI's efficiency. CECs Gill and Lyngdoh, who followed Seshan, were able to consolidate the gains in terms of the ECI's profile to implement measures to improve the conduct of elections.

The legitimacy gained by the ECI over the elections it had conducted, was reflected in a nationwide poll conducted in 1996 by the Centre for the Study of Developing Societies (CSDS), Delhi, for the Indian Council of Social Science Research and *India Today*, after the national elections in June–July 1996, and then again in another survey conducted in Delhi in September–October 2003. Both the surveys showed that people had a remarkably high degree of trust in the ECI. The 1996 poll showed that the ECI was ranked the highest among political institutions in terms of public support. Of the 15,030 respondents, 62 per cent rated the ECI as trustworthy, which was the highest score, followed by 59 per cent for the Supreme Court. The lowest-ranked were the police and the bureaucracy. The responses suggested that the ECI, more than any other institution, had remained true to its goal, that is, of guaranteeing free and fair elections.[72] The polls conducted in September–October 2003 showed that trust in the ECI had sustained. While only 8 per cent of the respondents thought the bureaucracy was trustworthy and 29 per cent found it completely untrustworthy, 38 per cent placed complete faith in the ECI.[73] A study conducted in 2008 found the ECI placed second only to the army in terms of people's trust in the institution.[74] The credibility of the ECI is not confined to the people. While the relationship between the ECI and political parties has remained uneven and often contentious, the criticism of the ECI by the Communist Party of India (Marxist) (CPI(M)) and the Left Front government in West Bengal being one of the several examples, political parties have always submitted to electoral outcomes.

[72] For a discussion of this survey result, see Peter Ronald de Souza (1998: 51–2, 2000: 200–10).

[73] The survey conducted by *Hindustan Times* and CSDS in Delhi on a sample size of 14,000, spread across 70 constituencies, also concluded that the poll panel was trusted most among people who are rich, educated, and have a high level of media exposure. In these groups, 41, 44, and 46 per cent of people trusted it fully. The poor (34 per cent) and uneducated (24 per cent) trusted it to a lesser extent. Only 20 per cent of people with no media exposure shared this sentiment, suggesting that media coverage, at last to an extent, could be responsible for the popularity of the ECI (see HT-CSDS Survey, 'Battle for Delhi, 2003,' *Hindustan Times*, 9 November 2003).

[74] Nearly 80 per cent of the people expressed trust in the ECI (SDSA 2008).

This, however, does not mean that there have been no controversies over the conduction of specific elections: the elections in Jammu and Kashmir, for example, have been seen as less than credible, and the state assembly elections in Assam in 1983 were the most violent in the history of electoral democracy in the country.

We may, of course, ask whether participation in the electoral process has merely paved the way for participatory democracy or has it also opened up spaces for transformative politics that is not limited by narrowly defined electoral allegiances and outcomes. In other words, does the consolidation and strengthening of the electoral system through rules and principles of governance, which have facilitated participation, have longer-term gains of strengthening democratic government? Writing in the 1990s, Yogendra Yadav argued that the institutional apparatus of democracy has not actually strengthened in a way commensurate with or reflective of the greater dynamism in politics brought by the democratic upsurge (Yadav 1997: 178). Indeed, if the waning of people's faith in representative, administrative, and political institutions is any indication, it would appear that institutions have in fact considerably weakened. Yadav (2000: 187) sees this waning of trust in the 1990s as an accentuation of 'the simultaneity of involvement and alienation which has characterized the Indian electorate'. The accentuation, he points out, reflects an intensification of tensions between two fundamentally conflicting tendencies in Indian politics. While the process of democratisation has advanced further with higher mobilisation and greater politicisation, particularly of the marginal sections, this democratic upsurge has not been translated effectively into the institutionalised world of politics. However, Yadav is not arguing that the democratic upsurge has led to institutional decay and distrust of people in political institutions; rather electoral volatility has opened up fresh possibilities without leading to transformative politics.

On the other hand, while arguing that political mobilisation may have 'often exceeded institutionalisation' affecting institutions adversely, Kapur and Mehta (2005: 4) suggest that it would be wrong to presume that that there is a direct proportionality between the two, and that Indian public institutions are 'severely stressed and weakening'. The impact of political mobilisation, they argue has been uneven and variable, strengthening some institutions, while weakening others.[75] Indeed, pointing at the increase in 'veto points' within the government, Kapur and Mehta identify the emergence of 'referee institutions', like the ECI and the Supreme Court, as one aspect of the strengthening of institutions. The choice of the expression 'referee institution' by Kapur and Mehta, as well as 'regulatory institution' used to refer to the ECI by the Rudolphs and following them, by Alistair McMillan, has significant implications. Both refereeing and regulating connote specific functions, but these may not be the roles that the ECI is expected to perform, or even what it is perceived to be performing. Indeed, it is debatable whether the performance of the ECI, which is perhaps one instance where an *institution* has 'exceeded' the role it was expected to perform, may be labelled as a refereeing function. A referee is someone to whom something is referred in case of a conflict or contest, who reaches a decision and settles the dispute by taking recourse to existing rules. The referee would also, as a person having the authority to do so, keep constant vigilance on the field of action to ensure that competing/contesting parties adhere to existing rules. In a sport or game, the referee, while regulating the game, is not a part of the game itself in the sense of being a player, but stands apart, to oversee and arbitrate within the frameworks of the rules that all sides have agreed to obey.

The discussions in the chapters that follow will show that the ECI, far from being a neutral arbiter and rule-implementing body, has become a prominent player in the electoral game by determining its rules; innovating, strengthening, and reinforcing them where they appear to be weak; and plugging gaps by devising new rules, becoming in the process, as a former CEC, James Lyngdoh (2004: 69–70), remarked, a 'pitcher' in the football game. The reference to a 'pitcher' is significant, since it alludes to the important function of initiating the game itself. Lyngdoh's remarks pertained not just to the change in the way in which the ECI perceived its own role in the electoral game, but also in the new 'defiance' it assumed and exhibited in the period immediately after the

---

[75] Kapur and Mehta (2005: 4) cite the reversal of the trend towards centralisation as an illustration of the strengthening of institutions. They also argue that the multiplicity of veto points has led to a greater need for consensus, which was reflected in the selection of K.R. Narayanan and A.P.J. Abdul Kalam as presidents of India.

Emergency. If the Emergency was the period in which all institutions suffered erosion, the period after the Emergency can in some senses be seen as one when institutions like the ECI recuperated and resurged, reinventing themselves by giving innovative interpretations to the powers that already existed in their inventory.

The democratic upsurge in the late 1990s opened up new political possibilities, but failed to transform political institutions. The dissonance between enhanced political participation and lack of trust among people in political institutions, led in 2012 to a movement in Delhi demanding robust institutional mechanisms for fighting corruption in public institutions. Notably, a primary reason for the decline in people's trust in political institutions, owed to the profusion of 'scam' charges against the political establishment, which included not just the then Congress-led coalition government of the UPA in the centre, but also the state governments, which were led by the main opposition party, the BJP. Asking for a law to set up an effective ombudsman (the Lokpal), a hunger fast by Anna Hazare, in the summer of 2012, saw an unprecedented mobilisation of men and women across the country, but more specifically in Delhi. While the hunger fast by Anna Hazare petered out after assurances from the government, the movement simmered on. Even as Anna Hazare and some of his associates were steadfast in dissociating themselves from 'politics', a strand from the movement led by former civil servant, Magsaysay Award winner and Right to Information activist Arvind Kejriwal, decided to congeal the energies unleashed by the movement into a political party—the Aam Aadmi Party (AAP; which can be translated literally to 'the common man's party'). When it decided to contest the Delhi Assembly elections in December 2013, the AAP was a four-month old party. In the electoral outcome, the AAP reduced the Congress party in Delhi, which had been in power in the state for 15 years, to a meagre tally of eight seats, and the BJP to a position where, although it gained the highest number of seats, it could not muster the required majority to form the government.[76] The fall

---

[76] Of the 70 Assembly seats in Delhi, the BJP got the highest at 31 seats, the AAP followed with 28 seats, the Indian National Congress with 8 seats, the JD(U) and Shiromani Akali Dal with 1 seat each, and an independent candidate with 1 seat. See the ECI website. Available at http://eciresults.ap.nic.in/; accessed on 25 December 2013.

of the coalition government of the Congress and AAP led to fresh state assembly elections in February 2015 in which the AAP won 67 out of 70 seats. The results of the state assembly election of Delhi in 2012 and 2015 may be read as a manifestation of the paradox in the contemporary moment in the biography of Indian democracy, where a phenomenon of the deepening of democracy occurred alongside declining trust in political institutions. The movement against corruption was emphatic in expressing its disenchantment with the state/government/political institutions and drew sustenance from the resources offered by democracy identified with the space of civil society, which it also claimed to be reinforcing through its struggles. This pitting of 'democracy' (civil society) against 'politics' (defined narrowly as the government and the institutional space of the state) did not, however, mean a corresponding decline of trust in the electoral system and institutions of electoral governance.

The chapters that follow trace the aforementioned problematic through an analysis of themes integral to the conduct of democratic elections. We have seen that question of the *pedigree* of the ECI's powers and contests around the constitutional and legal architecture of electoral governance cluster around Article 324 of the Constitution. The principle of procedural certainty (Mozaffar and Schedler 2002) is considered essential for electoral governance in societies that are 'democratising', but equally valid for long-sustaining democracies where elections have become 'routine'. The trust people have in the electoral system corresponds to the degree to which the body entrusted with the responsibility of administering elections is able to regulate electoral competition by ensuring procedural certainty. Apart from laying down the rules of the electoral game and organising them with procedural certainty, questions concerning whether the procedures designed to conduct elections are appropriate and can achieve the objective of democratic uncertainty of elections are also important. The evaluative frameworks for assessing the appropriateness of procedures concern themselves largely with the question, whether or not, and to what degree, the integrity of the electoral system is maintained. Chapter 2 of this book takes up for scrutiny themes that are integral to elections and democracy, especially, the right to vote, the relationship people have with this right, and the conditions that enable its meaningful exercise. The arguments are elaborated in consideration of another theme central to the conduct of democratic elections, that is, 'electoral integrity'. In addition, the debates over electoral rolls and innovations in 'voter education and awareness', which are often seen through the lens of electoral 'management', are discussed to show how they have become part of the deliberative content of election alongside the quest for 'procedural certainty' and 'democratic outcomes'.

The ECI's constitutional powers of superintending elections have over the years become more pronounced. This power has been contested by political regimes that have sought to limit it by invoking Parliament's powers to legislate on electoral matters. More importantly, by seeking extraordinary powers during election time, dipping into the 'reservoir' of powers, which Article 324 of the Constitution has vested in it, the ECI has marked out 'election time' as 'special time'. The expression 'special time', used by David Gilmartin, refers to the parameters of the 'conduct' of election, whereby the bureaucratic apparatus of the state both substitutes and defers the 'political' to enable unharnessed and un-coerced exercise of the sovereign act of voting by the citizen-voter (Gilmartin 2009). Chapter 3 focuses on the 'Model Code of Conduct' (MCC), an innovation of political parties, which was institutionalised by the ECI in later years, to argue that the model code constitutes the conditions of 'special election time', but simultaneously, it also provides 'supplementary legality' augmenting the legal exceptionalism of election time.

Electoral governance does not take place in a vacuum and unfolds in a political field that is structured in a way that produces vulnerabilities and participation and representation deficits. The ECI may be able to address them only in limited ways while conducting elections. The enrolment of voters, preparation of electoral rolls, ensuring a level playing field, and purity of elections by eliminating crime and money from influencing the electoral domain have presented challenges before the ECI. Chapter 4 in this book suggests that despite conflicts over the nature of the powers of the ECI and allegations of complicity with the ruling party, over the years, there has been a democratisation of the electoral space. This has given an ideological content to 'electoral trial', whereby the act of voting is taken beyond the 'here and now' to become a necessary part of democratic representation-projects (Urbinati 2000). Yet, the chapter also addresses deep-seated problems of conducting credible elections in contexts that are not conducive to and, indeed, distort the democratic representation-project. The promise of democracy and leap of faith, which marked the first general elections, would, however, serve as a reminder to future administrators and political leaders, of the need to preserve institutional integrity in order to enhance and entrench a culture of democracy. Chapter 1 concerns itself, therefore, with the manner in which the first general election was conducted and how the questions of procedural and substantive aspects of elections were addressed by the ECI, which lay down the brass tacks of electoral governance.

ೲ

1

The First General Elections

The Political and the Bureaucratic

On 18 February 1950, the first pages of most national newspapers were dominated by reports of the conclusion of a two-day meeting of the Congress Working Committee (CWC) in New Delhi. The meeting had ended with the announcement that social and economic reconstruction was to be the Congress' future plan for the nation. To work towards this, the CWC had appointed a five-member committee headed by Govind Ballabh Pant. The committee was to draw up a short-term programme of action for 12 months, which would dovetail with the First Five-Year Plan, to be formulated by the Planning Commission, which the government proposed to set up soon. The Congress' announcement of a plan of national social and economic reconstruction was largely being construed in newspaper reports as a design for revitalising the party by eliminating 'power' politics.

Simultaneously, however, the interim government led by the Congress party was also getting ready to install institutional structures to inaugurate the processes of competitive electoral politics in the country. A news item, tucked away inconspicuously at the bottom of the same page, informed the reader that preparations for the first general election under the new Constitution were being taken a stage further with the appointment of the election commissioner.

The government, the reader was informed, also planned to enact laws on the model of the RPA in the United Kingdom to assume the necessary legal authority for proceeding with the preparations for the elections as provided for under the republican Constitution. Even though the ECI was not yet functional, the election commissioner was yet to be appointed, and the legal framework for conducting the election was so far not in place, the secretariat of the ECI under P.S. Subramaniam had begun operating from its offices in the Parliament House. Indeed, the ECI's secretariat had already set in motion the process of conducting the first general election by sending circulars to state governments, alerting them to the necessity of expediting all the preliminary arrangements for holding elections early in the following year, that is, the beginning of 1951.

While it was not a constitutional and legal requirement, beginning with the first general election, the ECI adopted the practice of preparing a narrative report of every general election. This practice changed in 1983 to one where the ECI submitted a report annually to Parliament. In his prefatory comments to the first narrative report produced by the ECI, the CEC Sukumar Sen considered such reporting 'necessary and desirable' even when there was no provision in law requiring the preparation of a report on the elections.[1] For Sukumar Sen, the desirability of a narrative report stemmed from the necessity of preserving and disseminating 'an exhaustive record of the different aspects of [a] remarkable *administrative* task' (emphasis added),[2] giving the opportunity to the ECI, the body responsible for administering elections within the framework of the constitution, to review the working of election law and procedure, and also to offer comments and suggestions for their improvement.

Writing after the first general election, CEC Sukumar Sen emphasised the importance of appropriate laws and procedures to run an *efficient* electoral system. Several years later, writing after the mid-term elections of 1968, the then CEC S.P. Sen Verma preferred to highlight the importance of a politics of dialectics in democracy, which made it

---

[1] Election Commission of India, *Report of the First General Election of India 1951–52*, Vol. I. New Delhi: Election Commission of India, 1955, p. i.

[2] Election Commission of India, *Report of the First General Election of India 1951–52*, Vol. I, p. i.

imperative that opposite views should be heard in public discussions. The creation of such a deliberative space was to him more important than the actual act of voting itself. If, for Sukumar Sen, the problem of ensuring certainty of procedures appeared primary at a time when they were in an incipient stage, for S.P. Sen Verma, the problem of regulating electoral competition in order to compel political parties to submit to the 'moral order' of a code of conduct assumed primacy. For Sen Verma, the importance of a model code of conduct, which became relatively institutionalised in 1968, lay in providing the unconstrained space for prior discussion, so that the vote when it was finally cast had the quality of intelligent consent.[3] It may be recalled that the 1967 general elections were the last in India where the Lok Sabha and state assembly elections for all states were held simultaneously. It was also the election where the Congress's stronghold in the states weakened, with seven states including Gujarat, Orissa, West Bengal, and Kerala slipping out of its control. This was also the period when Indira Gandhi's leadership within the Congress party was challenged by strong contenders like Morarji Desai.

It was in these later years that the ECI also came to dominate the newspaper broadsheet during election time, as an active participant in the poll process, as the electoral rule-maker, enforcer, and adjudicator. In the months leading to the first general election, while reporting on different aspects of the electoral contest, the newspapers were silent about the ECI itself. This 'absence' of the ECI in public reporting of elections corresponds to the spirit of the first narrative report of the ECI, where the CEC appears to interpret the ECI's constitutional role in conducting election as one of *meticulous* and *efficient* bureaucratic administration. Acknowledging the press for generating and sustaining public interest in the election, and the All India Radio for helping to familiarise the electorate with the intricacies of election law and voting procedures, the ECI saw itself largely as a facilitator in a 'common task' for a 'national purpose', rather than a 'pitcher' in the election game. The 'pitcher' was the expression used by CEC James Lyngdoh to describe the 'active' role played by the ECI in the 1990s. In the first general election, the ECI's administrative task, by its own

---

[3] Election Commission of India, *Report on the Mid-term General Election in India, 1968–69*, Vol. I. New Delhi: Election Commission of India, 1970, pp. 9–11.

description, seemed to be concerned largely with putting in place the logistics leading up to the polling day. The task of preparing the electoral rolls was entrusted to the state governments and the decision on the dates for the election was taken by the central government.[4] The labour of preparing the ballot papers,[5] ordering the ballot boxes in suitable numbers,[6] setting up of polling booths, ensuring the security of the polling booths and the ballot boxes,[7] counting of votes, and declaration of results were the jobs assumed by the ECI.[8] In addition,

[4] Electoral rolls had already been printed in the Punjab, West Bengal, Orissa and Madras, while they were about to be printed in Bombay, Madhya Bharat, and Assam. In the states, electoral rolls prepared on the basis of adult franchise for election to the Constituent Assembly and the state legislature already existed in Mysore, Travancore-Cochin Union, and Rewa state of Vindhya Pradesh and were being revised for adoption. Good progress had been reported from Saurashtra, PEPSU, Bhopal, and Cooch Behar. 'Preparation for India's General Election: Election Commissioner may be Appointed Soon,' *The Times of India*, 18 February 1950, p. 1.

[5] A 180 tonnes of paper was used for six hundred million ballot papers, at the cost of Rs 1,077,401. Election Commission of India, *Report of the First General Election of India 1951–52*, p. 103.

[6] The ballot boxes were prepared by Godrej and Boyce Manufacturing Co. Ltd. Bombay, Hyderabad Allwyn Metal Works, Oriental Metal Pressing Works, Bombay, and paper seals for securing boxes against tampering were prepared by the India Security press, Nasik. About 2,600,000 ballot boxes were manufactured. Election Commission of India, *Report of the First General Election of India 1951–52*, p. 209.

[7] A total of 338,854 policemen were deployed for polling duties all over the country. Election Commission of India, *Report of the First General Election of India 1951–52*, p. 33.

[8] The ECI acknowledged a range of agencies: the Security Press, Nasik, which printed ballot papers and paper seals in enormous quantities at a short notice, the Council for Scientific and Industrial Research for their valuable contribution by manufacturing and supplying the indelible ink for the election, the Ministry of Commerce and Industry for releasing the steel for the manufacture of ballot boxes in spite of an acute shortage of steel in the country and for designing the inexpensive and fraud-proof ballot boxes, the Post and Telegraphs Department and the Railway Board for providing communication and railway transport. Election Commission of India, *Report of the First General Election of India 1951–52*, pp. 209–10.

through mock exercises and radio broadcasts, the ECI sought to familiarise the voters with what was an unfamiliar political activity for the majority of the population.

The reticence of the ECI in assuming a public persona was commensurate with the arduous constitutional responsibility of performing a political function, while remaining outside the political domain. It did not mean, however, that questions germane to the procedural and substantive aspects of electoral democracy and administering a democratic election were not actively being considered by it. Indeed, contestations over some of the core components of integrity in electoral governance, including questions of adequate representation, inclusive electoral rolls, and a code of conduct for political parties, among others, became crucial in the quest for procedural certainty. The resolution of these contests had ramifications within the political domain. The entrenchment of procedural certainties in the first general election took place through the bureaucratic apparatus of the state and political decisions taken by the government to address issues pertaining to representation and citizenship.

The Election 'Game'

I know of at least one fellow called Ramu whose house was in the proximity of an election-meetings ground. It was great entertainment for him while it lasted.... On the eve of voting Ramu and his friends spent long hours not only in vigorous demonstrations but also in excited discussion.

'My father has promised to take me too for voting', said one.

'Nonsense. We won't be allowed to go there; it is only for grown-ups.'

'It seems anyone can vote, didn't you hear what they said in the meetings?'

'Not everybody, only tall persons will be allowed to vote.'

'No. It is all wrong. What about our geography master? He is our height and I know he is going to vote.'

'What is a vote like?'

'My father said it is made of paper.'

'What is its shape?'

'We are not allowed to see it'.

'I am going to slip in somehow and see what it is like. They are going
to have it after all in our school....'

'You will be handcuffed if you go there, it is against the law to try and
see the vote. Don't you see how many police they have kept there?'....
Needless to say when the elders went out to cast their votes, they left
the children behind much to their chagrin, which increased when the
elders came back and displayed the little dot on their fingers. It made
a little girl Kamala very jealous, and she vowed, 'See if I don't get my
vote very soon. And when they put that dot on I will tell them to place
it between my eyebrows'. (Narayan 2000: 291–2)

Writing about the first general election in India in a short story
titled 'The Election Game', R.K. Narayan recounts the fever that seized
the people participating in what he called 'a large-scale rehearsal for
political life'. No one, young or old, was left untouched, 'as though
a sense of sovereignty [was] aroused even in the most insignificant
of us'.[9] The children too had adopted electioneering as one of their
games. The fictional rendition of the first general election by Narayan
reflects the enigma surrounding it, but it also underscores its historical and political significance. The exercise of franchise was an
unfamiliar experience for the large numbers of hitherto colonial
subjects deprived of political rights. Elections embodied the fundamental rupture that independence from colonial rule was to bring
in its wake, affirming the powerful imaginary of a sovereign nation
of citizens. Central to this imaginary was the creation of a political
community of citizens and a democratic public sphere. The exercise
of *universal* adult suffrage, which substituted the colonial practice
of *limited* franchise restricted by property and education criteria,
was an affirmation of political equality, and the promise that government was to be based on principles of popular sovereignty and
self-determination expressed through representative institutions. The
supplanting of a colonial regime with a democratic government was
hinged upon putting in place a system of rules and principles, laws,
procedures, and institutions that would affirm and substantiate
the powerful democratic imaginary of a sovereign nation of citizens.

---

[9] R.K. Narayan. 1952. 'The Election Game,' *The Hindu*, 3 February. The
story can be read in the anthology by R.K. Narayan (2000).

The first general election in India in 1951–2 was perhaps the most significant expression of national and popular sovereignty. The exercise of universal franchise was a powerful manifestation of horizontal equality, democratic citizenship and the modern public sphere. Not only was the government to be based on principles of sovereignty and self-determination which were to be expressed through representative structures, in a more fundamental sense, the democratic implication of this rupture was to be witnessed in the shift in the principle of rule from colonial governmentality to self-determination.

The expression of sovereignty and the demonstration of a capacity for self-determination through the exercise of universal adult franchise was, however, 'a colossal task', unparalleled in the history of humankind'.[10] The adoption of universal adult franchise was also, as the first narrative report of the ECI asserted, a 'massive act of faith'. While discussing the feasibility of universal adult suffrage, the Constituent Assembly had considered the kinds of problems that would emerge out of the magnitude of the task involved. The number of voters under adult suffrage, it felt, would exceed 'all reasonable bounds' involving 'too stupendous an administrative task'. Moreover, the illiteracy of the voters was likely to render the election 'a farce' unless an electoral system could be devised under which even an illiterate voter could cast his or her vote intelligently and in secret. This, CEC Sen argued, was an act of faith—'faith in the common man of India and in his practical common sense. This decision launched a great and fateful experiment, unique in the world in its stupendousness and complexities'.[11] This act of faith was implicit in a newly independent country's attempt to move straight into universal adult franchise, instead of incremental enhancement, which had hitherto been the practice in most other countries with respect to extension of franchise. The determination to put in place democratic institutions, in particular, a parliament embodying popular sovereignty, buttressed by the people's mandate to govern, was seen as essential

[10] See Ramchandra Guha. 2002. 'The Biggest Gamble in History,' *The Hindu Magazine*, 27 January.

[11] Election Commission of India, *Report of the First General Election of India 1951–52*, p. 10.

for marking a rupture from the past. The humungous nature of this task, which included at a fundamental level the constitution of an electorate and setting in motion the ponderous process of holding the first general election based on universal adult franchise, was depicted by the famous cartoonist Shankar in a series of cartoons reproduced in Figures 1.1 and 1.2.

Figure 1.1   'Adult Suffrage Was a Mighty Experiment'
Source: Pillai (1983: 74). Reproduced with permission from Yamuna Shankar, Children's Book Trust, New Delhi.
Note: Cartoon produced in the context of preparations for the first general elections to be held under the new constitution based on universal adult suffrage, dated 21 October 1951.

Figure 1.2   'The First Round'
Source: Pillai (1983: 56). Reproduced with permission from Yamuna Shankar, Children's Book Trust, New Delhi.
Note: Cartoon produced in the context of the postponement of the first general elections under the new constitution which were subsequently held in 1952, dated 19 November 1951.

The enormity of the task was so great and the political context in which the elections were held so unstable that popular affirmation, which Nehru desired, much to his anguish, could come only several months later in 1952.[12] The cartoon (see Figure 1.3) by Shankar depicts the continual deferral of the elections from its first assigned date of April 1951.

For the ECI, however, the trouble at the borders or, even as the cartoon seems to suggest, Nehru's indecisiveness stemming from Congress's own anxieties, were not issues the Commission had to grapple with. The size of the electorate at 176 million, of whom about 85 per cent could not read or write, the identification and registration of voters, designing and allocation of party symbols, preparation of ballot papers and ballot boxes for a mostly unlettered electorate, building of polling stations, recruitment of honest and committed polling officers, as well as providing ample time for political parties to compete and contest the first elections ever, was an exercise of massive proportions. The following description given by Ramchandra Guha helps us comprehend the magnitude of the exercise:

> At stake were about 4,500 seats; two lakh twenty four thousand polling booths had to be constructed and equipped with about two million steel ballot boxes made of 8,200 tonnes of steel. About 380,000 reams of paper were used for printing the electoral rolls; fifty six thousand presiding officers were recruited who were assisted by about 280,000 lesser staff. The election and the electorate was spread over an area of more than a million square miles. The terrain was vast, diverse and in some cases difficult to access. The nature of electorate required some innovations, e.g., the use of large pictorial symbols drawn from their daily lives by which the illiterate voters could identify their candidates, and the use of multiple ballot boxes. On a single ballot, it was feared

[12] Often 1951 is mentioned as the year the first general election in India took place. Polling was held in Himachal Pradesh from 25 October 1951 and the residents of Chini district in the state of Himachal Pradesh were the first to cast their votes. The rest of the country voted in February–March 1952. The exception was made for the hill state because of harsh winter conditions, when the rest of the country voted later in February (except Kashmir, which voted for the first time in 1967).

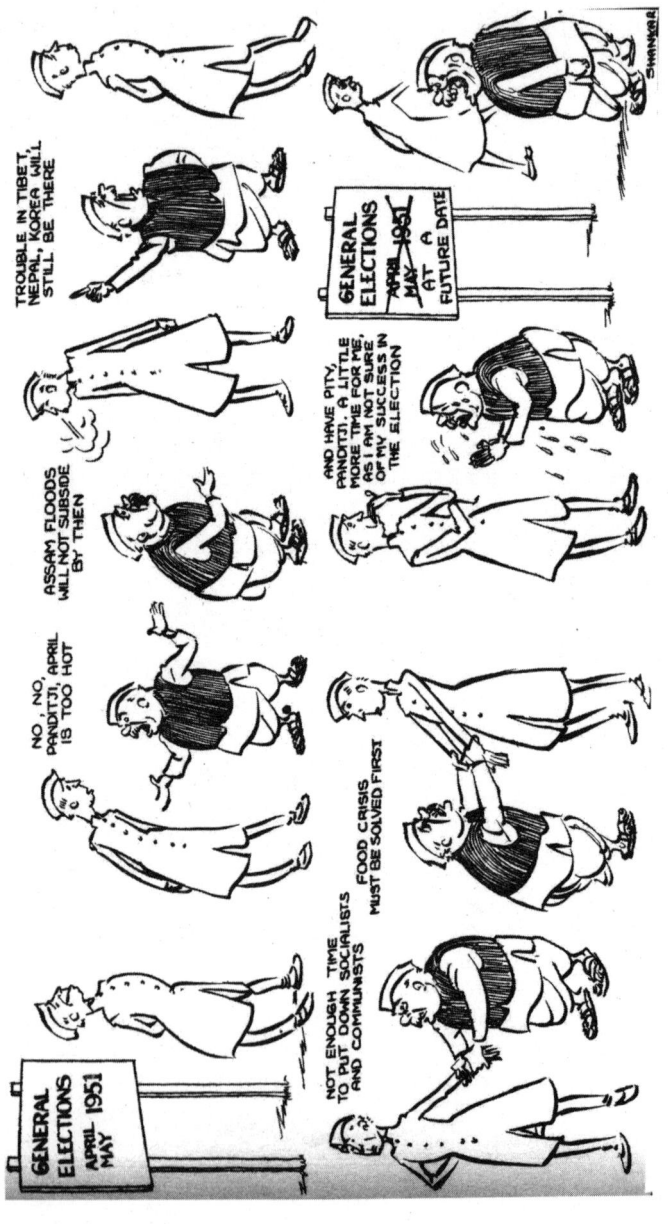

Figure 1.3 'The General Elections Have Been Postponed'

Source: Pillai (1983: 57). Reproduced with permission from Yamuna Shankar, Children's Book Trust, New Delhi.

Note: A cartoon etched in the context of the postponement of the first general elections, dated 26 November 1951.

the Indian voter was likely to make a mistake. Thus each party had a ballot box with its symbol marked in each polling station, the voter had to simply drop their paper in it. (Guha 2002)

Two days before polling took place in the constituencies in Himachal Pradesh, which voted a couple of months before the rest of India, *The Hindu* published an elaborate write-up on the 'The Ensuing Elections' as a 'Great Experiment in Democracy'. Commenting on the 'colossal' nature of the task, which had been made remarkably simple by the efforts of the electoral bureaucracy, the article went on to suggest that the working of adult franchise was a 'huge problem' and an 'interminable headache' not in the least because:

the universal adult suffrage granted by the Constitution has made half of India's population eligible to become voters, and the total number enrolled now is 170,000,000 ... When he was the President of the Constituent Assembly, Dr. Rajendra Prasad amused himself one day calculating what would be the thickness of the Indian electoral roll if you printed 40 names per foolscap-size page and bound the pages together—and arrived at the figure of about 400 feet.[13]

This huge electorate was to vote simultaneously (except in the states of Bilaspur, Kutch, Manipur, and Tripura, for which no state legislative assembly had been provided) for the Lok Sabha and the state assembly elections. There were, moreover, 666 double member constituencies, where an additional seat was reserved for the scheduled castes or schedule tribes, including two three-member constituencies. This basically meant that each voter had to elect more than two and often as many as three to five representatives at one and the same election. The process was not to end at this. After all the legislators were elected, an electoral college comprising all members of the central Parliament and the state legislative assemblies would choose the new president of the Republic of India. The task was unimaginably huge:

Besides the enrollment of an unbelievably large electorate, a staggering number of constituencies, 2438 single member and 666 multi-member

---

[13] 'Ensuing Election: Great Expectations,' *The Hindu*, 23 October 1951.

had to be delimited. This had to be done on the basis of the constitutional provisions regarding maximum and minimum number of voters and to the satisfaction of Parliament, at the same time avoiding gerrymandering or creation of pocket-boroughs and with due regard to administrative feasibility. An interesting point in delimitation is that the number of members in the local Legislative Assembly of a State are the exact multiple of the number of members from that State to the House of the People. Laws and rules had to be drafted and passed by Parliament to provide for orderly procedure, keeping in regard every aspect from electoral rolls to electoral returns and from qualification to election offences. Polling programme for the whole country extending from the Himalayas to Cape Camorin had to be planned keeping in view weather changes like snow and rain and agricultural operations and administrative effectiveness. Special measures had to be undertaken for keeping law and order, for providing postal and other conveniences to the candidates and parties and so on. Officials had to be trained in the mechanics of polling and electoral laws and rules, and directed to keep themselves impartial in their election work so as to ensure free and fair elections.[14]

On 19 April 1950, Prime Minister Nehru made a statement in Parliament that elections would be held in the Spring of 1951.[15] To facilitate and expedite the formalisation of the election procedure, the electoral law was enacted in two stages. Indeed, the final passage of the Bill happened as late as May 1951, when the Bill was discussed in Parliament well after the working hours to consider the select committee's recommendation and important amendments pertaining to disqualification of members and their code of conduct. The rush to take the Bill expeditiously through the second reading stage was precipitated by the discussion scheduled for the next day (that is, 29 May 1951) for the passage of the first constitutional amendment. The *Times of India* on the following day described these proceedings as follows:

The pigeons that inhabit the Council chamber by day had long gone home to roost and the bats had begun their tedious round of nocturnal

[14] 'Ensuing Election: Great Expectations,' *The Hindu*, 23 October 1951.
[15] Election Commission of India, *Report of the First General Election of India 1951–52*, pp. 22–3.

inquiry when Parliament adjourned at 9.30 tonight after the marathon extra five-hour evening sitting called solely to complete the second reading of the Electoral Bill. The hurry was provoked by the government's desire to take up the Constitution Amendment Bill tomorrow. It proved conclusive despite the urgent request of some members voiced by Pandit Kunzru, that they be given adequate opportunity to study the Select Committee's report on that most important measure. Notwithstanding the many informal meetings that have been held in the House, sitting in committees, and the Congress Parliamentary Party to thrash out amendments to the dozen odd clauses outstanding, there were several amendments moved to the 'agreed' amendments, which came up for protracted discussion [sic]. Accordingly, though the second reading could be accomplished, the third reading has had to be postponed till after the Constitution Amendment is through.[16]

The process of making the law to regulate the conduct of elections was described by CEC Sukumar Sen as 'piece-meal' legislation—a cumbersome and unsatisfactory procedure, but necessary for meeting the emergent conditions. The CEC wrote:

Although such piece-meal legislation were not quite satisfactory and may tend to leave a layman confused in the tangled multiplicity of legislative measures, there was hardly any other alternative. The difficulty was appreciated at the time and it has always been the intention to replace all this mass of dispersed law after the first general elections by a comprehensive Election Code and a body of consolidated Rules made thereunder. At present, certain piece-meal amendments of the election law are on the legislative anvil but no attempt has yet been made to codify the entire election law in a comprehensive manner. It is very desirable, however, that this work should be completed at least a year before the next general elections so that the election machinery, the political parties, the candidates and the individual voter may become fully conversant with the law under which the next elections will take place.[17]

---

[16] 'Electoral Bill Passes Second Reading,' *The Times of India*, 29 May 1951.

[17] Election Commission of India, *Report of the First General Election of India 1951–52*, p. 6. Under each of these two acts, statutory rules were made by the central government. These were respectively called the Representation of the People (Preparation of Electoral Rolls) Rules, 1950, and the Representation

While the massive task of conducting elections was initiated earlier with the beginning of the preparation of the electoral rolls,[18] the setting up of an election commission in January 1950 and the appointment of Sukumar Sen in March 1950 as the first CEC gave the process institutional form and coherence. The Constitution of India had laid down the institutional framework of electoral governance, but left it to Parliament to fill in the legal frameworks for conducting elections. The RPAs, 1950 and 1951, were subsequently passed by Parliament. Those aspects of electoral administration, which were to be addressed urgently, were incorporated in the RPA, 1950, passed by Parliament on 20 April 1950. The 1950 Act provided for the qualification of voters, the modalities of the preparation and publication of electoral rolls, the delimitation of constituencies, and the number of seats allocated to Parliament and the legislatures of different states. The provisions laying down the nuts and bolts of the actual conduct of elections were included in RPA, 1951, which was enacted as late as 17 July 1951. The second Act covered matters of qualification and disqualification of members of Parliament and state legislatures, and the micro-procedures for conducting elections at all stages, including the administrative machinery at all levels, the counting of votes, resolution of election disputes, and so on.

---

of the People (Conduct of Elections and Election Petitions) Rules, 1951. Subsequently, the two acts were amended by the following measures: The Representation of the People (Amendment) Act, 1950, The Representation of the People (Amendment) Act, 1951, The Representation of the People (Second Amendment) Act, 1951. Some amendments to the provisions of the two main acts were also made by the Government of Part C States Act, 1951, in order that some of the Part C states might be provided with legislative assemblies. Amendments were made in the rules from time to time as and when necessary (see 'Introduction'. Election Commission of India, *Report of the First General Election of India 1951–52*).

[18] A circular was sent to all provinces and states from the joint secretary of the Constituent Assembly Secretariat by 15 March 1948 with instructions for the preparation of the draft electoral roll on the basis of universal adult franchise, with the direction to start the work urgently (Shani 2018: 32). While the work on the electoral roll began before the constitutional provisions on citizenship had been confirmed, Shani (2018: 32) writes that the roll was pegged on the draft constitution and derived its legitimacy from it.

When the ECI started functioning under the new CEC, it assessed the state of preparedness of the electoral machinery for holding elections in 1950 and found it wanting. The electoral law was yet to be passed by Parliament. The scheduled castes and scheduled tribes had not yet been specified as required under Articles 341 and 342 of the Constitution to enable the assessment of their numbers in each state for the apportionment of reserved seats in the Lok Sabha and the state legislatures. The electoral rolls that were being prepared at the behest of the Constituent Assembly Secretariat were still 'informal' without any legal authority or sanction by the electoral law. The electoral rolls could, moreover, not be published for each constituency since the work of delimiting the constituencies could not be taken up in the absence of an Order under Article 387 of the Constitution for the delimitation of the population of the states and the different areas within the state. Furthermore, there was no uniformity in the level of preparedness of each state, so that even if elections could be held in some states in the winter of 1950–1, the rest of the states were way behind. Thus, even though the government hoped to hold an early election to give Parliament the stamp of popular sovereignty, firming of the laws governing the conduct of elections took place incrementally and in installments. Preparations for the first general election had, therefore, to be undertaken before the election law could be fully codified. This delay meant that the promise of a Spring 1951 election receded progressively.

Delimitation, Identification, and Enumeration

The provision of universal adult franchise and the constitutional right to vote set in motion a governmental activity of identification and enumeration of the voting population. This exercise of identification was, however, distinct since its objective was not the enhancement of the governmental power of the state, but the affirmation of popular sovereignty and transition to a democratic republic. In her book *How India Became Democratic* (2018), Ornit Shani examines the bureaucratic processes of the preparation of the electoral roll. In the course of her examination, Shani argues that Indians became voters before they became citizens. Indeed, it was in the course of the preparation of the preliminary electoral rolls, set in motion by 'the note' sent from the Constituent Assembly Secretariat to the various provinces and states of India on 15 March 1948, that the process of inserting 'the people' into the administrative structures of the state was initiated. It was the quest for a 'place in the roll', argues Shani (2018: 7), that prepared the ground for 'the conceptions and principles of democratic citizenship that were produced in the process of constitution making from above'. It was the implementation of universal franchise that elicited 'both a sense of Indianness and commitment to democratic nationhood' (Shani 2018: 2). Indeed, it was in the contestations and the language of interaction that was produced at the ground level, in the process of making the roll, that political imagination itself was democratised (Shani 2018: 6). Describing the electoral roll as a 'serialised epic', Shani suggests that preparation of the electoral roll on the basis of *universal* adult franchise became part of the 'popular narrative', and that through a process of consultation, the Constituent Assembly Secretariat (CAS) engaged public officials, people, and citizens' associations in the details of voter registration and citizenship, *mentoring* them into both the abstract principle and practices of electoral democracy, so much so that 'people and administrators began using the draft constitution to pursue their citizenship and voting rights, and they linked its abstract text to their everyday lives' (Shani 2018: 252–3). When Shani makes the point about Indians becoming voters before they became citizens, she is perhaps referring to the fact that the *legal* affirmation of citizenship happened *only* with the commencement of the Constitution. While there was a legal vacuum on who were Indian citizens (there were, in fact, two periods of such vacuum between 1947 and 1949 and then again between 1949 and 1955, when the Citizenship Act of India was passed by Parliament), it did not mean that questions of legal citizenship were not being addressed in 'problem' cases through instructions from the CAS. Indeed, the questions of legal citizenship were coming up and were being addressed primarily in the context of preparing the electoral roll, since only citizens could vote. Indeed, rather than a sequential development, one could perhaps see them as overlapping and simultaneous, taking shape through documentation practices of the state, and alongside the development of the institutions of the state and their functional differentiation. Indeed, over the years (and controversially so), resolution of the contest over citizenship in the preparation of electoral roll has come within the purview of the 'superintendence and control' of elections function of the ECI (under Article 324).

The affirmation of popular sovereignty involved identifying citizens, for the Constitution permitted only citizens to vote, and a process of constituting an electorate delimited into territorial electoral constituencies, spread across and juxtaposed onto the national territorial map of India. Since the next census was not due to take place until 1951, Article 387 of the Constitution authorised the president of India to determine the modalities of fixing the population of the country for holding an election during a period of three years from the commencement of the Constitution. Accordingly, the Constitution (Determination of Population) Order, 1950, was issued by the president, which required that the population of the states should be fixed by 1 March 1950 to facilitate the allocation of seats to different states through the RPA. The presidential order also laid down the procedure to be adopted for arriving at an estimate and to fix the population of a particular state. Under the procedure, the population of a state was ascertained by taking into account the population figure for the state in the census of 1941, which was to be adjusted by all available records regarding births and deaths in that territory, 'the mathematical projection of the trend indicated by the population figures of that territory as ascertained at the last five decennial censuses' and also 'the movement of displaced persons'.[19] Since the exact population figures could not be ascertained till after the next census, which would mean well after the exercise began in 1951, in the absence of precise population figures, it was the provisional electoral roll, being prepared across the country, that served as the base figure on which the population of a state was to be calculated. Clause 6 of the president's order under Article 387 laid down that for the purpose of the first general elections (to be held within a period of three years of the commencement of the Constitution), and the delimitation of constituencies for that election,

the population of any area within a state to be included in a constituency shall, unless in the case of any particular area or class of areas the

[19] Note for the Cabinet by K.V.K. Sundaram, Secretary, Ministry of Law, File no. F.2/12/50 MHA–Public, National Archives of India (NAI), 12 April 1950.

President otherwise directs, be determined by multiplying the number of voters entered in the provisional electoral rolls of that area by the total population of that state ... and then by dividing the product by the total number of voters entered in the provisional electoral rolls of the whole state.[20]

Explaining the need for fixing the population of a state for the purpose of delimiting constituencies, K.V.K. Sundaram, secretary in the law ministry, wrote the following in a note dated 12 April 1950:

The Constitution further requires that Parliamentary constituencies, as well as Assembly constituencies, shall be so delimited that the estimated population of the constituency divided by the number of members allotted to it is, so far as practicable, be the same throughout the territory of India in the former case and that of the state in the latter. Since correct population figures for specified local areas will not be available till some time after the next census, it is proposed that for the purpose of delimiting constituencies, the population of any area within a state should be assumed to vary in exact proportion to the number of persons included in the provisional electoral rolls for that area. This assumption must be correct within narrow limits since all persons over the age of 21 on a certain date are to be enrolled.[21]

The first narrative report of the ECI admits that the work of delimitation of constituencies had to be completed following a 'very tight time-table' to cover the various stages of the work. As it turned out, however, before the third session of Parliament in November 1950, when the ECI reviewed the state of preparedness for holding the elections, the delay in the issue of president's orders specifying the scheduled castes and scheduled tribes and determining their population in the different states, which in turn was dependent on the communication of the same to the president by the Parliamentary Advisory Committee, meant that the work on delimitation of constituencies could not take off immediately. In the meantime, however, the

---

[20] Draft Order, File no. F.2/12/50 MHA–Public, NAI.

[21] Note for the Cabinet by K.V.K. Sundaram, Secretary, Ministry of Law, File no. F.2/12/50 MHA–Public, NAI, 12 April 1950.

ECI had requested the state governments to send to it by May 1950, their proposals for dividing the units corresponding with the seats allotted to it for the legislative assembly and Lok Sabha. Some of these seats could be later paired to constitute two-member constituencies in which one seat could be reserved for the Scheduled Castes and Scheduled Tribes. These suggestions from the states took long in coming in, especially from the Part A and Part B states.[22]

Earlier, however, by July 1948, the Secretariat of the Constituent Assembly had made a *public announcement* of what it proposed to do regarding the enumeration of voters. In this announcement, it declared 1 January 1949 as the cut-off date for the preparation of the electoral rolls for each village or any other convenient unit. All such rolls from the units could be consolidated to put together the electoral rolls for each constituency, when the delimitation of constituencies was finally done. Since the electoral law was not yet in place, instructions were issued explaining how refugees were to be enumerated and the names of those who were serving sentences in prisons for criminal offences were to be included. While the statutory publication of electoral rolls could not take place until the electoral law came into existence, nonetheless, the states were asked to print the preliminary rolls, publish them, and receive claims for inclusion 'informally', so that the finalisation of electoral rolls when the election law was enacted could be done expeditiously. In his narrative report on the first general election, CEC Sukumar Sen noted that the 'pre-tentative' preparation of the preliminary electoral rolls was 'reasonably successful'.

When the RPA was enacted in 1950, it opened up new challenges. The electoral rolls, which were being prepared under the instructions of the ECI following the directives of the Constituent Assembly, had to now comply with the new procedures laid down in the RPA, 1950. The RPA had added a large age group hitherto not part of the electoral rolls, by bringing up the cut-off to 1 January 1950 (from the earlier cut-off date of 1 January 1949) for the purpose of registration of voters. The ECI subsequently had to take steps to prepare supplementary rolls for every town and village, delaying the publication of

[22] See Election Commission of India, *Report of the First General Election of India 1951–52*, p. 25.

the electoral rolls till the supplementary rolls were ready. The CEC appears, however, to have taken this delay as an advantage, since it gave the ECI time to scrutinise the draft rolls already prepared, addressing the allegations of large-scale omissions raised in Punjab and Assam, and personally visit each state in order to check the state of preparations for holding the elections.[23] In Punjab, for example, the ECI is reported to have revised the entire electoral rolls thoroughly to eliminate the numerous duplicate entries that had crept in as a result of the movement of displaced persons within the state during the preparation of the electoral rolls following the allotment of land to them. Bombay city, on the other hand, where the electoral rolls had been prepared and published only in the *Devanagri* script, was asked to publish it in English as well. Similar instructions were issued to the states of Bihar, Orissa, and Madras, to prepare bilingual electoral rolls.[24] The ECI directed that the electoral rolls of all constituencies, when finalised, be published and publicly displayed at a prominent place at the headquarters of the ERO.[25] Compounding the challenge for the ECI, when the delimitation of the boundaries of constituencies was finally done, these boundaries were different from those that had been envisaged by the ECI, making the collation of the electoral rolls labour- and time-consuming. This again contributed to the delay in the finalisation and publication of the electoral rolls any time before September 1951. Due to the different stages of preparedness of states, the ECI could not fix a single date for publication and display for all of them. The states, therefore, displayed the lists when they were ready, at different times, and the last rolls were published on 15 November 1951. Sukumar Sen notes that while the purpose of publication of electoral rolls was to give the voters an opportunity to object to the inclusion of names of those not entitled to be part of the rolls, and also present claims for inclusion in case their names had not been included—both within a specified period—which was later under

[23] Election Commission of India, *Report of the First General Election of India 1951–52*, pp. 22–4.

[24] Election Commission of India, *Report of the First General Election of India 1951–52*, p. 27.

[25] Election Commission of India, *Report of the First General Election of India 1951–52*, p. 67.

the law to be a period of 21 days, the ECI adopted a policy of flexibility in receiving objections and claims. Admitting that ordinarily a voter is 'apathetic', especially when the election date was still some time ahead, or as in the case of India where universal adult suffrage was still an unfamiliar exercise, the ECI 'liberally extended the date' for filing claims and objections in all states. Indeed, the ECI placed the responsibility to invoke interest in the electoral process and the procedures, which were involved in the conduct of election, with the political parties and their workers at the grass roots.[26]

On 10 October 1951, the CEC made an announcement in Bharatpur in Rajasthan that the time limit, which had been prescribed earlier for raising objections to non-inclusion of names, had been withdrawn, and any person whose name was omitted from the voters' list could get his/her name included anytime, even as late as the polling day itself by paying a penalty of Rs 50.[27] The following month, however, a notice was issued by the ECI in the press in response to the numerous requests the Commission was receiving through telegrams, letters, and phone calls by prospective candidates wishing to contest elections, for the expeditious inclusion of their names in the electoral rolls with the payment of the stipulated fine. The ECI clarified that the enrolment as a voter was not automatic, and before an order was issued, the Commission had to satisfy itself that the applicant was qualified to become an elector.[28]

The 'Descriptive' Women and Women Voters

According to the figures cited by CEC Sukumar Sen in the first narrative report, the total number of voters enrolled in the electoral rolls

---

[26] The maximum numbers of 'claims' were presented in Assam (102,339), and the maximum number of claims and objections were filed in Uttar Pradesh (765,521 claims and 344,227 objections). Altogether, a total of 1,658,428 claims and 731,750 objections were filed throughout the country, of which 1,393,526 claims and 712,802 objections, were allowed. (Election Commission of India, *Report of the First General Election of India 1951–52*, p. 70.)

[27] 'Electoral Rolls: Rectification of Omissions,' *The Hindu*, 11 October 1951.

[28] 'Enrollment of Voters,' *The Hindu*, 21 November 1951.

in the entire country, except Jammu and Kashmir, was 173,213,635, of whom about 45 per cent were women. According to the 1951 census, the population of India was 356,691,760, and the CEC estimated that 49 per cent of the total population was enrolled as voters. Considering that by the census figures, the percentage of adults, that is, those above 21 years of age (180,307,684) was 50–5 per cent of the total population, the CEC found the enrolment of voters 'reasonably' satisfactory. It may be noted that the CEC mentions 7,034,839 adults as having been left out, some of whom, he states, 'must have lacked the necessary qualifications'.[29] In the case of women voters, however, the ECI's narrative report admits that a large number of women voters had to be dropped from the rolls for reasons that were different.

In the course of the preparation of the electoral rolls, a large number of women voters enrolled in some states not in their own names but 'by the description of the relationship they bore to their male relations', for example, as someone's mother or wife, since they were not comfortable disclosing their names to strangers. When this phenomenon of enrolment of women voters through their male relatives came to the attention of the ECI, it issued the instruction that the name of the voter was an essential part of his or her identity and should be included in the electoral roll with all other essential particulars. Directions were issued to substitute relationships with proper names, and in case a woman refused to give her name, she should not be registered, and if she had already registered by description only, she should be dropped from the roll. Public appeals were issued to people to encourage them to give details and extensions of a month were given to EROs in various states, like Bihar which had a number of such 'descriptive' women, to reduce the number of women whose names were likely to be struck off from the electoral rolls. While Bihar was reported to have made good use of the extension, the response was not successful in Rajasthan and a large number of descriptive entries of women voters, which could not be substituted by their proper names, were deleted from the electoral rolls. According to the ECI, 'out of a total of nearly 80 million women voters in the country,

[29] Election Commission of India, *Report of the First General Election of India 1951–52*, pp. 68–9.

nearly 2–8 million eventually failed to disclose their proper names, and the entries relating to them had to be deleted from the rolls. Practically all such cases were from the States of Bihar, Uttar Pradesh, Madhya Bharat, Rajasthan and Vindhya Pradesh'.[30] The *Times of India* reported the CEC's statement to the press acknowledging that roughly 10 per cent of the total women electorate in five states had been struck off the list. The CEC, according to the report, welcomed the protest over their omission from the electoral roll, hoping that in the next annual revision of the electoral rolls, social prejudice and ignorance would be overcome, and of the 'stupendous' total of 17.5-crore voters, half would be women.[31]

Women MPs met the prime minister with an appeal to restore the names of those 'orthodox women' who were dropped from the voters' list for having registered as wives, mothers, or daughters. Describing the efforts of women parliamentarians, a report in *The Hindu*, on 25 August 1951 suggested that the 'progressive' women were in fact wary of the 'orthodox' women who did not register in their names. They feared that in case such women electors were also elected to Parliament, they may decide to vote against the Hindu Code Bill, which was to come up for Parliament's consideration.[32] On the other hand, Vidya Devi, president of the All India Mahila Sangh, made a statement in Varanasi, asking the ECI to restore the names of the 28-lakh disenfranchised women, who were merely following the sacred Indian traditional customs whereby a woman's identity is not derived only from her name but other relationships. To deny women the right to vote for such a 'trifling lapse', she argued, would amount to 'grave injustice'.[33] In the meantime, while it was the ECI that could decide the modalities of the inclusion of women's names, the government seemed to be in favour of allowing women to enrol as wives and to retain the names of women who had enrolled as such. Later, in response

[30] Election Commission of India, *Report of the First General Election of India 1951–52*, p. 73.

[31] '28,00,000 Women Voters Struck off Rolls,' *The Times of India*, 4 August 1951.

[32] 'Disenfranchised Women: Effort to Include Women,' *The Hindu*, 25 August 1951.

[33] 'Women's Right of Franchise,' *Hindustan Times*, 9 August 1951.

to a question in Parliament, B.R. Ambedkar refuted the charge that the disenfranchisement of lakhs of women had taken place because the officials in charge of preparing the electoral rolls were not given proper instructions. On the contrary, the ECI had given specific instructions to register women in their proper names. It sought the help of the state governments to ensure that these instructions were communicated and followed, and of the public to assist the officials in the preparation of the electoral rolls.[34]

The ECI's refusal to register women 'descriptively' was couched in a language that appeared to make it the responsibility of the woman to register 'appropriately', failing which she would bear the penalty of the removal of her name from the electoral roll. Unlike the system that prevails in countries like the United States of America, the RPA endows a positive responsibility on the EROs to enumerate voters in the manner required under the prevailing laws, rather than expect the voters to 'conform to the registration process' (Singer 2007: 80). The 'non-disclosure' of their names by women, leading to their removal from the electoral rolls, was partly due to the requirement in the registration forms to report kinship relation for the purpose of verification. The process of registration of voters required a house-to-house movement by the registration officers to fill out forms that listed the names of eligible voters in the house, along with the names of their husbands (in the case of women) and fathers.

When polling began, there were reports of women voting enthusiastically, even in those constituencies where polling was reported to be in general 'extremely dull'. In parts of Orissa, for example, particularly the hilly areas of Mayurbhanj and other constituencies of Puri district, there was poor voter turnout. The *Times of India* reported relatively active voting in coastal areas. While some Adivasi women placed the ballot paper near the boxes rather than inserting them inside the box, at Athgarh, the majority of voters who exercised their franchise were women.[35] The *Times of India* on 24 December, covering the polling in Hyderabad, had the following headline: 'Women Voters Preponderate in Election', noting in particular the

[34] 'Non-inclusion of Women Voters,' *The Hindu*, 26 September 1951.

[35] 'Poor Polling in Orissa: More Women Voters,' *The Times of India*, 26 December 1951.

Table 1.1 Women Voters as Percentage of Total Electors

	Total electors	Men electors	Women electors	Total who voted	Men who voted	Women who voted	Percentage of women electors who voted
1952	173,213	95,267	77,946	80,709	51,997	28,732	36.8
		(55%)	(45%)		(64.4%)	(35.6%)	
1957	193,652	102,206	92,141	91,329	55,924	35,405	38.7
		(52.8%)	(47.2%)		(61.2%)	(38.8%)	

Source: The Reports on General Elections, Statistical Volumes, for 1952, and 1957, available in Singer (2007: 81).

heavy polling in Aland, where 68 per cent of the voters exercised their franchise. 'Women Voters here', the newspaper noted, 'including *purdah* women, were much in evidence' and were 'preponderating in a number of rural areas'.[36]

When the second general election took place in 1957, the number of women voters had increased from 77,946 million, which constituted 45 per cent of the electorate, to 92,141 million, that is, 47 per cent of the electorate. Interestingly, in the 1957 general elections, as shown in Table 1.1, the percentage of men electors rose from 95,267 million to 102,206 million, which was, however, a slide from 55 per cent of the electorate in 1952 to 52 per cent in 1957. Significantly, the percentage of women who voted in the 1957 elections rose from 35.6 per cent in 1952 to 38.8 per cent. For the men, it fell from 64.4 per cent to 61.2 per cent.

Displaced Persons, Refugees, and the Predicament of 'Hustled' Constituencies

Interestingly, while recounting the difficulties of preparing the electoral roll, the election commissioner identified, among other things, the apathy and inexperience of eligible voters, and the manner in which the preparation of the rolls was left entirely to the government

---

[36] 'Women Voters Preponderate in Elections,' *The Times of India*, 24 December 1951.

bureaucracy. The political parties did little to help, even though they were in a position to do so. Among civil society groups, it was only the displaced persons' associations that took interest, pointed out the defects that existed in the enumeration of displaced persons, and took advantage of the special facilities that were being provided by the government for their enrolment.

We may recall that on 8 January 1949, the Constituent Assembly of India had adopted a motion by Prime Minister Nehru issuing instructions for the preparation of the electoral rolls and for taking all the necessary steps for holding elections as early as possible in 1950.[37] This required speedy enumeration of voters in a context where there were no prior existing electoral rolls based on *universal* adult franchise, and questions of citizenship remained liminal. The resolution of these questions involved officials from institutions as diverse as the ECI and the Ministries of Home, Law, Rehabilitation, and External Affairs. It was, however, as early as November 1947 that the Constituent Assembly had alerted the state governments of its decision to introduce adult franchise for elections and asked them to assess the administrative problems they foresaw in the preparation of a voters' list based on adult franchise. Indeed, as soon as the draft constitution was published on 21 February 1948, the Secretariat of the Constituent Assembly also made the states aware of the appropriateness of holding elections to both the central and provincial legislatures as soon as the new Constitution came into force. The Secretariat also issued detailed instructions for the preparation of the voters' list with regard to age, citizenship, and residential qualifications of a voter. Of these, the instructions on citizenship remained somewhat inconclusive since the Constituent Assembly had not taken any decision so far about the qualifications for citizenship. The provisions pertaining to elections and citizenship in the Constitution came into force on 26 November 1949, that is, the date on which the Constitution was finally passed by the Constituent Assembly, two months before the date of the commencement of the Constitution on 26 January 1950. In the interim period, the ECI faced the difficult question of enrolling the large numbers of displaced persons who had migrated from the

---

[37] Election Commission of India, *Report of the First General Election of India 1951–52*, p. 27.

territories that were now part of Pakistan after their citizenship status had been affirmed. The government advised the states that the names of all persons who had migrated to India must be included in the voters' list of a town or village 'on a mere declaration by them', that they intended to reside permanently there, irrespective of how long they had actually been residing there.[38]

For the ECI, the displaced persons posed a serious problem of enrolment, especially in West Bengal, Punjab, Assam, and Delhi, where the Partition had seen massive cross-border movement of population. This population, moreover, was not stationary but constantly on the move. In Delhi, for example, a large number of displaced persons, who resided in temporary shelters when the electoral rolls started being prepared, had by September 1951, when the rolls were finally published, shifted to colonies and townships set up for their rehabilitation. These voters were then not entitled to vote in the polling stations that were set up in the localities in which they came to finally reside. The localities where they were originally resident and were enrolled as voters now formed a part of another constituency. To overcome this problem of dislocation, the Delhi Transport Authority ran special buses on the polling day, to enable displaced persons to cast their vote.[39] Similar conditions prevailed in West Bengal and Punjab, two other states that had experienced large influx of persons displaced from Pakistan.

The Constituent Assembly had decided that the names of all displaced persons be included in the voters' list on the strength of their oral declaration. The states were instructed to enroll all such persons in the electoral rolls and place a distinguishing mark against their names, so that their citizenship status may be confirmed after the Constitution came into force. The narrative report of the ECI states that the third letter of the Urdu alphabet was used to mark such persons to distinguish them from others whose citizenship status was unambiguous. In finalising the voters' list after the commencement of the Constitution, the 'marked voters' presented a critical

[38] Election Commission of India, *Report of the First General Election of India 1951–52*, p. 21.
[39] Election Commission of India, *Report of the First General Election of India 1951–52*, p. 70.

administrative problem, since Article 6 of the Indian Constitution lay down that all those who came to India after the constitutional deadline of 19 July 1948 had to register themselves as Indian citizens. While a majority of persons who migrated from West Pakistan to India had arrived before the constitutional deadline and had automatically become Indian citizens, those who came later had not acquired Indian citizenship and could not vote. Following a public notice inviting such persons to apply for Indian citizenship, they were made Indian citizens, and citizenship certificates were issued to 8,051 persons, who were then enrolled as voters. Almost 1,100,000 voters were registered in the supplementary electoral rolls of Punjab, which included those voters also who had shifted from their original place of residence at the time of enrolment to the quasi-permanent allotment of land and houses to them in other parts of the state. Representations were received pertaining to a large number of duplicate entries because of the constant movement and rehabilitation of displaced persons. The ECI used the postponement of the election as an opportunity to eliminate duplicate entries and 82,497 such entries were removed from the voters' list.[40]

These questions continued to invoke concern and indecision even after the first general election. The official files in the Citizenship Section of the Ministry of Home Affairs reveal that the government issued directions for the facilitation of acquisition of Indian citizenship by displaced minorities from Pakistan. This was to be accomplished not just through their expeditious registration as citizens but also through their urgent inclusion in the electoral rolls, in time for the second general elections. Thus, when the draft citizenship rules were being framed in 1956, the deputy secretary (Home Affairs), issued 'urgent' instructions to various state governments asking them to make 'immediate arrangements' for the registration of displaced persons under Section 5(1)(a) of the Citizenship Act 1955, linking it up with the enrolment of voters for the next general elections. The letter, copied also to the Ministries of External Affairs, Rehabilitation, Law, and to the ECI, stressed the necessity of taking immediate steps so that the displaced persons who had migrated from Pakistan and

---

[40] Election Commission of India, *Report of the First General Election of India 1951–52*, p. 72.

had not yet become citizens of India could exercise their franchise in the next general election.[41]

In November and December 1951—the two months preceding the polls—the *Hindustan Times* carried a series 'Refugee Log' under the pseudonym 'kith and kin'. The log raised issues of disenfranchise-ment of displaced persons, focusing in particular on the administra-tive lapses and inadequacies in electoral law as far as the protection of voting rights of refugees in Delhi was concerned. A 17 December 1951 'log' referred to a pamphlet 'alluringly' titled *Your Rights as a Voter* brought out by the Publications Division of the Government of India. Much to the disappointment of 'kith and kin', the pamphlet did not mention anything about the right of the refugees to vote. It referred, however, to what it called the 'next best thing', since the 'ideal arrangement' of every voter voting from 'his own home' could not be made, which was increasing the number of polling stations and placing them as close as possible to the voters' homes. 'Kith and kin' remarked:

> But in India's capital nearly one lakh refugee voters have been, by state authorities or by State policy removed to suburban settlements situated at long distances from polling booths where they are supposed to exer-cise their votes—often 8 to 10 miles, sometimes quite 15 miles. Such a situation implies a wholesale disenfranchisement in effect and carries within it a great temptation for crimes of impersonation. The nearness of the booth is a basic assumption underlying the present election law. I am afraid this fact is not being sufficiently well realized. In dismiss-ing a refugee writ petition raising this question their lordships of the Simla High Court are reported to have observed that it being open to the refugee voters of Delhi's suburban settlements to go to the polling booths in the areas where they were registered two years earlier, no redress was needed [*sic*]. ... I had occasion last week to cite the provisions of the law intended to safeguard refugee's electoral rights in situations like the one in which suburban Delhi's displaced persons find them-selves. That provision has been made so little known and so little put to use that it is no better than a dead letter.... I cannot recall any reference to this provision in law in the educative broadcasts regarding the great

[41] Executive instructions issued in a letter from the Deputy Secretary (Home) dated 14 June 1956. File no. 10/1/56, MHA–IC, NAI.

enterprise to the general election, whether by the Prime Minister or by the Chief Election Commissioner.[42]

There were two aspects of the problem of disenfranchisement of refugees as expressed in the 'Refugee Log' by 'kith and kin'. The loss of franchise because of rehabilitation/relocation to refugee colonies was only one aspect of the problem. The second related aspect was the loss of representation, which occurred partly because of disenfran-chisement as an outcome of rehabilitation, but also because of the manner in which constituencies were crafted in Delhi, particularly for the assembly elections. Assembly constituencies in Delhi, as was argued in the log, were 'hustled' constituencies, rather than 'natural' constituencies that would follow the logic of 'shared interest'. A correspondent from Jangpura refugee township reported that large numbers of refugee families living there had been 'transplanted' from areas in the walled city or from New Delhi's central areas where they lived at the time the electoral rolls were being prepared. In order to cast their votes, they would now have to travel to polling booths about 10 miles away from their present place of residence. This applied also to refugee 'townships' like Lajpat Nagar, Malaviya Nagar, and Kalkaji, all of which had relocated inhabitants whose polling booths were 10–15 miles away. In some cases, voters were registered in Patiala and East Punjab States Union (PEPSU) and Punjab, but would have liked to vote in Delhi (in the legislative assembly elections), where they were residents now. Indeed, 'kith and kin' argued that the electoral rolls of Delhi were not truly representative of the constituencies, since a large number of people were not enrolled in their constituencies of residence, having been 'forcibly evicted to remote townships'.[43]

In an interesting espousal of the idea of 'natural' constituencies, the refugee log saw the 'refugee townships' forming natural con-stituencies 'just by themselves or readily so with small additions from areas on their periphery' for the state assembly election. One gets a sense of the distinction being made by 'kith and kin' between

[42] 'Your Rights as a Voter: D.P.'s Grievances,' *Hindustan Times*, 17 December 1951.

[43] 'Delhi Divided into 42 Constituencies,' *Hindustan Times*, 21 November 1951.

a 'natural' constituency and a 'hustled' constituency from the official
description of the 42 assembly constituencies that were carved out in
Delhi following a territorial grid. In each case, the description showed
a pattern of territorial demarcation pegged around particular police
stations joined to other official places by straight lines and junctions,
interspersed with bazaars and roads. The description of the Ajmeri
Gate constituency is illustrative:

> Such of the area of Hauz Qazi Police Station as is bounded by the
> straight line starting from the junction of Kucha Pati Ram with Bazar
> Sita Ram, along Bazar Sita Ram to its junction with Lal Kuan Bazar up
> to its junction with Mohalla Rodgran and along Mohalla Rodgran to its
> junction with G.B. Road and then along G.B. Road towards North up
> to its junction with the boundary of Kotwali Police Station and then an
> imaginary straight line up to G.I.P. Railway Line up to its junction with
> New Delhi Municipal Committee boundary and then along with the
> New Delhi Municipal Committee boundary to its junction with Kucha
> Pati Ram to its junction with Bazar Sita Ram—starting point [sic].[44]

The problem of disenfranchisement had its roots in what the All
India Refugee Association saw as nearly two lakh refugees being
'virtually thrown out' of the places where they were enrolled and
relocated to the 30,000–35,000 residential units established by the
Ministry of Rehabilitation. The All India Refugee Association alleged
that since the law required a 180-day period of residence for a person
to be registered as voter in a constituency, most refugees being new
residents were not registered. Since entire townships were inhabited
by refugees, this basically meant that the electoral rolls did not take
notice of certain townships at all. These townships did not exist as
far as the electoral rolls were concerned, and the delimitation process
was 'carried out not in its natural way but as dictated by the serial
order in the electoral register', either losing sight of these townships
completely or noting them as 'uninhabited land':

> There is no sense in urging that the electoral map divided with 42 divi-
> sions includes the area of the township also—that of course it does,

[44] 'Delhi Divided into 42 Constituencies,' *Hindustan Times*, 21 November
1951.

but it includes this area as uninhabited land! This means that townships which have a natural aspiration for being treated as constituencies by themselves or as the essential core of constituencies are treated by the electoral map as the least important part of their respective constituencies! And if the election is based on such a map for 5 years these townships may continue to go virtually unrepresented in the Assembly. They will not be able to claim anyone as their representative who will pay special heed to their peculiar problem ... A prospective Congress candidate was telling me a short while ago about his difficulty in the choice between two possible constituencies for he did not know whether a particular slice of special interest to him falls in one constituency or the other.... The Delhi State Legislature is of special interest to the refugee cause as the refugee population is nearly 45 per cent of the total population (emphasis added).[45]

The argument being made was that the ECI had acted with 'unreasonable haste' rather than 'reasonable speed' in announcing the delimitation for Delhi State Assembly constituencies, with the result that it had 'short circuited' the basic procedure. A far more satisfactory procedure would have been to invite claims and objections pertaining to the electoral roll of each constituency. The authorities, however, to save time, labour, and money, used the parliamentary roll prepared two years ago to elect four members to represent Delhi in Parliament, when there was no intention of setting up a state assembly of 48 seats. The artificial delimitation of constituency assemblies was undertaken with each parliamentary constituency being divided into 12: 'This may sound easy arithmetic and at first thought it may promise neat geometrical divisions. Actually havoc has been wrought by such allurement'.[46]

The refugee log reported a special representation drive for refugees in West Punjab (in Pakistan) where a substantial proportion of the refugees who fled from India were rehabilitated, and a plan was devised for every constituency of 100,000 with 10,000 refugees to have at least one refugee representative. The representatives of displaced persons cited the West Punjab example as something that could be

---

[45] 'Refugee Townships Disenfranchised,' *Hindustan Times*, 19 November 1951.

[46] 'Assurances Not Enough,' *Hindustan Times*, 26 November 1951.

emulated in India, and any constituency with a refugee population of 40 per cent or more in the electoral roll could be treated as a 'refugee constituency'. The 'unnatural limitation that has been forced on Delhi by a hustled programme for the general election', precipitated by the Act giving a state legislature to Delhi two months back, had meant that for the next five years, 'such natural constituencies may remain without proper representation in the State Legislature.... If you consider these refugee townships, the situation is something like this. The electoral roll is just a *haphazard catalogue* in which voters from all localities have been indiscriminately jumbled. Cutting up of such a haphazard list roughly into 17000 entries apiece is being named delimitation' (emphasis added).[47]

Indeed, as pointed out by the refugee log, the RPA already provided that the requirement that a person should have been 'ordinarily resident' for at least 180 days during the qualifying period in the constituency in which he or she was to be registered be relaxed in the case of displaced persons. Section 20 laid down the meaning of 'ordinarily resident', but Section 20(7) made 'a very special and significant provision for safeguarding the electoral rights of the displaced persons'. It recognised the unsettled conditions of their lives by making an exception in the meaning of 'ordinarily resident' in their case. Accordingly, 'a person who was a citizen of India and had migrated from the territory of Pakistan into the territory of India before the 25th day of July 1949 on account of disturbances or fear of disturbances in the former place of residence would be deemed to have been ordinarily resident during any period or any date in the constituency in which he was resident on the said date or in any other constituency is specified by him in this behalf in the prescribed form and manner, in that other constituency too [sic]'. Indeed, the refugee log alleged that when an official of the All India Refugee Association personally called the electoral authorities in Delhi to enquire whether claims under Section 20(7) in the prescribed form had been invited and what was the last date for their submission, 'the staff concerned seemed to know nothing and referred the inquirer to the Election Commission's office'.[48]

---

[47] 'Delhi Divided into 42 Constituencies,' *Hindustan Times*, 21 November 1951.

[48] 'Raw Deal for Displaced Persons,' *Hindustan Times*, 10 December 1951.

The ECI, however, differed from the Refugee Association on the legal position. In its response to a memorandum sent by the Refugee Association, the ECI responded that the law provided for revision of electoral rolls under clause 3 of Section 25 of the RPA, 1950. Such a revision had to be 'an all-out revision for the general public and not merely for any particular section'. Any procedure of revision, even for exceptional cases, would follow the same procedure as the annual revision of electoral rolls. This could take months to finalise and may not be accomplished in time for the 1952 election. The Refugee Association, however, disagreed and argued that Section 25 did not refer to an 'all-out' revision *only* but also to a constituency or a part of a constituency, if there were 'special reasons' for doing so. It charged the ECI of thinking of revision only in terms of 'a prescribed routine', rather than in substantive terms, and refusing to frame new rules or modify and relax existing rules to address the special circumstances of the refugees.[49]

Draft Electoral Rolls and the Dilemma of Dates

Recounting the challenges generally faced by the ECI in the preparation of electoral rolls, the CEC noted that in some states like Madhya Pradesh, Bihar, Bombay, Uttar Pradesh, and Rajasthan, serious defects had occurred in the electoral rolls. In Madhya Pradesh, two villages were left out of the enrolment process. In Bihar, five villagers in the Sadar sub-division of Palamau district were left out, and in Bombay, around 3,000 persons found that their names had not been included in the rolls of the Pimpari Camp; in Rajasthan and Uttar Pradesh too, entire villages were left out completely. The CEC noted:

> Although the Commission was anxious to rectify these defects even before the final publication of the rolls, this was not possible, as the powers vested in the Commission by virtue of section 25(a) could not be invoked before the final publication of the rolls. No action could,

[49] 'Delhi Assembly Rolls—Injustice to D.P.s,' *Hindustan Times*, 3 December 1951. To push its argument on the relaxation of rules, the log referred to the draw of lots done the previous week by the rehabilitation ministry for the 'much deferred allotment' of flats and shops in Khan Market and the formal inauguration of Kamla Market.

therefore, be taken until after the rolls had been finally published. The delay in delimiting the constituencies led necessarily to delay in the final publication of the rolls and eventually, when the rolls were finally published, there was not sufficient time left for completing the revision of the rolls of these areas in time for the general elections. Under the procedure prescribed by the Rules, a revision of rolls requires a minimum of about two months. In order that the all-India programme for the general elections might not be upset, the Commission had to decide that the revision of these defective electoral rolls should not be undertaken. While the above instances demonstrate that it is necessary for the Commission to have the power of ordering the revision of rolls wherever necessary, such power would prove virtually ineffective unless a more speedy and summary procedure is made available. The law should therefore be suitably amended in this respect.[50]

The estimated requirement of paper for the printing of the rolls was so considerable that the Government of India had to make special arrangements for its supply in time for printing. In all, 384,215 reams of paper were used for the printing of the rolls, including supplementary rolls and the lists of additions and corrections. The considerable volume of printing work, coupled with the pressure to conform to the election programme, prompted the state governments to distribute the work to a large number of private presses along with the government press. The magnitude of the task to be completed within a prescribed period necessitated the payment of comparatively higher charges. As the boundaries and extent of the constituencies had not been settled at the time when the printing of rolls commenced, the printing presses were required to print the rolls separately for each village or town. After the constituencies had been finally delimited, a good deal of detailed and careful work had to be done to collate the rolls printed unit-wise, into sets of electoral rolls, constituency-wise. Some idea of the magnitude of the work can be formed from the fact that 16,523 clerks were employed for the purpose all over the country over a period of nearly 6 months.[51]

[50] Election Commission of India, *Report of the First General Election of India 1951–52*, pp. 79–80.
[51] Election Commission of India, *Report of the First General Election of India 1951–52*, p. 75.

We know from the earlier discussion that the draft rolls were being prepared on the instructions of the Constituent Assembly. The preliminary rolls could not, however, be published as the process of delimitation was still incomplete and it was not possible to publish the rolls without reference to specific constituencies. The draft electoral rolls were, however, published before the final delimitation of constituencies. If the publication of the rolls was postponed until the constituencies had been finally delimited, the delay would have had ramifications for the election schedule. On 1 November 1950, an amendment was made to Section 22 of the RPA, 1950, to allow for the preliminary publication of electoral rolls according to the administrative units without any reference to the constituencies.[52]

Interestingly, when all state governments were asked to give feedback on their state of preparedness and suggest a convenient date for the election, all states, apart from Uttar Pradesh, suggested October–December 1951 as the appropriate time. For Uttar Pradesh, however, January–February 1952 was the preferred choice.[53] The editorial in the *Hindustan Times* of 2 August 1951 was scathing in its criticism of the central government's inability to decide on the election date:

> It is not edifying for the Chief Election Commissioner to keep on eating his words. The fault is, of course, not his. The Government of India keeps on changing their mind regarding the dates for the coming general election. It is a far cry from April last, the date originally fixed by Mr. Nehru to January next. State Governments tend to relax when the Central directive is not firm and when such an issue is left to their discretion they naturally give weight to such considerations as the weather or the cultivator's convenience. Presumably, the President in his opening address to Parliament will explain why the firm announcement he made in his previous address has had to be modified.[54]

The ECI finally announced the dates of the elections for 18 out of 26 states publicly on 5 September 1951. The ECI announced that

[52] Election Commission of India, *Report of the First General Election of India 1951–52*, p. 30.

[53] Election Commission of India, *Report of the First General Election of India 1951–52*, p. 27.

[54] 'Election Problems,' *Hindustan Times*, 3 August 1951.

elections for these states were be held between 3 and 24 January 1951, with the precise dates of elections for each state to be recommended by each state government to the ECI, taking into account their local conditions.[55] Soon after the announcement of the election dates, the Government of India issued an 80-page booklet prepared by the law ministry in consultation with the ECI, giving details of the rules of procedure to be followed in the conduct of elections. Apart from the provision of postal ballots for the armed forces and diplomatic personnel, the booklet lay down in detail the ceiling on election expenses for candidates contesting the election for parliamentary and state assembly seats. These expenses calculated on the basis of the number of voters were different for single and multi-member constituencies, and for Part A, B, and C states.[56] To ensure that mail intended for the ECI at New Delhi would reach it without delay, the director general offered the facility of special bags. This was to ascertain that mail intended for the ECI did not get directed to any other post office in Delhi.[57]

Franchise Deferred

The institutional frameworks for the conduct of elections were taking form alongside the development of legal frameworks of citizenship as well as the statutory frameworks for ensuring representation through the electoral system. There were contestations over appropriate legal frameworks and institutional modalities through which effective representation could be achieved. We are already familiar with CEC Sukumar Sen's concerns over the 'piecemeal' manner in which electoral law on representation of the people was being enacted. The sites in which these contests played out reflected the uncertainties surrounding the statutory frameworks of elections. These sites ranged

[55] Except for the states of Himachal Pradesh, Travancore-Cochin, Madhya Pradesh, Orissa, Bhopal, and Bilaspur, which were to go to polls earlier than other states due to various reasons, all other states were to go to polls in January. 'Dates for General Elections Fixed,' *The Times of India*, 6 September 1951.

[56] 'Ceilings Fixed for Election Costs,' *The Times of India*, 14 September 1951.

[57] 'Special Post Bags for Election Commission,' *Hindustan Times*, 6 December 1951.

from Port Blair where people were dissatisfied with having been left out of the electoral process to specific states where the structure of electoral governance appropriate for the state were being debated.

On 28 March 1951, a public meeting of the local citizens of Port Blair in the Andaman and Nicobar Islands was called in the Netaji Club Hall at five in the evening. The reason for calling this meeting was the newly enacted RPA, 1950, which allocated seats to all the states and union territories of the country. Andaman and Nicobar Islands, which had the status of a union territory, was given a single seat. This seat was to be filled through nomination by the president of India, rather than by direct election through the exercise of universal adult franchise.[58] At the public meeting, an overwhelming sentiment of hurt prevailed. Sri Ratnam, secretary, Andaman Indians Association, spoke at the meeting, expressing that there existed no justification, 'moral or legal', 'to deny the people of these Islands the benefits of democracy', and suggested that the Government of India be approached through the chief commissioner of the Islands to demand that the people of Andamans too should 'enjoy the same rights as have been allowed to other states' in India.[59]

---

[58] Allocation of seats to all Part A and Part B States (excluding Jammu and Kashmir) in the Lok Sabha was made on the basis that one seat would be allotted for every 720,000 of the population, which was the average population for each seat in all these states taken together. The estimated population, as on 1 March 1950, was divided by 720,000 in respect of each of the states and the quotient gave the number of seats to be allotted to the state in the House. A fraction of more than one-half was rounded off to the next higher integer and entitled the state to an additional seat, while smaller fractions were ignored. In this way, 470 seats were allotted to the Part A and Part B states under Section 3 of the RPA, 1950, including the 6 seats allotted to Jammu and Kashmir. Under the same section, read with Article 82 of the Constitution, 25 seats were allotted to Part C states and 1 seat each was allotted to (a) the Andaman and Nicobar Islands and (b) the Part B tribal areas of Assam, making a total of 497 seats. The average population of 720,000 did not apply to Part C States or the aforesaid areas which, in fact, got a good deal of weightage in this respect. Election Commission of India, *Report of the First General Election of India 1951–52*, p. 51.

[59] Proceedings of the public meeting held on 28 March 1951, enclosed in File no. 55/20/51, A.N., NAI.

The response by the Government of India vacillated between reiterating the colonial argument that franchise must be deferred when people were incompetent to exercise political choice, and on the other hand, the practical difficulties of administering elections in a dispersed cluster of islands. A communication from the Government of India, sent in response to the recommendation by Chief Commissioner A.K. Ghosh that the 'representative of these Islands in the House be elected as in the rest of India', gave a set of reasons why the representative from the Andaman and Nicobar Islands would continue to be unelected. Dated 27 August 1951, the communication by Mr Iyenger, secretary with the Ministry of Home Affairs, conveyed to the chief commissioner that the 'A & N islands *have not yet reached the standard* required for direct election' (emphasis added), necessitating that a suitable person be nominated by the President. A note, dated 28 August 1951, by R.N. Philips, deputy secretary with the Government of India in the same file of communications, elaborated:

> The one seat allotted for Andaman and Nicobar Islands shall be filled by a person nominated by the President. This procedure was perhaps deliberately put in by the framers of the Act having regard to *the relatively low standard of the people of Andamans* for shouldering responsibilities vis-à-vis those on the mainland. The people in the Islands have not had any experience in exercising their individual votes even for electing members to Municipal Councils or District Boards since these institutions have not yet been constituted in the islands. It will not be correct to make such people suddenly exercise their rights for election of a member of parliament. Such changes should be imposed on them by slow stages (emphasis added).[60]

The following month, in a letter dated 6 September 1951, N.L. Nagar, undersecretary to the Government of India, explained the inability of the government to propose an amendment to the existing provisions of the RPA, 1950, which provided for a nominated candidate, 'in view of the difficulty for Govt. and for the candidate of conducting a proper election for *one seat* in the *widely dispersed* islands of the Andaman and Nicobar group'.[61]

[60] File no.55/20/51, AN, NAI.
[61] File no.55/20/51, AN, NAI.

As a result of these two positions taken by the central government on why the people of the islands could not exercise the franchise (they were not mature enough) and needed to be represented through a choice exercised by another person on their behalf, and the administrative problems involved in conducting an election in a geographically scattered space, the candidate for Andaman and Nicobar Islands continued to be nominated till 1968. In 1968, the first elected candidate was sent from the islands to the Lok Sabha. K.R. Ganesh, who was elected in 1968, had participated in the public meeting in March 1951, and along with R.L. Saha (who the proceedings noted was active with the Youth Congress movement in Delhi), had been designated by the meeting to represent the citizens of Port Blair on the question of obtaining an elected seat for the Islands. Evidently, the estrangement from politics for the people of the islands took place along the familiar route of disenfranchisement that was part of the colonial practice of ruling, and sustained through the dominant logic of bureaucracy as distinct from the political logic of democracy.[62] Indeed, the deferred representation for the people of the Andaman and Nicobar Islands remained confined to bureaucratic communication and did not figure in the domain of political contestations, which animated the discussions on the electoral system and its governance in newspapers. It is in this context that the attention given in the newspapers to adult franchise, civil liberties, and the MCC, the role of the bureaucracy and the missing women in the electoral rolls become important.

The Nuts and Bolts and the Brass Tacks

Electoral Officers

Commenting on the state of preparedness of the three parliamentary constituencies of Delhi to go to the polls, the *Hindustan Times* on 18 August 1951 suggested that preparations for holding elections were complete—the staff of the Chief Electoral Officer (CEO) was working in the belief that the election will be held in November 1951

---

[62] Apart from Andaman and Nicobar Islands, the Part 'B' tribal areas of Assam, and Jammu and Kashmir were excluded from direct franchise, which amounted to around 2.5 million voters. See Shani (2018: 224).

(even though they were eventually held in January 1952). Polling stations had been selected and the electoral rolls were being finalised for publication in the first week of September. Even at this stage, however, the state of preparedness was being assessed keeping in mind the parliamentary elections. In case—the newspaper surmised—parliamentary elections were to be held alongside the state assembly elections, the scenario would be completely different. The problem of disenfranchisement expressed by the refugees and displaced persons discussed in the earlier section is an illustration. The newspaper anticipated the problems Delhi would face and projected it onto the much larger scale of poll preparations in the country as a whole:

> Another 6000 ballot boxes will have to be purchased. The number of polling officers and assistants would have to be doubled and a number of copies of the electoral rolls will have to be prepared for different areas. ... the staff of the Local Administration, it is stated, will not be able to cope with the work and the Government of India will be approached for securing the services of the Secretariat staff for the elections. All Ministries have been approached in this connection and names of about 703 presiding officers, 2024 polling officers, 1006 women polling assistants and 3,343 clerks have already been received and tabulated and they only await assignment to different stations.... It is proposed in certain cases one presiding officer would supervise two or more polling booths ... the local bodies it is understood are experiencing difficulty in getting suitable buildings for polling stations ... in areas where suitable buildings are not available, it is stated, use would be made of Delhi Premises (Requisition and Eviction) Act 1947 and they would be made available for being used as polling booths. ... The Local Administration, it is understood, suggested to the Election Commission to sanction 6,400 ballot boxes but the number was reduced to 5000 and in case of any shortage the Election Commission would have to make necessary arrangements. The Delhi Municipality and the District Board, it is stated are getting a few thousand boxes made for their own use. These ballot boxes are different in design from the one approved by the Election Commission but in case of non-availability of boxes from the Election Commission, the only alternative would be to use the boxes from these two local bodies.[63]

[63] 'Delhi Arrangements for Holding Elections,' *Hindustan Times*, 18 August 1951.

The legal-institutional edifice of electoral governance for the entire country was still fuzzy at the time preparations for the first general election were being made. When the Constituent Assembly communicated with the state governments on the question of the preparation of electoral rolls, it felt the need for creating an election office in each state with an officer who was to be in over-all charge of the work. Officers with varying designations were accordingly appointed by all the state governments. Some of them were appointed as officers who were responsible for electoral work full time, but in some states, those who were appointed performed electoral duties in addition to their other administrative responsibilities. To ensure uniformity, the ECI subsequently suggested to all states that the officer designated with the responsibility of conducting the election in the state be called the 'chief electoral officer'. To invest the CEO with a legal status, the term was inserted and defined in the Representation of the People (Preparation of Electoral Rolls) Rules, 1950, to mean the officer appointed by the state government to perform the functions of the CEO under the Rules [Rule 2(b)]. The state governments were thereafter requested to make formal appointments under the rule, except Part C states, in which the CEO was to be appointed by the central government or the chief commissioner of the state. Subsequently, however, an amendment made on 6 May 1952 required that the appointment of a CEO should be made with the concurrence of the ECI.[64]

Following the suggestions made by different state governments, the ECI notified the appointments of 1,652 EROs in the states under the amended law. The EROs were drawn from the ranks of revenue officers of the status of collectors, deputy collectors, and *tehsildars*. Judicial officers were appointed as revising authorities to resolve disputes, claims, and objections to the draft rolls after their preliminary publication. In order to do so, the ECI had to acquire the permission of the high courts to allow for appointment of officers as revising authorities within their jurisdiction. Indeed, since a large number of claimants would in all probability be living far away from the offices of the revising authorities, the ECI decided to appoint officers who would simply receive claims and forward it to the revising

[64] Election Commission of India, *Report of the First General Election of India 1951–52*, p. 29.

authority. According to the CEC, the appointment of these receiving and forwarding officers proved very convenient for the public and also enabled the speedy disposal of claims. All these functions pertaining only to the preparation of electoral rolls involved a large number of EROs, revising authorities, returning officers, and assistant returning officers, who were drawn from the state government bureaucracy.[65] A substantially larger number of persons were required, however, for appointment as presiding and polling officers to be in charge of the actual conduct of polls. Aware of the magnitude of the task and appre-hensive of the difficulty it might encounter in getting suitable persons in appropriate numbers, the ECI set about the task of identifying such persons reasonably early. In a request sent to state governments on 8 April 1950, it asked them to assess their requirements for presiding officers, polling officers, and policemen, and to map out plans for meeting them.

The CEC stated in his report that the number of presiding and polling officers required for the 132,560 polling stations with 196,084 booths was extremely large. The appointment of all officers had to be done from among the officers of government and government-aided institutions after careful scrutiny.[66] The ECI placed the requirement of polling-booth personnel at close to 900,000 and felt the need to employ teachers from private educational institutions to make up for the deficit. As far as securing the polling booths was concerned, the state governments deputed the policemen at each polling station on the polling day. While ordinarily an assistant sub-inspector of police or head constable and three police constables were deployed, the number of such policemen depended upon the local requirements. The police also helped in the transportation of polling material includ-ing ballot boxes and ballot papers, both before and after the polls. In the first general election, the ECI reports to have used the services of 338,854 policemen across the country.[67]

[65] Election Commission of India, *Report of the First General Election of India 1951–52*, p. 32.

[66] Election Commission of India, *Report of the First General Election of India 1951–52*, pp. 32–3.

[67] Election Commission of India, *Report of the First General Election of India 1951–52*, p. 33.

'Mock' Elections

Given that the officers deployed to conduct the polls were inexperienced, the ECI decided to make them familiar with the modalities of conducting an election, by holding 'mock' elections on a wide scale all over the country. This was done not only to enable the officers to acquire 'sufficient familiarity with the relevant provisions of the law, and receive necessary training in the practical conduct of polling' but also to elicit public interest in voting and the election. The first such polling rehearsal was held in Udaipur in Rajasthan on 5 August 1951. Chief Election Commissioner Sen recounts:

All the District Electoral Officers of Rajasthan, and the Election Officers of the Ajmer State, attended this rehearsal. The Chief Election Commissioner personally supervised the arrangements and all the legal formalities were gone through during the demonstration of the polling procedure. The rehearsal succeeded in its main objectives, namely, creating public interest in the elections and, at the same time, giving practical experience to the election officers in their future task. The rehearsal attracted country-wide attention and was followed by a series of similar rehearsals in Rajasthan and in every other State. The Chief Election Commissioner attended at least one polling rehearsal almost in every State in order to ensure that the procedure followed all over India was uniform and properly understood and that no mistakes were made or misapprehensions entertained in any State. The rehearsals also gave an opportunity for examining the suitability of the provisions of the law laying down the election procedure. The rehearsals were extensively held in every State that, so far as practicable, almost all prospective election officers received adequate training.[68]

The *Hindustan Times* followed the mock elections held in the District Board School in Nangloi on the Grand Trunk Road (then 10 miles from Delhi). The newspaper carried a small notice informing that the mock elections would begin at eight in the morning and was open to the public and representatives of political parties alike.[69] Its report of the 'mock' elections the next day spoke of the lessons learnt

[68] Election Commission of India, *Report of the First General Election of India 1951–52*, p. 34.

[69] 'Mock Elections at Nangloi,' *Hindustan Times*, 2 September 1951.

and the challenges that needed to be addressed before the polling day arrived. The mock elections were conducted by the deputy commissioner and other local officials in the presence of CEC Sukumar Sen. Nangloi was a double-member constituency, with one general seat and one reserved seat for a scheduled caste candidate. The newspaper report makes for an interesting read:

A crowd of several thousands, mostly villagers, gathered in the belief that Mr. Nehru accompanied by some diplomats would visit the area. Although the Prime Minister could not come, being away in Kashmir, the report of his intended visit did the trick of collecting a large crowd. The task of educating voters and of making polling officials do their job was not easy. Loudspeakers helped but not much. Villagers did not quite understand the purpose of symbols. The ballot boxes were too small and some voters failing to notice where votes were to be dropped, left them on the table. In one case a voter was seen putting four papers in the ballot box. When asked he said the others were the votes of his family members who could not come.... Symbols like the buffalo, box of matches, book and conch were displayed outside the polling booth. These symbols it is stated, will, however, be not used in the regular election. The significance and the procedure of the election were explained to the villagers by means of a loudspeaker fixed in a jeep which was moving around inside the school compound. By 8.30 a.m. the school compound was almost full with men and women from adjoining villages seemingly ignorant of the procedure to exercise their right to franchise ... At about 9.30 a.m. when the polling attained its requisite pitch, it was learnt 30 votes were cast in ten minutes which resulted in an average of three votes in a minute. The authorities appeared satisfied that all voters came with identity slips, about a thousand votes could be polled in a day in each polling station.[70]

Another mock election held 10 days later in the Municipal Hall in Karnal to 'educate' the voters in Karnal town and Baldhi and Phoos Garh villages was, however, reported differently by the same newspaper. Political parties like the Congress, Jan Sangh, Hindu Mahasabha, and Akalis participated in the two-hour exercise. Thousands of voters turned up and cast their votes in what the newspaper called

[70] 'Educating Voters in Delhi: Many Lessons Learnt in Nangloi Mock Election,' *Hindustan Times*, 3 September 1951.

'real election atmosphere'. The mock election was held under the supervision of the home secretary and the state election commissioner, all of whom were satisfied with the 'speed and disposal' of the votes.[71] Unlike the Nangloi mock election, it appears from newspaper reports that other mock elections were limited affairs. A report of another mock election in Lucknow, for example, shows that the exercise began in the evening, in which three political parties participated with their 'mock symbols'. Hundred and six votes were cast in a span of one hour, which was described by election officers as a 'splendid' rate.[72] In Allahabad, district election authorities launched a mobile election booth to train personnel through mock elections in different tehsils of the district.[73]

'Multi-member' Constituencies

Despite their attempt to anticipate and cover all aspects of administering the elections, in the actual conduct of elections, the ECI encountered several unanticipated problems. One of these problems pertained to multi-member constituencies, which were almost double the area and population as compared to the single-member constituencies, and had to return more than one candidate to Parliament. The *Hindustan Times* on 1 December 1951 carried a write-up explaining how voters could cast their votes in a double-member constituency in which one of the seats was reserved. All voters in these constituencies would have two votes, but unlike popular perception, it was not essential that both the votes had to be cast—one of them for a candidate contesting the 'general' seat, and the other for a candidate contesting from the reserved seat in the constituency. The voter in a double-member constituency with a reserved seat could exercise any of the following six options: (a) cast one vote according to his/her preference and return the second ballot paper without casting a vote for a second candidate (b) cast both votes—one for a candidate from the reserved seat and the second for a candidate from a general

---

[71] 'Mock Elections in Karnal,' *Hindustan Times*, 14 September 1951.

[72] 'Mock Election in Lucknow,' *Hindustan Times*, 22 November 1951

[73] 'Mobile Booths for Mock Elections,' *The Times of India*, 3 November 1951.

seat (c) cast both votes for two general candidates (d) cast both votes for two reserved candidates (e) cast both votes in the same ballot box in which case, however, one of the votes would be declared invalid at the time of counting (f) refuse to vote at all and return the ballot papers.[74]

The problem in such constituencies, as far as the candidates were concerned, was one of the scale of organisation of the campaign. For the ECI, however, the problem was of a different order. A large number of voters cast all their votes into the ballot box of the same candidate, leading to cumulative voting and rejection of their votes by the returning officer.[75] The maximum number of rejections took place in the North Bengal parliamentary constituency. In addition, the counting of votes in such constituencies took much longer. In a two-member constituency in Uttar Pradesh, it took almost 20 days for the counting to be concluded, even when the counting took place well beyond the usual hours. In his narrative report, the CEC explained that in multi-member constituencies, the counting of votes was a more complicated process since cumulative votes had to be identified and excluded. To exclude cumulative votes, the ballot papers in each ballot box had to be arranged in a serial order and whenever more ballot papers than two with the same serial number were found in the same box, all but one of them had to be rejected. In one constituency in Bihar, there were as many as 78,000 cumulative votes. Counting of votes in such constituencies, therefore, took a longer time.[76]

Ballot Boxes and Election Symbols

Single-member constituencies with large numbers of candidates presented problems as well. In the Mylapore constituency of Madras, 14 candidates were nominated to contest the single-member legislative assembly seat. The large number of candidates made it necessary to put up 14 ballot boxes of different colours. The ECI was apprehensive

[74] 'Double Member Constituency,' *Hindustan Times*, 1 December 1951.

[75] Election Commission of India, *Report of the First General Election of India 1951–52*, pp. 137–8.

[76] Election Commission of India, *Report of the First General Election of India 1951–52*, pp. 52–3.

that this could be potentially confusing for the voter, who may find it difficult to distinguish and identify the ballot box in which the ballot paper could be inserted. This prompted the ECI to opt for the 'symbol system' whereby each ballot box would bear a distinctive symbol and the voter would place her ballot paper in the box bearing her preferred symbol. Subsequently, the ECI decided that the symbols should be familiar to the voters and 'have no religious or sentimental associations'. The cow, temple, the national flag, and the spinning wheel were considered symbols likely to elicit such sentiments. The allocation of symbols was done on the basis of consultations among state governments, 'all the organised political parties', and the ECI in a conference held in Delhi on 30 July 1951, presided by the CEC.[77] Reporting on the allocation of symbols, the *Times of India*, on 15 August 1951, held that the major political parties had chosen symbols with the intention of wooing rural voters. The Congress was allotted two bullocks with a yolk, and the Socialist Party, a tree. The Communist Party of India had given hammer and sickle as its first preference and ears of corn with hammer and sickle as their second. The ECI assigned them the ear of corns, without the hammer and sickle. Incidentally, the Congress' preference for two bullocks with a plough, followed by the Congress flag with a charkha, was disallowed for a clash with the Socialist Party's first preference (a plough) and the confusion the Congress flag would create due to its resemblance with the national flag.[78] Interestingly, it was at this stage that the ECI received claims from 29 parties for recognition as national or state parties, which the ECI had to decide on an *ad hoc* basis since no data on party performances was available.[79] On the advice of the ECI, the state governments printed 42.1 million symbols, which included copies to be pasted inside and outside ballot boxes for display outside the polling station and booth.[80]

[77] Election Commission of India, *Report of the First General Election of India 1951–52*, p. 81.

[78] 'Symbols to Woo Rural Voters,' *The Times of India*, 15 August 1951.

[79] Election Commission of India, *Report of the First General Election of India 1951–52*, p. 81.

[80] Election Commission of India, *Report of the First General Election of India 1951–52*, p. 91.

The design of ballot boxes was approved by the ECI with the objective of inspiring public confidence as entirely tamper-proof. Yet, the design also had to be cost-effective. The ECI decided that steel boxes of specified dimension be designed in a way that they would not require locks. The following specifications were prescribed by the ECI:

Every box should measure 8″ high × 9″ long × 71/2″ wide, the lid being fixed by inside hinges. It should be made of steel of 20 gauge. Unpickable locking should be provided to secure the lid to the box, and a slot about 2″ long and 4″ wide should be provided in the lid, for the insertion of ballot papers. The box should be so made that when the lid is locked the slot can be left fully open for polling and can later be effectively closed against any further insertion of ballot papers once polling is over. The general construction must be such as to make the box fraud-proof. It must not be possible to insert ballot papers through the edges where the lid shuts, upon *the* box, or through any surface or joint of the box—the slot in the lid being the only opening for inserting ballot papers. All exterior fittings, including the handle, should be so accommodated that no part may project beyond the six surface planes of the box. This was to ensure that the ballot boxes may be packed together or stacked upon each other compactly. Public notice was given inviting manufacturers to submit designs of ballot boxes to the Commission for approval. Several firms submitted their designs which were subjected to severe tests.[81]

The selection of ballot boxes from the approved designs and suppliers was done by the respective state governments, which ordered the boxes based on their requirements, which was estimated at 1,905,324 for the entire country on the assumption that each polling station would on an average require four ballot boxes.[82] Despite these calculations, 111,095 wooden ballot boxes were rushed to Madras, and to almost every state, additional boxes were supplied at short notices since the number of ballot boxes required in each polling station surpassed the estimated four. The ECI put the cost of the ballot boxes at Rs 12,287,349. The steel required for the ballot boxes

---

[81] Election Commission of India, *Report of the First General Election of India 1951–52*, pp. 95–6.

[82] Election Commission of India, *Report of the First General Election of India 1951–52*, p. 97.

was facilitated by the Ministry of Industry and Supply, and 816,545 tonnes of steel was used to meet the demands of ballot boxes for all the state governments.[83] Since the polls for both the Lok Sabha and the state legislative assemblies were being held together, two sets of ballot boxes were made in two different 'groups of colours', which for the Lok Sabha was in different shades of green (Olftre, Meadow, Pale, or Brunswick) and for the state assemblies, chocolate, mahogany, teak, tan, or bronze.[84] Significantly, as the CEC pointed out in his report, the slot for inserting the ballot paper was emphasised and made prominent by printing it in white so that the voter when she went to cast her vote would know exactly where she had to insert her ballot paper. It was considered desirable by the ECI to have uniformity in the design of ballot boxes for the convenience of both the voters and those who were administering the polls at the booth level, and it issued instructions to all state governments to requisition them from the same firm. Paper seals for securing the ballot boxes were designed in consultation with the master, India Security Press, Nasik, and an intricate design for the seal was agreed upon that could not be replicated and would make the boxes tamper-proof. Since the seals also served the purpose of locks, the ECI expressed satisfaction at having avoided the considerable expenditure on expensive locks.

The ballot papers were printed on watermarked paper by the India Security Press in Nasik. The ballot papers for Lok Sabha elections were marked by a thick vertical bar of olive green to distinguish them from the ballot papers for the state assembly elections, which were marked similarly with a chocolate-coloured bar. The ballot papers did not mention the names of the candidates and carried a serial number that was prefixed by two letters, which indicated the particular state in which the ballot paper was being used.[85] In the months leading to the polling day, questions were raised regarding the secrecy of the ballot. Many were apprehensive that the secrecy of the vote will be

[83] Election Commission of India, *Report of the First General Election of India 1951–52*, p. 98.

[84] Election Commission of India, *Report of the First General Election of India 1951–52*, p. 99.

[85] Election Commission of India, *Report of the First General Election of India 1951–52*, pp. 100–2.

vitiated by the requirement that the serial number of the ballot paper will be recorded in the electoral rolls by the polling officer against the name of the voter to whom it was issued. The ECI allayed the fears of the voters by issuing a press note to say that the serial numbers of ballot papers were recorded under the RPA to ensure that 'full facts' of the poll may be available for presentation before an election tribunal in case of a dispute on an election result. The ECI assured that the electoral roll on which the serial numbers of the ballot paper issued to electors were recorded would be sealed by the polling officer and the candidate's agents, immediately after the conclusion of the poll. The seal could not be opened unless authorised by an order of 'a competent authority of an election tribunal'.[86] The indelible ink to mark the fingers of voters was manufactured by the Indian Council for Scientific and Industrial Research and so was the special adhesive to stick the election symbols on the ballot boxes. The ECI provided the states with the indelible ink (a total of 389,816 phials which cost Rs 227,460). The ECI rejected claims that the ink could be removed upon the application of chemicals and confirmed its reliability.[87]

Polling Booths

The decision on numbers and location of polling stations was made following certain principles. These included their location to serve what the narrative report mentions as 'a well defined geographical area', to cater to not more than 1000 voters, who should not be required to travel more than 3 miles to vote,[88] with separate booths for women if required.[89] The ECI noted that the setting up of polling booths in hilly

---

[86] 'Ballot Secrecy Not Endangered,' *Hindustan Times*, 8 January 1951.

[87] Election Commission of India, *Report of the First General Election of India 1951–52*, p. 105.

[88] Election Commission of India, *Report of the First General Election of India 1951–52*, p. 126.

[89] The ECI, noted the following:

As a rule, men and women voters voted at the same polling station or booth. At least one woman was appointed to assist the presiding officer at every polling station as far as possible. Wherever it was felt that on account of local custom women voters would find it difficult to appear

and desert terrains presented the additional problem of low density of population, which made it difficult to provide a polling station for every 1,000 voters within 3 miles of the voter's home. As a result, the number of polling stations had to be increased so that the smallest polling station catered to only nine voters in the area. The *Hindustan Times* of November 1951 reported that in the North Kanara district where dense teak forests covered almost 60 per cent of the area, with isolated communities dispersed across it in small pockets, compliance to the rule that no voter should travel more than 3 miles to cast the vote meant that this district had 361 booths for an electorate of 256,343. Of these, there were at least 15 booths with less than 100 voters, and in one case, 27 voters had an entire booth to themselves.[90]

A press statement by the CEC on 3 August 1951 announced that since social customs pertaining to purdah were followed unevenly across the country, a separate booth would be set up for women in places where the practice was strictly followed. In other places separate queues would be made, or men and women would vote in separate batches.[91] The polling stations were to be located in public buildings, no places of religious worship were to be used, and private establishments could be used as polling stations only after consent of the owners was obtained upon payment of compensation if required. 'Inexpensive temporary structures' were built using the 'cheapest available material' and 'improvised' furniture in around 16,000 cases. Lists of polling stations were published to enable the voters to know where to head to cast their votes. According to the ECI figures, 132,560 polling

---

at polling stations and cast their votes unless special facilities were provided for them, arrangements were made to set up separate women's booths. As far as possible, women polling officers were employed at such booths. At polling booths where both men and women voters voted, they were formed into separate queues and allowed to vote in alternate batches. A total of 27,527 booths were reserved for women voters all over the country. (Election Commission of India, *Report of the First General Election of India 1951–52*, p. 124.)

[90] 'Smallest Number for Polling Booth,' *Hindustan Times*, 5 November 1951.
[91] '28,00,000 Women Voters Struck Off Rolls,' *The Times of India*, 4 August 1951.

stations were set up with 196,084 polling booths in the country.[92] To administer the polls at these large numbers of stations and booths, personnel 'of a minimum standard' were required by the ECI. The paucity of such personnel in some cases led to the polls being staggered over a number of days. In big cities like Calcutta, which had 826 polling stations with 1,918 polling booths, the poll was conducted in a day with the help of 4,175 polling officers and 11,052 policemen.[93] In some states like Rajasthan, particularly in districts such as Barmer, Jaisalmer, and Jodhpur, the difficulties in arranging the logistics of transportation and communication presented problems. Yet, in none of these places was the polling adjourned, it was completed according to schedule under the guidance of control rooms set up under the CEO in Jaipur.[94] Indeed, in Orissa, the wireless system maintained by a police department was expanded to sustain communication during the election period. In the absence of telegraph offices and communication facilities in the area, even in the sub-divisional headquarters, the state wireless service, the *Hindustan Times* reported, was being 'powerfully' supported by a pigeon service with about 700 'winged messengers'. The Koraput district in the Eastern Ghats had the largest number of over a 100 such messengers. These 'flying messengers' had been trained in the 'boomerang service' of carrying messages and bringing back replies.[95]

In the hilly forest areas of Assam, the polling party had to go on foot with the porters to reach their polling stations. Advance parties were sent ahead to ensure that the polling party did not lose its way.[96] The CEC credited the large voter turnout (51.15 per cent, where out of a total of 173,213,635 voters, 88,612,171 voters turned up to cast their votes) to the efforts of the ECI. Inexplicably, however,

[92] Election Commission of India, *Report of the First General Election of India 1951–52*, p. 123.

[93] Election Commission of India, *Report of the First General Election of India 1951–52*, p. 127.

[94] Election Commission of India, *Report of the First General Election of India 1951–52*, p. 127.

[95] 'Pigeon Post During Elections,' *Hindustan Times*, 6 December 1951.

[96] Election Commission of India, *Report of the First General Election of India 1951–52*, p. 127.

not a single vote was cast in four polling stations in the country; these were Nurpur in West Bengal, Intali in Rajasthan, Juni-Chhapri in Saurashtra, and Kitchner Road (Tents) in Delhi.[97] Newspapers reported of a polling station in Kalamgadia located in the densely forested Kaptipada constituency, which also returned the polling boxes empty. One vote each was cast in Kutling and Poradiha, two other polling stations in the same constituency. The polling staff at Kutling had the peculiar experience of 'unwelcome visitors' at their camp in the night where a wild elephant and, later, two tigers hovered around their camp till daybreak.[98]

Law and Order

Law and order violation was an additional anxiety, which the CEC expressed in his report. As the campaign gained momentum, and the polling day drew close, possible breach of peace were seen as likely—with the administration stretched to its limit, even ordinary crimes were expected to rise, if 'anti-social elements' took advantage of the situation:

> The arrangements for the maintenance of law and order had there-fore to be planned with extreme care. Sufficient numbers of policemen were provided at each polling station and wherever necessary, village chowkidars or home-guards, etc., were made available for such duties. Apart from the police force provided at the polling stations, additional forces were kept in reserve at suitable points to serve as striking forces for meeting any unforeseen developments. Mobile parties of police were detailed in some states for going round excitable areas in order to inspire public confidence. Special precautions were also taken in respect of likely trouble-spots. The law prohibits public meetings on any polling day and canvassing near a polling station. These provisions proved very salutary. All these arrangements had the desired effect and 88.6 million voters actually cast their votes in a perfectly peaceful atmo-sphere. In fact, in most areas the cities, towns and villages wore almost a festive appearance and there was perfect discipline and good humour

[97] Election Commission of India, *Report of the First General Election of India 1951–52*, p. 131.

[98] 'Ballot Boxes Empty,' *The Times of India*, 26 December 1951.

all round. An additional cause for gratification was that there was no increase in the incidence of crime during the entire period of the elections. No breaches of law and order occurred at any of the polling stations in most of the States.[99]

On 5 November 1951, *The Hindu* carried a comprehensive write-up as 'do's and don't's for the 'scrupulous observance' of both the candidates and the voters for the ensuing 'free' elections.[100] The *Times of India* similarly carried columns titled 'Do's and Don'ts for Voters', convincing the voter that 'the vote' mattered in a democratic election and the voter could assert so as to not become a mere pawn, and elect the best candidate through fair, legal, and correct means.[101] Of the candidates, the newspaper expected a 'scrupulous observance' of the code of conduct, which was to give free and fair choice to the electorate to vote for whoever it favoured, and to abide by the rules and regulations of the electoral laws, which may appear irksome but whose sole purpose was to ensure democracy.[102]

A few 'minor breaches of law' were reported at 80 polling stations. Electoral offences were 1,250, which included disorderly conduct at election meetings; convening, holding, or attending public meetings within a constituency on a polling day; illegal hiring or procuring of conveyances for the transport of voters; canvassing within a 100 yards of a polling station; disorderly conduct in or near polling stations; impersonation of voters; fraudulent defacing or destroying or removing a list or notice or other document fixed by or under the authority of a returning officer; fraudulent insertion into ballot boxes of anything other than a ballot paper; destroying, taking away, or otherwise interfering with ballot boxes or ballot papers; fraudulent defacing or destroying ballot papers or the official mark on ballot papers; and fraudulent taking of or attempting to take ballot papers out of a

---

[99] Election Commission of India, *Report of the First General Election of India 1951–52*, p. 134.

[100] 'Ensuing Free Elections,' *The Hindu*, 5 November 1951.

[101] "Do's and Don'ts' for the Elections,' *The Times of India*, 30 October 1951.

[102] 'Code of Conduct for Candidates,' *The Times of India*, 1 November 1951.

polling station. Of these, the largest numbers booked were for impersonation (817), followed by fraudulent taking of ballot papers (106),
and canvassing within 100 yards of the polling station (100). These
numbers were, however, considered insignificant by the ECI given
the humongous nature and span of the exercise.[103] Interestingly,
apart from persons eligible to vote through postal ballots (which
included members of the armed forces and those in the service of the
Government of India and posted outside the country, among others),
a separate list of persons under preventive detention was also prepared and arrangements were made to enable them to vote through
postal ballot. In the case of the armed personnel, the postal ballots
were returned undelivered in large numbers. The postal ballots, even
in cases where they were delivered, were not effective, since the ballot papers did not carry the names of candidates, and in most cases,
the voters were not able to vote 'intelligently' because of unfamiliarity
with the candidates in their constituencies.[104]

Counting the Vote

It was, however, the counting of votes, which proved to be most
tedious. The ballot boxes had to be collected expeditiously from the
constituencies, taken to the counting centre, and sorted out candi-
date-wise. A directive issued by the ECI (as a set of revised rules under
the RPA) on counting of votes as reported by the *Hindustan Times*
provided that the counting of votes for a parliamentary constituency
could not be done at more than five different places. In an assembly
constituency, however, the counting was to take place in one place
within the constituency. Only under special circumstances could the
counting be shifted to another constituency.[105] The ECI noted in the
narrative report that the deputation of the same person as returning
officer for several constituencies made it impossible for the counting to begin the same day after the polling was over. There were

[103] Election Commission of India, *Report of the First General Election of
India 1951–52*, p. 135.

[104] Election Commission of India, *Report of the First General Election of
India 1951–52*, pp. 136–7.

[105] 'Directive on Counting of Votes,' *Hindustan Times*, 28 December 1951.

suggestions favouring simultaneous counting, so that counting could take place only after polling in the entire state was over, so as to not 'unduly influence' the voter in a constituency where polls had not taken place and results for another constituency were declared. This opinion did not find favour with the ECI. The CEC alluded to the different strategies being followed by the states, which though uneven, were effective. He favoured, however, the manner in which states like Madras and Bombay, through 'well-planned administrative arrangements', were able to commence the counting immediately after the polling, and not the arrangement followed by states like West Bengal and Mysore that did not begin counting until all the votes were cast.[106]

When the counting of votes concluded and all results had been declared, the *Times of India* published an interesting 'review' of election statistics while announcing the majority that had been garnered by the Congress:

Parliamentary elections were held for 489 seats and of these the Congress has claimed 363. Eight more seats, six from Jammu and Kashmir, one from Andaman and Nicobar Islands, and one from tribal areas in Assam are yet to be filled to complete the strengthening of the House of the People. The Indian electorate chose its 489 representatives from among 1800 candidates. Actual contests were, however, only for 479 seats. Ten members—seven Congressmen, two independents and one KMPP candidate—having been returned unopposed to the House. The total number of votes cast in the election to the 479 seats ran to over 107,578 million, of which nearly 205,200

---

[106] There were some instances of unjustifiably protracted counting as well. For instance, in one two-member Parliamentary constituency in Uttar Pradesh, counting of votes took as many as 20 days. Similarly, in Travancore-Cochin, counting of votes in a two-member Assembly constituency took 12 days. In two-member Assembly constituencies it took, on an average, as many as 15 working hours to count the votes. The preparation of the statement prescribed for the record of rejected ballot papers (Form 15) took considerable time, prompting the ECI to consider devising means for materially reducing the clerical labour involved in preparing the statement. (Election Commission of India, *Report of the First General Election of India 1951–52*, pp. 137–8.)

or 1.90 per cent had to be rejected. Besides the Congress President Mr. Nehru, the only other head of an all-India political organization who was successful was Dr. Shyama Prasad Mukherjee, President of the Jan Sangh.[107]

Allegations were, however, made from some quarters that the 'astounding success' of Congress candidates in some places like Bangalore and Mysore cities was achieved 'by organised booth tampering during the unnecessarily long period during which they had been stored between polling and counting of votes'. These views were expressed in a memorandum submitted by the Standing Committee of all parties opposing the Congress, to the Mysore government, with the request to be forwarded to the ECI. The memorandum alleged that ballot papers were transferred from non-Congress to Congress candidates in the period during the unusual delay in counting made possible by the inadequate security of the ballot boxes:

> The seals used for ballot boxes and on locks in strong rooms, where the ballot boxes had been stored till the counting of votes were those of the Election commission of which there were a hundred on the State and no proper security of the seals had been ensured; the keys for locks of strong rooms were not in the personal custody of returning officers; at the time of the counting of votes rules had not been followed in Bangalore City; sufficient opportunity had not been given to candidates to examine the paper seals on ballot boxes, which did not bear the signature of either the agents or the candidates.[108]

Indeed, the memorandum stated that it was possible to open the ballot boxes without breaking the seals, which the parties claimed they could demonstrate. A major dispute erupted between Amul Desai, a Socialist candidate, and Morarji Desai, a Congress candidate and home minister of Bombay, over the recounting of ballot papers in the Bulsar-Chikli Assembly Constituency for which both were contenders. Amul Desai had led the first count by 179 votes, but a recount was ordered after torn ballot papers were recovered near the

---

[107] 'Congress Secures Overall Majority,' *The Times of India*, 3 March 1952.

[108] 'Alleged Tampering with Ballot Boxes,' *The Times of India*, 2 February 1952.

counting centre. The result was not declared since the returning officer wanted to 'tally and tabulate figures'. Amul Desai protested the recount, asking that the first count should be treated as final, alleging 'fraudulent destruction' of his ballot papers by the Congress agent, an act which, he argued, amounted to an offence of theft. A second round of counting under the circumstances, according to him, would be illegal, and if at all recounting was done, ballot papers of all boxes should be counted simultaneously. Amul Desai won the seat with a lead of 19 votes in the recount. In the last hour of recounting, the *Times of India* reported 'intense excitement' with the crowds waiting 300 yards away from the place of counting, shouting for results'.[109] In the narrative report, the CEC reports the incident as having been satisfactorily resolved. The framing of the episode and the sequence of events leading to the dispute were, however, different from the newspaper report:

A careful scrutiny of the ballot paper accounts received from all the polling stations revealed that in respect of the ballot papers from the Vankal polling station, there had been a mistake during the first count in recording the number of votes polled by Dr. Amul Desai. Dr. Amul Desai had actually polled 168 votes at this polling station and not 268 as wrongly recorded during the first count. A similar check of ballot paper accounts from other polling stations resolved the remaining discrepancies between the first and the second counts.... The pieces of the torn ballot papers were reconstructed and it was found that they made up 13 ballot papers only. Their serial numbers showed that they related to the Faldhara and Tankal polling stations of the constituency.... It was found that all but 14 ballot papers issued at these two polling stations had been found in the ballot boxes received from those stations. As against this shortage of 14 ballot papers, 13 ballot papers had been recovered in torn condition and one ballot paper only thus remained unaccounted for. These facts made it clear that 13 or 14 ballot papers had been somehow obtained by some mischief-maker at some point of time before the first count and torn into pieces which were thrown near the premises in order to create suspicion against the honesty of the counting and the correctness of the result when it came to be declared.... Fortunately, the

[109] 'Dr. Amul Desai Still Tops Polls in Bulsar,' *The Times of India*, 18 January 1951.

number of ballot papers involved in this attempt at creating mischief was too small in any case to affect the result of the counting in any way; ... No sufficient materials could, however, be collected to support a criminal charge against any person and the matter had to be finally dropped.[110]

Towards a Code of Conduct

While the MCC in elections came into existence only later in 1968, the idea that free and fair elections required strict adherence to rules was being presented through different platforms by political parties. The political parties addressed themselves to the electoral bureaucracy, reminding them of the importance of bureaucratic neutrality in holding free and fair elections to ensure that the party in power is not placed at an advantage in the election. There were, moreover, attempts to ensure fairness of election through legal provisions incorporated in the RPA itself. Amidst allegations of misuse of official machinery by the ruling party, Nehru reminded all political parties to adopt the right means, in order to ensure fairness in electoral outcome.

A minor strand in the chorus of free and fair election was represented by the Bharatiya Jana Sangh, which addressed itself to the party in power, through the idiom of civil liberties. Speaking at the All India Civil Liberties Conference in Nagpur on 25 August 1951, Shyama Prasad Mukherjee claimed that the protection of civil liberties (by the government) was a component of free and fair elections. Significantly, Mukherjee and N.B. Khare, the national convenor of the conference, were speaking in the context of the first amendment to the Constitution of India, which had inserted restrictions on free speech by constraining Article 19(2) of the Constitution of India. Mukherjee, a former Hindu Mahasabha member and the founder of the Bharatiya Jana Sangh, had asserted the right to criticise the Partition of India and had sought its annulment. Arguing that the party in power could manipulate and influence the elections in its favour, Mukherjee linked free and fair elections with freedom of speech and warned

[110] Election Commission of India, *Report of the First General Election of India 1951–52*, pp. 139–42.

against 'bogeys of upheavals and perilous consequences raised to justify the arbitrary exercise of power by government'. Attributing the 'suppression of civil liberties in India' to 'one party rule' more than anything else, Mukherjee exhorted the press, the bureaucracy, and judiciary to be free and independent of the party in power, and made a case for making freedom of expression the 'test issue' in the coming general elections. Claiming that the amendment had been made with the purpose of appeasing Pakistan, Khare asked the voters to vote only for those candidates who would 'give a firm promise to work with singleness of purpose for the restoration of these funda-mental rights'. He advised political parties to put this demand in their party programmes and use the elections as an opportunity to educate people on the question of civil liberties.[111]

In other quarters, however, it was bureaucratic neutrality that was being considered essential for free and fair elections. The chief minister of Madras province, for example, underscored 'bureaucratic efficiency' and 'absolute impartiality'. Referring to the forthcoming elections as a 'severe test', he called upon officers of the state 'of all ranks' to 'rise equal to the occasion'. Preparations made 'carefully and well in advance' were required to ensure the success of what he described as 'the largest democratic elections ever attempted so far in any country in the world', which would be 'an exacting but appropriate test of our fitness for the ambitious and up-to-date democratic consti-tution that we have framed for ourselves'. Acknowledging that the task of efficient organisation of the 'elaborate arrangements necessary for holding these gigantic elections' fell 'naturally' on the officials, the chief minister promised the officials cooperation of the public and the political parties. Stressing upon 'absolute fairness and impartiality' in the conduct of elections, the chief minister advised the officials that they were free to exercise their own vote according to their judgment, but their activities as officers responsible for the conduct of elections 'must be confined to the careful and thorough carrying out of all the duties entrusted to [them] by the competent election authorities ... governed by rigid statutory provisions'. Exhorting the officers to give the elections the topmost priority 'from now on until the elections are

---

[111] 'Civil Rights in India: Steps to Ensure Free Elections,' *The Hindu*, 26 August 1951.

over, and see that there is no delay at any stage', the chief minister promised that 'the efficiency displayed by an officer in his election work will be an important item to be taken into account in judging his record during the year and for assessing his merit for promotion ... performance will figure in personal files'.[112] The Bombay government similarly issued orders to all government servants to observe the 'strictest neutrality', to refrain from doing anything that may even remotely be construed as indicating their preference for any particular political party, not to take part in canvassing support for any candidate, whether affiliated to a party or independent, and neither accompany ministers to meetings that are likely to be political meetings, nor attend such meetings.[113]

Speaking in the course of his election campaign in Akola, in Maharashtra, Nehru made similar statements reminding public servants to stay neutral. Nehru's statement was, however, in the nature of what he called a 'warning': 'It had come to his notice', he said, that 'officials here are trying to create trouble and are taking sides in election matters. I warn them this is not a threat that a full inquiry will be instituted against any officer who does an improper thing or interferes in election matters. Officers all over India have been given strict instructions to keep away from electioneering and if any official is found guilty of misconduct, he will be severely dealt with'. Nehru's warning was received with prolonged cheers from the crowd, to which he responded: 'From your cheers it is clear that you also feel that officials are creating trouble here'.[114]

Indeed, the exhortation for neutrality came in a context where charges were made by opposition parties of possible or actual use of the governmental machinery and bureaucrats for the promotion of the interests of the party in power. Asoka Mehta, the general secretary of the Socialist Party, expressed his apprehensions in a statement issued in Bombay. In his statement, Mehta alleged that fair and free election was compromised in Surat, where a senior police officer called a meeting of the village *patels* of some areas, including

---

[112] 'Ensuring Free Elections: Responsibility of Officers—Chief Minister's Call,' *The Hindu*, 26 September 1951.

[113] 'Neutrality in Elections,' *The Times of India*, 15 November 1951.

[114] 'No Interference by Officials,' *Hindustan Times*, 18 December 1951.

that of Morarji Desai's constituency, advising them 'to remember their loyalty to their chief and his party'. The statement was carried on the first page of the *Times of India* along with the major news item of the day—the validation of the first constitutional amendment by the constitution bench of the Supreme Court and the confirmation of the power of the provisional Parliament to amend the Constitution.[115]

In November 2017, Krishna Prasad, the director-general of the Post and Telegraphs Department, assured that complete neutrality will be observed in his department's policies towards political parties. As an evidence of this, he promised in a press conference that his department would be 'most impartial' in its service to all candidates irrespective of their political affiliation. As an evidence of this, he released a brochure titled 'How We Can Serve', and promised that all contesting candidates would receive temporary telephone connections expeditiously, if they desired, to facilitate their electoral work. In addition, the brochure declared, special measures were being taken for quick and efficient delivery of election material including election manifestos and postal ballot papers for the armed forces personnel and those posted in embassies.[116]

Earlier in May 1951, when amendments to the RPA, concerned mostly with the qualification of MPs, were being discussed, the question of fairness and impartiality in the conduct of elections came up as a matter that could be addressed through law, the RPA itself. Two members of the Assembly, Ram Narain Singh and N.G. Ranga, raised concerns about the use of government machinery and administrative officials by ministers for their election campaigns and suggested that 'the established government may be set aside for the interim period during which elections could be held'. This, however, was considered 'wholly unfeasible' by the law minister, B.R. Ambedkar, who argued that there was nothing in the Constitution that provided for the suspension of the government since the head of the state could act only on the advice of the council of ministers, and in the absence of such advice, there could not be any legal administration. If the civil administration had become politically corrupt, the remedy lay not in

---

[115] 'Govt. Servants and Elections,' *The Times of India*, 6 October 1951.
[116] 'P & T Facilities in Election,' *Hindustan Times*, 8 November 1951.

law, but in public morality: 'The most effective sanction lay in public morality'.[117]

On 28 May 1951, when the second reading of the RPA concluded, along with the decisions on what would constitute disqualification for members contesting election to the Lok Sabha and state legislative assemblies, two 'other amendments of substance' were introduced in the Bill. These pertained to the conduct of candidates and voters on polling day and electoral expenses of political parties. Reporting on the amendment, the *Times of India* informed:

> A candidate may use a conveyance on the day of the poll to carry himself, his family and election agent. Electors may jointly hire a 'vehicle or vessel' provided it is not propelled by mechanical power. The use of public transport at the electors' own expense is permitted. In the matter of election expenses, a political party apart from conducting general propaganda in furtherance of its own platform may support and further the candidature of individual candidates without expenses incurred on this latter account having to be debited to the election expense of the individual candidate in question.[118]

In October 1951, the Home Ministry sent detailed instructions to government officials of all states explaining how they must conduct themselves during the tours of ministers in the course of their election campaigns. The instructions required all government servants to desist from taking part in any election campaign on behalf of any political party, advising them to take 'scrupulous care' not to 'lend [their] position and authority to assist one group or another'.

---

[117] In the course of the same discussion, another member proposed that the exercise of franchise must be construed a duty rather than a right, as was the case in countries like Australia and Belgium. A fine of Rs 100 was to be paid by any person who failed to vote. Opposing the proposal, Ambedkar proposed that it was the 'Brahmins' (who had too much to lose) and the 'Harijan' (who had everything to gain) who were the two classes which voted. It was the electorally apathetic middle class which had to be mobilised by those from the political class who represented them. ('Qualifications of India's Law Makers: Parliament Discusses Clauses of Representation Bill,' *The Times of India*, 15 May 1951).

[118] 'Electoral Bill Passes Second Reading Stage,' *The Times of India*, 29 May 1951.

Considering that the ministers were likely to be from the Congress party and there was possibility of slippage between a public meeting and an electoral campaign, the directive made it the responsibility of the concerned minister to inform the officials of the nature of the meeting. In case of an election meeting, the arrangements were to be made on behalf of the minister, but 'non-officially', that is, without using the official machinery, with the expenses borne by the minister himself. In all such meetings, the government officials were advised to limit their roles to maintaining law and order and offering protection to the minister. There was no requirement for the official to be present in the meeting itself. The directive acknowledged, however, that in election time, it was difficult for any public meeting to not be an election meeting itself, and there could be difficulties in its implementation.[119]

The question of the conduct of bureaucrats and their responsibilities as officials responsible for making the arrangements for elections at the ground level seemed to be a subject of official discussions and declarations as well. A three-day conference of police officers and officials of the district administration at Phillaur near Jalandhar focused on the different aspects of maintaining peace during elections. At the same time, the officials took what a newspaper called 'important decisions' to ensure free and fair elections. Among these was the declaration by the Punjab governor, Chandulal Trivedi, a former civil servant himself, to shift his headquarters from Shimla to Jalandhar to ensure the smooth and impartial conduct of election.[120]

In a broadcast to the nation carried on the front pages of newspapers, Prime Minister Nehru stressed the need of 'propriety' in elections. The prime minister's broadcast was in the nature of an exhortation to the people, who he described as being 'mostly unfamiliar' with the electoral process but 'enthusiastic' to be part of the democratic elections:

All of you know something about the general election and there is naturally a great deal of interest in the country on this subject. It is right

[119] 'Election Campaign: Centre's Directive to Govt. Servants,' *Hindustan Times*, 13 October 1951.
[120] 'Peace During Elections: Trivedi's Appeal to Officials,' *Hindustan Times*, 20 November 1951.

that each one of you should take interest as a citizen of the Republic of India whose future will no doubt be affected to some extent by these elections. Democracy is based on the active and intelligent interest of the people in national problems and affairs and in these elections that result in the formation of governments.[121]

For a large part, however, Nehru's broadcast to the nation was addressed to 'all political parties and every candidate'. The election was, indeed, said Nehru, 'a test for all of us', who must understand it thoroughly, comprehend the magnitude of the responsibility to be borne, and to bear it with propriety and decorum:

I have given you a simple and rather bald account of these elections. I should like you, however, to try to visualize the inner significance of this great adventure of the Indian people. Imagine hundreds of millions of people on the move all over India to determine the future government of this country. They do so or should do so peacefully and will drop their voting paper in tens of thousands of ballot boxes indicating their choice. Out of these voting papers, will emerge the members of Parliament and of the State Assemblies, and we shall accept the result of this election, whoever wins or loses. That is the essence of democracy.... There has been a long argument especially in India about means and ends. Do wrong means justify right ends? So far as we are concerned in India, we decided long ago that there can be no right end if the means employed were wrong. If we apply that to this business of elections, we come to the conclusion that it is even better for the wrong person to win by dubious methods. If such dubious methods are employed, then the rightness of the right person itself fades away. I lay stress upon it because it is important and because there is a tendency during election time, to forget normal standards of behaviour. I earnestly hope that every candidate and those who support him will remember that, to some extent, he has the honour of India in his keeping and will conduct himself accordingly.[122]

In the months leading up to the election day, accusations pertaining to official pressures for collecting funds for electoral campaign

[121] 'Need of Propriety in Elections: PM Asks People to Avoid Wrong Means,' *Hindustan Times*, 23 November 1951.

[122] 'Need of Propriety in Elections: PM Asks People to Avoid Wrong Means,' *Hindustan Times*, 23 November 1951.

against the ruling party were made. The Socialist leader Asoka Mehta accused the minister of Civil Supplies in United Provinces, Chandra Bhanu Gupta, of using his position as a minister to collect funds for the Congress party. Similar charges were made by him against Morarji Desai, the home minister in the Congress government in Bombay province and the Congress treasurer, of demanding a 'levy' from mill owners and textile magnates in Bombay for Congress funds. In both cases, the ministers concerned refuted the charges and stated that the electoral funds for the Congress came from all sections of society and they were in all cases voluntary.[123] The *Times of India* carried the allegations made by Asoka Mehta as its front-page news—carrying the statement made by Mehta as he opened his campaign with a press conference in Poona, where he charged Morarji Desai of using his influence, especially as the chairman of the Textile Control Committee to charge a levy on loom workers in mills.[124]

The MCC, which was drawn later in the 1960s, to provide a mutually agreed framework for the conduct of candidates and political parties during elections, and the question of election expenses, have been riddled with contestations. It is clear from newspaper reports during the first general election that these matters were seen as integral to the conduct of fair and free elections. In the course of the election campaign, concerns regarding bias in favour of the ruling party in state-owned media and election campaign by political parties were raised in Parliament. Following a decision by the Government of India, political parties were not allowed to use the state-owned broadcasting facilities to campaign for election. H.V. Kamath raised a question in Parliament whether a system allowing a sharing of broadcasting space and time, which existed in Britain, could be introduced in India. In his response, the Information and Broadcasting minister referred to the specific problems of large number of languages and the difficulty of defining a political party, which were numerous in the case of India, to argue that any arrangement of the kind that existed in Britain would be difficult to adopt in India. He admitted, however, that apart from the ECI, government officials and ministers had

---

[123] 'Congress Election Funds,' *The Hindu*, 11 October 1951.

[124] 'Mills asked to Pay for Election Work,' *The Times of India*, 8 October 1951.

spoken on what he called 'educative subjects' like the provisions of the Constitution and the importance of democracy on the All India Radio. The minister assured Kamath that such broadcast would remain free from party bias.[125] The investigative weekly newspaper *Blitz* made similar charge of misuse of official publicity machinery in its issue on 6 October 1951.[126] In the process of refuting the charge, especially those pertaining to the use of Armed Forces Public Relations Directorate for Congress propaganda among the armed forces, and the charge that the All India Radio had been giving 'blazing publicity' to Prime Minister Nehru's election speeches, the Ministry of Information and Broadcasting outlined the policy of the government in these matters:

> AIR has been giving publicity to the electoral policy of all parties on the basis of their election manifestoes and speeches and statements of their leaders. Coverage is governed by various factors, more especially the publicity value of any particular speech. It is well known that Mr. Nehru's speeches attract vast audiences and a still vast number of people are interested in what he says. The speeches also deal with government policy. The reference of Blitz to the work of the Films Division is also wrong. Documentaries produced by the Films Division cover either the activities of the various Ministries of the Government of India or subjects of general social or cultural interest, but exclude politics.[127]

As per newspaper reports, Jawaharlal Nehru was visiting all the states in the course of the Congress party's election campaign. The Central Election Board of the party had released a documentary titled 'Pandit Nehru Speaking', a gramophone record with Nehru's speech in Hindi on one side and the national anthem on the other, and a handbook detailing the role of the Congress party in the freedom movement and the achievements of Congress ministries in the

[125] 'Election Campaign by Parties: No Broadcasting Facilities,' *The Hindu*, 31 August 1951.

[126] An investigative weekly newspaper published and edited in the form of a tabloid by Russi Karanjia, *Blitz* started in 1941 in Bombay.

[127] 'Use of Official Machinery: India Government Refute Charges,' *The Hindu*, 23 October 1951.

states.[128] Indeed, in the first narrative report, CEC Sukumar Sen stressed the importance of regular broadcasts in the All India Radio to educate voters about the modalities and importance of voting in elections. At the same time, however, he was of the opinion that it was ultimately the political parties that could reach out to the people and motivate them through their vigorous campaigns in the field to come out and vote in large numbers. Writing in the first narrative report, the CEC noted:

One welcome result of such campaign was to enthuse and educate the electorate. As the bulk of the electorate was illiterate, a good deal of educative propaganda was required to be carried out before they could fully understand the true meaning of the elections and appreciate their own role therein. Vast areas had been left untouched in this regard even after all the efforts made by the Press, the Radio and the governmental machinery. It was the party workers and the candidates who, in the ultimate analysis, largely performed the invaluable task of familiarising the mass of the electorate with the process and the mechanics of polling and the implications thereof. This task had to be accomplished within a very short time, and under great physical handicaps arising from vast distances and poor communications in many areas. It is remarkable how well the task was done for 51–55 per cent of the voters actually exercised their franchise at the polls—a fairly good percentage even for countries with long established democratic traditions.[129]

The ECI sought the cooperation of political parties to accelerate the pace of polling by facilitating the identification of voters at the polling station on polling day. The ECI made arrangements for the issue of official 'identity slips' to the voters at the entrance of the polling stations. Political parties distributed identity slips to the voters with essential details, as a 'time-saving devise' so that on the polling day, the process of identification of voters could take minimum time.[130] The regional election commissioner speaking in a press

---

[128] 'Nehru to Visit States,' *The Hindu*, 11 October 1951.

[129] Election Commission of India, *Report of the First General Election of India 1951–52*, p. 189.

[130] Election Commission of India, *Report of the First General Election of India 1951–52*, p. 190.

conference in Ahmedabad stressed the importance of political parties distributing identity slips to the voters at the time of campaigning. The identity slips mentioned the serial number of the voter, the page of the electoral roll on which the name figured, and the polling station where the vote had to be cast. This, the CEC felt, would speed up and smoothen the process of voting, particularly in large cities where there were numerous polling stations.[131]

This practice of political parties distributing identity slips to the voters continued until 2010, when the Information, Education and Communication (IEC) division was set up by the ECI, which later developed into Systematic Voters' Education and Electoral Participation (SVEEP). With the objective of providing information to voters and educating and mobilising them to vote in large numbers, the SVEEP became almost a mission with the ECI and its officials at the district levels. One component of this programme was to excise the role of political parties as conduits between the voters and the election administrators, so that it was electoral officers who reached out to the voters, distributed the identity slips, and ensured that the communication with the voters was free from political intervention and interference.

The polling day in 1951–2 was 'a day of silence'—to provide repose to the voters to make up their minds in silent contemplation—as they *walked* to their polling booths, which the *Times of India* of 3 January 1952 informs, was 'likely' to be close by. In an interesting aside, the newspaper informs the reader that walking was perhaps the only and perhaps the 'safest' option for the voters for a variety of reasons. While the candidates themselves were forbidden to transport voters, taxis were not an option since all available vehicles had been 'commandeered' either by the government or by political parties and candidates for the elections. The voters could drive their own cars or other modes of conveyance, but they could not offer a lift to other persons. Two families could travel in one vehicle only if they had paid for it jointly. The vigilance in and around the polling booths was such that in Srirampuram, a person distributing pamphlets advertising Godrej Company, which had manufactured the steel ballot boxes, was removed from the vicinity of the polling booth. A group of people

---

[131] 'Identity Slips for Voters,' *The Times of India*, 5 December 1951.

wearing shirts with small imprints of Nehru and Gandhi were asked to remove their shirts.[132]

Elected Detenus and the Right to be Released

The question of release of detenus upon their election to the representative bodies became a matter of debate and contestation following the announcement of the election results. The question was precipitated by letters written by detenus who had contested and won elections, requesting their release. In its discussions on the matter, the Government of India seemed inclined to go with the parliamentary practice in Britain where no such privilege would reside with members of Parliament, if they were a 'danger to the Commonwealth'. The detenus, the government believed, were in detention because they were a 'danger to the Indian Union'. Their election did not make them any less dangerous or diminish their offence, and there was indeed no distinction between a detenu and an underground offender, who if he or she were to surrender would be placed under detention. It was only a legal review as provided by law, and not the fact of their successful election that would provide the conditions for their 'lawful' release.[133]

While the ECI was not concerned with the question of their release, it is noteworthy that the detenus, most of whom were communists detained under the Preventive Detention Act of 1950, presented a curious dilemma of democracy within the electoral space. Towards the end of 1951, when the electoral process had begun, various state governments and high courts were faced with the question of releasing detenus to enable them to contest elections. The *Times of India* on 8 November 1951 reported that political prisoners all over India had decided to launch a 'passive offensive' against the state governments to demand their release so that they could take part in the general election. In Bombay, the detenus presented a memorandum to the state government informing the government that they would go on a hunger strike if their demand for immediate release was

---

[132] 'Identity Slips for Voters,' *The Times of India*, 5 December 1951.

[133] 'Release of Election Detenus: Govt. Statement Likely,' *The Times of India*, 5 February 1952.

not acceded. Indeed, the detenus accused the state government of intensifying its 'repressive measures' against communists.[134] Similar memoranda were presented by detenus to other state governments demanding parole or release to enable them to campaign in the elections. Demands for trial in an open court were also being made.[135] While holding that there was nothing to prevent 'political workers' in prison from contesting elections, B.C. Roy, the chief minister of West Bengal, stated that the decision of their release to enable them to participate was one that could be taken only by the central government. Speaking at a press conference on the question of release of political prisoners, he stated that those convicted by law courts could be released only under orders of magistrates or the judiciary but those detained without trial would be 'given the facilities and the right to cast their votes from within the jail'.[136] The West Bengal government gave permission to leaders of political parties to visit detenu candidates in jail in connection with the arrangements for their election campaigns.[137] While an official communication on other facilities pertaining to the election campaign had not been issued, there were cases where some of these detenus were shifted to jails closest to the constituencies from which they were contesting elections. In Tamil Nadu, for example, P. Ramamurthy, a detenu, was brought to Madura Central Jail from Vellore since he was contesting the state assembly election from Madura North. Following his transfer, there were demonstrations by his supporters at the railway station and in front of the jail, pressing for his release.[138]

In the meantime, in Hyderabad, which was among those states that had the largest number of detenu candidates contesting elections, the government released four 'top-ranking communist leaders'

[134] 'Election and Detenus: Release Demanded,' *The Times of India*, 8 November 1951.

[135] 'Political Prisoners Demand Release,' *Hindustan Times*, 8 November 1951.

[136] 'Release of Detenus for Elections,' *Hindustan Times*, 13 November 1951.

[137] 'Election Facilities: Detenus,' *Hindustan Times*, 30 November 1951.

[138] 'Detenu Candidate Shifted to Madura,' *Hindustan Times*, 30 December 1951.

of Telangana on parole for three months to enable them to contest elections for the Lok Sabha. The government issued the following press release: 'Representations were made to the Government on behalf of the Peoples' Democratic Front that candidates put up by them for the General Election, who are under detention may be released. After careful consideration the Government has decided that in the interests of fair and free election they should accede to this request'. Ravi Narayan Reddy, one of the detenus released on parole, was reported as having expressed surprise at the continued arrest of their workers. Restoration of civil liberties was required if the elections were to be fair and free, he felt, and the ban on the Communist Party and the Andhra Mahasabha should be lifted, a measure which was being negotiated with the government.[139] A deputation of the Hyderabad People's Defence Committee met the home minister, to request the release or extension of about 500 detenus who were now out on parole. The latter could be done after consideration of their adherence to the terms of their 'undertaking', which is to say, their conduct while on parole.[140] By December, both West Bengal and Bihar governments released 17 and 5 detenus, respectively, on parole, to enable them to contest elections to the Lok Sabha and the state legislative assemblies.[141] The Orissa High Court released a detenu, B.K. Patnaik, to enable him to contest in the state legislative assembly elections.[142] The Madras High Court, however, dismissed the application of T. Nagi Reddy, a detenu who was contesting the assembly election against N. Sanjiva Reddy. While T. Nagi Reddy pleaded his case on the ground that he had a fundamental right to contest the election, the judges decided against releasing him by arguing that his right was subject to the legal process, which could not be 'dodged'.[143]

---

[139] 'Four Telangana "Red" Released,' *The Times of India,* 5 December 1951.

[140] 'Detenus on Parole,' *Hindustan Times,* 8 December 1951.

[141] 'Bihar to Release 5 Communist Detenus,' *Hindustan Times,* 8 December 1951; 'Bengal to Release 17 Security Prisoners,' *Hindustan Times,* 8 December 1951.

[142] 'Orissa High Court Releases Detenu,' *Hindustan Times,* 6 December 1951.

[143] 'Detenu's Application Rejected,' *Hindustan Times,* 6 December 1951.

In January, the following year, when the electoral process was close to completion and results were available for several seats, the *Times of India* wrote a scathing critique of the Preventive Detention Act declaring that the 'whirligig of the elections had brought a queer revenge'. Pointing towards the results from three southern states of Travancore-Cochin, Hyderabad, and Madras, the editorial argued:

> seldom had electors in any country chosen as their representatives so many detenus and fugitives from the law.... Their elections carries with it the stigma of a two-pronged censure. Not only have the voters rejected the candidates of the party in power but by a queer quirk of irony they have expressed their confidence in persons whose freedom Authority regarded as a threat to law and order and who in many cases were not able to face their electorate and run their campaign.... What makes their continued detention invidious at this juncture is that they are detained merely on suspicion.[144]

Suggesting that they should be tried publicly and not detained without trial, the editorial also made the argument that the electoral law that allowed detenus to contest will make no sense if those who were elected were not allowed to sit in the legislatures:

> The Congress finds itself poised perilously on the horns of a dilemma largely of its own creation ... to prevent the opposition parties from functioning constitutionally will lay it open to the charge that ever hungry for power, it is now determined to seize it by all means. Thereby it must make the maintenance of law and order more difficult and ultimately render more easy another devastating Communist sweep at the polls'.[145]

Nominations, Election Petitions, and the Contest over Jurisdiction

Some of the nominations filed by candidates hoping to contest the elections were rejected, prompting them to approach the courts for redress. In the process, the constitutional and statutory provisions

---

[144] 'The Detenus Dilemma,' *The Times of India*, 22 January 1951.
[145] 'The Detenus Dilemma,' *The Times of India*, 22 January 1951.

pertaining to elections were called into question and their interpretation became a matter for the courts to decide. Article 329(b) of the Constitution, which became the focus of contest, provided that no election to either House of Parliament or to the state legislative assemblies could be questioned 'except by an election petition'. The authority to which the petition was to be submitted and the manner in which it was to be done would be determined by the law framed by an appropriate legislature. In a case of eight petitions filed before the Bombay High Court, the petitioners whose nomination papers had been rejected pointed at a *vacuum* in the rules laid down for the conduct of elections in the RPA. The Act had not provided for any remedy in case of 'improper' rejection of nomination by returning officers. Indeed, the procedure which the Act laid down in Section 100(C) required that a candidate must establish that his or her nomination papers had been 'wrongly rejected' and also give evidence that the rejection had 'materially affected' the election result. The latter condition, the petitioners argued, was beyond the competence of any candidate to establish.

The advocate general was, however, of the opinion that an election tribunal set up under the Constitution would be competent to deal with such questions, and not the High Court. He further argued that the expression 'election' in Article 329(b) referred to 'all stages of the election', and any remedy would be available only at the *conclusion* of the election. Recourse to the court before the conclusion of an election would 'seriously upset the election machinery'.[146] The absence of a legal provision to respond expeditiously to what was considered an unfair provision that led to the exclusion of candidates at the threshold, without providing a remedy till it was too late, brought up the demand for the examination of electoral law. John Matthai, former finance minister, whose nomination papers filed as an independent candidate were rejected on the ground of him being a member of the board of directors of the House of Tatas, which made profit out of its government contracts, asked for such an examination. Matthai argued that the rejection of his papers had 'created a dangerous precedent' whereby he could exercise his franchise but

---

[146] '8 Petitions to Set Aside Nomination Rejections: Bombay High Court Hears Arguments on Jurisdiction,' *The Times of India*, 4 October 1951.

not contest an election.[147] In the course of the hearing of his case in the Travancore-Cochin High Court, the advocate general argued that the right to franchise was merely a statutory right, which was not protected by the power of the courts to issue writs. The petitioner argued, however, that such a writ was available to him on the ground that 'the election had been materially affected by the improper acceptance or rejection of the nomination'.[148] Campaigning in Travancore-Cochin, Jai Prakash Narain was concerned at the rejection of nomination papers by returning officers on what he called 'flimsy grounds'. Indeed, his own party, which expected to do well in the region, had suffered 11 rejections on technical grounds, which he thought could be condoned, considering that people (in this case, prospective candidates) were still unfamiliar with electoral democracy in the country.[149]

The Travancore-Cochin High Court decided 'in view of Article 329(b) of the Constitution and Section 170 of the Representation of the People Act the decision of the Returning Officer in reject-ing the nomination paper could not be called in question except by the presentation of an election petition under the aforesaid Act'. Such a petition could be presented, moreover, only after the result had been announced.[150] An editorial piece in the *Hindustan Times* lamented that a crucial suggestion by B.R. Ambedkar at the time when the RPA was being discussed, regarding the disposal of disputes over nomination before the commencement of elections, was not accepted. The present situation, where all contests over improper decisions pertaining to nomination papers were to be raised and resolved at the conclusion of the electoral process, would lead to unnecessary and avoidable waste of time, energy, and money. Indeed, even as the Travancore-Cochin High Court made a decision

---

[147] 'Need to Examine Electoral Laws,' *The Times of India*, 1 November 1951; 'Petition of Dr. John Matthai,' *The Times of India*, 3 November 1951.

[148] 'Dr. Matthai's Petition,' *Hindustan Times*, 10 November 1951.

[149] In one case, the nomination papers of a candidate were rejected on the ground that he or she had not given three alternative symbols, even when the returning officer was presented with the ECI instructions that this could be condoned ('Election of Nominations,' *Hindustan Times*, 12 November 1951).

[150] 'Election Law Anomalies: Legal Reform,' *Hindustan Times*, 25 November 1951.

within the frameworks of the existing law, it referred to the 'material inconveniences' that were caused by precluding relief to the affected persons at an earlier stage in the electoral process. It recommended, therefore, that the state should devise a suitable mechanism for considering the legality of the decisions of the returning officer before polling begins.[151]

Other high courts were interpreting the rules differently. The Bombay High Court admitted several petitions from different parts of the state challenging the rejection of nomination papers by returning officers on technical grounds ranging from failure to name an agent to not mentioning one's age. The petitioners argued that the rejections were illegal and disregarded Sections 33(3) and 30(4) of the RPA, which stated that the returning officer should not reject any nomination paper on the ground of any technical defect that was not of a substantial nature. Admitting the petitions, Justice Gajendragadkar provided interim relief to petitioners and passed injunctions against returning officers.[152] Another candidate appealed before the Allahabad High Court to 'restrain' the returning officer in Allahabad, who had declared the nomination papers of Prime Minister Nehru and Sri Prakasa, minister for scientific research and natural resources, contesting elections from the Allahabad constituency valid, despite objection raised by the petitioner. The high court admitted the petitions and issued notices to Nehru and Prakasa.[153] The Lucknow bench of the Allahabad High Court admitted a petition filed by Hargovind Dayal Srivastava, a Jan Sangh candidate contesting the Lok Sabha election, challenging the validity of the nomination papers of Vijaylakshmi Pandit filed for a parliamentary seat in Lucknow on the grounds that 'she was not in India when the nomination papers were available and she signed them long before they were called for'. The judges issued notices for the papers to be placed before them for an early disposal of the case.[154]

---

[151] 'Election Law Anomalies: Legal Reform,' *Hindustan Times*, 25 November 1951.

[152] '2 More Election Petitions,' *Hindustan Times*, 1 December 1951; 'Rejection of Nominations Challenged,' *The Times of India*, 1 December 1951.

[153] 'Nomination of Mr. Nehru,' *The Times of India*, 30 November 1951.

[154] 'Nomination of Mrs. Pandit,' *Hindustan Times*, 5 December 1951.

A variety of issues were generated when nomination papers were rejected, ranging from the right of the candidate to contest election to the lack of clarity on what constituted disqualification at the stage of nomination, especially how and when it could be resolved. While the ECI issued orders periodically on what was within the purview of technical rejection, ambiguity on the matter remained, which was compounded by uneven responses by different high courts. Ultimately, however, all these issues were resolved with the decision of the Bombay High Court concurring with the Travancore-Cochin High Court that these matters were outside the jurisdiction of the high court since the judiciary was specifically barred from intervening in the electoral process until it was over, and a judicial remedy was available to petitioners only after the election had concluded.[155] Dismissing the petitions filed in the Bombay High Court, Justice Gajendragadkar held that under Article 329(b), the jurisdiction of the Court to hear petitions relating to or connected with election matters had been taken away. The *Hindustan Times* reported the order as one where the judges considered the RPA as being part of a legal 'scheme' that gave 'finality' to the 'different stages of elections'. By itself, Section 117 of the RPA was not sufficient to 'oust' the jurisdiction of the high court to issue writs under Article 226 of the Constitution of India. As long as Article 226 remained unamended, no law could abridge the jurisdiction of the high courts. It was then only the Constitution that could provide for any curtailment. Article 329(b) of the Constitution, which provided that no election to either house of the legislature could be 'called in question except by an election petition presented to such authority and in such manner as may be provided for by or under any law made by the appropriate legislature', in the opinion of the judge, excluded the jurisdiction of the courts to issue a writ under Article 226 in election matters. The newspaper reported:

> Their lordships added: 'To the extent that the Constitution has excluded jurisdiction of courts in election matters referred to in Article 329(b), the power of the high court to issue writs has been taken away.... The substantial question to be decided by the court was meaning of the

---

[155] 'Election Petitions: High Court's Right to Hear Questioned,' *Hindustan Times*, 5 December 1951.

expression 'election'. Their lordships held that the word had a wider connotation than the more restricted meaning of the result of the election or of counting of votes. The word election meant all matters relating to election from the time of notification till the final result was announced. It was the whole continuous integrated procedure.... It seemed to their lordships that the whole object of enacting Chapter 15 of the Constitution and the Representation of the People Act was to set up a machinery whereby elections could take place as far as possible within scheduled time and there should be no interference or interruption in the proceedings by any court of law. It might in some cases cause hardships but their lordship thought that the scheme of the RPA was not contrary to the larger interests of the state. Their lordships also held that although their power of superintendence and control has been taken away with regard to election matters, under Article 227, the high court could interfere in case the election tribunal were to act without jurisdiction and or in excess of the power conferred on it by statute.[156]

An editorial on electoral reforms in the *Times of India* lamented that the exclusion of the courts had prevented them from providing the much-needed interim relief to candidates who were adversely affected by the wrongful rejection or acceptance of nomination papers. A scrutiny of the number of rejections showed that only 5 per cent of over 30,000 nominations filed were rejected and 'a microscopic proportion of these were invalidated on dubious grounds'. The editorial advised that experience should serve to remind the future law-givers that they take good care to study the law and observe the simple rules about nominations, and also the returning officers to read the law well, so that the rejection of nomination papers, for 'some inscrutable reasons' like being 'unable to spell their fathers' names correctly', may not occur at all.[157]

Justice Bose of the Calcutta High Court dismissed a number of petitions on the ground of jurisdiction and observed at the same time that the provisions of the RPA must be 'suitably amended to provide for the final decision of the question pertaining to rejection of nomination paper before the polling began. Otherwise, his lordship

---

[156] 'Election Please & High Courts,' *Hindustan Times*, 6 December 1951.
[157] 'Legal Petitions,' *The Times of India*, 6 December 1951.

remarked, the returned candidate would be deprived of the fruits of his election after he had incurred considerable worry in getting through the election, merely because the Returning Officer had come to an erroneous conclusion'.[158] The ECI received the first election petition on 23 December 1951 when the bulk of the country was to still go to polls. Ironically, the petition concerned 'improper rejection' of nomination papers. Prabhuda Ramjibhai Mehta of Bhavnagar in Saurashtra challenged the rejection of his nomination papers for Talaja-Datha, an assembly constituency, which led to his rival being elected unopposed.[159]

A petition by B. Ponnuswami, dismissed by the Madras High Court 'for want of jurisdiction', reached the Supreme Court. The petition was dismissed by the high court on the ground that the candidate, B. Ponnuswami, had not filed five separate forms for appointment of the election agent, although one form had the required authorisation. Rajagopala Aiyangar, the counsel for Ponnuswami, questioned the interpretation of Article 329, which referred to interference by the courts, to say that the word 'election' in the article meant only the 'returns at the polls' and not the earlier stages of election. While upholding the decision of the high court, the judges took the view that 'the word "election" used in Part XV of the Constitution should take in the entire process to be gone through to return a candidate to the legislature and that it should have the same meaning wherever that word is used in the said part of the Constitution'.[160]

* * *

When the first Lok Sabha was elected in India, an entire edifice of legal-institutional machinery for conducting elections in the most populous democracy in the world was put in place. The exercise was colossal, but it also unleashed the colossus of democracy, which would refuse to be harnessed. Tracing unchartered territory, the electoral machinery had to grapple with administrative and political logics of

---

[158] 'Electoral Law Needs Change,' *The Times of India*, 7 December 1951.

[159] 'Unopposed Return Challenged,' *The Times of India*, 24 December 1951.

[160] 'Jurisdiction of Courts,' *The Times of India*, 8 January 1952.

holding an election on the basis of universal franchise. While delimitation of constituencies and enumeration of voters were part of the bureaucratic exercise, the RPA provided the legal frameworks within which the electoral game was to be played. The first general elections were all about a quest for certainties of procedures thus laid down, to ensure that the outcome was not predetermined, the electoral competition was fair, and the result was, therefore, democratic. The contests over appropriate representation as well as over the fairness of the procedures themselves made their appearance in the first general election, and have continued to be debated in various forms through all these years.

౫✕ౚ

2

Electoral Roll, the 'Vote', and Democracy

In the Bollywood film *Newton* (2017), the presiding officer deputed to a remote village in the state of Chhattisgarh is given the charge of conducting polls in a polling booth of 76 Adivasi voters who, for various reasons, have never voted before. The polling booth is located in the Dandakaranya forests dominated by the Maoist insurgents who have given a call for poll boycott. Airdropped into the village where the polling booth is located, the presiding officer and his assistants are escorted by the Central Reserve Police Force (CRPF) to a dilapidated room in a forest clearing, where they set up a polling booth and wait for the villagers to arrive and cast their votes. Gun-wielding CRPF men stand guard outside the booth as the threat of a Maoist attack lingers in the air. The young presiding officer, a 'rookie' on his first election duty, has a stubborn streak of integrity. Much to the chagrin of the CRPF personnel accompanying the polling party, the presiding officer takes his task of making the Adivasis vote seriously and suspects that the voters are likely to stay away because of intimidation by both the CRPF and the Maoists. The inertia of waiting for voters in the polling booth is interrupted when the director general of police (DGP) sends word to the CRPF officer of his visit to the polling booth with the press, including foreign press, to showcase how deep democracy ran in India. The news of the DGP's impending arrival precipitates a flurry of activities. The CRPF men scoop onto the Adivasi villages, round up the villagers, bring them to the polling booth, and compel them to vote.

This is where the irony of electoral democracy is on stark and poignant display. The Adivasis have never voted before and are strangers to the electoral process. Not familiar with political parties and their manifestoes, all they wish to know is what recompense voting will bring to them. After all, they are risking their lives by lining up to vote: 'Will the prices of *tendu* leaves be raised in their favour?', they ask. The returning officer tries explaining to them how to use the EVMs and their responsibility as citizens to cast an informed vote. But he remains inscrutable to them; ironically, it is the CRPF officer who makes things simpler and comprehensible—the EVM machine was nothing but a toy, he says. The Adivasi could press any button he or she wished, to hear the beep. The Adivasis queue up to vote, presenting a spectacle of democracy, which impresses the foreign press—much to the satisfaction of the superior officer. Compelled to abandon the polling booth after what appears to be a Maoist attack but turns out later to be a red herring staged by the CRPF, the polling party leaves. On their way back to the CRPF camp, however, the presiding officer takes his revenge by allowing four Adivasis, who were on their way to vote from work, to exercise their franchise 'voluntarily', even as the CRPF is unwilling to stop. The presiding officer is a stickler for rules: the official time to vote is not over, the polling booth cannot be abandoned, and the Adivasi must vote. Allowing the Adivasi to vote against the wishes of the CRPF officer is, however, not easy. Ultimately, it is the presiding officer who exercises force, snatches the gun from the CRPF officer, and trains it against him and his men, creating a space of freedom for the unfettered exercise of franchise.

Newton opens up for scrutiny themes that are integral to elections and democracy, especially, the right to vote, the relationship people have with this right, and the conditions that enable its meaningful exercise. The questions—who can vote, whose votes count, and what makes the vote effective, raise concerns around representation and inclusion, which have been debated largely within the normative frameworks of democratic theory. Questions of procedure in relationship to the exercise of franchise are often relegated to the perplexing

domain of electoral outcomes, and not seen as relevant for the normative frameworks of democracy. Yet, as the film *Newton* reminds
us, franchise is an activity fraught with ethical and moral questions,
which is true not only for conflict situations, which the film portrayed,
but also for 'normal' times. These contests are often sought to be
resolved at the level of procedures, that is, at the level of essential,
and not sufficient, conditions. The question whether or not the procedures facilitating franchise lead to democratic outcomes needs to be
addressed in the specific contexts in which rules and procedures are
put in place as efficient models for administering an election.

Who Can Vote? Electoral Roll and the Right to Vote

The right to vote is a constitutional right in India, which is available
only to citizens. Exercised periodically in each election, the right to
vote is contingent upon the procedural requirement of enrolment of
citizens as voters. Unlike the practice followed in the United States
and elsewhere, the ECI has been given an affirmative responsibility
under the Constitution of India to prepare the electoral roll. Article
324 of the Constitution and RPA, 1950, provide the procedure for the
preparation of electoral roll. The debates in the Constituent Assembly
show that the ECI was envisaged as a constitutional body entrusted
with the task of giving effect to the principle of equality of the citizen-
voter, and ensuring that no eligible voter was excluded from the
electoral roll on grounds of religion, race, caste, or gender. Yet, the
ECI's constitutional role of preparing the electoral roll has unfolded
in uneven and contradictory ways. While playing the role of a protec-
tor and facilitator of franchise, in specific contexts, the ECI has also
opened itself to charges of discrimination. This contradiction is made
manifest in particular in those contexts where the ECI has been implicated in disputes over citizenship. The preparation of the electoral
roll is not an exercise of identifying citizens, and the determination
of citizenship is outside the jurisdiction of the ECI. Disputes over
electoral rolls show, however, that the task of 'superintending' the
preparation of the electoral roll has, in specific contexts, translated
into the power of the ECI to identify 'legitimate' voters and to sift out
for that purpose the citizens from non-citizens. A stern adherence
to procedures has also led the ECI on a collision course with specific

state governments, following the ECI's initiative to check the validity
of voters, emerging from what the ECI saw as a 'suspicious' increase
in the number of voters.

The role of the ECI in citizenship decisions first emerged in the
period immediately following the Partition and Independence. In the
unsettled conditions following the Partition and the large-scale migration of people, the passage of 'displaced persons' from Pakistan into
Indian citizenship became an issue of central importance—and one
in which the citizenship rights of Muslims as a minority were sometimes undercut by the religious assumptions underlying Partition
itself. Yet the ECI's position was not initially controversial, as it was
assumed that enrolment as voters would follow enrolment as citizens.
In subsequent years, however, contests over citizenship erupted in
ways that seemingly tied the ECI's authority directly to citizenship
issues. Three key moments may be identified in this process, beginning in the 1980s. Each of these three moments threw up a situation
in which the increase in the number of voters in the electoral rolls was
attributed to the presence of illegal migrants, particularly Muslims,
whose names were deleted from the voter list. In 1984, in the context
of disputes over the electoral rolls in the state of Assam, a Supreme
Court judgment instructed the ECI to interpret its role differently, laying down the modalities by which the ECI, in preparing the electoral
rolls, could also become the arbiter of citizenship. In the wake of this,
the role of the ECI in citizenship matters—particularly in relation to
the position of minorities—became an increasingly contested one.

Article 325 of the Constitution is crucial in so far as it gives direction regarding the nature of the responsibility of the ECI in preparing
the electoral rolls under Article 324(1). The Article gives effect to the
constitutional principle of equality of the citizen-voter, stating that no
person can be excluded from the electoral roll on grounds 'only of
religion, race, caste, sex or any of them'. Accordingly, there is a single
general electoral roll for every territorial constituency for election to
either House of Parliament or to either House of the legislature of
a state, and no person is ineligible for inclusion in any such roll on
grounds of religion, race, caste, or sex.[1] Article 326 lays down the
principles of voter eligibility, stating that elections to the Lok Sabha

---

[1] *Poudyal* v. *Union of India*, (1994) Supp.(1) S.C.C. 324 (para 206) C.B.

and to the legislative assemblies of states are to be on the basis of adult suffrage.

While franchise is not explicitly included as a fundamental right in Part III of the Constitution, the right to adult suffrage may nevertheless be understood as a constitutional right incorporated in Articles 325 and 326 of the Constitution. This constitutional right has two components: the right to vote and the right to contest elections.[2]

---

[2] Undated note (2007) by Professor Upendra Baxi, responding to the proposal by the law ministry on electoral reforms, particularly those pertaining to disqualification of candidates standing for elections, on grounds of criminal chargesheets against them. Baxi expressed his anxiety:

at this demotion of a constitutional right to a mere statutory privilege. I do not here address the perilous, if I may with respect say so, future impact of the Law Ministry mindset. There is no need in India to emulate the American Supreme Court holding in Bush v. Gore that held the right to adult suffrage merely as a statutory privilege. The Indian constitutional scheme is far more advanced on this count than the American and it is simply impermissible to convert a constitutional right into a mere statutory privilege, especially after six decades of the Indian constitutional development.

In later years, however, the judiciary interpreted the right to vote differently. In 2013, the Supreme Court of India upheld a 2004 decision by the Patna High Court to confirm that the right to vote was a mere statutory right: 'the law gives it, the law takes it away'. The decision came in the context of the question whether or not persons convicted of crimes 'can be kept away' from elections to the legislature (state assemblies and Parliament) and all public elections. The courts decided that persons in lawful custody of the police (except those under preventive detention) cannot be voters under the law and, therefore, cannot be 'electors' who can contest public elections:

The Law temporarily takes away the power of such persons to go anywhere near the election scene. To vote is a statutory right. It is privilege to vote, which privilege may be taken away [sic]. In that case, the elector would not be qualified, even if his name is on the electoral rolls. The name is not struck off, but the qualification to be an elector and the privilege to vote when in the lawful custody of the police is taken away.

The Supreme Court decided: 'a person who has no right to vote by virtue of the provisions of sub-section (5) of Section 62 of the 1951 Act is not an

Following the 61st amendment in 1988, every citizen of India who is not less than 18 years of age, and not otherwise disqualified, on the grounds of non-residence, 'unsoundness of mind', or 'crime or corrupt or illegal practice', is entitled to be registered as a voter at any such election. Article 327 gives Parliament the power to make provision with respect to elections to legislatures and Article 328 confers similar powers on state legislatures with respect to state elections.[3] But it is significant that the power of Parliament has been made subject to other provisions of the Constitution including Article 324, which makes the 'superintendence, direction and control' of elections the primary responsibility of the ECI.[4]

The electoral rolls are revised and updated from time to time by the EROs either on an application by persons or on their own. No person can be registered in more than one constituency and no person can be registered more than once in the same constituency and should be 'ordinarily' resident in that constituency (Sections 17 and 18, RPA, 1950).[5] Before every general election to the Lok Sabha or the state

---

elector and is therefore not qualified to contest the election to the House of the People or the Legislative Assembly of a State.' (See *Chief Election Commissioner etc.* v. *Jan Chowkidar (People's Watch) & Others* [civil appeal 30140-3041 of 2004, decided on 10 July 2013].)

[3] Parliament may, from time to time, by law make provisions with respect to all matters relating to, or in connection with, election to either House of Parliament or to the House or either House of the legislatures of a state including the preparation of electoral rolls, the delimitation of constituencies, and all other matters necessary for securing the due constitution of such House or Houses.

[4] *Sadiq* v. *Election Commission*, AIR 1972 S.C. 187.

[5] Triggering off a debate on the violation of the 'principle of local representation', the Representation of the People (Amendment) Act, 2010, allows a non-resident Indian (NRI)—that is, a person who is a citizen of India and who has not acquired the citizenship of any other country and is otherwise eligible to be registered as a voter, and who is away from his or her place of ordinary residence in India due to employment or for education—to be registered as a voter in the constituency in his or her place of residence as mentioned in the passport. Under the hitherto existing law, an NRI who stayed out of the country, and therefore, the constituency in which his or her name occurred in the electoral roll, was not allowed to vote. The amendment was

legislature, or before a by-election, an intensive revision of the roll is carried out. The qualifying date for the year for which the electoral rolls are being prepared is 1 January, but the registration of voters is in a sense an ongoing exercise, and the insertion of names of eligible voters may continue till the last date of the nomination of candidates in an election.

The electoral roll for every parliamentary constituency consists of the electoral rolls for all the state assembly constituencies that fall within that parliamentary constituency. Thus, there is a single, and not separate, roll for national parliamentary and state assembly constituencies (Section 13D, RPA, 1950). In preparing the rolls for each assembly constituency, the ECI subdivides it into parts, each corresponding to one polling booth. No polling booth is to have more than 1,200 electors. The polling booths are, in turn, identified in a

---

the result of a promise made to the Indian diaspora by then prime minister Manmohan Singh at a *Pravasi Bharatiya Divas* commemoration in 2009. Under the amended Act, an NRI could vote if he or she was present in the constituency on the polling day ('The Right to Vote,' *Economic and Political Weekly* (2010). The NRI community, however, pressed for e-voting rights, and petitioned the Supreme Court in 2014 for the restoration of their right to vote. Nudged by the Supreme Court and pushed by the BJP, in August 2017, the government approved a proposal to further amend the RPA to allow NRIs to vote through 'proxy'. Under the system of voting by 'proxy', the NRIs can register themselves as voters online and appoint a person as their proxy to vote. If Parliament passes the proposed amendment to the RPA, states like Punjab, Kerala, and Gujarat would be impacted the most by this decision since a substantial percentage of the diaspora belongs to these states. Parties like the Congress and the CPI(M) have been critical of 'proxy' voting, because of its susceptibility to violation of secrecy of ballot and trust deficit. ('Government Clears Proxy Vote Move for NRIs,' *The Indian Express*, 3 August 2017.) A year later, the Lok Sabha passed an amendment in the RPA by voice vote to approve proxy voting by NRIs. Concerns continued to be raised. The CPI(M) preferred that the amendments be referred to a select committee for detailed discussions, and the regional parties were apprehensive that large and resourceful parties would benefit from the change. ('Bill to Allow Proxy Voting Passed by Lok Sabha,' *Economic Times*, 9 August 2018. Available at https://economictimes.indiatimes.com/news/politics-and-nation/bill-to-allow-proxy-voting-by-nris-passed-by-lok-sabha/articleshow/65343623.cms; accessed on 15 August 2018.)

way so that no voter may have to travel more than two kilometres to reach the polling booth.[6] The Constituent Assembly envisaged the ECI as a body that could play an active role in facilitating and ensuring equality and fairness in the electoral process. Unlike the practice in many other democracies, the task of 'superintendence, direction and control of the preparation of electoral rolls', vested in the ECI under Article 324, has in practice evolved as an affirmative responsibility of the ECI to enrol voters. For the ECI, this has included a constitutional obligation to encourage, as it says on its website, the '*actual* exercise of franchise by eligible citizens' (emphasis added).[7] While encouraging 'eligible citizens' to exercise their franchise, the ECI reminds them that to be able to vote, the 'first and foremost requirement' is that their names should be registered in the electoral roll. The 'duty' of the citizen in this matter extends, however, *only* to 'finding out' whether or not his or her name appears in the electoral roll. The actual task of registering citizen-voters, as the 'guidelines to voters' on the ECI's website indicates, is undertaken by the ECI itself. The registration of voters takes place through a process of 'intensive revision' involving 'house-to-house enumeration', whereby the enumerators go 'physically from door-to-door' to collect information about electors. While the process of intensive revision is undertaken every five years, summary revisions are done every year, when those electors whose names do not figure in the electoral rolls, or those who have shifted to a new constituency, are given the opportunity to register themselves, by filling out a form (Form 6).[8] This is very different from the practice

---

[6] Election Commission of India. 2006. 'A Guide for the Voters,' New Delhi, available at https://www.eci.gov.in/eci_main/ECI_voters_guideline_2006.pdf; accessed on 13 July 2011.

[7] Election Commission of India. 2006. 'Why Should You Vote?,' New Delhi, p. 1, available at https://www.eci.gov.in/eci_main/ECI_voters_guideline_2006.pdf; accessed on 13 July 2011.

[8] During the process of preparation or revision of electoral roll, an appeal against the decision of the ERO may be made to the deputy commissioner/district magistrate/DC. During the continuous updating of the rolls, an appeal against any order of the ERO, under Section 22 or 23 of the RPA, 1950, can be made before the district magistrate/DC or the additional district magistrate and a further appeal against the order of the appellate authority may be made before the CEO.

that exists in the United States, for example, where responsibility for registration lies with would-be voters rather than the state.

To facilitate the process of revision, an important innovation of the ECI has been the appointment of BLOs at the lowest level of the administrative machinery of the electoral system.[9] A BLO is a local, lower-level government or semi-government officer, who is familiar with the local electors and is also a voter in the same polling area. The usefulness of the BLO in updating the electoral rolls is seen to lie in his or her knowledge of and familiarity with the locality, which is seen as effective for collecting actual field information for the purpose of revision of electoral rolls.[10] While revising the rolls, the BLO is expected to make frequent field visits to the villages or 'tolas' of that part of the electoral roll he or she is responsible for, interacting with the local people, particularly village elders and grass-roots-level elected representatives, and identifying the names of the dead, relocated, and duplicate voters in the roll, which need to be removed by the ERO under the relevant provisions of law.[11] Following the

---

[9] The following are some of the lower-level government and semi-government officials who may be appointed as BLOs by the DEO: teachers, anganwadi workers, patwari/Lekhpal, panchayat secretary, village-level workers, electricity bill readers, postal workers, auxiliary nurses and midwives, health workers, midday meal workers, contract teachers, corporation tax collectors, clerical staff in urban areas, and the like. While BLOs continue to discharge their duties in their parent organisations, when involved in the task of revising the roll, they are considered on deputation to the ECI and subject to its disciplinary control. Above the BLOs are supervisory officers who monitor and maintain checks on the quality of work done by them. Each supervisory officer has 10–20 BLOs under his/her supervision.

[10] The BLO is not a full-time electoral officer, and his or her responsibility of assisting in roll revision is seen as rendering a civic duty. Each BLO has one or two polling station areas under his or her jurisdiction.

[11] The handbook for the BLOs published by the ECI describes him or her as 'a friend, philosopher and guide of the local people in matters relating to the roll'. The BLO is expected to use his or her familiarity with the locality to do the following jobs, which are seen as important for effective revision of the rolls: receiving claims and objections; house-to-house visits and checking of overlapping, migration, transfer/shifting, identification of shifted/dead/non-existing electors; checking inclusion and exclusion errors; checking details of

intensive revision, a draft roll is prepared and published at every polling booth. The publication of the draft roll is done with the purpose of verification of the list, so that eligible voters who have been left out can apply to the ERO for the inclusion of their names, and conversely, so that objections to the names of ineligible or non-existent voters can be raised for deletion by filling up another form (Form 8A). After processing the claims and objections, the ECI prepares a supplementary electoral roll, which is subsequently published. The electoral roll is continuously updated, and registration of names can take place up to 10 days before the last date notified by the ECI for the filing of nominations of candidates in an election.[12]

To ensure accuracy and facilitate modification, the ECI undertook the computerisation of the electoral rolls throughout India. For adequate publicity and accessibility of information, the electoral rolls

---

spellings, entries of duplicate names, photos, and the like of electors in the roll; collecting photos of electors; collecting mobile numbers of electors (optional); submitting reports to EROs so that notice can be issued to the persons whose names have to be deleted; display of draft roll/prescribed notices at designated locations; reading of rolls in gram/ward *sabhas*; liaison with resident welfare associations (RWAs) in urban areas for registration; electronic photo identity cards (EPICs) for voters; distribution (after preparation) to the right person and not to any other intermediary; maximisation of EPIC coverage and enrolment; SVEEP (for example, street plays, dramas, wall writings, and so on); National Voters Day (NVD) activities; administering NVD pledge and exhorting voters at NVD time; correct serialisation of the houses and correct arrangement of sections falling within the part; detailing of forms received; impart simple voter education at registration time; distribution of voters slip before election. (For details, see Election Commission of India 2011).

[12] 'A Guide for the Voters,' Election Commission of India, New Delhi, 2006, available at http://www.eci.gov.in; accessed on 13 July 2011. During the process of preparation or revision of electoral roll, an appeal against the decision of the ERO may be made to the deputy commissioner/district magistrate/DC. During the continuous updating of the rolls, an appeal against any order of the ERO, under Section 22 or 23 of the RPA, 1950, can be made before the district magistrate/DC or the additional district magistrate and a further appeal against the order of the Appellate Authority may be made before the CEO.

of all are available on the website of the ECI. Moreover, to improve the accuracy of the electoral rolls and prevent electoral fraud, in the middle of the 1990s, the ECI introduced EPICs,[13] though this process generated considerable controversy.[14] In 2004, 'to improve the fidelity of the electoral rolls and to evolve methods to eradicate impersonation during the poll', the ECI started the process of incorporating photographs in the electoral rolls to ensure proper identification of electors at the polling stations.[15] In 2015, the ECI launched the National Electoral Roll Purification and Authentication Programme (NERPAP) where it proposed to link the EPIC with the Aadhaar number of the registered voter in order to remove duplication and create an error-free voter identification system. The programme was launched on 3 March 2015.[16] NERPAP was, however, put on hold in August 2015, after the Supreme Court of India passed an interim order putting the Aadhaar on hold, prohibiting Aadhaar from being used for any purpose other than the government programmes of public distribution of food grain, cooking fuel, and liquid petroleum gas (LPG) (Supreme

[13] All the EPICs issued by the ECI were assigned a unique number, which was also printed on the EPIC. Subsequently, under the directions issued by the ECI under Rule 4 of the Registration of Electors Rule, 1960, the EPIC number was incorporated in the electoral rolls.

[14] Sridharan and Vaishnav (2017: 449) point out that this process is administratively complex and expensive. In addition, the insistence of then CEC T.N. Seshan that elections would be delayed till all voters had EPICs, attracted criticism for holding the elections 'hostage to a personal crusade carried out by a single individual'.

[15] Election Commission's letter No. 23/ER-Revised Format/ 2003/PLN-II, addressed to the Chief Electoral Officers of all States and Union Territories on the Subject: Pilot projects for printing electoral rolls along with the photographs of electors, 21 January 2004. Pilot projects were undertaken in two assembly constituencies in Kerala and two in Haryana, following which the ECI decided to expand this exercise incrementally in all states and union territories. (See Election Commission of India 2006, available at http://www.eci.gov.in; accessed on 13 July 2011.)

[16] Press Information Bureau, 'Election Commission Launches National Electoral Roll Purification and Authentication Programme (NERPAP) from Today,' press release, 3 March 2015, available at http://pib.nic.in/newsite/PrintRelease.aspx?relid=116280; accessed on 18 December 2017.

Court order dated 11 August 2015, in writ petition [civil] no. 494 of 2012, *Justice Puttaswamy [Retd.] & Another* v. *Union of India & Others.* Available at http://indiankanoon.org/doc/116396036/; accessed on 30 August 2015).

While the ECI halted its programme immediately after the Supreme Court delivered its order, a report in *The Wire* based on right to information (RTI) requests revealed that in the course of the process of seeding, the ECI had 'skirted the boundary between responsible data sharing practices and outright violation of privacy and user consent', by adopting a range of strategies to 'rapidly link' millions of voter IDs to Aadhaar numbers. The ECI had access to the National Population Register in at least four major states of the country and also employed the DBT Seeding Data Viewer (DSDV) tool, which allowed third parties to access non-biometric identity data stored by the Unique Identification Authority of India (UIDAI). Indeed, as declared publicly by the ECI, in the few months that the NERPAP was active, the ECI had been able to link 320 million voter IDs to Aadhaar.[17] The then CEC O.P. Rawat and his predecessors A.K. Joti and H.S. Brahma, who had endorsed the linkage programme, apart from other serving electoral officials, were, however, of the opinion that consent was implicit in the process and had, in fact, been obtained. According to CEC Rawat, 'the process involved voters going online voluntarily and completing the linkage after agreeing to the terms and conditions', which 'naturally' involved consent.[18] Following the Supreme Court judgment of 26 September 2018, restricting Aadhar linkage to certain basic services backed by an appropriate law, the ECI has revived its efforts to establish linkage between Aadhar and voter IDs, in order to purify the electoral roll. The ECI hopes to make this linkage mandatory with the help of an

[17] Anuj Srivas. 2018. 'How did the EC Link 300 Million Voter IDs to Aadhaar in Just a Few Months,' *The Wire*, 9 November.

[18] 'Linking Voter ID with Aadhaar: Pleas in Madras High Court Revives Concerns About Privacy, Consent,' *Scroll.in*, 18 December 2018. A petition seeking that voter IDs be linked with Aadhaar, was admitted by the Madras High Court on 5 October 2018. Admitting the petition filed by M.L. Ravi, the head of a political group called Desiya Makkal Sakthi Katchi, the High Court issued notices to the Centre and the UIDAI. The Election Commission had already informed the court that it supports the plea.

amendment in the RPA, 1951, which would provide effective legislative support for the linkage.[19]

Another newspaper report based on interviews with serving and retired election officers in Delhi, Punjab, Rajasthan, and Andhra Pradesh and examination of internal documents concluded that the linking of voter identification card with Aadhaar led officers to defer their judgement to algorithms that they themselves did not understand. Indeed, investigations carried out by a team of journalists in Andhra Pradesh and Telangana revealed that in these two states that were to serve as the template for a wider national project for electoral roll purification and authentication, 'software could have played a role in the elimination of 2.2 million voters from Telangana's electoral rolls'.[20] The concerns around 'missing' names raised by a number of political parties, including AAP in Delhi, were attributed to 'multiple reasons' by the ECI. The CEO of Telangana, for example, cited not just the 'new software' as a reason for the deletion of names, but also the possibility of a number of voters living in Telangana choosing to vote in the neighbouring state of Andhra Pradesh.[21] In Delhi, Chief Minister Arvind Kejriwal requested that all the names deleted from the electoral rolls since 2015 be put on ECI's website and verification of rolls in Lal Kuan and Harkesh Nagar constituencies, affected by the deletions, be done to instil confidence among the voters. This, then CEC O.P. Rawat assured, had been done expeditiously.[22] Yet, issues of procedural impropriety, especially with respect to the security of

[19] Anubhuti Vishnoi. 2018. 'Linking of Aadhar & Voter ID May be Made Mandatory,' The Economic Times, 13 December, available at https://economictimes.indiatimes.com/news/politics-and-nation/linking-of-aadhaar-voter-id-may-be-made-mandatory/articleshow/67069414.cms?from=mdr; accessed on 16 May 2019.

[20] Rachna Khaira and Aman Sethi. 2018. 'UIDAI's Voter Linking Plan May have Cost Millions Their Vote,' Huffington Post, 9 November, available at https://www.huffingtonpost.in/2018/11/08/election-commission-uidai-plan-to-link-aadhaar-to-voter-ids-may-have-robbed-millions-of-their-vote_a_23584297/; accessed on 17 December 2018.

[21] Khaira and Sethi, 'UIDAI's Voter Linking Plan May Have Cost Millions Their Vote'.

[22] 'O P Rawat: Note Ban Had Absolutely No Impact on Black Money,' The Indian Express, 16 December 2018.

the information on Aadhaar already received by the electoral officers in various states and districts, and the normative question of
preservation of the citizen's constitutional right to vote, continued to
be raised.

The Contest over Citizenship

In theory, as we have seen, no otherwise qualified citizen is excluded
from the electoral roll on grounds of class, caste, gender, or religion.
The ECI is entrusted therefore with the responsibility of ensuring that
in the preparation of the electoral rolls, there is no abuse or deviation from procedural norms. The Constituent Assembly expected the
ECI to be vigilant in protecting socially disadvantaged groups from
exclusion or elimination from the rolls. Yet the ECI was not initially
given the constitutional authority to determine citizenship. As the
ECI's authority has evolved, its task of enumeration of voters has
come to overlap with the executive task of identifying citizens, which
has immersed the ECI at times in some controversy. The Supreme
Court's decision in *Inderjit Barua & Others* v. *Election Commission
of India* (1984) first held that the task of preparing electoral rolls
included the power to identify citizens. The decision came in the
specific context of a petition challenging the electoral rolls in the state
of Assam, with reference to the legislative assembly election in the
state held in February 1983. The validity of these elections was challenged on the ground that large numbers of non-citizens, migrants
from Bangladesh, had been included on the rolls. In deciding this,
the Supreme Court upheld the ECI's 'power to decide individual cases
raising questions of citizenship' while superintending the preparation of electoral rolls under Article 324(1) of the Constitution and the
RPA, 1950. In effect, the Supreme Court turned the ECI's responsibility and the authority to superintend the preparation of the electoral
rolls under the Constitution and the RPA, 1950 and 1951, into the
power to decide—whenever there was a contest, or whenever in the
opinion of the ECI there were grounds to suspect the citizenship of
a person—whether those who claimed to being eligible to vote were,
in fact, citizens.

A reading of the text of the Constitution and the RPA, 1950 and
1951 shows no such overlap of functions between registering voters

and determining citizenship. There appears, on the contrary, a clear separation of the two tasks: while citizenship is an essential qualification for voters/electors, the task of the ECI is confined to preparation of the national rolls of electors. The question as to who is a citizen of India, as set forth in Chapter Two of the Constitution (Articles 5–11), is to be addressed ultimately by Parliament, which enacted the Citizenship Act of India in 1955 under the provisions of Article 11 of the Constitution. But the blurring of the two functions came about in contexts where the question of citizenship was a politically vexed one, as was the case that led to the Supreme Court's 1984 decision.

It is important to stress that from the very beginning, questions of legal citizenship in India were difficult and often fuzzy. Though the Constitution contained provisions for determining citizenship, the large-scale migrations following India's partition left the issue in considerable flux until the passage of the Citizenship Act of India in 1955.[23] In the wake of the Partition, there was movement of people across

[23] Under Articles 5–8 of the Constitution, the following categories of persons became the citizens of India at the date of the commencement of Constitution: (a) those domiciled and born in India; (b) those domiciled, not born in India, but either of whose parents was born in India; (c) those domiciled, not born in India, but ordinarily resident in India for more than five years; (d) those resident in India, who migrated to Pakistan after 1 March 1947 and returned later on resettlement permits; (e) those resident in Pakistan, who migrated to India before 19 July 1948 or those who came afterwards but stayed on for more than six months and got registered; (f) those whose parents and grandparents were born in India but were residing outside India. The constitutional provisions may be seen as laying down the terms of citizenship for two broad categories of people: (a) those who were 'found' to be residing in India at the time of Independence and 'became' Indian citizens, and (b) those who, unlike the earlier category, moved across the borders—a category that again had different patterns of movement: (a) those who migrated from Pakistan to India after the Partition and before 19 July 1948, (b) those who migrated from Pakistan to India after 19 July 1948 but before the commencement of the Constitution and registered themselves as citizens of India before the concerned authority, and (c) those who went to Pakistan and returned to India under a permit for resettlement or permanent return issued by competent authority.

borders on a variety of travel documents, entry permits, and long-term settlement visas. In the absence of a clear legal framework, executive orders and instructions from the Home Ministry were conveyed to multiple institutions, including the ECI, the Indian Citizenship Section of the Home Ministry, and the Ministry of Rehabilitation, in order to deal with the indeterminate citizenship of those persons still in the process of moving across the newly created national borders. The preparation of electoral rolls following Independence, as discussed earlier, were set in motion by the Constituent Assembly Secretariat in March 1948, even before the ECI was set up and electoral laws were enacted. The enrolment of electors to the future Parliament saw officials grappling with the modalities of registering those who had 'migrated' to India and constituted the administrative category of 'displaced persons', who were to be registered on their declaration that they intended to stay in India. The conundrum over the registration of displaced persons continued well after the first general election, in a context where the constitutional provisions pertaining to citizenship (1949), the Citizenship Act (1955), and the RPA (1950, 1951) were in place. Communications among officials focused in particular on the question of the legal accommodation of displaced persons. These communications reveal that it was 'understood' among official circles that the legal confirmation of Indian citizenship of displaced (largely Hindu) minorities from Pakistan was to be facilitated and expedited. Moreover, their complete absorption in the fold was to be accomplished not just through their expeditious registration as citizens but also through their immediate inclusion in the electoral rolls. Thus, when the draft citizenship rules were being framed in 1956, the deputy secretary (Home Affairs), issued 'urgent' instructions to various state governments asking them to make 'immediate arrangements' for the registration of 'displaced persons' under Section 5(1)(a) of the Citizenship Act 1955, 'as this was linked up with the enrolment of voters for the next general elections'. The letter, copied also to the Ministries of External Affairs, Rehabilitation, Law, and to the ECI, stressed the necessity of taking immediate steps so that the displaced persons who migrated from Pakistan and had not yet become citizens of India were enabled to obtain their franchise in the next general election. Their names could not, however, be included in the electoral rolls now under preparation, unless they were registered as Indian citizens. All necessary arrangements were, therefore, to be made to complete the registration of displaced persons as Indian citizens 'with all possible dispatch'.[24]

Indeed, the government made assurances 'that the registration of such persons [as citizens] will be effected with the least inconvenience to them'. This basically meant, as the letter specified, making arrangements for their registration, 'in all places where they are residents in reasonably large numbers, e.g., towns, villages, refugee camps, settlements etc'. The state governments were 'requested to take immediate steps' for the selection of registration officers, and indicate their 'full names, designations, and the areas which will be under their charge' by 25 June 1956. Moreover, since the number of persons who would offer themselves for registration in each state was not immediately clear, the letter asked that the application forms be printed as quickly as possible 'according to the requirements of each State'. No fee was to be charged from displaced persons for registration under Section 5(1)(a) of the Citizenship Act and the expenditure incurred in connection with registration was to be borne by the central government.[25]

The easing of the conditions of citizenship for expeditious enrolment as voters for those who migrated from Pakistan to India, in particular, the 'displaced' Hindus from East Pakistan, was in sharp contrast to the 1980s when the presence of large numbers of 'unauthorized immigrants' from Bangladesh in the electoral rolls in the state of Assam became a politically contentious issue. In a speech to state-level election officers before the 1979 general election, then CEC S.L. Shakdher referred to the 'alarming situation' arising out of

[24] Executive instructions issued in a letter from the Deputy Secretary (Home), File no. 10/1/56, Ministry of Home Affairs—Indian Citizenship, National Archives of India, 14 June 1956.

[25] Executive instructions issued in the letter from the Deputy Secretary (Home), File no. 10/1/56, Ministry of Home Affairs—Indian Citizenship, NAI, 14 June 1956. In response to the Ministry of Home Affairs' letter, in a letter dated 19 June 1956, the deputy secretary, Ministry of Rehabilitation, stated that they 'had no comments to offer except that the provision of Displaced Persons and Muslims who have returned to India from Pakistan on the strength of permanent resettlement permits or long-term visa, which is only up to 30th September 1956, would appear to be too short.' (File No. 13(25)/55—N, National Archives of India.)

unprecedented inflation in electoral rolls in Assam due to 'large-scale inclusions of foreign nationals'.[26] This statement catapulted Assam's electoral rolls into the centre of a political storm, embroiling the ECI in that state's ethnic conflict.[27] This was the context for the previously mentioned Supreme Court decision, *Inderjit Barua & Others* v. *Election Commission of India* (1984), which transformed the ECI's role in the citizenship process. The case focused on a cluster of writ petitions challenging the validity of the elections to the Assam Legislative Assembly held in February 1983 on the ground that the electoral roll had not been properly revised before the elections. This, the petitioners argued, was in contravention of the provisions of the RPA, 1950, which required intensive revision of the electoral rolls before each election. The petitioner called attention to the ECI's instruction to electoral authorities in charge of revision of electoral rolls, 'not to

---

[26] See Weiner (1983: 282–5) for a discussion on and estimation of the growth in the population of Assam, and Baruah (1986) for the difficulty of estimating the number of foreigners/immigrants in Assam. Baruah (1986: 1189–90) identifies the reasons as the absence of official records, the problems with using the census data (no census data for 1981 due to political turmoil as well as misreporting by respondents on questions of birthplace and language), and estimates from the natural rate of population growth in Assam, which make no distinction between immigrants from within and outside India.

[27] Shakdher stated:

I would like to refer to the alarming situation in some states, especially in the North Eastern region, wherefrom reports are coming regarding large-scale inclusions of foreign nationals in the electoral rolls. In one case, the population in 1971 census recorded an increase as high as 34.98 per cent over 1961 census figures and this was attributed to the influx of large numbers of persons from foreign countries. I think it may not be a wrong assessment to make that on the basis of increase of 34.98 per cent between two censuses, the increase likely to be recorded in the 1991 census would be more than 100 per cent over the 1961 census. In other words, a stage would be reached when that state may have to reckon with the foreign nationals who may in all probability constitute a sizeable percentage if not the majority of population in the state. (Speech at the Conference of the Chief Electoral Officers of states held on 24 September 1978, in Ootacamund, Tamil Nadu [Hussain 1993: 102].)

delete the names of any persons from the electoral rolls on the ground of lack of qualification of citizenship, since the question of citizenship was not one which could be decided by the electoral authorities'.[28]

Another petition also challenged these instructions as calling into question the validity of the electoral rolls of 1979, and asked that 'the electoral rolls on the basis of which the forthcoming elections to Parliament from Assam would be held should be revised before the holding of such elections as required by Section 21 [2(a)] of the RPA 1950'.[29] These petitions must be viewed in the context of considerable anxiety over the presence of large numbers of 'foreigners' in the state of Assam, due to the large-scale migration from Bangladesh that occurred during and after the 1971 Bangladesh liberation war. Several hundreds of thousands of Hindu and Muslim refugees fled from East Pakistan into Assam in 1971. Not all refugees returned to Bangladesh, and more continued to cross the border into Assam and other parts of India in

---

[28] *Inderjit Barua & Others* v. *Election Commission of India*, AIR 1984 SC 1911, 1984 (2) SCALE 441 (1985).

[29] About a year after the Supreme Court decision, the central government under Rajiv Gandhi and the leaders of the Assam movement reached an accord in August 1985 which, among other things, focused on resolving the question of 'foreigners' in the state. To implement this aspect of the Assam Accord, the Citizenship Act of India was amended in 1986, and Section 6A was inserted in the Act to make way for a specific category of citizenship pertaining especially to the state of Assam. Section 6A provided that (*a*) all persons of Indian origin who came to Assam before 1 January 1966 from a specified territory (meaning territories included in Bangladesh) and had been ordinarily resident in Assam would be considered citizens of India from the date unless they chose not to be, (*b*) (*1*) person of Indian origin from the specified territories who came on or after 1 January 1966 but before 25 March 1971 and had been resident in Assam since, and (*2*) had been detected in accordance with the provisions of the Foreigners Act, 1946, and Foreigners (Tribunals) Orders, 1964 (*3*) upon registration, will be considered as a citizen of India effective 10 years after the date of detection as a foreigner. In the interim period, such a citizen would enjoy all facilities including an Indian passport, but would not have the right to vote. The rest, that is, those who arrived in India after 25 March 1971, were illegal aliens, identified under the provisions of the Illegal Migrants Determination by Tribunals (IMDT) Act 1983, and deported from the country.

search of livelihood. Within Assam, the presence of large numbers of foreigners instilled a sense of unease at the change in demography, culture, and language, and competition over access to resources, primarily land, and employment. While initially these anxieties remained subterranean, a strong movement against the presence of 'foreigners' was set off in the context of a by-election held in 1979 in Mangaldai parliamentary constituency. The revision of the voter list for the by-election drew attention to the extraordinary increase in the number of voters since the previous election. In the process of revision, objections were raised against 70,000 people, of whom 45,000, constituting about one-sixth of the total electors, were declared foreigners under the Foreigners Act, 1946. The CEC S.L. Shakdher, as mentioned earlier, also raised an alarm over the large-scale presence of foreign nationals in the electoral rolls. The All Assam Students Union (AASU) organised a mass rally on 6 November 1979 in Guwahati demanding the immediate settlement of the 'foreigner' issue (Barpujari 2006: 3–4). The anti-foreigner movement in Assam led by the AASU, and supported by several regional parties and major literary associations of Assam, demanded the screening of the electoral rolls prepared by the ECI to eliminate illegal migrants, and called for a civil disobedience movement, pushing the state into prolonged political turmoil. There was, as Sanjib Baruah points out, a 'palpable breakdown of the distinction between citizens and aliens', as large numbers of unauthorized immigrants were 'able to access full *de jure* citizenship rights' (Baruah 2011: 594), in particular, the right to vote. Both Sanjib Baruah and Kamal Sadiq suggest that the 'widespread use of illegally acquired identity documents' (Sadiq 2009: 168) by migrants to legitimise their stay and access public benefits was a critical feature of the situation.

In an apparent reversal of the process of enrolment as voters, in which citizenship is the basis for enumeration as a voter, illegal immigrants became 'visible' as citizens through a cumulative process of documentation, each additional document, including registration on the electoral roll, adding a layer of legitimacy to their attempt to secure citizenship (Sadiq 2009: 113). Seeing a potential political benefit for themselves in the inflation of the rolls, successive Congress governments in Assam and in the centre 'adopted an open-to-all approach' towards the electoral roll (Baruah 2011: 594, 599). It was against this backdrop that the Supreme Court in 1984 affirmed the validity of the

1983 state assembly election, rejecting the plea that the electoral rolls used for that election 'suffered from legal infirmity'. Responding to the specific charge in the petition pertaining to the ECI's directive 'not to delete' names from the electoral rolls on the ground of lack of qualification of citizenship, the Supreme Court interpreted the ECI as simply proceeding 'on the basis that those whose names were already included in the previous electoral rolls should be prima facie regarded as satisfying the qualification of citizenship'. In upholding the rolls, the Court noted that the electoral rolls of 1977 were used in the 1978 Assam Legislative Assembly elections, without being challenged any time before in a court of law. But while affirming the 1983 state election, the Court went further and effectively instructed the ECI to include a review of citizenship in future electoral roll revisions. In its submission to the Supreme Court, the ECI had assured the Court that before the approaching elections to Parliament, intensive revision of the electoral roll would be undertaken where practicable, and a summary or special revision where intensive revision was not possible (Judgment, *Indrajit Barua* case, paragraph 6). The ECI also informed the Court of the procedure it would follow to ensure accurate revision, especially where the confirmation of citizenship status of the voters was concerned. In the existing system, the electoral card used to collect the details of electors from the head of each household did not require the disclosure of whether the would-be voters were citizens.

The ECI therefore proposed to substitute the word 'citizen' for the word 'elector' in the electoral card. This change, it argued, would ensure that the person signing the electoral card would have to 'state and validate' that the persons being included in the electoral rolls were citizens. Significantly, the ECI attempted to avoid any direct investigative responsibility by placing the responsibility of disclosure on the citizen-voters themselves. The powers of investigation into whether or not a person was a citizen still lay with tribunals which had specified powers of investigation under the Foreigners Act, 1946. Yet the shift in the ECI's responsibility was nevertheless important, for it marked the first time that the ECI took on responsibility for ensuring that only citizens appeared on electoral rolls.

However focused this case was on the specificities of Assam, this shift in the ECI's role had wide-ranging ramifications for its subsequent operation. In Assam itself, the government amended portions of the Citizenship Act applying specifically to the state of Assam to confer Indian citizenship on all those who had migrated before 1971, but defining new procedures for the identification and expulsion of 'illegal migrants' who had arrived after that date. The use of this date was not an accident. Before 1971, migrants were largely Hindus, whose migration could be seen as a continuation of the migrations that had begun at Partition. But through much of the late 1970s and 1980s, the majority of migrants were Bangladeshi Muslims, and their labelling as non-citizens fed into larger anxieties associated with the rise of Hindu nationalism and the increasing ethnic marginalisation of Muslims more generally, who were increasingly viewed as dangerous to the security of the Indian state. In the years which followed, illegal immigration, was not seen as an anxiety confined to the state of Assam and was projected onto the country as a whole.

Illegal migration from Bangladesh came to be seen as 'an act of aggression' posing a threat to national security. The potentially perilous consequences of these ideas for Muslim voting rights became clear in 1995 in a cluster of petitions in *Lal Babu Hussein & Others* v. *Electoral Registration Officer*.[30] These petitions arose out of three cases in which names were deleted from the electoral rolls, as the result of two directives issued by the ECI in August and September 1992, respectively. On 21 August 1992, the ECI issued the first directive, which empowered DCs to determine whether or not a person was a foreigner. According to the directive, this information was to be collected and consolidated by enumerators and conveyed to the collectors who were required to get the information verified through the police/intelligence agencies, and then decide whether or not a person was a citizen of India. On the basis of this information, the ERO was expected to prepare a draft roll, which was to be published for validation, objection, and inclusion in case a person was enumerated but his or her name was not included in the electoral roll.

The ECI issued the second directive on 9 September 1992, vesting the ERO with the power to 'identify and declare the names of foreign nationals and delete their names from the electoral roll', with the instruction that the burden of proving citizenship lay with the

---

[30] *Lal Babu Hussein & Others* v. *Electoral Registration Officer*, 1995AIR 1189, 1995 SCC (3) 100.

person seeking to have his or her name listed in the electoral roll. Following these directives, extensive searches were undertaken in 39 police stations of Greater Bombay, and the police issued notices to around 167,000 people 'suspected' of being foreigners. These people were required to prove their citizenship by producing specified documents, which included (a) birth certificates, (b) passports issued by the Government of India, (c) certificates of citizenship, and (d) entries made in the register of citizenship by the Government of India. Most of those who received the notices were Muslims. The recipients saw the notice and the instructions as a move to harass them because of their religion and ultimately to disenfranchise them. The other two writ petitions arose from similar large-scale deletions of names from Motia Khan in Paharganj, New Delhi, and Sanjay Amar Jhuggi Jhopri Colony in Matia Mahal constituency in Delhi, both comprising slums and *jhuggi-jhopri* localities with large Muslim populations. In September 1994, in the course of the revision of the electoral roll and the issue of voter identify cards, the ERO of Matia Mahal constituency issued a general notice stating that all the residents of that colony were suspected to be foreigners, directing about 18,000 of its poor, illiterate residents, whose names figured in the electoral rolls of the polling station, to appear before the concerned authorities with documentary proof of their citizenship.[31]

It was in these circumstances that the Supreme Court now made it clear that there were constitutional limits to the ECI's efforts to

---

[31] The petitioners contended that they, like other residents of the slums, were migrants from Uttar Pradesh and Bihar who had come to Delhi in search of livelihood, and had been voters in the constituency for the past decade. While they had settled in the area several years ago and had several documents, such as ration cards, past electoral rolls, school records, and the like, to show that they were bona fide residents of the locality, they did not have the precise documents that the ERO required them to produce. The insistence on certain documents to the disregard of others, the petitioners felt, was intentional, done with the purpose of excluding them from the electoral rolls. The ERO refused to accept copies of their ration cards and jhuggi tokens issued by the Delhi Administration or letters from their native village *Pradhans/* legislators, and asked them instead for copies of their passports, citizenship certificates, or birth certificates. As a result of this special revision, in early 1995, the names of 16,454 voters were removed from the electoral rolls.

purge non-citizens from the rolls. According to the Court, 'whenever any authority is called upon to decide even for the limited purpose of another law, whether a person is or is not a citizen of India, the authority must carefully examine the question in the context of the constitutional provisions and the provisions of the Citizenship Act'. The Court overturned the orders of the Bombay and Delhi High Courts, both of which had upheld the deletion of names from the voters list. The notices issued by the ECI were not justified, the Court concluded, because they were 'sweeping' in nature, 'covering the entire populace of the area without there being any inquiry as to the citizenship of an individual'. Though the Supreme Court did not specifically refer to its judgment in the *Inderjit Barua* case a decade earlier, the ECI's action conflicted with that case's understanding of the ECI's powers as limited to the resolution of individual cases of disputed citizenship in preparing the rolls. In the three cases before the Supreme Court in 1995, by contrast, electoral officials challenged the citizenship of everyone within certain localities and deleted their names en masse from the electoral rolls.

In *Inderjit Barua*, the Supreme Court had explicitly abstained from issuing instructions on how the ECI could go about preparing the electoral rolls, leaving it to the ECI to do so in accordance with the provisions of the RPA, 1950. By contrast, in *Lal Babu Hussein*, the Supreme Court issued explicit instructions to the ECI. Emphasising the 'sweeping' manner in which the 'entire populace of the area' was deprived of its voting rights, the Supreme Court laid down in precise terms the procedural norms that the ECI must follow in deciding disputed cases. While the Supreme Court had enhanced the powers of the ECI in *Inderjit Barua*, it emphasised the boundaries of the ECI's powers in *Lal Babu Hussein*. According to the latter decision, the ECI's power flowed from the 'limited purpose of another law' and was subject to 'the constitutional provisions and the provisions of the Citizenship Act'. The Court therefore concluded that any decision to delete voters' names must meet the requirements of both 'procedural fairness' and 'principles of natural justice' (emphasis added).[32]

---

[32] The Supreme Court found it surprising that while specifying the document, the ECI overlooked the fact that 'the addressees were by and large uneducated and belonged to the working class, particularly those who

For these requirements to be met, the 'opportunity to be heard' for those whose names were being deleted had to be both 'meaningful' and 'purposive', according to the Court. In other words, those whose names were being removed had the right to be informed why a suspicion had arisen regarding their status as citizens and to be given an effective opportunity to remove those doubts.[33] The Court thus directed the ECI to initiate fresh proceedings on the basis of specific guidelines laid down by the Court, which included disclosure of material that formed the basis of suspicion. The ECI was also required to hold a quasi-judicial enquiry, in which all possible evidence pertaining to the affected person's status would be allowed. Subsequent to this judgment, all guidelines issued by the ECI for the revision of electoral rolls have made explicit reference to the requirements that the Supreme Court laid down in *Lal Babu Hussein*.[34]

The Supreme Court's judgment in *Lal Babu Hussein* (1995) made no reference to its earlier judgment in *Inderjit Barua* (1984), and explicitly stated that the special provisions of the Citizenship Act applied in Assam were of no concern to it. But despite the Court's rebuke of the ECI, *Lal Babu Hussein* can nevertheless be understood as affirming the powers of the ECI and electoral officers in matters of citizenship, first acknowledged in *Inderjit Barua*. Specifically, the 1995 decision acknowledges the ECI's power to determine citizenship in the process of preparing the rolls, while at the same time enforcing the constitutional and legislative constraints on that power.

---

lived in jhuggi jhopris.' The Supreme Court found it particularly disturbing that the EROs did not apply their minds to individual cases, abdicated their functions to the police, and merely added their seals to their reports. This, notwithstanding the fact that these persons were voters in previous elections and hence it would ordinarily appear that their cases were verified before their names were entered in the electoral rolls. (*Lal Babu Hussein & Others* v. *Electoral Registration Officer*, 1995AIR 1189, 1995 SCC (3) 100, judgment, paragraph 13).

[33] *Lal Babu Hussein & Others* v. *Electoral Registration Officer*, 1995AIR 1189, 1995 SCC (3) 100, paragraph 6.

[34] See Guidelines Section 8.13 Disposal of Claims and Objections and Printing of Supplements Summary Revision of Electoral Rolls, with reference to 1 January 2005 as qualifying date, in Election Commission of India (2006: 48–9).

The Problem of Exclusion

As discussed before, the Constituent Assembly favoured a centralised electoral machinery to ensure protection of religious, caste, and
ethnic minority groups against discrimination and exclusion from
the electoral rolls. In the exercise of its powers of 'superintendence,
control and direction' over the preparation of electoral rolls and the
conduct of elections, the ECI often attracted the charge of exclusion.
The contest over citizenship and electoral rolls discussed earlier was
one such example. Since the 1990s, another area of contestation
opened up over the ECI's initiatives with respect to identification and
'purification' of electoral rolls. In order to prevent impersonation and
fraudulent voting, in 1993, the ECI under T.N. Seshan decided that
all voters should be issued the EPIC. In January and February 2002,
the ECI issued orders specifying that voters without EPICs could vote
only if they presented one of 18 alternative documents.[35] The findings
of a survey conducted by the CSDS in the 2004 parliamentary election
showed that around 71 per cent of those who had voted possessed a
valid EPIC. While the data was uneven for different states, with states
like Kerala, Orissa, Haryana, Mizoram, and Gujarat, among others,
showing a higher percentage of EPIC possession as compared to
states like West Bengal, Assam, Bihar, and Manipur, the possession
of EPICs was uneven across different groups as well. Only 64 per cent
of Muslims among the respondents possessed an EPIC. Indeed, only
about 1 per cent of the voters contacted by the survey team had been
unable to vote because they did not possess any identity documents. In
certain states (Haryana, Rajasthan, Andhra Pradesh, Delhi, and Uttar
Pradesh, among others), the number of persons who could not vote
was double the national average. Among the social groups, of the total

---

[35] The 18 alternative identity documents specified by the ECI were passport, driver's license, service identity cards, bank/*kissan*/post-office passbooks, ration cards issued prior to 1 January 2002, SC/ST/OBC certificates,
student I-cards, property documents, arms license, conductor license, pen-
sion documents, ex-servicemen's widow/dependant certificate, railway/
bus passes, handicap certificate, freedom fighter I-cards, I-cards issued to
advocates, certificate of residence issued by village administrative officers.
'Supreme Court Stays Allahabad High Court Order on Photo I-cards,' Press
Trust of India, 12 February 2002.

number of Muslim women who could not vote for a variety of reasons, 17 per cent could not do so because they did not possess any identity proof (Rao 2004). Significantly, a Supreme Court decision upheld the ECI's instructions regarding voter identification, even in circum-stances where they might prevent some eligible citizens from voting. In a public interest litigation filed against ECI orders in the Allahabad High Court, asserting that the list of permitted identity documents was too narrow, the high court ordered that voters in Uttar Pradesh be allowed to vote if they could produce any valid identifying document at the polls—not just one of those specified by the ECI (Venkatesan 2002). Challenging the high court's verdict in the Supreme Court, the ECI argued that the court could not interfere with the election process after a notification announcing elections had been issued. Citing the risks of bogus voting, the Supreme Court upheld the ECI's instructions, reversing the Allahabad High Court ruling.

The 2005 assembly election in Bihar provided the context within which the electoral roll became a focal point of contestation between the ECI and state government—in this case, the ruling party in the state, RJD, led by Lalu Prasad Yadav. The conflict centred on the ECI's drive to clean up the electoral roll of 'fake' and 'nonexistent' voter names, which could be used to cast bogus votes. In the course of this exercise, the ECI deleted the names of nearly two million dead, relocated, or residual 'fake voters'.[36] The ECI's initiative, however, opened it up to charges of being biased against the 'weaker sections' (the largely poor, lower, and backward castes) and Muslims who formed the base of RJD's support in the state. The RJD spokesperson alleged that the ECI was treating Bihar differently and that its policies in the state were clearly discriminatory and biased along caste lines. Specifically, the party contended that (a) by making photo identity cards compulsory, the ECI was stopping the weaker sections from exercising their constitutional rights since it was mostly members of the weaker section who were without identity cards, and (b) the ECI

---

[36] Of these, 100,000 names were deleted in Patna, while 50,000 to 60,000 names were deleted in Darbhanga, Begusarai, and Muzaffarnagar districts. Simultaneously, however, the ECI also had identity cards distributed to 80 per cent of voters in the state. 'EC Deletes 20 Lakhs Names from Rolls,' *Indian Express*, 22 September 2005.

shifted officers without 'valid reasons' and all such officers belonged to the weaker sections.[37]

The ECI claimed, however, that its actions in Bihar were part of a wider initiative to revise the electoral rolls and followed the accepted procedure for checking the validity of voters, which was also being pursued in other parts of India. In Tamil Nadu, for example, the ECI sent a team to Chennai to enquire into the sudden rush of applications for inclusion in the electoral roll in the summary revision being carried out in the state. The rise in applications exceeded the 'normal' limit of 4 per cent, going up to more than 10 per cent in some constituencies, giving reasons to the electoral officers to suspect 'stuffing', primarily because the bulk of applications had no signatures or addresses.[38] In West Bengal, the ECI reported 'glaring irregularities' in the issue of EPICs to voters where assembly elections were due in

---

[37] Interview of Shivanand Tiwari, spokesperson, RJD in 'Biased EC Officials Will Try to Defeat Us. But We Believe in People's Court,' *The Indian Express*, 9 October 2005.

[38] 'Electoral Rolls Revision: Officials Alarmed at Rush of Bulk Applications,' *The Hindu*, 2 June 2005. In June 2005, the ECI sent a team to Chennai to enquire into the sudden rush of applications for inclusion in the electoral rolls in the summary revision of electoral rolls being carried out in non-tsunami-affected districts of the state. The CEO of the state, Naresh Gupta, reported that the receipt of applications on the last day, that is, 30 May, was particularly high, prompting the officials to pursue the applications and enquire into their genuineness. Five assembly constituencies, in particular, registered receipts of Form 6 application of over 10 per cent (Erode 17.79 per cent, Tiruchengode 10.05 per cent, Pollachi 11.71 per cent, Dindigul 11.48 per cent, and Villupuram 10.05 per cent). Anything above 4 per cent is considered 'abnormal' by the electoral officers and if it exceeded 6 per cent, the electoral officers had reasons to suspect 'stuffing'. Preliminary investigations showed that the bulk of applications had no signatures or addresses. The CEO's office in the state issued instructions to the EROs 'not to segregate the bulk applications for distribution to field staff, but instead after numbering them serially and indicating the name of the party/organization filing them send them to the District Election Officers where, with the available computer infrastructure and the software devised for the purpose, it will enable a search to be made whether the applicants are already registered somewhere else or neighbouring Assembly constituencies'.

May 2006. The ECI alleged that although 92 per cent of the voters had been issued EPICs in the state, the cards were distributed in bulk in several places instead of being given to individual voters, in violation of the ECI's instructions.[39] Close to the Delhi Assembly elections in December 2013, which resulted in a hung assembly, a study conducted by the Janaagraha Centre for Citizenship and Democracy located in Bangalore found that nearly 20 per cent of the names in the voter list of Delhi were 'phantom names', of people who were not residents at the specified addresses. Arguing that the electoral roll is a 'key factor' in electoral outcome, the continuation of large numbers of 'phantom voters' on the list, even after the ECI had revised and updated the roll in preparation for the approaching election, opened up the possibility of voter fraud. In absolute numbers, the phantom voters added up to 23 lakh of the 1.23-crore registered voters in Delhi, a number which could become significant in results with small margins of victory, in case, even when it had become increasingly difficult to do so, fraudulent voting were to take place against the names of non-existent voters. An important conclusion of the study pertained to the challenges of preparing 'error-free' voter lists in 'a new order'—of 'a dynamic, mobile, urban citizenry overwhelming an electoral system designed for a different electoral demographic'.[40] Indeed, electoral list management

---

[39] 'Irregularities in the Issue of Voter ID Cards in West Bengal,' *The Hindu*, 28 December 2005. The random checks made by the ECI's special teams sent to the state to check the records of EPIC distribution at the offices of the BDOs showed that the EPIC cards had been handed over to one person under his or her signature, or in cases almost all cards distributed with acknowledgement receipt obtained in the form of a thumb impression, which had not been duly verified by any official.

[40] Ebony Bertolli, Santosh More, and K.R. Prasad. 2013. 'The Phantom Voters,' *The Indian Express*, 13 December. As part of its Proper Urban Electoral (PURE) List maintenance initiative, over the past one and a half months, Janaagraha had been conducting a systematic survey in Delhi. Subsequent surveys conducted in Delhi by Janaagraha in 2015 before the Legislative Assembly elections in, showed a 22 per cent error rate in the voter list in Delhi. See, 'Voter List Errors Can Impact Poll Outcomes: Janaagraha,' *The Hindu*, 28 January 2018, available at https://www.thehindubusinessline.com/news/national/voter-list-errors-can-impact-poll-outcomes-janaagraha/article6831041.ece.

for urban areas, especially those which experienced population mobility, within and into the city, presented challenges before the ECI of frequently updating the voter list, with the help of population mapping technology.

Requirements of voter identity cards have generated debates arrayed along the fault lines of 'ballot security' and 'access to voting'. Arguments in favour of voter IDs make a case for stringent provisions for voter identification to prevent election fraud. On the other hand, equally strong arguments are made that such steps are likely to disenfranchise voters, especially those who are poor and belong to other vulnerable groups like the elderly, religious and ethnic minorities, persons with disability, and women, who are more likely not to be in possession of an appropriate or valid ID. Debates on the desirability of voter ID, especially a standard voter ID, have occurred in other democracies, including the United States of America. A study by American University's Center for Democracy and Election Management found that in Indiana, Mississippi, and Maryland, three states with ID requirements, only a small percentage of registered voters—about 1.2 per cent—did not have a photo ID. While this was a small percentage of the voting population, the disconcerting part of the findings was that a disproportionate part of those without an ID were women and African Americans.[41]

As has been the case in India, contests on the constitutional validity of restrictive voter identification laws, passed by different state governments in the United States of America, have been brought before the judiciary for scrutiny. In April 2008, for example, the Supreme Court decided on the constitutionality of voter ID laws in Indiana, which was one of the states that had passed restrictive voter ID laws.[42] In a 6–3

---

[41] Jimmy Carter and James A. Baker. 2008. 'A Clearer Picture on Voter ID,' *The New York Times*, 3 February.

[42] The Indiana voter identification law was among a series of state laws that were enacted in the wake of the Help America Vote Act of 2002 (HAVA) enacted by the Congress. HAVA laid down voter identification requirements for first-time voters, who at the time of registering or voting, had to produce a valid photo identification, or other specified documents for identification including utility bills, bank statements, or any other government document which showed the name and address of the voter. The HAVA asked states to

decision, the US Supreme Court rejected a challenge to Indiana's voter identification law in the American Civil Liberties Union's (ACLU) case, *Crawford v. Marion County Election Board*[43] (consolidated with *Indiana Democratic Party v. Rokita*), which was an appeal against two lower court decisions that upheld the state's law requiring voters to present government-issued photo IDs in order to vote. The ACLU had argued that the Indiana law created an unconstitutional burden on voting rights.[44] The court upheld Indiana voter identification law,[45] in a decision which was criticised by the editorial of the *New York Times* as an attempt to solve 'a nearly non-existent problem by putting major barriers between voters—particularly minorities—and the ballot box'.[46] By upholding the law, the editorial argued, the court reversed its position that the right to vote is so fundamental that a state cannot restrict a citizen's right to vote 'unless it can show that the harm it is seeking to prevent outweighs the harm it imposes on voters'.[47]

While the verdict was fractured with three out of nine judges deciding to disagree with the majority judgment, by affirming the law,

---

enact similar or stricter laws. It was to this invitation that Indiana responded, and in 2005, it enacted a law with the general requirement for all voters, and not just the first-time voters, to present a government-issued photo identification at the time of voting. Before the changes were proposed in the 2005 law, voters in Indiana simply had to sign in at the polls and their signatures were compared to the ones on file. Under the changes proposed, voters were required to present a current government-issued photo ID, generally a driver's license. Unlike HAVA, private ID cards like those issued by educational institutions, employee ID cards, and utility bills were no longer acceptable (Foley 2008).

[43] 553 U.S. 181 (2008).

[44] For details of this case, see http://www.aclu.org/scotus/2007term/3259 2res20071106/32592res20071106.html. More on the work of the ACLU Voting Rights Project, available at http://www.aclu.org/voting-rights; accessed on 12 July 2011.

[45] Linda Greenhouse. 2008. 'In a 6-to-3 Vote, Justices Uphold a Voter ID Law,' *The New York Times*, 29 April.

[46] 'The Court Fumbles on Voter Rights,' Editorial, *The New York Times*, 29 April 2008.

[47] 'The Court Fumbles on Voter Rights,' Editorial, *The New York Times*, 29 April 2008.

the judgment set out a standard for other states to follow and set in motion a process of accumulation of similar laws. In March 2011, the Ohio Fair and Secure Elections Act, one of several proposals the Republican Caucus in Ohio planned to bring in the state to combat voter fraud and ensure a smooth legal process for casting ballots, was introduced. While the Bill was described by its proponents as 'a long overdue, important first step toward securing the integrity of the electoral process' that was 'necessary to make sure every legitimate vote is counted', it was criticised by those who saw the Bill in its current form as making it more difficult for eligible citizens to vote.[48] In Missouri, the contest over voting rights expanded as the state contemplated proposing a constitutional amendment that would enable election officers to ask anyone registering to vote to furnish proof of citizenship.[49] With the setting up of the Presidential Advisory Commission on Election Integrity by President Donald Trump in May 2017 to enquire into 'the registration and voting processes', and the 'vulnerabilities' that could lead to 'voter fraud', the debate over electoral rolls opened up another dimension—that of 'national security'. A strand of opinion, however, saw the Commission as 'perpetuating the myth of mass fraud', initiated by President Trump himself, who alleged that non-citizens and illegal immigrants voted in large numbers in the 2016 presidential election. The myth of voter fraud, according to its critics, facilitates 'voter intimidation and suppression, including selectively purging of voter rolls', which is equally a threat to national security because it makes the exercise of franchise difficult to access in a hostile environment of suspicion.[50]

The purging of electoral rolls to weed out illegal immigrants and non-citizens who could masquerade as legitimate voters posing

---

[48]   See John Michael Spinelli. 2011. 'OSU Voting Law Prof Says GOP Voter ID Bill "Another Great Embarrassment for Ohio",' Columbus OH, 21 March, available at Columbus/governmentexaminer.com; accessed on 4 June 2011.

[49]   Ian Urbina. 2008. 'Voter ID Battle Shifts to Proof of Citizenship,' *The New York Times*, 12 May.

[50]   Jake Laperruque. 2017. 'Voter Access, Not Voter Fraud, Is a Pressing National Security Issue,' *Just Security*, 13 July, available at https://www.justsecurity.org/43062/voter-access-voter-fraud-pressing-national-security-issue/; accessed on 7 December 2017.

thereby a threat to national security, raises concerns similar to those discussed earlier in the section on citizenship and electoral rolls in Assam. Indeed, the weeding out of 'Doubtful' or D voters has become a pressing issue in what are construed as 'sensitive' districts in Assam. Marked as 'doubtful' in the door-to-door surveys conducted by the ECI in the 1990s, following the suspicion that large number of illegal immigrants, largely Muslims from Bangladesh, had managed to enter the electoral rolls, the D voters were deprived of their voting rights till they could prove their citizenship. In a document stating the challenges of preparing the electoral rolls in one such 'sensitive' district—Karimganj—the CEO of Assam pointed to the complications arising out of the 'judicial nature' of sifting out doubtful voters by tribunals implementing the Foreigners Act of 1946. The identification itself, the document states, can be difficult since the 'so called 'doubtful citizens' possess all legally valid documents, otherwise contrary to the genuine citizens, who fail to produce and seldom have any kind of document'; even when identified as doubtful, the judicial proceedings on the verification of their status take long to conclude.[51] The preparation of the National Register of Citizens (NRC) underway in Assam under the supervision of the Supreme Court of India, to separate citizens from 'aliens' and those who may have 'infiltrated' into the electoral rolls, relies on specified documents to trace the lineage of those residing in Assam to Indian citizens. The enumeration of Indian citizens in Assam under the NRC and the cleaning of electoral rolls—both are processes which rely on sifting out those who cannot prove their citizenship. In the process, as reports have pointed out, large numbers of people, mostly Muslims in Assam, have felt that they have been randomly marked out as doubtful, disenfranchised, and forced to live in a state of deferred citizenship and suspect legality.[52]

[51] M. Angamuthu, deputy commissioner, Karimganj and Hemanta Narzary, CEO, Assam's presentation before the ECI on 'Challenges in the Management of Electoral Rolls ...'

[52] According to one report published in the *Wire*, till October 2016, 621,688 people, mostly Muslim, were either branded as doubtful voters or reference cases were registered against them under the Foreigners Act, 1946. As a consequence, they were denied access to government-sponsored welfare schemes, the right to vote, and other rights that are enjoyed by an Indian

Coming back to the contest over voter identification, pertaining especially to access to franchise as discussed earlier, studies on voter identity laws in the United States of America have shown that adequate dissemination of information about the requirement, and the details on how to acquire IDs, especially among those groups which are likely to be most affected by the law, has had the consequence of increasing voter turnout.[53] Other studies too have sought to direct attention from the conflict over voter identification to the ways in which voter registration, identification, and participation may be enhanced by ensuring clarity in voter identification laws, increasing thereby the effectiveness of state and local officials in not just enforcing them, but also ensuring that voters have acceptable identification documents (Chambers 2016). The appeal to shift focus to the role of electoral officials in ensuring registration and identification of voters for the efficient conduct of election is in line with the idea that bodies conducting elections primarily perform the function of *administering* elections. Yet, bodies conducting elections are often also engaged in *reforming* elections. As electoral reform bodies—at different times and in a range of contexts—they collaborate and supplement, but sometimes also confront the legislative bodies that are entrusted with the responsibility of framing electoral laws and also reforming elections through their law-making functions. In the context of the ECI, the reforming and administering

---

citizen. In February 2017, according to the government of Assam, the cases of 444,189 people were referred to tribunals, of which 201,928 cases were still pending with them. Of the cases which were decided, 92 per cent were able to prove their Indian nationality. The majority of the remaining cases where the person was declared as foreigner were ex-parte judgments. As per the white paper on foreigners published by government of Assam, 88,192 cases were disposed of between 1998 and 2012. Out of 88,192 cases, only 6,590 cases were declared as foreigners. (See Abdul Kalam Azad, 'The Struggle of "Doubtful Voters" has Intensified in BJP's Assam,' *The Wire*, 12 July 2017).

[53] See Citrin, Green, and Levy (2014) who studied the effects of voter ID requirement on voter turnout in the run-up to the 2012 general election in counties along the Tennessee-Virginia border and in heavily African American precincts in Roanoke and Knoxville, and found out that information to voters of a new identification requirement raised turnout.

functions have often converged.[54] One such site of convergence can be seen in the ECI's innovative programme—SVEEP.

Treading the Last Mile: Educating Voters through SVEEP

While conducting the first general election, the CEC Sukumar Sen wished that political parties had taken the responsibility of reaching out to the voters to ensure their registration in the electoral roll and exhorting them to come out and vote, more seriously. The Constitution itself places no such responsibility on political parties, and it is the BLO, a functionary of the ECI at the grass roots, who performs the task of reaching the remotest village to ascertain that all eligible voters were enumerated and enrolled. Until recently, political parties took the responsibility of distributing voter slips to all households before the polling day. The voter slips mentioned the enrolment numbers and polling booth details of voters, to facilitate and expedite voting on polling day. From the perspective of the political parties, the distribution of voter slips was another opportunity to contact the voter at home. Later, however, amidst widespread allegations of political parties not distributing voter slips to those who were not likely to vote for them, the task of distribution reverted to the ECI and in particular to the ECI's foot soldier in the field—the BLO. By 2014, completing a process begun in 2011, the ECI put in place a structured system of distribution of voter slips with photographs of voters to ensure what it called 'transparency' in the system. The authenticated voter slips were to reach all voters at least five days before the polling day, and their receipt was to be logged on the register of voters carried by the BLO. According to the instructions issued by the ECI to the CEOs of all states and union territories, the booth-level agents of political parties were not required to accompany the BLOs but could do so if they wished, and the BLO was to maintain complete neutrality in the distribution of voter slips.[55]

---

[54] Detailed insight into voter registration and voter education programme of the ECI can be found in former CEC S.Y. Quraishi's book *An Undocumented Wonder* (2014), especially Chapters 4 and 8.

[55] Instructions of Chief Electoral Officers, No.464/INST-VS/2014-EPS, dated 21 March 2014.

The excision of political parties from what was considered earlier a desirable role they played in exhorting and enthusing the electors to vote by contacting them directly can be seen as part of a process of entrenchment of what are called electoral best practices in the conduct of elections. The invocation of best practices is part of a tendency in election administration that sees the conduct of elections as efficient management, transforming the election commissions into Election Management Bodies (EMBs). The EMBs are expected to manage elections as 'enforcement enterprise'. One component of this enterprise is SVEEP, a 'best practice' which the ECI describes as being distinct for having a 'different character'—which is one of 'election *development*' (emphasis added).[56] As a voter *education* programme, SVEEP was expected, through what the ECI called officers with 'a distinct social orientation and collaborative approach', to deliver the objectives of taking voter participation to the next higher level. The objective of enhancement of voter participation was to diminish the 'democracy deficit' that it acknowledged had seeped into democracies across the world.[57] If one were to look at enhanced electoral participation as indicative of diminishing democracy deficit, one would also expect that electoral development perceives 'the active voter' to be someone who is not apathetic towards the electoral process, and is, in addition, a politically engaged citizen. Such an engagement makes the act of voting an essential component of other possibilities that the political landscape offers, to bridge the democratic deficit through a 'ceaseless process of political education in citizenship' (Urbinati 2000: 758). The complexity of modern societies has made the directness of democracy impossible, and the distance between the processes of ruling and those being ruled gets more pronounced as one moves up across the layers of government. The participatory model of democracy, however, continues to be influential as an ideal form, embodying an elusive state of perfection that one must constantly aspire to emulate, and wherever possible, replicate.

The shift in the paradigms of government, with direct participation in ruling giving way to being ruled through representatives, has not eroded the normative value of direct democracy—ironically as

---

[56] Election Commission of India (2013).
[57] Election Commission of India (2013).

something that the 'moderns' can never have, and yet cannot cease to want (Dunn 1993: 28). An uncritical nostalgia for directness in democracy generates corresponding concerns about the inadequacy or deficiency of modern representative forms of democracy.[58] These concerns have become more pronounced with questions around issues of equality in representation, forms of representation of groups, and the appropriate ways of achieving adequate representation, becoming progressively more significant. Anxieties around thin and passive citizenship, which accompanied the shift from participatory and direct democracy to representative democracy, have also been raised. A lament of 'crisis' in representative democracy emerged subsequently, stemming from the assumptions of democratic deficiency and political passivity in representative democracy. Critics of representative democracy consider it a weak form of democracy, a poor substitute for self-government and active citizenship.

The concerns around indirectness and political deficit may be seen as having been addressed in two ways, each approaching the relationship between representation and participation in divergent ways. The manner in which the question is addressed at each level has a special resonance for excluded groups and their engagement/ relationship with politics. A universality approach may be seen as looking at the relationship between representation and participation as a continuum in which an articulated public sphere is created through and in the intervening period between elections, bridging the spatial and temporal gap, and the absence of simultaneity between voting and decision-making. Seen from this vantage point, the emphasis on the deliberative character of modern democracies is seen as providing the institutional and socio-cultural space within which the various components of political action—from opinions and will formation to decision-making—take shape (Urbinati 2000: 759). Another approach, however, sees representation and participation as separate and having distinct characteristics, and would, therefore, not consider devising ways by which representative democracy could as closely as possible replicate participatory democracy. It would make the problems and patterns of exclusion, rather

---

[58] Nadia Urbinati (2000) points out that nostalgia may foster resignation, but it may also encourage a realistic disenchantment towards what is actual.

than the participatory deficit that representative democracy might entail, central (Plotke 1997: 19). It would consider 'political representation as both necessary and desirable' concerning itself with exclusion and group-differentiated citizenship (Kymlicka 1996; Young 1989, 1997: 352).

When the ECI launched SVEEP in 2008–9 in a limited way in Jharkhand and then proposed to pursue it in its diamond jubilee year in 2010 around the theme 'greater participation for a stronger democracy', the ECI termed this initiative as one of 'educating voters'.[59] Apart from bridging the 'knowledge gap' among voters between what they 'should know' and what they 'actually know' about the electoral process, the ECI professed that it was its responsibility to 'tread the last mile' to remove indifference and apathy among voters. This was to be done by persuasion and motivation rather than compelling voters to vote through a law of Parliament enforcing compulsory voting. To some extent, the emphasis by the ECI on voluntariness in voting as distinct from coercion through the force of law can be seen, as in the case with the MCC, consonant with ECI's enhancement of its own powers of administering elections within the capacious frameworks of Article 324. At another level, however, in the absence of an explicit law enforcing mandatory voting, the ECI may be seen as having interpreted its role of administering elections as also one of enhancing democracy, by promoting voluntary civic engagement of citizens,

---

[59] The SVEEP Compendium states:

There were planned IEC (Information, Education and Communication) interventions in the Jharkhand elections of end-2009 and subsequently carried forward in the form of SVEEP (Systematic Voters' Education and Electoral Participation) in Bihar Assembly elections of 2010 and assembly elections of Tamil Nadu, Kerala, Assam, West Bengal and UT of Puducherry in 2011. This continued for the 5 State elections of UP, Goa, Punjab, Uttarakhand and Manipur and again in the twin general elections in Himachal Pradesh and Gujarat in 2012 and election to NE states of Tripura, Meghalaya and Nagaland in early 2013 with the main components of SVEEP intervention as IMF i.e. Information, Motivation and Facilitation. The second phase of SVEEP, SVEEP-II, is being rolled out, based on the learnings of Phase-I and the identified tasks ahead and allocation of additional resources. (Election Commission of India 2013: 3)

with an emphasis on enhancing participation and eliminating exclusion.[60]

In countries such as Australia, which have compulsory voting, the compulsion to vote is preferred as a defence against seismic changes that can be brought about by a minority of voters, and protection against swing to extreme forms of politics. Compulsory voting is also considered valuable as a measure to prevent political parties from playing up to particular groups of voters that form a party's base to the exclusion of others, and for its ramification not merely on the voter turnout, which seems to get the most attention, but also on who contests elections, and what kind of policies are eventually made.[61] Detractors would, however, claim that while it compels people to vote to avoid penalty, mandatory voting does not necessarily make a voter politically engaged and civic minded.[62]

For the ECI, the SVEEP was not about opening up a deliberative space, nor about correcting the ways in which political parties approach the electorate with policy issues. It may rather be seen as part of the tendency in the ECI to exercise its responsibility of conducting elections through innovations that do not flow directly from any parliamentary statute, but draw from its 'reservoir of powers' under Article 324—quite like the ECI's implementation of the MCC to release the electoral space from political interference during election time, and the enforcement of the voter's right to know about the background of the candidates to facilitate informed voting. Yet SVEEP is also distinctive because it moves away from placing the ECI's functions within a framework of enhancing the electoral space as an arena of political morality, and

[60] In November 2014, Gujarat became the first state in India to make voting in the election to all local bodies compulsory. The Gujarat Local Authorities Law, which makes voting mandatory in the election to local bodies and lays down penalty to enforce the law, was rejected in 2012 during the tenure of then Chief Minister Modi. Returning the Bill to the state assembly, the then governor of the state Dr Kamla had stated that compulsory voting violated Article 21 of the Indian Constitution. 'Gujarat Makes Voting Compulsory in Local Polls,' *Business Standard*, 9 November 2014.

[61] Waleed Aly. 2017. 'Voting Should Be Mandatory,' *The New York Times*, 19 January.

[62] Eryk Bagshaw. 2017. 'Time to Rethink Compulsory Voting Says Australian-US Research Institute,' *Sydney Morning Herald*, 16 July.

couches it in the idiom of efficient governance. It is possible that it is for this reason that SVEEP has not attracted the kind of criticism and political contestations, which both the MCC and the Right to Know did. Indeed, SVEEP initiatives in different districts of the country have been listed on the ECI website under the category 'best practices' and some of them have been nominated for, and received, the Prime Minister's Award for Excellence in Public Administration. Couched in the idiom of 'best practices' in voter education, SVEEP managed to dispel the suspicion and adversarial responses that earlier attempts by the ECI at extending its presence in the electoral space have experienced. To quote the ECI on the objectives of SVEEP:

> ECI envisaged systematic, strategic and scientific processes in understanding the voter participation and engagement dynamics so as to facilitate the processes of increased and informed participation. It was felt that voter education needed to be imparted through specific and targeted interventions, backed by scientific research carried out by professional agencies/institutes. There was a strongly felt need for a scientifically designed policy frame-work, clear guidelines, effective implementation combined with widespread publicity and importantly a well-established feedback mechanism for assessment of the impact made by the interventions. This would help in suitably modifying future strategies, programmes and interventions to educate the voters on all aspects of democratic and electoral processes. Effective partnerships with educational institutions like Universities, Colleges, Senior Secondary Schools, Vocational Institutes etc. needed to be carefully built in order to educate the students on subjects related to democratic electoral practices and participation. Large segments/sections of the electorate who were not covered by the formal educational system or those who had developed an apathetic attitude or those who are physically cut-off from the mainstream due to various reasons needed to be brought under the ambit of focused voter education. (Election Commission of India 2013: 3)

The ECI engaged in what it called 'voter behaviour surveys' through survey agencies in all states that were going to elections, Jharkhand onwards, to understand the reasons for under-registration, and instructed CEOs of states to frame and implement state- and district-level SVEEP plans. While these plans were to be intense for the election period, they were to be sustained over an entire year, with CEOs and DEOs allowed flexibility for innovation appropriate for their states and districts. The ECI's foundation day, 25 January 2017, was designated as the NVD, to be observed as a day when the new voters were felicitated by the BLOs in a public function where the EPICs were handed over to them along with a badge with the slogan 'Proud to be a voter—ready to vote'. As part of its voter education and awareness programme, the ECI and CEOs of states issued a series of posters, some of which can be seen in Figures 2.1–2.4.

Jashn-e-Jamhuriat[63]

One such innovation in SVEEP was carried out in Reasi district in Jammu and Kashmir. 'Jashn-e-Jamhuriat' (translated as 'celebrating democracy'), as the Reasi innovation was named, won the Prime

Figure 2.1   SVEEP Poster 1
Source: Election Commission of India website.

[63] The innovation was also nominated for the National CSO Award for Best Campaign on Voter's Education and Awareness, 2014 by the ECI. The DC Shahid Iqbal Choudhury was given the Governance Award 2014 for exceptional contribution to development work, including contribution to electoral governance.

Figure 2.2   SVEEP Poster 2
Source: Election Commission of India website.

Figure 2.3   SVEEP Poster 3
Source: Election Commission of India website.

Minister's Award for Excellence in Public Administration for the DC in 2015. We toured the district in the middle of December 2014 to study electoral governance at the district level. The visit took place almost six months after the parliamentary elections of April–May 2014, and coincided with the state assembly elections of December 2014. The primary purpose of the visit was to study the extraordinary performance of the district in the promotion of the objectives of the SVEEP programme for voter awareness. According to official ECI

Figure 2.4   SVEEP Poster 4
Source: Election Commission of India website.

figures, voter turnout in the district for the parliamentary election in April–May 2014 had doubled from the previous elections held in 2009, from 43 per cent to 81 per cent. Hitherto excluded groups (nomadic populations like the Gujjars and Bakerwals, migrants and those displaced by conflict, women, and persons with disability) were included into the electoral process through what the official SVEEP report for the district presented as 'innovations', leading to an unprecedented enhancement in their participation. We hoped to study the sustainability of the 'Reasi model' devised for the parliamentary election, in the state assembly elections which were held in the Reasi district on 2 December 2014, a few days before our visit. We also visited the adjoining Kathua district in Jammu and Kashmir, where the polling for state assembly election was scheduled a few days later, on 20 December. Incidentally, the DEO/DC under whom Reasi had achieved unprecedented voter turnout was now posted in Kathua district. The purpose of visiting Kathua was to study how the model designed for Reasi could be replicated in another district of Jammu and Kashmir, and to observe the model at work in the ongoing electoral process.[64]

---

[64] Reasi witnessed an equally high electoral turnout in the state legislative assembly elections of December 2014. Importantly, the system was replicated in another district of the state—Kathua—where the then DC of Reasi, Shahid

Officially called Jashn-e-Jamhuriat, the SVEEP project in Reasi was initiated by the DC of Reasi and his team in June 2013. Reasi was carved out of Udhampur district in 2007 and is known for the Vaishno Devi shrine at Katra, which attracts thousands of pilgrims and generates a variety of jobs and revenue for the local population. One-third of the population of Reasi lives below the poverty line. The district had a history of low voter turnout for a variety of reasons. The most significant reason had perhaps been the outbreak of militancy in this region in the 1990s, especially in the Pir Panjal hills, which cuts across Reasi and is inhabited by the nomadic Gujjar and Bakerwal communities. Electoral trust in Reasi had been fragile because of the long-drawn political conflict and frequent calls of poll boycott given by militant groups and political organisations, and political and sectarian violence (including the massacre of Hindu migrants by militants in 1998) leading to mass displacements. For the reasons mentioned above, specific sections had either been entirely excluded from the electoral rolls (for example, migrants) or under-represented (for example, women, persons with disability, militancy-affected groups), or had not exercised their franchise because their life cycles did not correspond with the electoral cycles (for example, nomadic groups), or faced problem of accessibility because of the hilly terrain.

The task before the district electoral administrators, as they mentioned to us, was to reach out to the excluded sections, instil trust among citizens, and educate them on the ethics and the importance of voting for democracy.[65] Among the special measures they adopted for

---

Iqbal Chaudhary, was the DC. Kathua too achieved 81 per cent of voter turnout, which along with Reasi, surpassed the average of 65–8 per cent of the state (which was 5 per cent more than the average for 2008–9).

[65] Reasi district may described as socio-economically backward, with more than one-third of its population living below poverty line and dependent on agricultural activities, Mahatma Gandhi National Rural Employment Guarantee Act (MNREGA), and religious tourism (including pilgrimage to Vaishno Devi shrine in Katra, Reasi). It has poor literary rate (58 per cent), nomadic population (31 per cent), less than 50 per cent of its area is connected with roads. It has a predominantly hilly terrain with inclement weather in the higher reaches and problem of access in large numbers of polling booths (119). In addition, two of its assembly segments are identified as having insurgency threats. Out of 301 polling stations, 177 were sensitive and 44 hypersensitive.

inclusion were, improving: the 'roll gender ratio' by enrolling women, the 'electoral population ratio' by ensuring that the names of those eligible to vote were on the electoral roll, and the 'EPIC ratio' by ascertaining that all those whose names were on the electoral roll were also in possession of the EPIC.[66] In our conversations with the DC/DEO of Reasi (now of Kathua) and the deputy election officer and subdivisional magistrate (SDM) of Reasi, we were told that a systematic plan for achieving these goals was laid down. These included the establishment of 'voter enrolment network at village, hamlet and household level', planning for 100 per cent electoral literacy and electoral participation, and addressing concerns of inaccessible areas, hilly terrain, hypersensitive areas, and insurgency-prone pockets by establishing infrastructure and facilities for electoral participation, and 'building a stronger network of partner organisations for sustained investment in strengthening democracy, and for an overall encouraging and positive atmosphere for development'.[67] At the local level, a convergence of the existing bureaucratic apparatus for local administration with that of the electoral machinery was expected to generate an efficient bureaucratic system for administering the election. The DC was the DEO responsible for monitoring election-related work, that is, addition/deletion/modification in voter lists during annual revision of electoral

[66] Special measures to include specific sections of the population after the Jashn-e-Jamhuriat SVEEP programme was put in place in Reasi show the following results, as per Shahid Iqbal, DC, Kathua:

	September 2009	April 2014
EPIC	68%	96%
EP ratio	50.12%	57.72%
Roll gender ratio	887	907
New voters	NA	16% increase (26,000 new voters—14,000 female and 12,000 male)

[67] For the first time after 1998, militancy-affected groups residing in camps in Talwada voted in polling stations where their names were registered, and were transported to these areas in specially arranged buses. Under the 'Rehbar' scheme for persons with disabilities and the aged, 1,506 voters were accompanied by assistants provided by the district administration to facilitate voting.

rolls starting from September each year. Special summary revision of electoral rolls is carried out in the election year. The assistant commissioner revenue/SDM is designated the ERO, who accepts or rejects the enrolment form. Tehsildars are the assistant EROs who control the BLOs and are responsible for enrolment forms to be filled up by the latter and recommending to the ERO for approval. Booth-level officers are mostly teachers drawn from the education department, but they also include junior engineers, officials of departments like agriculture, patwaris of revenue department, supervisors, and so on. This convergence envisages routine election work as an ongoing process and the chart below reflects the revenue administration, which is also the electoral administration. In Lok Sabha elections, DCs are designated as returning officers and ACs/SDMs as assistant returning officers. In state assembly elections, ACs/SDMs are designated as returning officers and tehsildars as assistant returning officers. The convergence between the bureaucratic apparatus for local administration and electoral administration is illustrated in Figure 2.5.

While the 'Reasi Model' put in place measures that addressed the specific concerns of the district of Reasi, it also aimed to lay down general principles of inclusive electoral system and democratic participation, which the 'Reasi team' argued was evident in the extraordinary enhancement in voter turnout in the region.[68] The model had to address challenges of not just long-standing voter apathy, but also their antipathy. Asserting that parliamentary elections in Jammu and Kashmir did not arouse the same kind of enthusiasm as the state

[68] While electoral turnout increased in Reasi from 43 per cent in the 2009 elections to 81 per cent in the parliamentary election in 2014, the sectoral increase was as follows (Conversation with Shahid Iqbal, DC/DEO, Kathua):

	2009 (%)	2014 (%)
General electoral turnout	43	81
Women's turnout	34	79
Gender gap/electoral sex ratio	20	1
Participation of the Gujjar/Bakerwal community	23	81
Participation of the migrants (militancy-affected) population	0	91
The disabled and the aged	NA	100

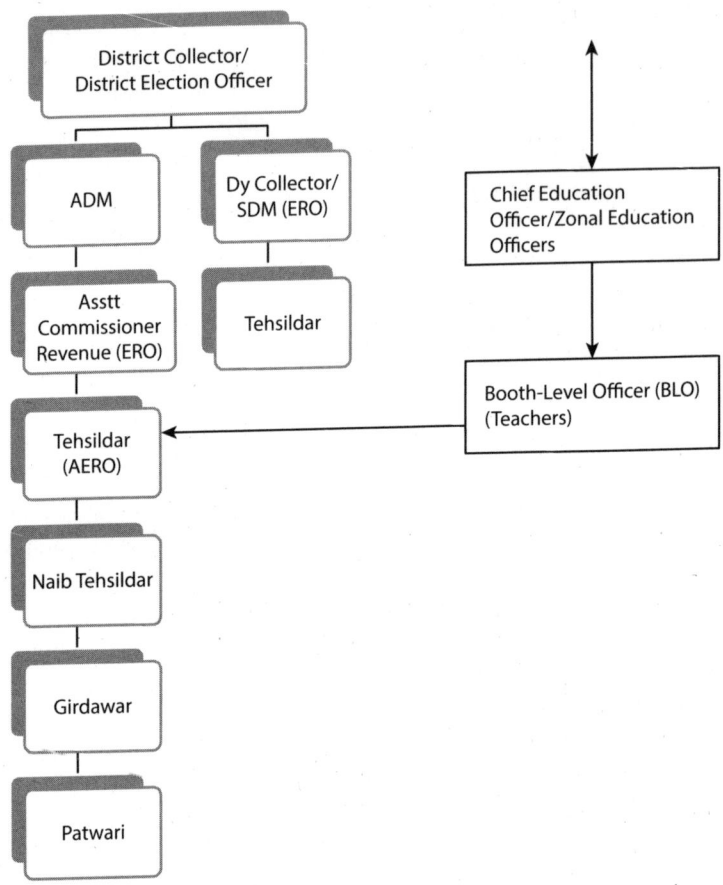

Figure 2.5   Convergence in District and Electoral Administration
Source: Courtesy Shahid Iqbal, DC/DEO, Kathua district (earlier posted in Reasi district).

assembly elections, it was a measure of the success of their model that they had managed to enrol and persuade the voters in Reasi to vote in the parliamentary election.

In the literature on electoral governance, the relationship between elections and democracy is seen as established through the entrenchment of procedural certainty and electoral integrity. Procedural certainty may be regarded as the principal task of electoral governance, helping to ensure the democratic principle of uncertainty of electoral outcome. The credibility/trust in the electoral system is assured through rules and structures of governance that ensure electoral integrity. The literature on electoral integrity suggests that the EMBs, responsible for the conduct of elections, must ensure that the following standards of electoral integrity are met: legitimacy, independence, impartiality and fairness, integrity and honesty, transparency and openness, efficiency and effectiveness, and professionalism and public service.[69] These require putting in place systems that strengthen public confidence in elections and institutional trust, strengthen voter turnout and civic engagement, weaken violent political protest, and accommodate excluded groups. Viewed within such a framework, electoral administration through SVEEP was not only about voter awareness and education, which is an important objective, but also about the consolidation of electoral and participatory democracy, especially in a region that had historically been alienated from the political mainstream because of a host of reasons, including a lack of trust in the electoral machinery and the political process in general. It is not surprising that James Lyngdoh, former CEC of India, titled his book published in 2004 *Chronicle of an Impossible Election*, referring to the ECI's experience of conducting elections in the state of Jammu and Kashmir.

A significant component of SVEEP was about making the 'pledge to vote' a ubiquitous message, by involving school and college students and organising public events to communicate that voting was a civic duty to strengthen democracy. The spectators at an international wrestling match at a sports stadium in Katra, for example, took a collective pledge to vote in the parliamentary election, street plays on the theme *'jaago* voter' (wake up voters) exhorted informed and ethical voting, rallies of students who were first-time voters were held in the city to converge at a central point for a collective pledge-taking ceremony, and mahapanchayats were held to remind the villagers of their duty to vote. During our visit to Kathua, we attended a *matdaan utsav* (vote festival) organised by the district administration in a school in the village Londi, attended by about 400 persons including school children. A popular poet recited poetry using local idioms to persuade people to vote not

---

[69] For more on electoral management and electoral integrity, see Karp et al. (2017).

as individuals but as groups. He urged them to bring with them their sisters, aunts, parents, and neighbours to the polling booth. Apart from these spectacles for voter exhortation, it was at the more banal level of routine activities that the persuasion was done—doctor's prescriptions were stamped with the reminder to vote and so were the bank passbooks and transaction receipts. Indeed, posters replete with wit and humour, such as those in Figures 2.6 and 2.7, were disseminated by the district administration to generate popular appeal.

More specifically, however, the 'Reasi Model' was also about efficient and effective governance, with important lessons on how convergence works in public administration by bringing together governmental branches, vertically and horizontally, to achieve a common objective. Significantly, this model was construed by the administration as one that was not specific to electoral governance, but could be transferred to other domains of governance. The officials discussed the details of convergence, sustainability, and transferability, which the model sought to achieve. The administration hoped to

Figure 2.6   SVEEP Poster 5
Source: District Election Office, Reasi.

Figure 2.7   SVEEP Poster 6
Source: District Election Office, Reasi.

do this by activating the existing channels of governance, reducing costs of elections without compromising on the objectives through public–private partnerships, through efficient utilisation of public funds and human resources in the existing government programmes (MNREGA, Integrated Child Development Services [ICDS] scheme, National Rural Health Mission [NRHM], Members of Parliament Local Area Development [MPLAD) Scheme MPLADs, and so on) and grass-roots institutions and community organisations like the panchayats and *jirgahs*, and also by building durable infrastructure for long-term community welfare (bridges and roads). The DC of Kathua explained how the model of convergence was employed in the 'Sadbhavna' programme through the activation of village and panchayat level organizations for the correction of the sex ratio in rural areas. At the crux of the model was the minimisation of costs by garnering funds for specific initiatives through sponsorships and, most importantly, using existing public funds and human resources in the public-welfare programmes and government schemes in ways that would interlock functions across schemes. On the patterns of (inclusion of the excluded or sensitive sections)

Reasi, the DC and his team had devised a plan for the border villages in Kathua, which we also visited, called '*Hifajat aur Jamhuriat*' translated as 'Security and Democracy'. These villages had recently come under shelling from across the border, leading to displacement of people who had to be moved to camps in other villages. While they were now back in their homes and appeared eager to vote, contingency plans had been created, including auxiliary and mobile pooling booths, which would enable the villagers to vote in the event of renewed shelling.

The website of the ECI is replete with innumerable initiatives under best practices, covering a wide range of activities carried out in different districts under the SVEEP programme. A number of them have been awarded by the ECI or by the Government of India for efficiency or excellence in governance. The success of such programmes ultimately depends on the efforts of particular individuals heading the district administration and collective efforts of his or her team in enhancing the trust of people in the electoral system in particular and democracy in general. Since the incorporation of excluded groups, particularly those impacted by conflict, was an important component of the initiative in Reasi, it was interesting to see how the nomadic communities of the Gujjars and Bakerwals perceived their integration into electoral democracy. During our visit to Reasi, we were constantly reminded by the district officials that the nomadic community had voted for the first time in a parliamentary election.

We journeyed into the hills up to Mahore tehsil in the Pir Panjal range, which was through much of the 1990s and into the 2000s strategically located along the route taken by insurgent/extremist groups to cross from Doda or Poonch to regions in South Kashmir.[70] The block development officer (BDO) accompanied us to Mahore tehsil headquarters through the difficult terrains of the Pir Panjal range. The villagers called them the 'walking hills'—an epithet that refers to the amorphous and unstable surface rocks of the hills, which were crumbling before our eyes, littered as rock and debris dotting our route. In the upper hill areas, one came across groups

---

[70] See for an insightful account of the strategic importance of the Pir Panjal range in Swami (2001).

of mostly men but sometimes also women belonging to the Bakerwal community, with their herds of goats. All of them without exception were carrying their voter identification cards, which they willingly displayed to us. We were told that the registration of Bakerwals and Gujjars as voters, the distribution of EPICS, and finally getting them to vote was part of the bureaucratic initiative. They had deferred their migration to the hills in the summer for 40 days to stay on in the plains and vote. To get them to vote was, however, also an act of subtle coercion. We learnt that the license issued to them by the collector's office to migrate with their flock to the hills for the summer season was withheld for a few days and handed to them only after polling had taken place. As a consequence, for the first time, there was 96 per cent voting by the Gujjars and Bakerwals in the election.

Upon reaching Mahore tehsil, we travelled further up to the village of Sungri, and attended a jirgah of the Gujjars and Bakerwals. In the presence of the BDO, the chief agricultural officer (CAO), the junior engineer, the sarpanch, and other members of the panchayat, a large number of men, women, and children had gathered. There was palpable energy in the gathering and a great deal of display and performance of collective and associational solidarity, put up for an audience that had come from the district headquarters and the national capital. After songs were sung and poems were recited, the CAO, followed by the sarpanch, rose and congratulated the community for their extraordinary performance of the duty of citizenship by voting in the Lok Sabha election. The voluntary and enthusiastic exercise of the franchise was lauded as evidence of their change of heart, and the way they *now* perceived the political regime in Jammu and Srinagar, and in Delhi. After the congratulatory address, often bordering on prescriptive sermonising by the officers from the plains, the people spoke—passionately and honestly. They had voted, and indeed through the vote, they had spoken to show that they were citizens, no longer caught in a bind. But the exercise of franchise was not an expression of sincerity and loyalty to the regime. This could be what 'Delhi' wanted and perceived. Indeed, in the perception of the Bakerwal and Gujjar community, they had always participated and believed in democracy. They claimed to have voted every year—but this year it was different: this year they had voted with what they called *jaddozahat* (effort), *jazbaat* (passion), and *shauk* (interest). It was now time that their vote was honoured (*kadra*), and their species (*naslein*)/children experienced development (*tarakki*) and were not deprived (*marhoom*) of hospitals, primary healthcare, schools, ration, and employment.

The voters wanted the local administration, the 'visitors' from Delhi, and through them the government in Delhi to be apprised of their needs—education, particularly schools for their children who trudged long distances to reach the nearest school, hospitals, and employment opportunities. The calculus was simple: the vote was not an empty exercise of support to be renewed after five years. It was a promise extracted by the people from those who asked them for their votes. The 'one day sultan', an expression used by David Gilmartin (2009) to describe the Indian voter, was not to be dethroned with ease. The guns had silenced the Bakerwals and the Gujjars, but the vote had made them vocal, and they had both expectations from the government and a sense of power to hold it accountable. In an article written in 1965 on the political culture in India, Myron Weiner discussed the features of the political order that was built in India following Independence. The new political order was characterised by, Weiner argued, 'a deliberate and successful dispersal and democratisation of power, which generated in post-independence India two political cultures operating at different levels of Indian society—an emerging mass political culture and an elite political culture' (Weiner 1965: 199). While the elite culture was homogeneous and the mass culture, fragmented and heterogeneous, the elite culture produced mass culture through the establishment of new governmental institutions and the expansion of governmental activities. These generated the socialising forces which changed the character of political attitudes and the political process. In such a framework, universal adult franchise played an important role in political socialisation associated with democratisation, making institutions subject to popular control and facilitating the dispersion of power to the local levels (Weiner 1965: 199). The jirgah in Sungri embodied, in the context of elections, the mobilisation and aggregation of interests along ethnic loyalties. The exercise of franchise enabled the articulation of collective demands by the community to persuade the government to provide schools for their children's education, economic assistance, housing sites, etc., making manifest the ways in which the 'popular' and the 'political' unfold at local levels.

* * *

In executing its constitutional responsibility of preparing the electoral roll, the ECI has come to play a role, which is sometimes also contested, in sorting citizens from non-citizens. Despite the fact that the ECI did not originally view the determination of citizenship as part of its mandate, the Supreme Court's 1984 decision in *Inderjit Barua* case thrust it into that role. The political imbroglio over the electoral roll in Assam left the ECI with decision-making authority in individual cases where citizenship was suspect. The Supreme Court's 1995 decision in *Lal Babu Hussein* case highlighted the danger of giving the ECI too much discretion in these matters. In that case, the Supreme Court felt compelled to lay down procedural safeguards for the protection of legitimate voters from overly zealous inquiries into citizenship that particularly threatened the Muslim minority. The ECI's role in determining citizenship arises from its larger constitutional responsibilities. It is charged with the conduct of elections in a fair and free manner, for which the preparation of a complete and accurate electoral roll is central. In preparing the electoral roll, the ECI must of necessity identify citizens. This has turned out to be an extraordinarily challenging enterprise due to the fluidity of India's population, with respect to both external borders, an issue central to citizenship, and internal migration. In the case of Assam, for example, the electoral roll and identification of citizens has consistently been a fraught issue.

The identification of citizens for purposes of voting is closely related to the larger issue of the position of minorities and other disadvantaged groups within India's body politic. Inclusion of one's name in the voter list has become a marker of citizenship, and since the 1990s, photo voter ID cards have become the most ubiquitous proof of identity for Indian citizens. At a more basic level, for the purpose of administering elections, the preparation and revision of the electoral roll is perhaps the most crucial aspect of electoral governance, requiring enormous resources, managerial skills, and vigilance. In times when people are likely to be moving from one place of residence to another, and sometimes displaced by violence, the prospect of voters being omitted from the rolls is as critical for democracy as the problem of duplicate and fake voters. Reconciling these competing imperatives remains a central challenge before the ECI. In recent years, the ECI has expanded its role of enumeration of voters, by interpreting it as an affirmative function of also encouraging an informed ethical voting. Thus, apart from ensuring that all persons eligible to vote are registered as voters, the ECI has encouraged 'best practices' in election management, which innovate measures to enhance voter turnout, especially those groups that are categorised as 'vulnerable' and have not been able to 'access' their right to vote. While directing attention in electoral governance to voter participation reinforces the procedural aspects of democracy, and shows how the processes of 'state-making' work by encompassing society, the meanings attributed to 'the vote' by the people, and the quality of representation achieved through elections remain within the deliberative domains of democracy. Our visit to Reasi showed that franchise makes people believe that popular control over political institutions is possible, and that the mobilisation of 'ethnic loyalties' has the potential of aggregating modern demands for schools, health, and employment—demands which are addressed to the paternal state and not necessarily couched in the language of democratic politics, of the dispersal and democratisation of power.

✂

3

'Election Time' and the Model Code of Conduct

Framed in 1968 by the ECI in consultation with political parties, the Model Code of Conduct (henceforth MCC) has evolved as an integral part of conducting fair and free elections. Intended for voluntary adherence, the MCC was the consummation of a progressively widening consensus over certain norms of behaviour during election time that were first drawn up by the Government of Kerala before the general elections of 1960. The acceptance of the MCC by all political parties appears, therefore, to be a manifestation of a voluntary act of political morality and collective ethics. Despite the fact that it emerged as a code for voluntary adherence, and was largely seen as having only a moral force to elicit compliance, over the years, the MCC has acquired 'supplementary legality', to fill up a vacuum that has existed in election law. Since the MCC itself does not have the force of law, in the absence of any statutory backing, it is enforced through executive decision-making. It remains, therefore, ambiguous, as far as the modality of its implementation and certainty of its execution are concerned. Consequently, the MCC has attracted innumerable disputes and contestations, largely over the enhancement of the disciplinary powers of the ECI during election time, which is construed under the MCC as 'special time'.

Election Time as 'Special Time'

In the literature on the substantive and procedural aspects of elections, one comes across three distinct, yet inter-related ways in which the expression 'election time' has been used. Dennis F. Thompson (2004) has referred to election time as having certain 'temporal properties' that structure the electoral process. These properties are grounded in the basic value that underpins all conceptions of democracy, that is, popular sovereignty. Election time, according to Thompson, is a moment in politics that marks a discontinuity from the normal and ordinary process of politics. As a moment of discontinuity, election time is characterised by a distinctive 'rhythm' constituted by the convergence of three temporal properties—periodicity, simultaneity and finality. All the three are important for and integral to the affirmation of popular sovereignty. The three temporal properties of elections—*periodicity*, that is, the property of elections taking place at intervals; *simultaneity*, that is, citizens voting on the same day; and *finality*, that is, the irrevocability of electoral outcome till the next election—are grounded in important values that any democratic process should promote. Contemporary democracies realise these properties in various ways and to different degrees. Thompson elaborates their importance in the following manner:

> Because elections take place periodically, current majorities can overcome the dead hand of past majorities. To the extent that voting takes place simultaneously, elections express the will of a determinate majority rather than the preferences of a series of different majorities. Because elections produce final results, they legitimate the authority of a current majority until the next election ... other democratic values, such as fairness and civic engagement, are also strengthened to the extent that the electoral process realizes these temporal properties. (Thompson 2004: 51)

An interesting formulation by the historian David Gilmartin describes elections as constituting 'special time' characterised by the *reversal* in the normal/ordinary working of power (Gilmartin 2009: 248). This reversal of power flows from, in, and through popular sovereignty, and constitutes special election time, whereby the normal/ordinary workings of power are suspended and replaced by a different regime of power. This regime of power defers normal power to provide the conditions for an unfettered exercise of popular sovereignty, which expresses itself through individual and collective acts of voting. In his study of the development of the MCC in India in the 1990s (more precisely, under CEC T.N. Seshan), David Gilmartin argued that the regulatory regime put in place by the ECI with the help of the MCC constituted 'special time'. This special time generated 'an electoral morality' that transcended 'everyday politics' (Gilmartin 2009: 252–3).

A third expression of election time is its characterisation as 'electoral trial', an ascription found in an article by Nadia Urbinati (2000) to refer to the electoral process. When she uses the word 'trial', Urbinati refers not only to the adversarial or competitive contents of elections, which are also relevant derivatives of the expression, but also to their ideological content. The ideological content is generated as issues are debated and thrashed out, and put to test, by taking them beyond the 'here and now' of the present political context, to their future ramifications. The prioritisation of the ideological content of elections ultimately leads to the contentious problem of appropriate representation. The electoral trial plays a necessary part in generating a process of deliberation whereby ideas are expressed and their representation is sought and achieved democratically.

Each of these different articulations of 'election time' focuses on the normative frameworks of democracy. At a fundamental level, however, the normative concerns are made dependent on the procedural frameworks of electoral governance, in particular the 'legal doctrine of electoral exceptionalism', which proposes that 'the electoral process may be subjected to more stringent regulation than ordinary politics' (Thompson 2004). All the three frameworks may be seen as establishing a relationship between the substantive aspects of democracy and the procedural frameworks of electoral governance, leading to the conclusion that an extraordinary legal regime for regulating elections is conducive to democracy. Their conclusions generate some significant questions pertaining to the statutory and institutional frameworks (of electoral laws and institutions), which constitute the template of such governance. These conclusions are, however, distinct from the framework of the 'extraordinary' in the 'state of exception' and must not be conflated or confused with it. For Agamben (2005), the state of exception is implicated in a political crisis and arises from a necessity that becomes an autonomous source of law. It is, moreover, reflective of a specific kind of politics that is largely adversarial and antagonistic, and is defined exclusively as a political contingency to the exclusion of law. The Agambenian state of exception reinforces sovereign power, since it is the sovereign's word that declares the existence of an extreme necessity not covered by law. The legal exceptionalism of election time is different, indeed, the opposite. Electoral legal exceptionalism suspends sovereign power, reversing the direction of the flow of power, in order to release popular sovereignty.

From the perspective of those who administer the institutional apparatus of electoral governance, elections are extraordinary times requiring efficient 'rule-implementation' so that the certainties of procedures generate democratic uncertainties of electoral outcomes. The players in the election game are placed under regulatory control, and political power is deferred until affirmed by passing through an electoral trial. On the other hand, even as electoral legal exceptionalism protects the autonomy of the electoral domain by giving pre-eminence to the bureaucratic apparatus of the state over the political, the electoral trial is not autonomous of the social forces and class interests, which frame the outcome of the trial in significant ways. Moreover, it is doubtful whether the exceptional legal regulation of elections and the specific forms of electoral governance it assumes are protective of other democratic values like freedom of expression. Similarly, in conditions of political crisis, where elections are expected to serve as surrogates or substitutes for a political resolution of the crisis, electoral legal exceptionalism may not be able to provide the conditions sufficient for the affirmation of popular sovereignty.[1]

---

[1] In such a context, rather than an autonomous body entrusted with 'enabling' the people to exercise an informed choice, the ECI may be seen as representing and furthering the hegemonic interests of the state, as opposed to the democratic aspirations of the people. The assembly elections in Jammu and Kashmir (September 2002), for example, opened up debates on the credibility of an election process in conditions that were not conducive to a free, fair, and importantly, fearless exercise of franchise. On the other hand, in Gujarat in the same year, the ECI managed to defer the state assembly elections for a few months, and ensure that elections were held when the moment of crisis had alleviated, but more importantly, to affirm its power of announcing the date of an election.

Between Moral Force and Supplementary Legality

In the writings on electoral reforms and electoral best practices, an MCC is presented as a set of minimum standards and rules of behaviour for political parties, their candidates and supporters, and the government of the day, to ensure free and fair electoral competition. The emergence of such codes is often seen, as it has been in a study by the International Institute for Democracy and Electoral Assistance (IDEA), as a response to challenges that countries may have faced in their transition to electoral democracies, or as a means of generating a political environment for an enduring commitment to multi-party pluralism and the democratic process (International IDEA 1999). There is difference of opinion, however, on the nature of such codes, in particular, whether they should be based on voluntary compliance and invocation of collective morality, or incorporated in and enforced as law, so that non-compliance would attract appropriate penalties.

A 1999 study by the International IDEA, for example, set out to develop a 'Code of Conduct' as a 'universal set of minimum standards' for political parties campaigning in democratic elections, after a review of several codes of conduct that were 'produced *recently*' in various parts of the world. Each of these reviewed codes, the study reports, was developed at a time when the democratic process in these countries was facing significant challenges of democratisation. The codes were formed and implemented in these countries, therefore, with the intention of 'minimizing conflict, eradicating intimidation, and encouraging a climate of open and fair competition during election time' to ensure 'multi party pluralism and the democratic process' (International IDEA 1999: 5–22). The countries whose codes of conduct were used in the study as reference documents were described as having developed their model codes in the 1990s, indicating a somewhat late and staggered process of democratisation. Among the countries listed is India, with the reference document Model Code of Conduct for the Guidance of Political Parties and Candidates (Election Commission of India 1991), along with countries like Bangladesh, Bosnia, Cambodia, Costa Rica, Ghana, Malawi, and Namibia.

The historical contexts in which the MCC emerged in India and the trajectory of its evolution tells a story that is different from what comparative studies of model codes in the world would lead one to believe. In India, the MCC was first developed in 1960 in the southern state of

Kerala. Emanating from a broad consensus among political parties in the state, the Code was designed for voluntary adherence. Despite the fact that the MCC has no statutory basis, over the course of years, it has evolved as an integral part of conducting fair and free elections in India as a whole. In the course of this evolution, it has ceased to be a shared moral code and has come to assume the status of a set of pre-scriptive rules codified and implemented by the ECI, drawing upon the powers vested in it by the Constitution of India. While the genesis of the MCC can be traced to an agreement among political parties, its application has led to contests over both its content and the modalities of its enforcement. The manner in which these contests have been resolved shows a distinct trajectory towards the entrenchment of the ECI from its initial role of being a 'referee institution'[2] regulating the conduct of political parties according to the rules that the political parties had framed[3] to one of a rule-making and rule-enforcing body, wresting from political parties and the political executive the power to determine the rules of fair play in the electoral game. The process of this shift may be seen as having passed through two distinct phases: the post-internal Emergency period (1975–7) and the ECI's initiative in 1979 to present its own version of the MCC, and the period from 1990 marked by the expansion of the powers of the ECI and leading to a period of consolidation of its powers in the following decades. In the course of this period of consolidation of the powers of the ECI, the MCC has emerged as an instrument of regulatory control but also one that enables the ECI to enforce the rules that it has authored. Not surprisingly, corresponding to the enhancement and consolidation of the powers of the ECI, the MCC has emerged as a terrain of contest where the political parties and the ECI have locked horns.

Before proceeding, it is necessary to explain the different rules or legal regimes at work during and after election periods. The RPAs

---

[2] Devesh Kapur and Pratap Bhanu Mehta (2005: 4) categorise the ECI and the Supreme Court as order-maintaining, referee institutions, exercising primarily the task of restraining other public institutions within a given framework of rules.

[3] Lloyd Rudolph and Susanne Hoeber Rudolph (2008: 279) note that the onset of economic reforms in India in 1991 paved the way for the regulatory institutions of the State, one of which was the ECI.

of 1950 and 1951, which provide the statutory framework for the conduct of elections in India, identify electoral offenses and corrupt practices that may be committed by *individuals* during elections.[4] The MCC, on the other hand, introduced an innovation by providing a *disciplinary regime for political parties*, empowering the ECI to call political parties to order, making them accountable for the conduct of individual members. Moreover, while the legal frameworks pertaining to electoral offenses and corrupt practices under the RPAs come into effect only after the electoral process is over, the MCC comes into play during election time, ensuring the direct disciplinary control of the ECI over political parties, offering a system of supplementary legality to plug the legal vacuum that exists during election time. It may be recalled that Article 329 bars interference by courts in electoral matters including election to either House of Parliament or a state legislature. Under the RPA, 1951, the power to decide election disputes vests in the high courts with a right of appeal to the Supreme Court. It should be noted that while election petitions under the RPAs must be made after the election process is over, and the MCC per se

---

[4] These offenses are listed as electoral offenses and corrupt practices. An electoral offense attracts penalty in a criminal code, whereas a corrupt practice disqualifies a candidate whose election can be set aside. The IPC, 1860, has declared certain actions in connection with elections as offenses. These are: promoting enmity, and so on, between different groups on grounds of religion, race, place of birth, residence, language, and the like (Section 153 A); imputations and assertions prejudicial to national integration (Section 153 B); bribery (Section 171 B); use of undue influence to interfere with the free exercise of any electoral rights (Section 171 C); personification at an election (Section 171 D); making false statements (Section 171 G); illegal payments (Section 171 H); failure to keep election accounts (Section 171); and making or circulating statements conducive to public mischief, enmity, or hatred and the like between different classes. While most of these provisions were part of the IPC before Independence, Sections 153 A and B were added in 1969 and 1972, respectively. Some of these offenses like bribery, undue influence, and promoting enmity on the ground of religion, race, and so on, have also been declared corrupt practices under the RPA, 1951 (Section 123), which also prescribes several other electoral offenses, such as holding a public meeting 48 hours before polling begins (Section 126), creating disturbances at election meetings (Section 127), and so on.

cannot be enforced as a law, corresponding offenses under the Indian penal and criminal codes, and other laws, can be invoked to book individual offenders during the electoral process.

Providing a Level Playing Field

Speaking at a conference on electoral reforms in Lucknow, in January 2011, then CEC S.Y. Quraishi pointed out an interesting paradox. While political parties, he said, are routinely criticised for the criminalisation of politics, it is the political parties that must be credited with the development of the MCC. Describing the MCC as the 'greatest' contribution of political parties, CEC Quraishi proceeded to explain the operation of the MCC as follows: 'enforced not by law but by an agreement made to this effect by all political parties [it] worked wonders as restrictions imposed under it are carried out by all governments and political systems without failure'.[5] A few days earlier, speaking at the valedictory function of the diamond jubilee celebrations of the ECI, the CEC had iterated that the MCC was indispensable for ensuring 'honest, free and fair elections', and despite the fact that it had no statutory backing, it continued to be effective because it elicited the 'moral sanction' of public opinion and had evolved virtually as a 'moral code of conduct'.[6]

Indeed, the history of development of the MCC in India shows that it came into existence on the eve of the state assembly elections in Kerala in 1960, when the state government in Kerala, representatives of major political parties in the state, and electoral officials drew up a code for voluntary observation by political parties. Reports

---

[5] 'Electoral Reforms Must to Purge System,' *The Times of India*, 31 January 2011. Available at http://timesofindia.indiatimes.com/city/lucknow/Electoral-reforms-must-to-purge-system/articleshow/7393944.cms#ixzz1HoIOl2kf; accessed 13 February 2011.

[6] Speech by CEC S.Y. Quraishi at the international conference on 'Best Electoral Practices' organised on the eve of the launch of NVD and valedictory function of the diamond jubilee celebrations of the ECI, on 21 January 2011. The speech is available on the web site http://equalityindia.wordpress.com/category/election; accessed on 20 July 2011.

by the ECI of the six general elections that it conducted between 1951–2 and 1977, scanned copies of which are available on the ECI's website, are a useful resource for gaining insight into how the ECI implemented the MCC in its formative years. A reading of the 1960 version of the MCC reveals a political consensus pertaining largely to how the time and space of the campaign was to be shared among political parties, making for a level playing field in electoral competition.[7] Addressing concerns around how political parties would carry out their campaigns in a mode of amicable cooperation and reciprocity, the 1960 MCC had five sections under the following headings: (a) meetings, (b) processions, (c) speeches and slogans, (d) placards, and (e) general. The sections covering meetings and processions laid down rules for holding meetings or carrying out processions with the knowledge and permission of local police and other authorities to ensure the smooth running of campaigns and the elimination of occasions of overlap and conflict in the election campaigns of different political parties. The section on speeches and slogans and the section on placards concerned themselves explicitly with the nature of the campaign, enjoining political parties 'to adopt an attitude of mutual tolerance and forbearance, especially in situations when the uncontrolled exercise of the right of free speech and expression [was] likely to stir up ill-feeling and lead to disorder and violence' and to avoid 'depreciatory or insulting remarks about the private lives, personal habits or physical peculiarities or handicaps of individuals', 'derogatory remarks on the religion, caste or community of individuals', 'statements that are likely to wound the religious susceptibilities of any section of the people in any manner', and 'statements and slogans suggestive of violent action against any members of other political parties'. The MCC made political parties responsible for ensuring adherence to these principles, entreating them to 'make earnest endeavors to instruct [their] followers on the above mentioned principles of conduct' and to openly dissociate themselves 'from any type of activity that [was] in contravention of

[7] For details of the MCC and its provisions, see the Election Commission of India, *Report of the Third General Elections in India*, Vol. I. New Delhi: Election Commission of India, 1962, pp. 58–61.

these principles', emphasising that 'there should be no hesitation on [their] part in taking necessary action against persons who deliberately disobey the party's instructions in this regard'.[8]

In the narrative report of the third general elections in India (1962), CEC K.V.K. Sundaram noted the 'usefulness' of the MCC in the 'hotly contested' election of 1960, and the decision the ECI subsequently took to circulate the code to all recognised political parties and to various state governments, asking them to secure acceptance for the code by all parties contesting elections in their state. Political parties and candidates in the country generally followed the code. As a consequence of this, the narrative report suggests, election campaigns were conducted in 'a peaceful and orderly manner almost everywhere'.[9] Adherence to the MCC was reiterated in Kerala in the 1967 election and model codes similar to the Kerala Code were drawn and adopted in 1966–7 in West Bengal, Tamil Nadu, and Andhra Pradesh, in conferences of representatives of political parties convened by the chief ministers of the respective states.[10] The annual report prepared by the ECI in 1983, which was the year in which the ECI started the practice of sending annual reports to Parliament in place of the earlier practice of reporting after each election, mentions that in 1966, the commissioner of police of (then) Madras city convened a conference of the representatives of political parties. In this conference, the political parties agreed to observe a code of conduct during the general elections of 1967. This was followed by another conference of party representatives convened by the chief minister of Tamil Nadu towards the end of December 1966. A standing committee of seven persons, representing different political parties, to whom complaints regarding any breach of the code could be made, was also set up at the conference. The peaceful conduct of elections in Tamil Nadu was largely attributed to the code of conduct. Early in 1967, political parties in Andhra Pradesh accepted a code of conduct drawn on the lines

[8] Election Commission of India, *Report of the Third General Elections in India*, pp. 58–61.

[9] Election Commission of India, *Report of the Third General Elections in India*, p. 61.

[10] Election Commission of India, *Report of the Third General Elections in India*, p. 61.

of the Madras Code. Kerala adopted the MCC it had developed in 1960 for the general elections in 1967 as well. A code similar to the Kerala Code was placed before a meeting of party representatives convened by the chief minister of West Bengal in January 1967. Though all parties did not fully accept the draft code, they unanimously resolved to ensure a peaceful election campaign and to assist the authorities in the smooth conduct of the poll.[11]

It was in 1968–9, in the context of the midterm election to the Lok Sabha that the ECI presented its own version of the MCC in the form of 'an appeal' to political parties 'to observe a minimum standard of conduct and behavior to ensure fair and free elections'.[12] In the narrative report of the midterm elections in 1968–9 for the state assemblies in Punjab, Haryana, Uttar Pradesh, Bihar, West Bengal, Nagaland, and Pondicherry, CEC S.P. Sen-Varma writes that the midterm elections were precipitated by the 'wind of swift change' that swept the country in the general elections of 1967.[13] It was in the general elections of 1967 that the Congress party lost its dominant position. The series of defections and re-defections among political parties, which followed, led to political uncertainty and president's rule in some states, which now faced midterm elections. The midterm elections, however, allowed the ECI the space to carry out some innovations, and drawing up an official MCC was one among them. The CEC convened a meeting with political leaders and party representatives in each state and made a 'personal appeal' to them to carry out the electoral campaign peacefully. In the narrative report, the CEC invokes theories of democracy to emphasise the importance of the politics of dialectics in a democracy. Such a politics made it imperative that opposite views

---

[11] Election Commission of India, *First Annual Report, 1983*. New Delhi: Election Commission of India, April 1984, p. 65.

[12] The ECI's MCC was titled, 'Role and Responsibilities of Political Parties during Elections: An Appeal to Political Parties for the Observance of a Minimum Code of Conduct during Election Propaganda and Campaign' (see Election Commission of India, *Report on the Mid-term General Election in India, 1968–69*, Vol. I. New Delhi: Election Commission of India, 1970, pp. 9–15).

[13] Election Commission of India. 1970. *Report on the Mid-term General Election in India, 1968–69*, Vol. I, pp. 9–15.

should be heard in public discussions. A citizen's choice was made through such discussion, and this process of making an informed choice was more important than the vote itself. For the CEC, the importance of the MCC lay precisely in providing the space for prior discussion, so that the vote when it was finally cast had the quality of intelligent consent.[14]

The ECI repeated its appeal at the time of the next round of general elections to the Lok Sabha and elections to state legislative assemblies in 1971–2. The two-page MCC embedded in the 245-page-long report, broadly reiterated the guidelines of the 1960 code, advising political parties against activities that would aggravate or create differences among caste and religious and linguistic communities, enjoining them to confine criticisms of political parties to their policies and programmes, and abstain from making unverified allegations and distortions. In addition, it cautioned the government officials that while they took measures to maintain law and order, they should resist from imposing 'undue restrictions on civil liberties' and not employ measures that would 'interfere with a satisfactory election campaign by parties'. In addition, there 'should be no appeal to caste or communal feelings' and 'mosques, churches and temples should not be used as a forum for election propaganda'. Any breach of code could be reported to a standing committee.[15] Interestingly, the 'narrative and reflective' report as the CEC S.P. Sen-Varma chose to subtitle the ECI's report on the 1971–2 election, is not optimistic about the impact such an appeal would have because of what he called 'extreme sense of selfishness' among political parties:

> But I may say without any fear of contradiction that such Code of Conduct is of little, practical value, because no party or no candidate observes the various rules and instructions laid down in such Code of Conduct at the crucial time, namely, election time. At that time every political party and every candidate is, so as to say, overpowered

[14] Election Commission of India, *Report on the Mid-term General Election in India, 1968–69*, pp. 9–11.

[15] See the Election Commission of India, *Report on the Fifth General Election in India (1971–72)*. New Delhi: Election Commission of India, 1972, pp. 151–2.

and overwhelmed with an extreme sense of selfishness and hardly hesitates to have recourse to means, fair or foul, to win the elections. Therefore the issue by the Election Commission of any Code of Conduct before an election is, more or less, a meaningless ritual in which high sounding jargons are formulated and published on every occasion.[16]

A revised MCC was circulated by the ECI in January 1974 on the eve of the midterm elections to certain state legislative assemblies, with instructions to the CEOs to set up standing committees at the district level with representatives of all recognised political parties to ensure broad cooperation and effective implementation of the MCC. A similar MCC was then drafted at the time of the general elections in 1977.

A reading of the narrative reports by the ECI suggests that up to the end of the 1970s, the ECI limited its role in the implementation of the MCC to eliciting consent from political parties, enjoining with them, and encouraging them to comply with norms, which the political parties had themselves evolved and resolved to follow. Yet, there also appears to have been an underlying concern around evolving a more comprehensive code, which would include special provisions to curb the privileges and powers of the ruling party. This would pertain largely to the use of official resources, which give the party in power an unfair advantage during the election campaign. The ECI felt that the ruling party required special restraints in light of the complaints it had received concerning the use and monopolisation of public maidans (grounds) for holding meetings, occupation of government rest houses and inspection bungalows, and the like, by the leaders of the ruling party, and the use of large-size advertisements in newspapers by the government to influence voters in favour of the ruling party. At a meeting of political parties convened by the ECI on 12 September 1979, chaired by CEC S.L. Shakdher, the representatives of political parties attending the meeting endorsed the ECI's suggestion for an intensive revision of the MCC.[17] Having

[16] Election Commission of India, *Report on the Fifth General Election in India (1971–72)*, pp. 151–2.

[17] See Election Commission of India (1979).

received the endorsement of all political parties, the ECI revised the 1974 Code thoroughly in October 1979. More comprehensive than the 1974 Code, the 1979 MCC was divided into seven parts with an entire part (Part VII) devoted to regulating parties in power in the centre and in the states.

The 1979 Code was modified from time to time in consultation with political parties, and was reissued in December 1983 in the form of a document titled 'Model Code of Conduct for the Guidance of Political Parties and Candidates'. It was in 1983 that Part VII of the MCC, pertaining to the 'party in power' and the rules of conduct it must follow to produce a level playing field, was further strengthened. It may be recalled that the 1983 report followed the elections to the legislative assemblies in five states, including Assam, Tripura, Karnataka, Andhra Pradesh, and Jammu and Kashmir. Apart from the MCC, the issues that were discussed in a meeting of political parties convened by the then CEC R.K. Trivedi had on its agenda the contentious issue of revision of electoral rolls in Assam with reference to the Illegal Migrants Determination by Tribunals Act (IMDT Act), 1983. Indeed, this meeting was also expected to discuss other crucial matters that would have ramifications for future elections, namely, the use of EVMs in the entire country by 1985, issue of photo identity cards to all voters, and revision of maximum limit of election expenses.[18] The participants in the meeting agreed in principle that apart from the already existing 'rules', the MCC should also prohibit the following: 'financial grants' in any form that may influence a voter; the use of official machinery, vehicles, and aircraft; and the entry of ministers in polling stations and counting halls, unless they were themselves candidates, voters, or authorised agents. Along with constraining the party in power through these measures, the ECI was also empowered to set up a monitoring cell to oversee the All India Radio and Doordarshan—the government-owned radio

---

[18] The meeting of the representatives of political parties was held on 3 December 1983 in the Secretariat of the ECI in New Delhi under the chairmanship of R.K. Trivedi, CEC of India. Forty-nine representatives of 7 national, 20 state, and 6 registered parties attended the meeting (Election Commission of India, *First Annual Report, 1983*, p. 88).

and television services—to ensure 'free and objective presentation of election news'.[19]

Since 1991, the MCC has come to be seen as an integral part of elections, making the electoral contest democratic by ensuring that the party in power and those who staked claims to power would abide

[19] Election Commission of India, *First Annual Report, 1983*, 88. A comprehensive MCC was appended to the annual report 1983. In a later meeting with the representatives of political parties with the ECI on 25 August 1984, following the BJP's complaint about the partisan news bulletins over All India Radio and Doordarshan in favour of the ruling Congress party, the MCC was expanded by amending clause [4(iv) of Item-VII] pertaining to party in power to state that 'advertisement at the cost of public exchequer in the newspapers and other media and the misuse of official mass media during the election period for partisan coverage of political news and publicity regarding achievements with a view to furthering the prospects of the party in power shall be scrupulously avoided' (Election Commission of India, *Second Annual Report of the Election Commission, 1984*. New Delhi: Election Commission of India, 1985, p. 41). In this meeting, the political parties also wanted a total ban on the use of official aircraft/helicopter by the ministers and other political leaders from the last date of withdrawal of candidatures till the date of poll, except in special or emergency situations. They requested the CEC to ask the chief ministers to avoid the use of official aircraft during the election period except for emergency administrative purpose. Following the recommendation of political parties, the CEC addressed letters to all chief ministers. On 17 June 1982, the ECI made a specific request to the secretary to the Government of India in the Ministry of Home Affairs that the contents of the MCC may be circulated officially to all the central ministries and departments for compliance. The home ministry had circulated the same vide its letter No. IV/14015/82: CSR, dated 24 August 1982. Some amendments and amplifications to the MCC, issued from time to time, were also forwarded to the central government by the ECI. Printed copies containing the consolidated and updated instructions, which had earlier been circulated, were forwarded by the ECI to the Cabinet Secretariat, Ministry of Home Affairs, and the Ministry of Law, besides the chief secretaries to the governments of all states and administrators of union territories vide letter No. 437/6/84/3963-4028, dated 16 November 1984. The political parties were also given copies of the same (Election Commission of India, *Second Annual Report of the Election Commission, 1984*, p. 42).

by certain rules, and by pruning the powers of the ruling party to reduce the advantage that it may have in the electoral arena. While the 1991 Code retained the form of the 1979 Code, its contents, particularly of Part VII, had undergone some significant changes, reflecting the spirit of the 1983 agreement between the ECI and the political parties. Part I of the Code stressed on certain minimum standards of good behaviour and conduct of political parties, candidates, and their workers and supporters during the election campaigns; Parts II and III dealt with the holding of public meetings and processions held by political parties and candidates; Parts IV and V described how political parties and candidates should conduct themselves on the polling day and at the polling booths; Part VI exhorted them to bring their complaints to the notice of the observers appointed by the ECI for remedial action; Part VII dealt with the parties in power, and may be seen as constituting the most crucial and contested component of the MCC.

If one examines the guidelines under the MCC issued in the later elections, that is, the 2009 and 2014 general elections, one can identify an underlying tendency to lay down general norms of dignified behaviour for all political parties. Such norms bar political parties from: (*a*) indulging in activities that may aggravate existing differences, create mutual hatred, or cause tension between different castes and communities, religious or linguistic, (*b*) criticising other political parties in matters related to their private lives, that is, matters not connected with their public activities, their policies and programmes, past record and work, (*c*) appealing to caste or communal feelings for securing votes, and using places of worship for election propaganda, (*d*) engaging in activities that are 'corrupt practices' and offenses under election law, such as bribing, intimidation, and impersonation of voters; canvassing within 100 metres of a polling station; and so on, (*e*) disturbing every individual's right to have a peaceful and undisturbed home life, that is, demonstrating or picketing before the houses of individuals because of their political opinions and activities, and (*f*) creating disturbances or obstructions to break up election meetings of rival political parties.

On the other hand, another set of norms specially designed to ensure a level playing field among political parties, with the implication that the party in power may not wield unfair advantage, can also be identified. In this context, the MCC prohibits the use of official resources, including aircraft, vehicles, machinery, and personnel in the 'furtherance of the interest of the party in power' (Section VII(i)(b)). More importantly, it restricts announcements of new projects under welfare schemes and government programmes, and puts conditions on the manner in which the existing projects may be carried out 'by civil authority and without associating political functionaries and without any fanfare or ceremonies whatsoever, so that no impression is given or created that such commissioning has been done with a view to influencing the electorate in favor of ruling party'.[20] It is in this context that the date on which the MCC comes into effect becomes important. It is from that date that the ECI's regulatory role becomes effective, the power of the political executive is suspended, the party forming the government can be bridled, and other political parties protected. It is not surprising, therefore, that the date on which the MCC becomes effective has become a matter of contest between the ECI and political parties constituting the government.

The End of Moral Consensus and Contest over Legality

As discussed earlier, the MCC was the consummation of a progressively widening consensus over certain norms that were first drawn up by the Government of Kerala before the general elections of 1960. While the aspects of voluntariness and moral force associated with the MCC have been important in the emergence of a political consensus over its desirability and appropriateness, there were, however, strains in this consensus, which became visible in the late 1970s and emerged more prominently during and after the 1990s.

---

[20] Election Commission of India (2009b: 7). See in particular the instructions issued by the ECI's letter No. 464/INST/2007-PLN-I, dated 7 January 2007 and addressed to the chief secretaries and the CEOs of all states and union territories, on the subject: 'Code of Conduct: Dos and Don'ts,' including detailed instructions on regulating the use of official machinery, the announcement of welfare schemes and governmental work, and the ban on transfer of government servants/bureaucrats (Election Commission of India 2009a: 3–10).

It may be reiterated here that the 1990s are often presented as the period when the ECI came into its own, owing to two inter-related developments that altered the nature of electoral politics in this period. First, a reconfiguration of the party system into a competitive multi-party system accompanied by the 'second democratic upsurge', which opened up spaces for marginal political parties and intensified electoral contests. Second, a progressive decrease in trust among the people in the political process and politicians, with commensurate increases in the credibility of non-elected public institutions like the ECI and the Supreme Court. Lloyd Rudolph and Susanne Hoeber Rudolph (2008: 279) also note that the onset of economic reforms in India in 1991, which witnessed a shift from centralised planning by an interventionist state 'towards market competition fostered by a regulatory state', has meant a 'diminished executive and legislature' and 'more scope' for institutions like the Supreme Court and the ECI. Regulatory institutions, they argue, are characterised by roles that are 'more procedural than substantive, more rule-making and enforcing than law-making and policy-making' (Rudolph and Rudolph 2008: 279). As a result of a combination of factors, in the course of the 1990s, one sees resurgence in the ECI's efforts to consolidate rules and procedures of electoral governance in a way that generates 'a radical uncertainty about authority' (Mozaffar and Schedler 2002; Singh 2004: 4). It does not remain, however, merely a regulatory institution of the state. Ensuring procedural certainties in the electoral arena, it also allowed momentum to build in the political arena for increased participation, releasing energies that led to mobilisation of new groups, unsettled existing power relations, and produced new openings.[21]

Significantly, while the moral force of the MCC was increasingly being reinforced through its projection by the electoral authorities as indispensable for the conduct of fair elections, this was also the period when the political consensus over the MCC was fractured owing to non-compliance by political parties, making it an increasingly deep terrain of contest among political parties on the one hand, and the

[21] Mehta (2003: 11) argues that the right to vote appears to be a meagre right, but it can bring about transformative change in people's social existence.

ECI and the political parties, on the other. Yet, the trajectory of the contest may be seen as having had its genesis further back, when in conformity of its constitutional mandate of superintending elections, the ECI asserted its responsibility of determining the rules of conducting the electoral game. The trajectory of the contest over the MCC may be traced along two broad periods—the post-Emergency period leading to the framing of the MCC by the ECI in 1979, where the beginnings of 'defiance' could be seen; and the period following the 1990s when the ECI reinvented itself through an incremental accumulation and consolidation of powers.

The Beginnings of Defiance

While the 1990s have been described as the ECI's 'activist' phase, often associated with the assertive personalities of CECs, in particular T.N. Seshan,[22] the emphasis on the 1990s occludes an earlier period of 'activism', which may be traced to the post-Emergency period and the 1977 general election.[23] In this election, alongside the posters with stencilled drawings of a farmer and plough, which was the symbol of the Janata Party, and the Congress graffiti of 'Support Indira Gandhi—Vote Cow and Calf of the Congress Party', were the ECI's posters exhorting the voter to vote without fear. Widely displayed all over India, the official poster produced by the ECI stated 'Vote without Fear—Your Vote Is Secret'. In the context of an election taking

[22] The ECI's activism refers to the phase especially in the 1990s with T.N. Seshan as the CEC (see Rudolph and Rudolph 2008; see also for discussions around this, Alistair McMillan 2010; Gilmartin 2010: 252–3; and Manjari Katju 2009).

[23] A state of national emergency was declared in India from 26 June 1975 to 21 March 1977, under the provisions of Part XVIII of the Constitution of India by the Indira Gandhi-led Congress government in the centre on grounds of political instability due to internal disturbances. The Emergency was marked by suspension of fundamental rights, large-scale arrest of the political opposition, deferral of general elections, and erosion of institutional autonomy of the judiciary. The lifting of the Emergency was followed by a general election to the Lok Sabha, in which the Congress was removed from power. The outcome of the election was seen as an indictment of the authoritarian regime during the period of the Emergency.

place after 21 months of national emergency and the suppression of civil rights, the exhortation to vote in the ECI posters had a distinct anti-government ring.[24] On 18 January 1977, Prime Minister Indira Gandhi announced that elections would be held in March the same year. The announcement came as a surprise to those who had thought that the Emergency regime would become the Indian version of Asian hereditary dictatorship. A year before, the tenure of Parliament had been extended beyond its normal life of five years by another year—an extension made possible under the conditions of a national emergency. Yet, even though elections were announced, detenus—the bulk of whom were political opponents of Indira Gandhi—were released, and press censorship and restrictions on public meetings was lifted to facilitate the election process, Indira Gandhi made it clear that the Emergency was not over. In her broadcast announcing the election, she declared that for the duration of the election campaign, the 'rules' of the 'emergency' will [only] be 'relaxed' (Weiner 1977: 1). It was

[24] In the paper 'The Indian Election: A Diary', Myron Weiner chronicles his observations of the momentous 1977 elections as follows:

Bombay, March 8. During the ride from Santa Cruz International Airport into the center of Bombay I could already see the sign of an election campaign. Every wall, large and small, seemed to be covered by an election poster or by graffiti. The Congress theme was simply 'For progress and stability vote Congress'. ... Many posters from the emergency with hortatory slogans persisted: 'Talk less, work more', 'There is no substitute for hard work' and 'Twenty point programme is a blueprint for progress'. Janata had fewer posters but more graffiti. 'Our pledge bread and liberty vote Janata' was a favourite slogan. Among other slogans I saw were 'save democracy—vote for Janata party', 'Problems are plenty—points are twenty, results are empty', 'We were curtailed freedom of speech, freedom of press, fundamental rights, freedom of association. To restore them forever vote for Janata party' ..., 'a ballot for Janata is a bullet for democracy' ... Banners and streamers were tied across streets ... in the early evening hours there were processions of young people shouting slogans. Later in the evening when the sun went down, and the temperatures dropped there were large public rallies, which often continued into the late hours of the night. (Weiner 1977: 9–10)

widely believed that the election was being held by Indira Gandhi to seek a democratic mandate and legitimacy for the changes that had been brought about during the Emergency. In a context where the opposition was enfeebled, and political institutions had been eroded, she was hopeful of victory (Weiner 1977: 1–2).

The outcome of the 1977 election, however, turned out to be a fearless popular indictment and rejection of the Congress, which ran a campaign on the plank of 'progress' buttressed by slogans pertaining to the disciplinary regime of the 20-point programme of the Emergency founded on 'hard work' (*kadi mehnat*) and 'determination' (*pakka irada*). For the first time in the electoral history of India, the Congress party was voted out of power by a unified opposition party (the Janata party), which contested the election on the twin slogans of democracy and civil liberties. The election achieved regime change through constitutional means. At a deeper level, however, the entire process also manifested people's faith in the electoral system, through which the citizen-voters could register their protest, and, as Partha Chatterjee (2006: 49) expressed it, 'established in the arena of popular mobilisations in India the capacity of the vote and of representative bodies of government to give voice to popular demands of a kind that had never before been allowed to disturb the order and tranquility of the proverbial corridors of power'. The entire process, moreover, brought the ECI into the public arena as an institution entrusted with carrying out the constitutional mandate of 'fair and free' elections. This was accentuated just prior to and during the Emergency, when the credibility of the courts had been eroded through political intrusions into judicial decision-making.

Writing in the prefatory note of the narrative report prepared by the ECI after the 1977 general election, CEC T. Swaminathan described the election as 'historic' for having obtained majority for the first time in 25 years for a party other than the Indian National Congress. While not naming the Emergency as having contributed to the substitution of the Congress party, the CEC says that the reasons for the outcome were subjects of academic study, which could be done by political scientists and historians. The ECI as an 'independent constitutional authority providing an agency for conducting a fair and free election was not, and should not be, concerned' with them. Yet, Swaminathan goes on to emphasise the role the ECI played in restoring democracy, as 'an independent, objective, honest and impartial agency', a role which he claims, was widely acclaimed in India and abroad. To CEC Swaminathan, the results were a vindication of constitutional wisdom and the free and fearless manner in which the electorate chose its representatives and the government.[25] Indeed, 'vote without fear' was the slogan the ECI chose to put on its posters exhorting voters to cast their votes freely.

As discussed in the earlier section, it was also during this period that the MCC experienced its passage from an 'agreed set of do's and don'ts' among political parties to a measure directed at restraining the party in power, in order to reduce its advantage during elections. In an important observation, James Lyngdoh (2004: 69–70), the CEC of India from 2001 to 2004, describes this transition in terms of the MCC becoming an instrument for '*pitching* into the party in power'. Correspondingly, the ECI assumed a role that was no longer confined to even-handed dispensation of rules of electoral competition, but one where it became an active player itself, and quite like the 'pitcher' in a baseball game, the initiator of the electoral game. The possibility of transition to a pitcher's role in preference to a referee's role, vis-à-vis the ruling party, emerged in the 1970s when electoral competition started becoming more plural due to the breakdown of the dominance of the Congress party in Indian political and electoral space. It is at this moment perhaps that the ECI may be seen as having put in place, more assuredly than ever before, the process of 'institutionalisation of democratic/electoral uncertainties' through the establishment of procedural certainty. We may recall from the discussion in the previous section that it was in 1974 that the ECI revised the MCC and attempted to make it effective by setting up bureaucratic bodies at the district level to oversee its implementation. The critical importance that the MCC assumed in the 1970s needs to be seen in the context of the paradox that exists in the Constitution of India, where the autonomy of the electoral process is sought to be maintained by imposing a bar under Article 329 to interference by courts in electoral matters during election time, giving primacy to Parliament's powers

---

[25] See the Election Commission of India, *Report on the Sixth General Election, 1977*, Vol. I. New Delhi: Election Commission of India, 1978, preface, pp. 81–2.

to legislate on them under Articles 327 and 328. Under Article 329(b) of the Constitution, an election petition could be placed calling into question an election of either House of Parliament or the state legislatures before an appropriate authority, in the manner provided by law. While the various high courts and the Supreme Court of India can hear election petitions, this power accrues from and is dependent on appropriate legislation.[26] It may be noted that while Chapter III of the RPA, 1951, lays down elaborate provisions for trial of election petitions, their disposal, specification of corrupt practices, election offenses, and so on, these provisions of the RPA, 1951, do not permit the presentation of a petition before 'the date of election of the returned candidate'.[27] As discussed in an earlier chapter, as early as 1952, in the case *N.P. Ponnuswami* v. *The Returning Officer*, Namakkal Constituency, dismissing the writ petition by a candidate challenging the cancellation of his nomination by the returning officer, the Supreme Court had affirmed that the word 'election' in Article 329(b)

---

[26] In 1974–5, Prime Minister Indira Gandhi was facing the charge of corrupt practices under Section 123(7) of the RPA, 1951. In June 1975, the Allahabad High Court passed an order finding Indira Gandhi guilty of corrupt practices in her 1971 election of Rae Bareilly, augmenting the problems for her beleaguered government. In the same year, Indira Gandhi's government sought to amend Article 329 of the Constitution by bringing in an exclusionary provision pertaining to the election of the prime minister and the speaker. Article 329 lays down that the election to the Houses of Parliament or the state legislatures may not be 'called in question except by an election petition presented to such authority and in such manner as may be provided for by or under any law made by the appropriate legislature' (Article 329(a)). Through the 39th Amendment Act, 1975, a new article (Article 329-A) was inserted into the Constitution to provide that the election to Parliament of a person who holds office of prime minister or speaker of the Lok Sabha at the time of such election or is appointed as prime minister or speaker after such election shall be called in question only before a specially prescribed authority [and not before the High Court under Article 329(b) of the Constitution]. The amendment was omitted by the 44th Amendment Act in 1978.

[27] The RPA, 1951, Section 81 (Presentation of Petitions)—(1) An election petition calling in question any election may be presented on one or more of the grounds by any candidate at such election or any elector within 45 days from, but not earlier than the date of election of the returned candidate.

was a 'compendious expression', which connoted the entire electoral process, commencing with the notification calling the election and culminating in the declaration of result. The bar on interference of the courts would thus apply to the entire electoral procedure, which once started could not be interfered with at any intermediate stage.[28] Moreover, post-elections petitions, which were allowed in the RPA, 1951, when presented in courts, were more likely to be dismissed than upheld by the courts for lack of evidence.[29]

The extraordinary nature of election time is characterised by both a bar on judicial interference and a corresponding legal vacuum explicitly laid down in RPA, 1951, for addressing issues that arise in the course of the conduct of elections. Significantly, it was in this period, in a context of political and democratic deficit with which the electoral system came to be characterised in the 1970s, that the ECI challenged the ruling party by asserting its constitutional mandate of being the

---

[28] *N.P. Ponnuswami* v. *The Returning Officer, Namakkal Constituency, Namakkal, Salem District and four Others* (The Union of India and State of Madhya Bharat Interveners), Supreme Court of India, (Civil Appellate Jurisdiction), Case No. 351 of 1951, (decision dated 21 January 1952) (Election Commission of India 1999).

[29] In *Ghasi Ram* v. *Dal Singh and Others* (1968), for example, Ghasi Ram made a petition before the Supreme Court against the elected candidate Dal Singh under Sections 123(1), (2), and (7) of the RPA, 1951. The petitioner, whose appeal had earlier been rejected by the state high court, alleged that Dal Singh, who was a minister in the ruling party, engaged in 'corrupt practice' by using discretionary funds to his advantage before the election. The petitioner claimed that the use of discretionary funds by Dal Singh for the construction of a sacred tank, the building of community centres, repair of wells for Harijans (term for members of scheduled castes that is infrequently used today), and providing irrigation facilities in some villages, and so on, was done with a view to securing support for his candidature, and amounted to 'bribing the voter'. Both the state high court and the Supreme Court dismissed the petition on the ground that there was no clear evidence to 'fully establish corrupt practice involving bribery', implying that the evidence must clearly show that the promise or gift directly or indirectly was made to an elector 'to vote or refrain from voting at an election'. *Ghasi Ram* v. *Dal Singh and Others*, decided on 7 February 1968 by a Supreme Court bench consisting of Justice M. Hidayatullah and K.S. Hegde.

primary institution responsible for superintending, directing, and controlling the conduct of elections. The revised MCC of 1979 was one aspect of this assertion, whereby the legal vacuum and absence of judicial redress, which obtained during electoral time, could be filled in with prescriptive rules enforced by the ECI. Another instance of this assertion by the ECI was the occasion of the Garhwal parliamentary constituency by-election in 1981. Discussing the Garhwal by-election in a chapter provocatively titled 'Beginnings of Defiance', former CEC Lyngdoh shows how the constituency, which had returned Hemwati Nandan Bahuguna to the Lok Sabha in the general elections of 1979 on an Indian National Congress (I) ticket, became a bone of contention between Bahuguna and Indira Gandhi when Bahuguna resigned from the party and his seat in the Lok Sabha following 'an ego problem' with Indira Gandhi. While Bahuguna was determined to win the seat again on his own, pressure was put on the then CEC S.L. Shakdher not to hold the by-election. Despite the pressure, the by-election was held in May–June 1981 (Lyngdoh 2004: 59–60). Interviews with CEC Shakdher during this intervening period, documented by the ECI, suggest a mounting rift between the ruling party and the ECI. In the ECI's compilation of press reports, the CEC's interviews show Shakdher addressing a series of questions pertaining to whether the ECI was assuming 'enormous powers' and more specifically to allegations being made on the floor of the Lok Sabha by the then law minister P. Shiv Shankar that the ECI was 'holding up' elections in the Garhwal constituency. The CEC appears strident in his responses, stating his preparedness to hold all elections 'right away' in any state, 'if the State Governments and the Centre do not put up excuses for further postponement and make all arrangements for the conduct of the poll'. On the specific question of the Garhwal elections, the CEC was clear that the presence of 'excess of policemen' on the orders of the government made conditions in the constituency non-conducive for holding 'fair and free elections'.[30]

In the debate in the Lok Sabha, however, the law minister asserted that the practice of inducting outside forces (as in Garhwal) had always existed, and the ECI did not 'come into the picture' in this

---

[30] *Sunday*, 21–7 February 1982, in Election Commission of India (1982: 88–90).

matter. The powers of the ECI under Article 324 of the Constitution, he pointed out, were 'confined to the electoral system', and did not give it jurisdiction over the maintenance of law and order during elections. He noted that the records of the home ministry did not show that the permission of or consultation with the ECI in this matter was ever required. The CEC responded that the ECI files showed evidence to the contrary:

> In the Election Commission files however, there are some eloquent 'crash' telegrams sent by the Union Home Secretary to the Chief Secretary of the Karnataka Government at the time of the Chikmaglur bye-election in mid-1978, regarding the deployment of a CRP battalion in the constituency 'as desired by the Chief Election Commissioner', copies of all communication between the State and the Centre in this respect were duly passed on to the CEC. If the Commission has no jurisdiction in respect of maintenance of law and order, I would say 'Wind up the Election Commission'. For, without such jurisdiction, it cannot do a thing.[31]

The assertion by the ECI of its constitutionally mandated special power of 'superintendence' of elections led to further contests through the 1980s and 1990s. The poster in Figure 3.1, possibly from the early 1990s, is a re-iteration and elaboration of the assertion that the ECI showed after the Emergency.

The 1990s and Consolidation of Special Election Time

In the 1990s, the contest between the ECI and the political executive continued to play out more aggressively around the two questions that had become the focus of disputes in the earlier phase, namely, the contours of the powers of the ECI under Article 324 of the Constitution, and arising out of this, the question of the juridical boundaries of 'election time'. More precisely, the contest had to do with the manner in which the constitutional powers of the ECI had both deepened and widened in such a way that its constitutional

---

[31] *The Statesman*, 8 January 1982, in Election Commission of India (1982: 101–2).

Figure 3.1   'Vote without Fear': Poster on Elections Issued by the Ministry of Information and Broadcasting (Possibly 1990–1)
Source: Courtesy Professor Wendy Singer's personal collection.

powers of superintendence and control of elections became more pronounced vis-à-vis competing claims of the political executive to limit it through its powers to legislate. Combined with this was the new assertiveness with which the ECI sought extraordinary powers during election time, drawing them from the 'reservoir' of powers which Article 324 vested in it. A significant aspect of this period was the marking out of election time as 'special time', to use Gilmartin's category, whereby the parameters of the 'conduct' of election were affirmed in a way that the bureaucratic apparatus both substituted and deferred the 'political' to enable the unharnessed and un-coerced exercise of the sovereign act of voting by the citizen-voter. The MCC played a pivotal role in this unharnessing, by plugging the legal vacuum produced by electoral law. In his study of the development of the MCC in the 1990s, David Gilmartin (2009: 252–3) points out that its extraordinary prominence in the early 1990s may be attributed to the appointment of T.N. Seshan as CEC, who sought to enforce the MCC 'in unprecedented ways' and brought it 'into public consciousness as a symbol of the underlying notion that elections required a different morality from everyday politics'.

The period during which T.N. Seshan was the CEC of India (12 December 1990 to 11 December 1996) was one of great volatility as far as political leadership was concerned. Seshan saw five prime ministers during his tenure—V.P. Singh, Chandrashekhar, P.V. Narasimha Rao, A.B. Vajpayee, and H.V. Deve Gowda. In the period immediately preceding Seshan's regime as CEC, significant changes had been introduced in the electoral law, including the reduction of the minimum age of voting to 18 years, the insertion of the 10th schedule of the Constitution to check defection,[32] the use of EVMs,[33] the provision

---

[32] The 10th Schedule of the Constitution added by the Constitution (Amendment) Act, 1985, was a subject of criticism both on political and legal grounds since its enactment. In *Kihota Hollohan v. Zachilhu* (AIR 1993 SC 412), the Supreme Court gave its final verdict on the validity of the 10th Schedule. For more details on the majority decision upholding the amendment and other legal aspects of the Amendment (see K.C. Sunny 2000: 226–9).

[33] The EVMs were introduced in 1982. However, in 1984, in *A.C. Jose v. Shivan Pillai*, the Supreme Court ruled that the action of the ECI in introducing EVMs was without jurisdiction, since the RPA did not provide for the use of a device other than ballots for voting. *A.C. Jose v. Shivan Pillai*, AIR 1984 SC 921.

of registration of political parties, the more stringent punishment for booth capturing, which was declared a 'corrupt practice' if practiced by a candidate or agent, and the decision to allow companies to make contributions to political parties. It was also in this period that the Goswami Committee on Electoral Reforms under the then law minister Dinesh Goswami made significant recommendations for reforms in May 1990.[34] Among these was the suggestion that the weakness of the MCC could be overcome by giving it statutory backing and making it enforceable through law.

The Goswami Committee suggested bringing certain areas within the ambit of electoral law and making their violation an electoral offense.[35] The government subsequently proposed an amendment to the RPA, 1951, to make the violation of some of the provisions of the MCC punishable as illegal practices. This Bill was, however, not passed, and lapsed on the dissolution of the Lok Sabha in 1996. The Goswami Committee's recommendation that the MCC be turned into law to remove weaknesses in its implementation did not come

---

In 1989, the RPA, 1951, was amended to include the EVMs as a mode of voting. All voting for the general elections from 2004, and the state assembly elections and by-elections from 2003, have been carried out using EVMs (see K.C. Sunny 2000: 225 and Alistair McMillan 2010: 104).

[34] Some of these recommendations were: (a) post offices should be the focal points for preparing electoral rolls, (b) a time-bound programme for issuing identity cards to voters, (c) prohibiting a person from contesting election from more than one constituency, (d) making certain provisions of the MCC statutory, (e) the committee did not support the Tarkunde Committee's recommendation regarding state governments functioning as caretaker governments during election periods, (f) banning donations by companies, (g) limiting financial assistance from the State to candidates of recognised parties, (h) amending the 10th schedule to the Constitution to provide that disqualification for defection should be decided by the governor or the president and not by the speaker of the Lower House or the chairman of the Upper House.

[35] See the Goswami committee report. Ministry of Law and Justice, *Report of the Committee on Electoral Reforms*. New Delhi: Government of India, May 1990, Chapter V, para 6. Available at https://adrindia.org/sites/default/files/Dinesh%20Goswami%20Report%20on%20Electoral%20Reforms.pdf; accessed on 8 February 2019.

to fruition. The position of the ECI itself has been ambivalent on the issue. In the mid-1980s, the ECI had suggested that provisions of the MCC, particularly Part VII dealing with the ruling parties, should be provided statutory backing by bringing a law on the matter (Devi and Mendiratta 2006: 639). In September 1982, the need to incorporate specific items in the MCC as corrupt practices in the RPA, 1951, was among the electoral reforms suggested by the ECI to the government.[36] In the annual report of 1983, for example, CEC R.K. Trivedi reported a consensus on the matter among political parties whose representatives had been called to meet and discuss the MCC: 'that the Commission should examine the legal and other implications of the suggestion that the Government should so amend the law that a breach of the Model Code of Conduct is treated as an electoral offence. The law should also authorise the Election Commission to issue suitable directions. Failure to comply with which should attract penal clauses'.[37]

By the 1990s, however, the ECI changed its position and withdrew its earlier recommendation of giving statutory backing to the MCC. Based on its experience of conducting the general elections during

[36] These were: (a) Ministers shall not combine their official tours with the electioneering work and shall not also [sic] make use of official machinery or personnel during the electioneering work; (b) Government vehicles, machinery, and personnel shall not be used for furtherance of the interest of the party in power; (c) Public places shall not be monopolised by the ruling party for holding election meetings. Other parties and candidates shall be allowed the use of such places on the same terms and conditions on which they are used by the party in power. As reported in Election Commission of India, *Second Annual Report of the Election Commission, 1984*, p. 42.

[37] Election Commission of India, *First Annual Report, 1983*, p. 88. Following its meeting with the political parties on 3 December 1983, the ECI had recommended to the government that specific provisions pertaining to the prevention of the use of temples, churches, or other places of worship as a forum for election purposes should be made in Chapter III of the RPA, 1951, and to prescribe suitable penalty for default. It further recommended the insertion of a new Section 133A prescribing suitable penalty to those persons who commit offences specified in Section 123(7) of the RPA, 1951, including those officials who abet in commission of such offences or who allow the use of official machinery for such purposes (Election Commission of India, *Second Annual Report of the Election Commission, 1984*, pp. 42–3).

the 1990s, the ECI concluded that bringing the MCC on the statute book would be a self-defeating measure. In order to be relevant in the context of an election, any violation of the MCC must have 'a quick reaction and remedial measure', the ECI argued. A quick response would not be possible if the matter had to be first taken to the courts, and then become the subject of examination in a regular judicial process, leading after a prolonged process to a judicial pronouncement.[38] More generally, the reluctance of the ECI to push forcefully for a legislated MCC has perhaps emerged from its understanding of its own powers and their consolidation through the 1990s and beyond. The implications of a statutory model code would be that while the MCC would have the force of law, the ECI would draw its authority to enforce it not from the residuary powers that devolve on it from Article 324, but from a 'preexisting parliamentary statute'.[39] In other words, a statutory MCC would open up the space of executive action on which the ECI hitherto had exclusive control, to be occupied by a statute, whose form and content would be controlled by Parliament, with the ECI's powers limited to its implementation.

Moreover, despite the non-statutory status of the MCC, the judiciary has more often than not been the ECI's ally in this quest. Through a series of cases, the Supreme Court has held that when the enacted laws are silent or make insufficient provisions to deal with a given situation in the conduct of elections, the ECI has the residuary powers under the Constitution to act in an appropriate manner. On the ECI's powers under Article 324, the Supreme Court held that the holding of elections 'is the exclusive domain of the Election Commission under Article 324 of the Constitution'. Article 324(1), construed liberally, may be seen as having residual powers relating to the electoral process, in areas unoccupied by legislation, empowering the ECI to issue all directions necessary for the purpose of conducting a smooth, free, and fair election.

James Lyngdoh's discussion of the MCC shows a preference in the ECI for the powers of 'superintendence and control' that accrue to it

---

[38] See the views of the ECI as conveyed to the government in July 1998 and December 1999 and circulated to all political parties (Devi and Mendiratta 2006: 639–40).

[39] See D.D. Basu (1999: 1061–2) for judgments pertaining to the limits on the powers of the ECI.

from Article 324 of the Constitution rather than powers drawn from a parliamentary statute, and a quick preventive action rather than deferral to a prolonged judicial procedure. Addressing the question, 'Would it have helped the commission if the Code of Conduct had been made into law?', Lyngdoh avers that the initial response within the ECI was yes, but it was soon realised that conducting elections, though occasionally involving quasi-judicial functions, was intrinsically an executive task. Moreover, he argued, looking at it from the perspective of the ECI and the special nature of the task of conducting elections, there appeared 'no point in prosecuting a person after he had committed the offence'. For a fair and free electoral campaign and outcome, what was required was 'a mechanism to take preventive action or to correct the course of events, insulating it from aberrating factors'. Unless the RPA, 1950, was restructured 'to include the anticipatory and corrective aspects', the MCC in its existing form was seen by him as reasonably effective for this purpose. Moreover, even if the MCC was inducted into the law, with anticipatory and corrective powers, the ECI's experience with law had been that it was 'remarkably negligent of political parties and their doings', and 'their increasingly abominable conduct' (Lyngdoh 2004: 79–80).

In the context of assembly elections in five states including Uttar Pradesh and Gujarat in February–March 2012, Pranab Mukherjee, then finance minister in the Congress-led UPA government, stated that the MCC was the biggest excuse to stall development projects. With this statement and the law minister's concurrence to it, the debate over the powers of the ECI and the need for electoral reform came up forcefully in the public domain. The law minister suggested that the MCC be made into a law. While denying that this was a move to curtail the powers of the CEC, the government maintained that it would consider this as a proposal for electoral reforms if the political parties wanted it. In keeping with its position in the past, the ECI opposed the move. Arguing that the present system worked effectively as 'quick action', 'like fire brigade dousing fire', CEC Quraishi cautioned: 'If such matters go to court, it will take six to seven years'. The CEC maintained that the so-called 'statutory power' was being given to the ECI 'forcibly' when it did not want it.[40]

[40] 'GoM Skips Discussion on Statutory Backing to Model Code of Conduct,' *Press Trust of India*, 22 February 2012.

The Compliance Conundrum

The question which then arises is this: How can, in the absence of legal backing, the ECI ensure that the MCC is observed by political parties? While the ECI has attempted to elicit compliance by showing displeasure over the conduct of politicians and handing out public censure, in some cases of serious breach of the MCC, it has also cancelled elections.[41] Cancellation of elections has been one of the more drastic responses by the ECI to ensure compliance, but it has resorted to a combination of measures, not all of them as extreme. The ECI has important disciplinary powers to assure that parties adhere to the MCC. Among them is Clause 16(A) in the Election Symbols (Reservation and Allotment) Order that gives the ECI the power to suspend or withdraw recognition of a political party 'for failing to observe the Model Code of Conduct or follow the lawful directions or instructions of the Commission'. In certain cases, action against specific candidates has been taken, through a public 'show of displeasure' and 'condemnation' by the ECI. In the 2007 election to the Gujarat state legislative assembly, the war of words between Narendra Modi, then chief minister of the state, and Sonia Gandhi, then president of the Indian National Congress, prompted the ECI to issue letters showing its displeasure to both the leaders. The condemnation of Sonia Gandhi by the ECI was with reference to her so-called 'maut ka saudagar' (merchant of death) speech in December 2007, referring to the then Chief Minister Narendra Modi's alleged role in the communal violence against Muslims in the state in February 2002. Narendra Modi received a similar letter of displeasure from the ECI for his retaliatory speech where he declared that Sonia Gandhi had insulted Gujarati asmita (pride). Asking that the MCC be strictly adhered to, the ECI took exception to both the speeches for aggravating communal differences and violating the spirit of the MCC, which was intended to maintain and uphold democratic traditions of 'issue-based' election campaigns. The letters sent by the ECI to both political

[41] The Kalka assembly by-election in Haryana in 1993, for example, was cancelled when the chief minister, whose son was one of the contestants, announced new development schemes for the area after the election had been announced. A similar cancellation of the Ranipet assembly by-election occurred in Tamil Nadu when the chief minister announced new schemes.

leaders were carried verbatim by some newspapers, and reported widely in the media.[42]

In the 2012 state assembly election, the ECI took exception to the poll promises being made by leader of the Congress party and then Union Law Minister Salman Khurshid,[43] who later suggested that the MCC should be reviewed. While campaigning for his wife, a Congress candidate from Uttar Pradesh, Khurshid promised that the Congress party would enhance the sub-quota for minorities to 9 per cent, out of the 27 per cent Other Backward Classes (OBC) reservation. The BJP complained to the ECI, which held that Khurshid had indeed violated the MCC. Expressing 'deep anguish and disappointment' over the violation, the ECI reminded him of the 'added responsibility' he had as the minister of law, 'of ensuring that the model code of conduct is observed in letter and spirit' and hoped that he would not repeat his actions.[44] Subsequently, however, Salman Khurshid denied that he had violated the MCC. In an unprecedented move, the ECI wrote to the president of India, Pratibha Patil, asking her to intervene in the poll process, expressing concern that 'Khurshid's action could vitiate free and fair poll in Uttar Pradesh'. The president forwarded the letter to the Prime Minister's Office for 'appropriate action'. The outcome of the episode was not only that the law minister was more careful in his promises; more generally, the ECI's censure and letter to the president embarrassed the government and the Congress.[45] The 2012 assembly elections also saw the MCC being implemented to rein in powerful political leaders like the chief minister of Uttar Pradesh belonging to the Bahujan Samaj Party (BSP). The ECI issued directives to cover up statues of elephants, hundreds of which were constructed by Chief Minister Mayawati during her tenure, in large

[42] See 'EC Displeasure over Modi, Sonia Speeches,' *The Hindu*, Delhi, 23 December 2007, p. 1; 'Ensure Adherence to Model Code in Future,' *The Hindu*, Delhi, 23 December 2007, p. 10.

[43] 'Salman Khurshid Defiant, Violating Model Code of Conduct: EC to President,' *Press Trust of India*, 12 February 2012.

[44] 'EC Censures Salman Khurshid for His Remarks on Sub-quota on Minorities,' *Press Trust of India*, New Delhi, 9 February 2012.

[45] 'Salman Khurshid Defiant, Violating Model Code of Conduct: EC to President,' *Press Trust of India*, 12 February 2012.

parks in Lucknow and Noida. The reason given by the ECI for draping the statues of elephants was that the elephant was also the election symbol of the BSP.

In some other cases, the ECI urged the concerned political parties to take action against erring candidates and party members. The latter has, however, often proved ineffective as in the much-debated Varun Gandhi case immediately before the 2009 general election. In March 2009, Feroze Varun Gandhi, a member of the BJP and its 'likely candidate' in the Lok Sabha election from Pilibhit parliamentary constituency in Uttar Pradesh, delivered communally charged and provocative speeches at two public meetings in the constituency. The DEO of Pilibhit brought this to the notice of the ECI and submitted a copy of the police superintendent's report of the meeting along with a CD containing the recording of the meeting.[46] The contents of the speech were reported widely in the print media, and TV channels repeatedly aired the video recordings. The ECI took suo motu cognisance of the incidents, issuing notices to Varun Gandhi and the central and state units of the BJP, asking them to furnish their responses immediately. It also directed the CEO of Uttar Pradesh to file a criminal case against Varun Gandhi under the provisions of Section 153A of the IPC (promoting enmity between different groups on grounds of religion), Section 295A of IPC (deliberate and malicious acts intended to outrage religious feelings of any class of Indian citizens by insulting their religion or religious beliefs), Section 505(2) of IPC (statements creating or promoting enmity, hatred, or ill will between classes), and Section 125 of the RPA 1951 (promoting enmity between classes in connection with elections).

It should be noted that the notification for election was issued on 2 March 2009, which would mean that the MCC was already operational. Pilibhit, however, was to go to the polls only in the third and final phase of the election on 13 May 2009. Moreover, Varun Gandhi, though a likely BJP candidate, did not become one until he filed his

---

[46] 'Notice to Shri Feroze Varun Gandhi and Bharatiya Janata Party for violation of the Model Code of Conduct on his offensive speeches on 7th and 8th March, 2009 in Pilibhit District, Uttar Pradesh,' signed by the CEC N. Gopalswami and the ECs S.Y. Quraishi and Navin B. Chawla, No. 464/UP-HP/2009, dated 22 March 2009.

nomination papers on 22 April 2009, more than a month after he delivered the 'hate speeches'. While the ECI accused Varun Gandhi of breaching the MCC, it could only *advise* the BJP not to field him as a candidate. Citing several Supreme Court cases to support its position, the ECI's notice to the BJP stated: 'In the considered opinion of the commission, the respondent (Varun Gandhi) does not deserve to be a candidate at the present general elections'. Yet, the notice also admitted that 'limitations under the law' did not allow the ECI to impose such disqualification on Varun Gandhi and debar him from contesting elections unless he was convicted by a competent court of law in an appropriate legal proceeding. Under the circumstances, the ECI could only 'strongly condemn' and 'censure' Varun Gandhi.[47] However, for the breach of specific provisions of the MCC, which were also punishable offenses under the IPC, the ECI could direct the district administration to file relevant cases. These cases were not, however, to be registered as electoral offenses or corrupt offenses pertaining to elections. Thus, even though an election petition cannot be filed until the electoral process is over, as seen in the Varun Gandhi case, the district administration can frame criminal charges during election time. One must remember that the district magistrate/collector, who is the head of the district administration, is the DEO during elections, responsible for the orderly conduct of polls in his/her district, and also, therefore, under the 'control' and 'superintendence' of the CEO of the state, and through the CEO, the CEC and the ECI. In its reply to the ECI's notice, the BJP expressed its commitment to the MCC and dissociated itself completely from the contents of Varun Gandhi's speech, stating that they did not represent the views of the party. While the BJP appeared to be tacitly admitting the complaint against Varun Gandhi, Gandhi himself cast doubts on the veracity of the evidence. He questioned the 'private and political motives' of

---

[47] 'Notice to Shri Feroze Varun Gandhi and Bharatiya Janata Party for violation of the Model Code of Conduct on his offensive speeches on 7th and 8th March, 2009 in Pilibhit District, Uttar Pradesh,' signed by the CEC N. Gopalswami and the ECs S.Y. Quraishi and Navin B. Chawla, No. 464/UP-HP/2009, dated 22 March 2009 (See also 'A Diff Perspective to UP Elections,' *BBC Hindi Election News*. Available at http://www.bbc.co.uk/Hindi_News; accessed on 10 February 2012).

those who 'photographed the event' and put together what he called a 'private unofficial tape', submitting him to a 'trial by the media to create an atmosphere of hostility against him'.[48]

The ECI on its part remained 'fully convinced and satisfied that the CD [had] not been tampered with, doctored or morphed' and placed the onus on Varun Gandhi 'to prove his allegation that the CD is not genuine or authentic'. It then set out to affirm its own authority in the matter by referring to a higher order morality of the Constitution and the collective conscience of the nation, which made it imperative 'to take note of [and] bring such violators of the Model Code of Conduct and electoral laws to book'. The ECI not only invoked constitutional morality and public reason, it also sought the backing of judicial authority of the courts, which had time and again affirmed 'secularism' as a higher order principle constitutive of constitutional and public morality.[49] In the opinion of the ECI, Varun Gandhi made

[48] See 'Notice to Shri Feroze Varun Gandhi and Bharatiya Janata Party for Violation of the Model Code of Conduct on His Offensive Speeches on 7th and 8th March, 2009 in Pilibhit District, Uttar Pradesh,' Election Commission Order No. 464/ UP-HP/2009, dated 22 March 2009. Available at http://www.eci.gov.in; accessed on 11 July 2011.

[49] The ECI cited in particular two cases, in which the Supreme Court upheld principles of secularism as sacrosanct in the Constitution and advised against whipping up communal hatred for electoral gains. In *Ziauddin Burhanuddin Bukhari* v. *Brijmohan Ramdass Mehra* (AIR 1975 SC1788), for example, the Court observed:

> Our Constitution makers certainly intended to set up a Secular Democratic Republic the binding spirit of which is summed up by the objectives set forth in the preamble to the Constitution. No democratic political and social order, in which the conditions of freedom and their progressive expansion for all make some regulation of all activities imperative, could endure without an agreement on the basic essentials which could unite and hold citizens together despite all the differences of religion, race, caste, community, culture, creed, and language. Our political history made it particularly necessary that these differences, which can generate powerful emotions, depriving people of their powers of rational thought and action, should not be permitted to be exploited lest the imperative conditions for the preservation of democratic freedoms are disturbed. Due respect for the religious

the virulent speeches in an area that was 'well known' for being 'highly communally sensitive', in 'utter disregard of the Supreme Court's advice regarding desirable behaviour during election', and in 'blatant violation of the provisions and spirit of the Model Code of Conduct and the law on the subject'. It also held that the speeches were 'highly dangerous, threatening the very survival of democracy and the communal harmony—the basic tenets enshrined in the Constitution of India', which deserved to be condemned in the 'severest terms'.[50] In the opinion of the ECI, therefore, Varun Gandhi did not deserve to be a candidate at the 2009 general elections. As events unfolded, however, the ECI became only one among several actors in the controversy around Varun Gandhi's speech and candidature. The then Mayawati government in Uttar Pradesh slapped the National Security Act (NSA) against Varun Gandhi and sent him to prison on 28 March 2009. Released on parole in April 2009, Varun Gandhi filed his nomination papers and became the new poster boy for the BJP in the state. The upshot of this episode was that the ECI could not wield any authority over restricting the BJP from choosing Varun Gandhi as its candidate from Pilibhit. Varun Gandhi campaigned and won the Pilibhit seat with a huge margin.[51]

---

beliefs and practices, race, creed, culture, and language of other citizens is one of the basic postulates of our democratic system. Under the guise of protecting your own religion, culture, or creed you cannot embark on personal attacks on those of others or whip up low herd instincts and animosities or irrational fears between groups to secure electoral victories.

In *Abdul Hussain Mir* v. *Shamsul Huda* (AIR 1975 SC 1612), the Supreme Court noted that 'religious appeal or communal appetite is stronger in a bigoted and backward population'.

[50] The ECI reiterated its opinion dated 15 October 1997 and 22 December 1998 in the cases of Dr Ramesh Yeshwant Prabhoo and Shri Bal Thackeray, respectively, and held that the speeches were 'also highly dangerous, threatening the very survival of democracy and the communal harmony—the basic tenets enshrined in the Constitution of India—and deserve to be condemned in the severest terms'.

[51] As far as charges under the NSA were concerned, on 8 May 2009, the Allahabad High Court cited insufficient grounds for pressing a case against

In an earlier case—*Dr. Ramesh Yeshwant Prabhoo* v. *Prabhakar Kashinath Kunte and Others*[52]—involving election speeches by Bal Thackeray and Ramesh Yashwant Prabhoo, the Supreme Court had held that the speeches made by Bal Thackeray appealing to voters on the ground of religious affinity with derogatory references to the members of the Muslim community amounted to 'promoting or attempting to promote feelings of enmity and hatred between different classes of citizens on the ground of religion and were of very serious and grave nature'. Both Ramesh Yeshwant Prabhoo and Bal Thackeray were disqualified for a period of six years, which is the maximum period for which they could be disqualified by the president under Section 8A of the RPA, 1951 (disqualification on the ground of corrupt practices).

While disqualification has not ordinarily been the outcome in such cases, the final decision-making powers have rested with the judiciary, in particular, the Supreme Court. Numerous cases are booked against violators of the MCC under specific sections of the IPC, the RPA, and the various state laws against defacement of public property, and convictions are handed out both during and beyond the time the MCC stays effective. In the state legislative assembly elections held in Tamil

---

Varun Gandhi under the Act. The state government appealed to the Supreme Court against the Allahabad High Court's order. On 14 May, the Supreme Court sustained the high court's order and asked the state government to withdraw charges under the NSA against Varun Gandhi. After the election process was over, the Congress candidate who was defeated by Varun Gandhi in the election filed an election petition in the Allahabad High Court. The petition asked for Varun Gandhi's disqualification as an MP for having made 'speeches during the election campaign in the name of religion [and] creating animosity and hatred between Hindu and Muslim community'. The case against Varun Gandhi for delivering the 'hate speech' continues in the court of the chief judicial magistrate of Pilibhit. The last information available on the case is a news item of July 2016 informing the reader that Varun Gandhi had been issued a notice by the court through the Lok Sabha speaker for non-appearance and the next hearing was scheduled for September the same year ('Hate Speech Case: Court Issues Notice to BJP MP Varun Gandhi,' *The Indian Express*, 8 July 2016).

[52] *Dr. Ramesh Yeshwant Prabhoo* v. *Prabhakar Kashinath Kunte and Others* (1996) 1 SCC 130.

Nadu in April 2011, for example, cases for violation of the MCC were registered under the IPC, RPA, and the Tamil Nadu Open Spaces (Prevention of Disfigurement) Act against functionaries of various political parties. Cases were registered for violations of different kinds: installation of flex boards and digital banners without permission, campaigning in convoys of vehicles without permission and blocking traffic, seeking votes in front of schools, installation of party flags and festoons on public property, taking out processions without permission, illegal distribution of money, and gifts to voters, and so on. Up to May 2011, a total of 633 cases were pending in the Tiruchi range, while 144 cases had resulted in conviction.[53] In Chennai city, police registered nearly 300 cases of violations of the MCC, which came into operation in the second week of February with the announcement of the election dates by the ECI. These ranged from distribution of money to gang clashes to defacing of walls. The Chennai suburban police registered 741 complaints and chargesheeted 701 cases for similar violations.[54]

A BJP MP Jagdambika Pal, who was charged with violation of the MCC on the ground of using more than the permissible number of vehicles in an election rally in Bansi in the 2014 general election, was given a one-month jail sentence and a fine of Rs 100 by the chief judicial magistrate in December 2017.[55] In the Uttar Pradesh Assembly election in 2017, the All-India Majlis-e-Ittehad-ul Muslimeen (AIMIM) chief Asaduddin Owaisi was booked for violation of the MCC under Section 171 of IPC (illegal payment in connection with an election). According to the police, the posters of AIMIM were pasted on the walls of public property, religious places, and private shops, which prompted the police to file a complaint against

[53] 'Over 140 Election Violation Cases End Up in Conviction,' *The Hindu*, 9 May 2011. Available at http://www.thehindu.com/2011/05/09/stories/2011050962430500htm; accessed on 20 July 2011.

[54] 'Over 1000 Election-Related Police Cases Filed in City and Suburbs,' *The Times of India*, 7 May 2011. Available at http://articles.timesofindia.india-times.com/2011-05-07/chennai/29520109; accessed on 20 July 2011.

[55] Pal was, however, granted bail by the Court immediately afterwards ('Jagdambika Pal Gets Jail Term for Poll Code Violation,' *The Hindu*, 24 December 2014).

him.[56] Earlier in 2014, the ECI registered a case against BJP's prime ministerial candidate Narendra Modi, because a sticker with his image was found posted on a pole at Tabha Ghat village. The sticker did not have the names of the printer and the publisher printed on it, which is mandatory according to the MCC guidelines issued by the ECI.[57] In the same election, an FIR was lodged against Narendra Modi for trying to 'influence' voters by holding a news conference near the polling booth, and displaying the BJP's election symbol, 'the lotus', as he emerged from the booth after casting his vote.[58] In December 2017, in the course of the Gujarat assembly election campaign, the ECI issued a show cause notice to Rahul Gandhi for giving a TV interview a day before the polls in the state. The ECI also issued an order to the election officers in Gujarat to file an FIR against the regional TV channels that aired Gandhi's interview and also restrain other channels from showing it till the poll process was over.[59]

Elaborating on the mode of implementing the MCC, a well-known expert on election law and a long-time consultant with the ECI, S.K. Mendiratta, emphasised the 'moral force' behind the MCC. Indeed, he argued, the approach of the ECI, even when it served a notice to a candidate was always 'cautious'. The intention of the ECI was to only 'embarrass', and not to have an impact on the campaign itself. An example of such an approach, he pointed out, was the 'advice' given by the ECI to the PDP president and then chief minister of Jammu and Kashmir, Mehbooba Mufti, not to campaign in the

[56] 'UP Assembly Elections 2017: AIMM Chief Asaduddin Owaisi Booked,' 17 January 2017. Available at http://zeenews.india.com/uttar-pradesh/up-assembly-elections-2017-aimim-chief-asaduddin-owaisi-booked_1967845. html; accessed on 20 December 2017.

[57] Nairita Das. 2014. 'Election 2014: Now, Narendra Modi Booked for Violation of Model Code,' 8 April. Available at https://www.oneindia.com/india/election-2014-now-narendra-modi-booked-for-violation-of-model-code-lse-1426666.html; accessed on 24 December 2017.

[58] '"Selfie" Modi Blooms Outside Booth, Slapped with FIR,' *The Telegraph*, 1 May 2014.

[59] 'Election Commissions Sends Notice to Rahul Gandhi for "Violating the Code of Conduct",' *The Economic Times*, 14 December 2017.

Anantnag by-election with the flag of the state on her car.[60] There may, however, be another way through which the ECI can take action under the MCC. If, for example, there was a case where a candidate was found distributing money, the action against the candidate may be two-pronged: the candidate would be served a notice for having violated the MCC—this could serve as a caution, but could also be in the nature of a public reprimand, which would be reported and made public by the ECI by uploading it on its website. Simultaneously, the district administration would be instructed to file a complaint against the candidate for having committed an electoral offence under Section 171 of IPC. In one such case, of which Mendiratta does not give details of names and the like, where such a charge was made against a candidate who belonged to the ruling party in the state, the court case was deliberately delayed and subsequently withdrawn at the magisterial level at the behest of the state government. The ECI, however, being the complainant in the case, pursued it with all seriousness and objected to its withdrawal. The state government appealed in the district court that the matter was between the state government and the candidate, in which the ECI had no role to play. The ECI persisted and appealed to the high court, which decided that the ECI had a locus standi in the case. The case continued to be heard for six years. Once the ECI files a complaint under the Code of Criminal Procedure (CrPC) or IPC, it follows the course of a regular trial in which the ECI is just a complainant and not the decision-making body. On the other hand, if a political party approaches the court, the ECI is not involved in the trial that follows, unless the ECI is made party to the case.[61]

The CEO of Bihar, Ajay Naik, concurred that the MCC is a set of guidelines to 'control the party in power', which may have the propensity to get rid of cases which may be brought up against them.[62] It was the duty of the ECI, according to him, to ensure that

---

[60] Conversation with Mr S.K. Mendiratta in his chamber at the ECI, New Delhi, on 23 June 2016.

[61] Conversation with Mr S.K. Mendiratta in his chamber at the ECI, New Delhi, on 23 June 2016.

[62] Conversation with Ajay Naik, CEO, Bihar, in his office in Patna on 28 June 2016.

no case related to election was withdrawn. The ECI and the CEO of states follow up cases through to the filing of chargesheets and the disposal of cases, even when they do not go into the 'nitty gritties', which is for the police to pursue. Indeed, all cases under the MCC, booked under various provisions of the law, have to be concluded before the next election—'brought to a zero'—when the status of all election-related cases are taken stock of in preparation for the next election. District-level data of chargesheets filed and disposal of cases is maintained. Thus, the MCC, is not just a code based on voluntary adherence, but is also enforced through penalties under IPC for violations of any law of the country. All laws are to be strictly followed, but for the ECI, the objectives are different from those which govern the administrator in ordinary times. Ordinary government may not have the same priorities, for example, for the ECI, defacement of property is an electoral offence to be followed strictly, but for the ordinary government, it may not be a matter of serious concern.

Naik emphasised his own autonomy as an officer responsible for the conduct of elections in the state, as an important aspect of electoral integrity. The appointment of CEOs is done by the ECI, which asks for a panel from the state government. But the ECI may include more names on its own to broaden its choice of appropriate and efficient officers. The CEO holds the rank of a principal secretary, but unlike other principal secretaries, the Annual Confidential Report (ACR) of the CEO is not written by the chief secretary, since in his case, the chief secretary is not the controlling officer. The CEO writes the ACR of all other officers in his office, and also receives reports: 'I am the principal secretary of the state, but not controlled by it. Chief Secretary is not my controlling officer—I write reports and also receive them [for my subordinate officers]. I am the Principal Secretary of the State but not controlled by them [that is, the state government]'.

CEO Naik stressed that the electoral governance for a particular state is specific to the state, and the tools employed by electoral officers are also relevant to the needs of the state. Other things will not be relevant: 'Bihar has specific needs: for example, the '*Pakistan bhaga do speech*' in the election campaign [in Bihar] was disallowed. But for Bihar this was not a prime concern, other things are more relevant.

For Bihar it is law and order which is more important—thus [action under] the Arms Act and ammunition surrender is immensely more important'. The CEO was referring to the statements made by Giriraj Singh, a BJP candidate from Navada constituency in Bihar, while addressing rallies in Deogarh and Bokaro in the Lok Sabha elections in April 2014. In his speeches, Singh said that those who opposed the BJP's prime ministerial candidate Narendra Modi should leave the country and go to Pakistan. The ECI subsequently disallowed Singh from campaigning. When Singh was making these statements in Bihar, the theatre of communal conflict, which Singh was evidently targeting, was Uttar Pradesh, which had experienced communal violence in Muzaffarnagar. Addressing rallies in Bijnor, Shamli, and Muzaffarnagar on 3 and 4 April, Amit Shah, the BJP's campaign in-charge of Uttar Pradesh, exhorted voters to reject parties with Muslim candidates and avenge the Muzaffarnagar riots by voting for BJP. Condemning Shah's 'revenge-speech' as appeasement on religious lines and an attempt at disharmony, the ECI imposed a ban on Shah's campaigning. The ban was lifted on 11 April 2014 after Shah promised to follow the MCC.[63]

Following the state assembly elections in 2015, the CEO's office in Patna, Bihar, released the comparative figures of MCC violation cases booked under different legal provisions. The figures released on 6 November 2015 compare the cases across three elections, the Bihar Legislative Assembly Election (2010), Lok Sabha Election (2014), and the Bihar Assembly General Election (2015). Tables 3.1 and 3.2 show not just the different laws that were invoked by the district administration across the state to ensure compliance with the MCC, but also what is construed as a 'violation' during election time.

While a comprehensive list of cases across states is difficult to find, our queries directed to specific state election commissions, under the provisions of the RTI Act of 2005, yielded limited results, not adequate to confirm a pattern. Interestingly, our queries sent to the state election commissions were directed by them to the police headquarters of the concerned states. Most of the responses therefore pertained to law and order aspects of elections,

---

[63] 'Speech Therapy: How Politicians Make Mockery of Model Code of Conduct,' *The Economic Times*, 27 April 2014.

Table 3.1 Comparative Report of MCC Cases

S.N.	Items	Bihar Legislative Assembly Election (2010)		Lok Sabha General Election (2014)		Bihar Legislative Assembly Election (2015)	
		No. of Cases	FIR Lodged	No. of Cases	FIR Lodged	No. of Cases	FIR Lodged
1	Defacement of Property Act (wall writing, posters, banners, and so on)	728	532	409	409	1,214	1,214
2	Misuse of vehicle (beacon light, flag)	579	188	344	129	321	309
3	Violation of Loudspeaker Act	54	54	78	75	58	58
4	Illegal, meeting/speech, and so on (without permission/speech promoting enmity, hatred, enmity, ill will)	113	97	69	63	85	82
5	Inducement/gratification to electors/cash, kind distribution	45	44	22	22	30	28
6	Others	490	270	141	134	380	376
	Total	2,009	1,185	1,063	832	2,088	2,067

Source: 'Press Release: Report of MCC Cases'. 2015. Nirvachan Vibhag, Mukhya Nirvachan Padadhikari, Bihar, 6 November 2015. Available at http://ceobihar.nic.in/press_release.html.

Table 3.2 Comparative Report of Law and Order

S.N.	Item		Bihar Assembly General Election (2010)	Lok Sabha General Election (2014)	Bihar Assembly General Election (2015)
1	No. of unlicensed arms/explosives seized				
	(a) Arms/weapons		791	743	1,040
	(b) Cartridges, explosives/bombs (quantity/ numbers)	Cartridges	17,222	2,636	3,853
		Explosives	18	14	1,025
		Bombs	73	200	177
2	No. of illicit arms manufacturing centres raided and seizures made		23	29	36
3	Licensed arms	Deposited	16,871	13,934	45,437
		Impounded		805	752
		Cancelled		515	11,416
4	No. of cases put up under preventive section of CrPc.				24,317
	(a) Of which no. of persons bound over under preventive section of CrPc			355,016	395,232
	(b) Of which no. of persons bound down under preventive section of CrPc		344,233	174,063	237,524

5	Execution of non-bailable warrants	(a) Executed	66,180	53,298	72,066
		(b) Pending	23,035	18,623	12,235
6	No. of incidents of violence related to poll campaign, political rivalry, and so on.				
	(a) No. of incidents		24	5	15
	(b) Total killed		6	5	0
	(c) Total injured		18	21	7
	(d) Damage to property (in lakhs)		9.52		
7	No. of incidents occurred under Atrocities Act, 1989 during election			2	0
8	Information regarding vulnerable hamlets				
	(a) No. of hamlets identified as vulnerable		17,672	9,586	24,791
	(b) No. of persons identified as probable source of trouble		71,632	46,078	81,432
	(c) Of which preventive detention taken against			24,833	76,716
9	No. of *nakas* operational			1,815	1,838

Source: 'Press Release: Comparative Report of Law and Order'. Nirvachan Vibhag, Mukhya Nirvachan Padadhikari, Bihar, 6 November 2015. Available at http://ceobihar.nic.in/press_release.html.

specifically to the number of persons booked under preventive detention. Tables 3.3–3.5 show the information on preventive detention cases received through RTI applications from the states of Uttarakhand, Goa, and Punjab.

The power of investigation, trial, and sentencing under the relevant sections of electoral offenses lies with the police and the judiciary, respectively. During the course of the special election time, however, it is only the ECI, through the MCC, which can hold political parties responsible for their actions by reprimanding, withholding candidature, or in some cases, cancelling elections. Thus, during election time, in the context of the suspension of legal and judicial authority of the courts, it is the ECI that supplements the absence of law through a strict implementation of the MCC. The question, when this special election time begins, becomes important, therefore, in terms of understanding the boundaries of the relative powers of the courts, the political parties and political class, and the ECI.

Table 3.3   Preventive Detention in Elections in Uttarakhand

State Assembly Election 2017	Number of Persons Booked
No. of cases booked under preventive detention section of CrPC	6,051
No. of persons bound over preventive detention section of the CrPC	44,439
No. of persons bound down preventive detention section of CrPC	38,858
No. of cases booked under any other preventive detention law	362
Lok Sabha Election 2014	
No. of cases booked under preventive detention section of CrPC	3,994
No. of persons bound over preventive detention section of the CrPC	32,767
No. of persons bound down preventive detention section of CrPC	28,459
No. of cases booked under any other preventive detention law	240

Source: Response dated 15 January 2018 from the Public Information Officer, Police Headquarters, Dehradun, Uttarakhand.

Table 3.4   Preventive Detention in Elections in Goa

State Assembly Election of 2017	Number of Cases
Mapusa Police Station	
Cases booked u/s 107 of CrPC	113
Cases booked u/s 110 CrPC	16
Total number of persons bound down (without arrest)	150
Pernem Police Station	
Cases booked u/s 107 of CrPC	93
Cases booked u/s 110 CrPC	04
Total number of persons bound down (without arrest)	97
Anjuna Police Station	
Cases booked u/s 107 of CrPC	128
Cases booked u/s 110 CrPC	08
Total number of persons bound down (without arrest)	153
Vasco Police Station	
Cases booked u/s 107 of CrPC	53
Cases booked u/s 110 CrPC	09
Verna Police Station	
Cases booked u/s 107 of CrPC	09
Cases booked u/s 110 CrPC	22
Mormugao Police Station	
Cases booked u/s 107 of CrPC	53
Cases booked u/s 110 CrPC	09
Porvorim Police Station	
Cases booked u/s 107 of CrPC	97 (without arrest)
Cases booked u/s 110 CrPC	Nil
Calangute Police Station	
Cases booked u/s 107 of CrPC	283 (without arrest)
Cases booked u/s 110 CrPC	03 (without arrest)
Saligao Police Station	
Cases booked u/s 107 of CrPC	115 (without arrest)
Cases booked u/s 110 CrPC	Nil (without arrest)
Margao Town Police Station	
Cases booked under preventive detention sections of CrPC	47
Total number of persons bound over	47

(Cont'd)

Table 3.4   (Cont'd)

State Assembly Election of 2017	Number of Cases
Maina Curtorim Police	
Cases booked under preventive detention sections of CrPC	19
Total number of persons bound over	19
Colva Police Station	
Cases booked under preventive detention sections of CrPC	17
Total number of persons bound over	17
Cuncolim Police Station	
Cases booked under preventive detention sections of CrPC	05
Total number of persons bound over	05
General Election of 2014	
Mapusa Police Station	
Cases booked u/s 107 of CrPC	20
Cases booked u/s 110 CrPC	17
Total number of persons bound down (without arrest)	63
Pernem Police Station	
Cases booked u/s 107 of CrPC	11
Cases booked u/s 110 CrPC	04
Total number of persons bound down (without arrest)	15
Anjuna Police Station	
Cases booked u/s 107 of CrPC	07
Cases booked u/s 110 CrPC	06
Total number of persons bound down (without arrest)	13
Vasco Police Station	
Cases booked u/s 107 of CrPC	46
Cases booked u/s 110 CrPC	08
Verna Police Station	
Cases booked u/s 107 of CrPC	03
Cases booked u/s 110 CrPC	24
Mormugao Police Station	
Cases booked u/s 107 of CrPC	11
Cases booked u/s 110 CrPC	01
Calangute Police Station	
Cases booked u/s 107 CrPC	28 (without arrest)

Margao Town Police Station	
Cases booked under preventive detention sections of CrPC	12
Total number of persons bound over	12
Cases booked under section 110 of CrPC	14; bound over 14
Maina Curtorim Police	
Cases booked under preventive detention sections of CrPC	12
Total number of persons bound over	12
Colva Police Station	
Cases booked under preventive detention sections of CrPC	20
Total number of persons bound over	20
Cuncolim Police Station	
Cases booked under preventive detention sections of CrPC	17
Total number of persons bound over	17

Source: Response dated 3 January 2018 from the PIO, office of the subdivisional police officer, Mapusa, Goa; response dated 29 December 2017 from the PIO, office of the subdivisional officer, Margao, Goa; reponse dated 28 December 2017 from the PIO, office of the subdivisional officer, Vasco-Da-Gama, Goa; response dated 23 December 2017 from the PIO, office of the sub-divisional police officer, Porvorim, Goa.

When Does the 'Special' Election Time Begin?

Delivering a lecture in Hyderabad, former CEC N. Gopalaswami lamented the loss of powers of the ECI to act on election-related offenses after the MCC ceased to operate.[64] The surveillance, under which the ECI puts candidates during 'election time', in particular those belonging to the ruling party, constitutes the most significant impact of the MCC, and the most contentious as well. In this context, the duration during which the MCC is effective becomes

---

[64] N. Gopalaswami pointed out that the cases were in the domain of the state governments after the polls and the ECI had no power to interfere with the administration once the code was inoperative ('Gopalaswami Opposes Telangana,' *The Hindu*, 25 June 2011).

Table 3.5   Preventive Detention Cases in Punjab

S.N.	Particular	No. of Cases	No. of Persons Bound Over	No. of Persons Bound Down
1	No. of cases under preventive detention sections of CrPC in state assembly elections 2017	3,576	2,827	1,991
2	No. of cases under preventive detention sections of CrPC during the general elections of 2014	4,374	6,581	2,691
3	No. of cases booked under preventive detention in state assembly elections 2017 under any other preventive detention law	217		
4	No. of cases booked under preventive detention in the general elections of 2014 under any other preventive detention law	213		

Source: Response dated 18 December 2017 from the office of the DGP, Chandigarh.

crucial. The question of the exact time of the commencement and termination of the MCC has generated acrimonious debates between the political parties and the ECI, compelling political parties to take recourse to courts of law to settle the issue. Political parties have thrown their weight behind reducing the duration of the MCC to the minimum possible extent, bringing into contention the meaning of the expression 'commencement' of elections, which is the date from which the MCC takes effect. The ECI has held to the position that 'commencement' indicates the day on which the ECI announces the election schedule, and the MCC, according to it, comes into operation on that day. Political parties across the spectrum, along with the central and state governments, in a rare show of consensus, construe 'commencement' to be the day on which a formal notification of the election is issued by the president or the governor, which comes after the announcement of the election has been made by the ECI. The political parties have argued that unlike the notification of elections, the date of announcement of elections is not a statutorily recognised date. Any concurrence on 'announcement' as the date on which the MCC becomes effective would, according to them, leave the initiative entirely with the ECI, which could 'arbitrarily announce the election on any date much ahead of the commencement of the "statutory process" [which began] with the issue of the notification'.[65]

The dispute over the commencement of the MCC was brought before the Supreme Court for settlement, in connection with a by-election to the Karnool parliamentary constituency in Andhra Pradesh. On 3 March 1994, the ECI issued a press note that the election notification for the by-election would be issued on 26 April 1994. Together with this, it sent a message to the state government that the MCC in the constituency would come into force on 3 March, that is, the date on which the ECI announced the holding of the election for the constituency. The Government of Andhra Pradesh filed a writ petition before the Supreme Court contending that the MCC could come into force only from 26 April 1994, which was the date of its notification. In an interim order, the Supreme Court decided that the statutory position and legal effect of the MCC was in dispute, that is, it was 'yet to be considered and decided'. It refrained, however, from 'expressing even a *prima facie* opinion on this aspect of the controversy'. It is interesting that the court should have directed the attention of the parties to the disputed legality of the MCC, and then refrained from settling it. More importantly, even as it reminded the contending parties of their constitutional obligations to discharge their respective duties with mutual respect, it steered clear of giving a firm opinion on what could be construed as 'commencement'. Yet, while appearing to remain a non-player in the electoral game, by asking the ECI to approach the court for 'directions' for legal action, the court opened up the possibility of becoming a significant player

---

[65] See Rama Devi and S. Mendiratta (2006: 634).

itself in the dispute.[66] While the above writ petition was pending before the Supreme Court, the ECI announced the schedule for the Andhra Pradesh legislative assembly elections. The Telugu Desam Party, which was in opposition in the state, filed a writ petition before the Andhra Pradesh High Court asking the Court to direct the state government, headed by the Congress party, not to undertake new schemes or relief measures in violation of the MCC after the announcement of the elections by the ECI. On 10 October 1994, a single judge bench, while issuing a notice to the respondents on compliance with the MCC, observed that the MCC would come into force from the date of notification and not from the date of announcement of the election schedule by the ECI. The ECI filed an appeal before a division bench of the high court, contesting the order. The elections were completed before the disposal of the writ petition. Elected to power, the Telegu Desam Party withdrew the writ petition, and the high court subsequently dismissed the petition as withdrawn. While giving the order of dismissal, the court left the question of the date of enforcement open, to be decided in an appropriate case in the future.[67]

A definitive judicial pronouncement on this issue was not made until 1997 in the case *Harbans Singh Jalal* v. *Union of India and Others.* Harbans Singh filed a writ petition in the Punjab and Haryana High Court on behalf of the Government of Punjab, with the central

---

[66] On 25 April 1994, a day before the election notification was scheduled, the matter was heard by the Supreme Court again. In its order, the court revisited the question of legality, which it had raised in its interim order, clarifying that the writ petition itself did not dispute either the 'desirability' of the MCC or the 'requirement' of its enforceability. The court desisted, however, from ordering on the question of the date of enforceability of the MCC, leaving it to the ECI to enforce it after the start of the statutory process. The Supreme Court finally disposed of the writ petition on 8 November 1994, leaving the question raised in the writ petition open for decision in the future, even as the state government withdrew its petition on the ground that the question had become purely academic since the by-election had already been completed without the ECI taking any action adverse to the state government's interests (*State of Andhra Pradesh* v. *Election Commission of India* Writ Petition No. 260 of 1994).

[67] Order dated 12 December 1994 of the *Andhra Pradesh High Court in Election Commission of India* v. *Ramakrishnudu and Ors* Writ Appeal No. 1347 of 1994.

government as a party supporting the petition, against the MCC and other instructions issued by the ECI in relation to the state assembly elections of 1996.[68] In its petition, the state government argued that the election procedure commenced only with the issue of a notification by the governor. The ECI, therefore, had no power to interfere with the implementation of schemes that had been announced by the state government prior to the announcement of the election, and could not control the activities of the government during the period between the announcement of the election schedule by it and the notification of the election by the governor of the state.[69] Unlike the ambiguity and deferral witnessed in the two cases pertaining to elections in Andhra Pradesh, the high court of Punjab and Haryana affirmed the ECI's position that it was entitled to take the necessary steps even anterior to the issuance of notification, that is, from the date of announcement of the election itself, for the 'conduct of free and fair election', which the Court interpolated, 'should be pure as well': 'On the eve of election, political parties or candidates may come forward with tempting offers to the electorate to win their favour. If such a course is allowed to be resorted to by the parties or the candidates contesting the elections, *it will certainly undermine the purity of elections.*'[70]

Unhappy with the decision, the central government went on to appeal before the Supreme Court.[71] The prolonged legal wrangle and the involvement of the central government in the imbroglio upset the then CEC M.S. Gill, who, in June 2000, wrote to the prime minister, asking him to dissuade his government from pursuing the appeal in

[68] Along with the announcement of the election schedule, the ECI informed the state government that the MCC had come into effect on 30 December 1996. Prior to the announcement of the election schedule by the ECI, the ruling party in the state had announced certain welfare measures and schemes on 22 December 1996, which were to be implemented by the state government from 1 January 1997.

[69] *Harbans Singh Jalal* v. *Union of India and Ors* (Civil Writ Petition No. 270 of 1997). The Union of India was arrayed as one of the respondents to the writ petition in support of the petitioner's position.

[70] Judgment delivered on 27 May 1997, *Harbans Singh Jalal* v. *Union of India and Ors* (Civil Writ Petition No. 270 of 1997).

[71] *Union of India* v. *Harbans Singh Jalal and Ors* SLP (Civil) No. 22734 of 1997 before the Supreme Court, decided on 26 April 2001.

the Supreme Court and to settle the matter through dialogue.[72] The legal wrangle, in the CEC's view, detracted from India's democratic culture, in which the MCC figured prominently as 'a unique voluntary political agreement, which [had] served the country well in difficult times, and earned the admiration of the democratic world'.[73] In his letter to the prime minister, the CEC reminded him of the Supreme Court's advice that the government should settle the matter directly in a dialogue with the ECI rather than pursue the legal course. The CEC also expressed surprise that the union law ministry should have kept the ECI in the dark for nearly two years about its appeal before the Supreme Court, and that successive prime ministers and law ministers should have allowed the pursuit of the case against the ECI. CEC Gill found it paradoxical that while political parties continued to agree with the ECI on enforcing the MCC, the governments formed by them have 'from time to time' continued to pursue a 'parallel litigation' to 'diminish the effectiveness of the Code'.[74]

After a prolonged and protracted dialogue between the ECI and the central government, an agreement was ultimately reached between them on 16 April 2001. The parties agreed that the MCC would come into force from the date the ECI announced the schedule for any election, but with the rider that the duration of the interval between the announcement and the notification would not normally exceed three weeks (Lyngdoh 2004: 78–9). As part of such agreement, it was also decided that the inauguration of any completed project or the laying

[72] 'Code of Conduct: Govt. Urged to Withdraw Plea in SC,' *The Hindu*, 13 June 2000.

[73] 'Decks Cleared for EC to Enforce Model Code of Conduct,' *The Indian Express*, 19 September 2000.

[74] While the matter was still before the Supreme Court, an all-party meeting was convened by the ECI in September 2000. At that meeting, it was agreed that the MCC should take effect from the date of announcement of the polls. Parties from Tamil Nadu, where assembly elections were due early next year, expressed certain reservations, but agreed after M.S. Gill spoke to them. Significantly, they agreed with the ECI's proposal and the high court decision, which had been contested by the union government, to enforce the code from the date of announcement of the poll, but felt that the gap between the announcement and the notification should be less than a month. ('Decks Cleared for EC to Enforce Model Code of Conduct,' *The Indian Express*, 19 September 2000).

of foundation stones, and the like, of new projects could be done by the civil servants so that public interest may not suffer because of the application of the MCC. The MCC was amended by the ECI to give effect to this agreement, and on 26 April 2001, the Supreme Court disposed of the petition filed by the central government.

There are those who believe that even this curb on the ruling party is not enough. Abhishek Singhvi, lawyer, Congress MP, and one of the spokespersons for the party, felt that the decision to go for elections, especially before the completion of a full term, vests in the government of the day. The genesis of that decision occurs at least a couple of months before the elections and is followed by dissolution of Parliament and then the fixing of the actual dates by the ECI. This interregnum between the decision and the fixing/announcing of dates is of crucial importance because it allows the government of the day to announce a spate of schemes that may give it an unfair advantage in the ensuing elections.[75] James Lyngdoh, however, argues that the entire process is something like a 'prolonged battle of wits' between the ECI on the one side and the government on the other, especially since the ECI has stopped consulting the government on the dates for the elections in its effort to protect the MCC. Until the interval between announcement of elections and its notification was fixed at 21 days, it was a question of whether the ECI could get in an announcement of the elections earlier, or the governments their sanctions and appointments (Lyngdoh 2004: 79). A controversy of a different order over poll announcement erupted in the context of the dates of assembly elections for Himachal Pradesh and Gujarat, two states which went to polls towards the end of 2017.[76] The controversy erupted when the ECI did not announce the dates of Gujarat election, which was ruled by the BJP, but announced those of Himachal Pradesh, ruled by the Congress party. The Congress alleged that the ECI delayed the announcement of dates for Gujarat polls to allow the

[75] See Abhishek Singhvi. 2004. 'Killing the Spirit,' *Hindustan Times*, 28 January, p. 12.

[76] See *Jansatta*, 'NDTV Anchor Ravish Kumar Attacks on Election Commission over Gujarat Elections,' [Hindi] *Jansatta*, 14 December 2017. Available at https://www.jansatta.com/trending-news/ndtv-anchor-ravish-kumar-attacks-on-election-commission-over-gujarat-elections/518041/.

ruling NDA in the centre to make welfare announcements with an eye on the poll outcome. Congress leader and MP, P. Chidambaram, accused the ECI of going on 'an extended holiday' after announcing the dates for Himachal Pradesh, and the ruling NDA expressed concern that a constitutional authority was being questioned.[77] The ECI was, however, compelled to explain why it deviated from the long-standing practice where election dates of states that go to poll within six months of each other were announced together.[78]

'Orwellian Power' or 'Cleaning Up Democracy'

As discussed before, three 'temporal properties'—periodicity, simultaneity, and finality—distinguish 'election time' from ordinary politics (Thompson 2004). All of these affirm popular sovereignty. Popular sovereignty[79] is also unharnessed through a reversal in the working of power in the course of the 'special time' of elections (Gilmartin 2009: 248;

[77] *The Hindu*, 2017. 'Election Commission on Extended Holiday Says Chidambaram', 20 October 2017.

[78] Gujarat went to poll on 9 and 14 December and Himachal Pradesh on 18 December. The date for Himachal Pradesh was, however, announced by the ECI earlier. The CEC explained that the weather and festivities were taken into consideration while announcing the dates separately (see 'Gujarat Elections Delayed,' *Hindustan Times*, video. Available at http://www.hindustantimes.com/assembly-elections/gujarat-elections-delayed-date-announcement-to-hardik-patel-video-5-controversies/story-LuaQU1rcNnRtBxuriyBRIL.html; accessed on 1 January 2018). There were allegations that the delay was deliberate to enable the prime minister, Narendra Modi, to visit Gujarat on 16 October, giving him the opportunity to announce new schemes. Former CEC T.S. Krishnamurthy felt that the controversy could have been avoided through better management (Gaurav Bhatnagar. 2017. 'Chidambaram Slams Election Commission over Gujarat Poll Issue,' *The Wire*, 20 October. Available at https://thewire.in/189151/chidambaram-slams-election-commission-gujarat-poll-issue/; accessed on 1 January 2018).

[79] David Gilmartin (2007: 55) points out that while the concept of the 'people', which has taken many forms and many genealogies, has played a central role in the universalist imaginings of modernity, few theorists have carefully examined the actual operations of elections (and of voting) as a clue for understanding the underlying structural meanings of the 'people' in the history of modern India.

Hauser and Singer 1986). The suspension of normal power in election time is seen as essential for generating conditions in which popular sovereignty may be released. This is facilitated by the invocation of another form of power, which is the power of the ECI 'to set with full discretionary authority the time parameters of the election campaigns during which its special powers (and the Model Code) would be in force' (Gilmartin 2009: 254). While the MCC has no statutory or legal basis, its appeal to a higher moral order establishes the authority of the ECI and the exceptional powers that flow from it. The acceptance of the principles of the MCC by all political parties is often presented as a remarkable voluntary act of political morality and collective ethics.[80] In addition, the MCC constitutes a moral force emanating from the normative concerns pertaining to the conduct of political parties in a democratic exercise such as elections, in order to 'ensure fairness between all contesting parties'.[81] The principle of fairness is invoked in particular to address the need to harness those in power— who 'naturally have the opportunity to help themselves'.[82]

In the course of its journey since the 1960s, the MCC has not remained a set of normative rules designed to elicit voluntary conformity. It has come to assume a relatively autonomous instrumentality and supplementary legality to plug a vacuum that had existed in electoral law. It may be argued that the MCC occupies that indeterminate zone of powers that Article 324, as interpreted by the Supreme Court, gives to the ECI. It may be recalled that in a series of cases beginning with the judgment of a constitutional bench of the Supreme Court in 1978, the Court had decided that Article 324(1) may be construed as not merely vesting all residuary powers in the ECI, but also envisaged as a 'reservoir of powers', 'where law [was] silent'.[83]

[80] Abhishek Singhvi. 2004. 'Killing the Spirit,' *Hindustan Times*, 28 January, p. 12.

[81] In the words of M.S. Gill, the CEC who oversaw the conduct of two general elections (1996 and 1998) ('What More Can Be Done? Election Commission Cannot Create Law,' *The Indian Express*, 22 November 1998).

[82] 'What More Can Be Done? Election Commission Cannot Create Law,' *The Indian Express*, 22 November 1998.

[83] These judgments are *Mohinder Singh Gill* v. *The Chief Election Commissioner*, New Delhi, 1978 (SCC 405), *Vineet Narain and Others* v. *Union of India and Another* (1998 SCC 226), and *Union of India* v. *Association for Democratic Reforms & Another* (SC 249/2002).

The ECI's powers to regulate elections have, however, not always been seen as 'pure governance unsullied by politics' (Gilmartin 2009). Partha Chatterjee (2006) prefers to describe the ECI's powers as unfolding into an 'Orwellian drama' during elections. For Chatterjee, a 'robust and impartial' ECI, which he describes as a 'useful' institution, even though not essential for liberal democracy, has swung the pendulum 'too far in the other direction', which may be ultimately harmful for Indian democracy.[84] The transformation in the modalities of superintending elections through unprecedented forms of surveillance including videographing of campaigns, the substitution of the political with bureaucratic authority, and 'area domination to ensure undisturbed polling', and so on, Chatterjee would argue, have had the lamentable consequence of sanitising and demobilising the political space. Indeed, the change in the 'ground rules' of elections, have constrained the traditional methods of campaigning, including wall writing, which he argues, are undemocratic, since they give an unfair advantage to the 'largest, most organised and most resourceful party', which will be the quickest not only to adapt to the new conditions but also to invent new techniques to reach the constituents and reap the maximum benefits from the new system. The act of voting would consequently become the private act of private citizens, with the erroneous prioritisation of the 'bourgeois individual, propertied and educated' as the typical Indian voter.[85] Similar sentiments were expressed in poll-bound Bihar in 2015, when the notification of the MCC before the state assembly election in October–November 2015 was seen responsible for the 'loss of flavour' of the Dussehra and Durga Puja festivals in the state in which political cartoons and tableaus depicting political leaders had become a regular feature.[86]

[84] Partha Chatterjee, 'Cleaning Up Democracy,' *The Telegraph*, 16 March 2006.

[85] Chatterjee cautions that it is no coincidence that the law against defacement of walls was enacted in 1976, in the darkest days of the Emergency, and long since forgotten (Chatterjee 2006).

[86] 'Poll Code Takes the Shine off Bihar's Pandals as Political Jokes Get Censored,' *Daily Mail Online*, 21 October 2015. Available at http://www. dailymail.co.uk/indiahome/indianews/article-3283401/Bihar-pandals-lose-satirical-edge-poll-restrictions-force-censorship-controversial-displays.html; accessed on 1 January 2018.

Indeed, Chatterjee's apprehension regarding the indifference and immobilisation of the political space finds validation in Mark Brewin's study of the 'Election Day' in Philadelphia city in USA. Mapping the changes in American political culture, Brewin points at what he calls the 'disappearance' of the election day as a day of public celebration and its 'transformation' into a media event—more specifically a 'mass mediated ritual' limited to a form of television genre (Brewin 2008: 1–2). In the Indian context, while television shows like 'election nama', 'chai pe charcha', and 'Ravish ka road show' took their audience along the campaign trail in the 2014 general election, the public spectacle of road shows of political leaders have continued unabated. On the other hand, as Thompson (2004) argues, there is a normative value attached to certain aspects of electoral administration, which may otherwise appear to be arbitrary or merely a procedural requirement. The regulatory regime of the ECI may appear to constrain the freedom of speech at a time when it is expected to generate exchange of plural political points of view to fully unleash the ideological and deliberative content of elections. If one were to focus only on the debate on the ban on exit and opinion polls in India, it may be useful to see how Thompson might respond to it, weighing it against one of the temporal properties of election time—*simultaneity*. Thompson distinguishes between two aspects of simultaneity—voting at the same time, and voting without regard to how others vote. The former, that is, the practice of citizens casting their votes at more or less the same time, 'rested partly on the value of popular sovereignty'. It also rested on the democratic principle of fairness, since citizens voting simultaneously would exercise their franchise with access to the same information.

> The more that voting is concentrated in time, the more that the election expresses the will of a determinate majority ... The outcome can then be seen as the result of a single collective decision rather than the product of a series of decisions made by different majorities ... Simultaneous voting in this way creates a more coherent popular sovereign. Simultaneity rests even more importantly on the democratic value of fairness. If citizens vote at the same time (or have only information they would have had if they were voting at the same time), the value of each citizen's choice is no greater than any other citizen. All make their choices with equal access to relevant information. Election projections

deny some voters information that other voters have ... fairness is not the only value at stake in simultaneous voting. When citizens go to the polls on the same day, publicly participating in a common experience of civic engagement, they demonstrate their willingness to contribute to the democratic process on equal terms. Going to the polling station and standing in line with one's neighbours may not rank among the most exciting moments in life, but election day voting serves an important expressive purpose in a democracy. ... The second aspect of simultaneous voting is independence of voting—a norm that holds that citizens should not adjust their votes according to how others have voted. This partly rests on fairness. An election that enables citizens to adjust their votes in this way privileges strategic voting. Strategy of course has a place in the campaign, but the value of a vote should not depend on the strategic savvy of the voter. (Thompson 2004: 57–9)

Going by Thompson's reasoning, the publication of opinion and exit polls would influence the deliberative and ideological content of elections by making electoral outcome the pre-eminent concern, rather than the collective act of voting itself.[87] A general election for the Lok Sabha is held in several phases across the country, diminishing fairness associated with simultaneity. The 2014 general election, for example, stretched for over a month and went through nine phases. The task of ensuring that the voter in Assam and Tripura voting in the first phase would vote on the same footing and with the same information available to them as those who voted in the last phase in parts of Bihar, Uttar Pradesh, and West Bengal then becomes important on the test of fairness, which requires that the voter is not influenced by another person's vote. Indeed, the question of fairness becomes crucial if one recalls that the BJP released its manifesto for the 2014 Lok Sabha elections on 7 April 2014, the day Assam and Tripura went to poll in the first phase of the election. The timing of the release could be interpreted in two mutually contradictory ways: for the BJP, the voters in the two states were inconsequential, or, conversely, by

[87] Thompson emphasises the critical importance of the electoral campaign, rather than the electoral outcome, pointing to the 'heightened value-debate and political opinion formation' and 'periods of heightened opportunity for citizens to transmit these values to their representatives' (Thompson 2004: 57–9).

ensuring national media attention and discussion around its mani-festo, the BJP managed to circumvent the restriction on campaigning on the polling day in the two states. The ECI closely monitors the polling day, with restrictions on campaigning in the vicinity of the polling booth, with a 48-hour period of repose before polling day, a convention followed in most democracies. The Indian polling booth is a highly secured and surveilled space.[88] Indeed, one of the reasons for staggered elections in the country is to enable the movement of the paramilitary forces from one part of the country to another to ensure their presence on polling day in sufficient numbers.

'Policy Paralysis' or 'Efficient Governance'?

The MCC has become a terrain of contests that emerge from local electoral competition. These contests are, however, ultimately about the fundamental principles of electoral governance. Ironically, the 'citizen-voter'—the 'little man' who the Supreme Court had sought to arm with the 'right to know'—figures in these contests as losing out on entitlements and benefits, and even disadvantaged because of the MCC. The reinstatement by the Kerala High Court in March 2011 of the 'Rs. 2 per Kilogram rice scheme' initiated by the Left Front government, which had been stopped by the ECI on the ground that it would influence voters, was indicative of this logic.[89] A division bench comprising Chief Justice J. Chelameswar and Justice Ramachandra

[88] In the 2009 general election, for example, almost 2000 joint-secretary-level observers were posted in various constituencies. Almost 141,000 micro observers, also senior officials, were deputed to these polling stations which the opposition or independent candidates felt insecure about, and video and still cameras recorded the poll process (see Navin B. Chawla. 2013. 'AAP's Victory Makes a Strong Case for Public Funding of Election,' *Hindustan Times*. Available at https://www.hindustantimes.com/ht-view/aap-s-victory-makes-strong-case-for-state-funding-of-polls/story-WcCCrwUTUFO5GyW3lMlXuL.html; accessed on 12 December).

[89] The bench also accepted the petitioner's plea that the scheme was imple-mented much before the announcement of election schedule. Incidentally, the scheme that was only for BPL card holders till February was extended to all cardholders just three days before the MCC came in force ('Kerala High Court Reinstates Kerala Rice Scheme,' *Hindustan Times*, 21 April 2011).

Menon observed that the poor could not be punished in the name
of elections. The stay of the high court's order by the Supreme Court
a month later was, however, an affirmation of the ECI's role as a
'pitcher' in the electoral game. Putting a stay on the implementation
of the Kerala High Court order, the Supreme Court concurred with
the ECI that irrespective of the technicalities concerning the duration
of the MCC, the objective of the MCC was to ensure that no action
that could disturb the level playing field should be taken by the party
in power close to the date of the announcement of elections.[90]

In the Lok Sabha election of 2014, with its communication to the
cabinet secretary and the chief secretaries of state governments and
the union territories and the CEOs of all states that the MCC had
come into play immediately upon the announcement of the election dates and would stay in place till the completion of the electoral
process, including the announcement of results, the ECI effectively
subjected governmental decision-making to the scrutiny of the ECI.
Among the regular instructions concerning the norms of conducting
the campaign and the restrictions on the announcement of financial
grants and the use of electronic media was a 'total ban' on the transfer
of all officers who were involved in the administration of elections.[91]
Significantly, these officers, including the commissioner of police
and the DC, are under the administrative control of the ECI for the
duration of the election. The ban on transfer imposed by the ECI
does not, however, foreclose the possibility of the ECI itself ordering
transfers to enable the conduct of 'fair and free' election. This power
of the ECI to control the movement of officers during election time
became contentious in the 2014 election. On 26 March 2014, the ECI
ordered the transfer of 44 top officials in Uttar Pradesh, including
district magistrates and police chiefs, who it said were likely to be
influenced by the Samajwadi Party, the ruling party in the state.[92]

---

[90] J. Venkatesan. 2011. 'Supreme Court Stays Kerala Rice Scheme Order,'
The Hindu, 31 March, p. 9.

[91] Election Commission Circular No. 437/6/1/2014-CC & BE. Available at
www.eci.nic.in; accessed on 14 March 2014.

[92] The transfer was announced following the visit by ECI officials in
Lucknow and their meeting with different political parties ('Election Commission
Transfers 44 Senior Officers in UP,' *Press Trust of India*, 26 March 2014).

A similar order for transfer of seven officers in West Bengal, following a visit by the election commissioners to the state, was met with stiff resistance by the state government. The chief minister of West Bengal, Mamata Banerjee, refused to implement the order of transfer of officers and their replacement with officers suggested by the ECI. Banerjee claimed that the ECI was attempting to suppress regional parties to promote the interests of dominant national parties. The ECI responded by threatening to cancel the polls in the state. A compromise was reached with the state government agreeing to transfer the officers named by the commission, but choosing their replacements from a panel suggested by the state government and approved by the ECI.[93]

It is often contended that by deferring decision-making during election time, the MCC puts government in the 'pause mode'. In the 2014 election, for example, there were reports of movement of files in government departments and ministries becoming slow and desultory, with important decisions being held up for the approval of the ECI. The Ministry of Information and Broadcasting asked the ECI's permission for its secretary to attend a FICCI programme, and its minister Manish Tiwari to participate in a National Community Radio Sammelan. Manish Tiwari was denied permission by the ECI.[94] The defence ministry referred its decision to appoint the next army chief to the ECI, seeking its approval to make the appointment.[95]

Indeed, the idea that Lok Sabha and state legislative assembly elections should be held simultaneously, which has been debated intermittently over the past few years, has largely been buttressed by the argument that the 'policy paralysis and governance deficit' associated with the implementation of the MCC during election time, needed to be overcome. In December 2015, a parliamentary standing committee recommended that simultaneous elections were necessary to enable India to compete with other nations 'in developmental agenda on real

---

[93] 'Poll Panel Transfers Eight Officers, Mamata Refused to Obey,' *Business Standard*, 7 April 2014.

[94] 'UPA-II Ministries Hit Pause Button, Keep Files Pending for New Government,' *The Indian Express*, 7 April 2014.

[95] 'Election Commission to Consider Army Chief Appointment Issue,' *The Hindu*, 3 May 2014.

time basis as a robust, democratic country'. The BJP manifesto of 2014 had mooted the idea earlier and Prime Minister Modi supported it in TV interviews and in his communication with party workers, calling upon the ECI to take the idea forward. Those favouring the reform argue that it would also reduce the cost associated with multiple elections, including the different kinds of disruptions caused to normal public life and the constant diversion of public resources and personnel including the armed forces for the conduct of elections.[96]

Electoral officers heading electoral administration at the level of the states differ on the association made between the MCC and paralysis in governance during election time. Indeed, they argue that election time produces an extraordinary convergence at the local level between the existing bureaucratic apparatus for local administration and the electoral machinery, generating an efficient system of governance. Ajay Naik, CEO of the state of Bihar at the time of this conversation in 2016, termed electoral governance during election time 'a pristine form of government'. The 'pristine' nature of government was because of the 'distinct identity' of the ECI as a body that was 'inside but also outside government'. To a large extent, however, it was also because, in election time, as Naik puts it, the ECIs 'writ runs'. Ironically, however, when the ECI does its job properly, which would mean that it constrains the party in power effectively, this would not be liked by the government. But for the ECI, it was 'not [only] what the EC does but the kind of picture the EC wishes to present to the people. It is a statement of perception'. Indeed, governance in election time is marked by remarkable 'efficiency'. Naik points out that individual officers may be efficient in normal times, but such officers are dispersed unevenly across the state, and the general administration shows 'huge variation': 'During election time, however, there is an accepted minimum which every official is expected to perform and the EC conducts election at the specific minimum level of efficiency, there may be some variations but not a lot'. While real-time IT-based

[96] Louise Tillin. 2016. 'Elections and the Governance Deficit: Does the Answer Lie in Streamlining India's Electoral Process?' *Scroll.in*, 18 July. Available at http://scroll.in/article/810995/is-holding-simultaneous-elections-for-lok-sabha-and-state-assemblies-necessarily-a-good-idea; accessed on 20 December 2017.

tools ensure efficiency, and a daily stock taking of work—'*kitna kaam hua*' [how much work was accomplished]—helps in monitoring the work, it is the maintenance of law and order that is the most visible aspect of election time government: 'Detention is often the pillar of election measures—*jila bahar karna, sandehaspad logon ko nazarband karna*—implementing the gun control act, deposition of arms, prosecution under crime control act'. All these measures make law and order effective. The absence of political interference and control helps. Documentation and administration capacity is enhanced through various measures and administration is 'restored' to its pristine form. The 'restitution period' involves 'keeping the morale of officers high and the bureaucratic apparatus efficient by constantly improving your system—any procedural violation is dealt with immediately. ... EC will extract accountability and internal audit of efficiency and lapses is done'.[97] How does the same bureaucracy perform better during election time? We wonder. Naik feels that self-perception and commitment comes into play: 'All the officers see themselves as the upholders of the Constitution ... there is nothing between them and the Constitution, which is morally binding for the bureaucrat too. You create your own system, which you have to make capable of delivering. It is a costly affair requiring high level of efficiency—[we show that a democratic] government can do it [and not just authoritarian governments]'.[98]

Sanjay Kumar Agrawal, district magistrate of Patna, who had won the ECI's Best Practices Award for conducting election in 'naxal affected area' of Gaya in 2014, talks about the 'innovations' which he had implemented in the ongoing panchayat elections. In addition, he speaks of the level of efficiency achieved in the state assembly elections held in Bihar in general and Patna in particular in 2015. The enhanced security, maintenance of law and order, in short, more 'vigilance', had generated almost a 'curfew like situation' to ensure fair elections. The 'curfew' was largely meant to keep away 'anti-social' elements from the electoral space, but more importantly to ensure 'MCC compliance' (for example, the Defacement of Property Act), which was very high, primarily because in most cases of violations, it

---

[97] Interview with Ajay Naik, CEO, Bihar, 28 June 2016.
[98] Interview with Ajay Naik, CEO, Bihar, 28 June 2016.

was not just an FIR that was filed but also a chargesheet to ensure that the legal process was immediately rolled out.

The views expressed by both Naik and Agrawal find resonance in Beatrice Jauregui's ethnography of the everyday life and work of the police in Uttar Pradesh. The police in Uttar Pradesh, Jauregui (2017: 11–13) argues, wield 'provisional authority', which is distinct from the legal-bureaucratic authority associated with an 'ideal-typical liberal democracy'. The provisionality of authority is characterised by contingency and variability across time and space and emerges from a host of conditions including its location in an amorphous and multidimensional social field. One aspect of provisionality of authority was witnessed during the 2007 state assembly election in Uttar Pradesh that coincided with Jauregui's fieldwork. Amidst the large-scale transfer of police officers by the CEC including the DGP of the state, to ensure that non-partisan police officers occupy key posts during the polls, an Indian Police Service (IPS) officer, who had just replaced the district police chief, talked to Jauregui about the distinctiveness of Indian democracy, indeed, its greatness when compared to China. Yet, he knew his present position was 'ephemeral': 'When the election is finished, I will be kicked out and the new government will appoint a "party man" to take my place'. But it was the 'present' that made him feel confident. He would ensure that the democratic process went well under his 'watch': 'I answer only to the CEC, not to the CM. ... I am not getting calls from any politicians trying to apply pressure on me' (Jauregui 2017: 114). The moment of authority the police officer referred to as 'ephemeral' was also the source of self-assured confidence, which Jauregui did not find in other police officers, who complained of constant harassment by politicians of all ranks, in non-election time.

Preventive detention, which Naik had earlier referred to as one of the most effective measures for maintaining law and order during election time, is explained by Agrawal as consisting of a 'range of actions' and not necessarily detention in prison, which would deprive a person of his or her voting rights. One such 'action' consists of 'bonds of good behaviour' signed by persons 'detained' as a preventive measure but not imprisoned till the time they adhered to the norms of good behaviour. Similarly, the data on 'execution of warrant' under the Crime Control Act is maintained in the police headquarters on a daily basis. Indeed, preventive detention is critical to mapping of vulnerability of constituencies. The ECI's Manual on Vulnerability Mapping (2016) states that the objective of vulnerability mapping is to ensure 'fearless and seamless' participation of electors in the electoral process and involves mapping the susceptibility of voters or groups of voters to intimidation, which may prevent them from participating in the elections. Agrawal informs us that vulnerability mapping involves identifying who is causing the vulnerability and is to be kept under watch. Often the CRPF is employed, which conducts a flag march of all the hamlets that are vulnerable.

On the question of efficiency of the government before and after election, Sanjay Agrawal was of the view that efficiency during election pertains to one aspect of the government—'the focus is on one thing, the sole objective is the conduct of election ... at other times the District Magistrate is dealing with a hundred subjects, and the same level of compliance is not possible'. Moreover, during election time, it becomes possible for him under the powers given by the RPA to draw [efficient] officers from all areas—'the result is visible, the response is immediate and visible'. Moreover, it is not just the priority areas identified by the electoral/district bureaucracy during election, but also the resources (including human) during election time that are available in plenty and are also optimised (unlike plural and competing priorities at other times and dispersal of resources). Like other officers, Agrawal too points at the absence of political interference as an enabling factor alongside the enhanced powers of the administration under MCC to put political leaders under the scanner. Interestingly, certain actions taken under specific laws during election time may seep into non-election time because of their usefulness. The implementation of curfew times for playing of loudspeakers during election time under the Loudspeaker Act whereby no loudspeakers were allowed to play after 10 in the night (no band, *baajaa*, *baaraat*), was appreciated so much by the residents of Patna, that it was allowed to linger on beyond election time.[99]

Showing us around the election headquarters set up in the DC's office in Kathua in Jammu, DC Shahid Iqbal had echoed the sentiments

---

[99] Interview with Sanjay Kumar Agrawal, district magistrate, Patna, in his office on 29 June 2016.

expressed by other electoral officers in Patna on the reasons why election time produces efficient government. Apart from the freedom to focus on one 'sector' and not being distracted into administering a huge number of other departments, all energy is concentrated on the management of elections and exceptional results are produced. According to Iqbal, there is extraordinary team work during election— 'team work and leadership' which works itself into a 'mission mode':

> When you work in a mission mode, for example, when you are control-ling floods, you realise that you have so many efficient officers who you did not know of earlier ... you know their work and you call them dur-ing election time to make an extraordinary team ... IAS probationary officers have shown an inclination to have the experience of conduct-ing elections and have worked day and night, one of them has been appointed as Assistant Returning Officer.

Indeed, it is important to see how the idea of being on 'mission mode' during election time has invigorated other departments as well, so much so that it would be wrong to say that development is impeded during elections. An example is the manner in which the 320 (mostly non-functional) *anganwadi* centres in Reasi district, where Iqbal was the DC earlier, were also designated as women's voter registration centres. This had the 'double effect' of activating them as voter registration centres as well as anganwadi centres. Indeed, ordinary departments may be seen as actually functioning during election time.[100]

As the election headquarter and the nodal centre for administer-ing elections in the district, the DC's office in Kathua was segmented for the duration of the elections into several units, each taking care of various aspects of 'daily administration of election'. The DEO's office received all mails from the ECI and the CEO of the state, and marked it to the different cells/offices to which they pertained, which were housed in the same office building. The monitoring of TV news channels, filing of clippings from newspapers and press releases of political events and all election-related activities, and expenditure

---

[100] Interview with Shahid Iqbal, DC of Kathua in Jammu and Kashmir, on 14 December 2014.

of political parties as gauged from the events were monitored on a daily basis. In case a specific news item was identified as favouring a particular candidate, a notice was issued to him or her, and a committee decided whether indeed the item constituted paid news, which could then be added to the expenditure of the candidate. Monitoring of MCC was being done by a separate unit that received complaints of violations, investigated them, and filed reports on action taken, within 24 hours. The files contained details of the date of complaint, the name of the person who filed it, the name of the person against whom it was filed, action taken and enquiry report, all of which were then uploaded on the website. The DEO/DC showed us files with documents relating to permissions given to candidates to hold meetings, for helicopters to land in designated areas for the purpose of the meeting, and the conditions in which the meeting could be held. Any deviation from these conditions would be construed as a violation of the MCC. The expenditure-monitoring cell received the details of expenditure filed by the candidates, but its shadow teams (which include flying squads, video surveillance teams, expenditure observers, and the like) kept watch on and maintained their own register of what according to them constituted the expenditure of the candidate. The shadow observer's register maintained the daily estimate of the candidate's expenditure on the basis of a rate list fixed and notified by DEO's office (for example, rates of different kinds of vehicles used for the rally, the podium, the shamiana, the advertisements, posters, and the like, for which the candidate should have already taken permission). A week after an election rally, the candidate is called by the monitoring team to discuss the expenditure.[101]

Indeed, as part of the surveillance on expenditure during elections, based on confidential reports by the district administration and electoral officers, the ECI declares those constituencies as 'expenditure-sensitive', which may be susceptible to increased expenditure by parties and candidates. Constituencies that are declared expenditure-sensitive are subjected to increased surveillance and monitoring by the ECI. According to the DEO of Bhatinda district where three

---

[101] Interview with Shahid Iqbal, DC of Kathua in Jammu and Kashmir, on 14 December 2014.

assembly constituencies were declared expenditure-sensitive by the ECI in the state assembly elections of 2017, such a declaration was followed by a series of stringent vigilance measures. These included increased number of flying squads and check posts, the fixing of prices of 142 election items by the ECI, which ranged from a meagre Rs 3 to Rs 1.5 lakhs for expenditure on a range of things including the engagement of reputed singers in poll campaigns.[102] An application to the ECI under the RTI Act, 2005, yielded information on the number of such constituencies from the ECI, which have been cumulated in Table 3.6. Out of 543 constituencies for which elections to the Lok Sabha were held, 166 constituencies, that is, almost 31 per cent of the total, were declared expenditure-sensitive. In three states, Tamil Nadu, Andhra Pradesh, and Telangana, all constituencies were declared sensitive. While more focused research is required to study the effectiveness of the surveillance mounted on these constituencies and the electoral outcomes, it is interesting to study the list itself as presenting a pattern.

Priyanka Sinha is the DEO whose office is part of the larger building of the office of the CEO of Bihar. She dispels the notion that election administration is confined only to those few weeks or months of election time. While elections are held periodically, the work of election management continues unabated: 'You cannot always be on war time alertness—geared up—but there is always also continuous work going on over the years to step up to the state of preparedness when required'. The national electoral rolls are 'purified' and updated continuously, polling stations are altered and relocated, and the preparation of EPICs is carried out throughout the year, every year: 'The entire process requires deployment of information technology, GIS based mapping of polling stations, CAD based maps of polling stations, and the rationalisation of polling stations so that a maximum

---

[102] The items included per day hiring of furniture, tent houses, light and sound system, cycle rickshaws, three wheelers, cabs of all kinds, mini buses, trucks, printing material, paper caps, printed caps, cloth banners, flags, compact disks, videos, cutouts, hand bills, pamphlets, posters, hotel room and guest tee-shirts with and without sleeves, hotel rooms and guest room accommodations, and so on ('Three Constituencies Declared Expenditure-Sensitive,' *The Tribune*, 7 January 2017).

Table 3.6 Expenditure-Sensitive Constituencies in the 2014 General Election

S.N.	Name of State/UT	No. and Name of Parliamentary Constituency	No. of Constituencies
1.	Andhra Pradesh and Telangana	All parliamentary constituencies (25 in Andhra Pradesh and 17 in Telangana)	42 (100%)
2.	Arunachal Pradesh	1 – Arunachal Pradesh (West) 2 – Arunachal Pradesh (East)	2 (100%)
3.	Assam	2 – Silchar H.P.C. 4 – Dhubri H.P.C. 7 – Gauhati H.P.C. 9 – Tezpur H.P.C. 13 – Dibrugarh H.P.C. 14 – Lakhimpur H.P.C.	6 (out of 14, 42.85%)
4.	Bihar	4 – Sheohar 6 – Madhubani 7 – Jhanjarpur 8 – Supaul 9 – Araria 11 – Katihar 12 – Purnia 13 – Madhepura 15 – Muzaffarpur 16 – Vaishali 17 – Gopalganj (SC) 18 – Siwan 19 – Maharganj 20 – Saran 21 – Hajipur (SC) 27 – Banka 29 – Nalanda 30 – Patna Sahib 31 – Patliaputra 32 – Arrah 34 – Sasaram (SC) 35 – Karakat 36 – Jehanabad 37 – Aurangabad 38 – Gaya (SC) 39 – Nawada 40 – Jamui (SC)	27 (out of 40, 67.5%)

(Cont'd)

Table 3.6   (Cont'd)

S.N.	Name of State/UT	No. and Name of Parliamentary Constituency	No. of Constituencies
5.	Chhattisgarh	5 – Bilaspur	3 (out of
		6 – Durg	11, 27.27%)
		8 – Raipur	
6.	Gujarat	1 – Kutch (SC)	23 (out of
		2 – Banaskantha	26, 88.46%)
		3 – Patan	
		4 – Mehsana	
		5 – Sabarnkantha	
		6 – Gandhinagar	
		7 – Ahmedabad East	
		8 – Ahmedabad West (SC)	
		9 – Surendranagar	
		11 –Porbandar	
		12 – Jamnagar	
		13 – Junagarh	
		14 – Amreli	
		16 – Ananad	
		17 – Kheda	
		18 – Panchmahal	
		19 – Dahod (ST)	
		20 – Vadodara	
		21 – Chhota Udaipur (ST)	
		22 – Bharuch	
		24 – Surat	
		25 – Navsari	
		26 – Valsad (ST)	
7.	Haryana	2 – Kurukshetra	3 (out of
		7 – Rohtak	10, 30%)
		10 – Faridabad	
8.	Madhya Pradesh	1 – Murena	13 (out of
		2 – Bhind	29, 44.82%)
		4 – Guna	
		6 – Tikamgarh	
		7 – Damoh	
		11 – Sidhi	
		18 – Vidisha	
		19 – Bhopal	
		23 – Mandsor	

		24 – Ratlam	
		25 – Dhar	
		26 – Indore	
		29 – Batul	
9.	Nagaland	1 – Nagaland	1 (100%)
10.	Punjab	1 – Gurdaspur	4 (out of
		2 – Amritsar	13, 30.76%)
		10 – Ferozepur	
		13 – Patiala	
11.	Pondicherry	1 – Puducherry	1 (100%)
12.	Tamil Nadu	All Parliamentary	39 (100%)
		Constituencies	
13.	Damn and Diu	1 – Daman & Diu	1 (100%)
14.	Lakshadweep	1 – Lakshadweep	1 (100%)
Total constituencies declared expenditure-sensitive			166

Source: Response No. 4/RTI/191/patra/karyatmak/Bha.Ni.AA/2017/106, dated 26 October 2017, from the PIO, Secretariat of the ECI, New Delhi.

of 1,200 to 1,400 persons are allotted to each polling station. In Bihar, the ratio was still 1,600 per polling station', she explains.[103]

* * *

The two modes in which the MCC has unfolded—as a moral code and through supplementary legality—has corresponded with the specific ways in which the ECI has sought adherence to it: through 'voluntary observance', and alternatively by compelling observance through public censure and legal action. The voluntariness (of observation), which the MCC embodied in its 'foundational moment', has gradually given way to norms that have assumed the semblance of legal force through executive dictates and judicial interpretations. The latest addition in the ECI's repository of powers has been the Supreme Court's decision to bring the election manifesto of political parties within the purview of the MCC and thereby the scrutiny of the ECI. The decision taken by a bench of Justice P. Sathasivam and

[103] Interview with Priyanka Sinha, DEO, Patna, in her office, on 29 June 2016.

Justice Ranjan Gogoi concluded that party manifestos have a tendency to promise 'freebies' before elections, which 'shake the root of free and fair elections to a large degree'. Since there existed no law to govern the content of an election manifesto, the judges directed the ECI to frame guidelines for the same in consultation with all recognised parties and include a separate head on manifestos in the MCC for the 'guidance of political parties and candidates'.[104] The augmentation of the regulatory powers of the ECI through the stretching of its oversight over manifestos is extraordinary. No other election commission except those in Mexico and Bhutan, where the law requires the manifestos to be approved by the election regulatory body, has similar powers of scrutiny. Electoral officers we spoke to believed that the regulation of the manifestos could be used to the advantage of voters, who can now receive the information whether what is being promised to them is financially feasible. Political parties, for example, as one electoral officer remarked, could not promise the moon, without explaining where the funds would come from.

At the same time, however, the ECI has been wary of substituting statutory law for the MCC through which it currently wields such considerable power over the political executive during election time. While a statutory MCC would take it from the domain of supplementary legality to explicit legality, if such a law were to be passed, it would likely constrain the ECI's powers, in particular limiting its ability to take immediate action against violators.

In the writings on the ECI's regulatory powers, the constituent power of the commission to produce conditions conducive to an uncoerced and unbridled popular sovereignty has been seen as ranging from 'Orwellian drama'[105] to 'pure governance unsullied by politics'. The legal structuring of the first general election was in continuation

---

[104] Election Commission of India, 'Letter to Recognized Political Parties Regarding Meeting on Election Manifesto', No. 437/6/Manifesto/2013, dated 2 August 2013.

[105] In March 2011, the Hooghly district administration stopped the staging of a play called 'Poshu Khamar', adapted from George Orwell's novel *Animal Farm*, citing the MCC as justification. Largely seen as a critical take on the hegemonic politics of the CPI(M) and its allies, the administration acted on a complaint from former CPI(M) MP Rupchand Pal. He contended that

with the emphatic constitution of the collective political subject—
'we the people'—as the source of authority of the constitution. The
MCC is reflective of the sustained importance of unsullied politics
as the most appropriate condition in which popular sovereignty may
be produced, and the importance of legal-institutional measures, to
achieve this condition. Perhaps more so than in the early years of
the Republic, the protection of the electoral domain as a space of fair
competition—the assurance that representatives are elected legiti-
mately, can be made accountable to those who elect them, and would
want to be adequately informed to make competent choices—has
come to be seen as a function and effect of firm, appropriate, and efficient electoral laws. Indeed, the regulatory regime of electoral laws,
from the right of the voter to information, which was affirmed by the
judiciary in 2002, to the disqualification of those convicted of crimes
from contesting elections in 2013, the electoral space is replete with
purgatory laws.

Yet, it is the MCC that makes for special election time, transforming the modalities of superintending and controlling elections. The
MCC is, however, no longer left to voluntary observation, but requires
unprecedented forms of surveillance including videographing of campaigns and the securitisation, sanitisation, and cleansing of political
space. The voluntariness (of observation), which the MCC embodied
in its moment of inception, has gradually given way to norms that
have assumed the semblance of legal force through executive dictates
and judicial interpretations. The latter has resulted in a continual
enhancement of the repertoire of the ECI's powers, accompanied by
the accumulation of the vast paraphernalia of instructions, which the
ECI issues to ensure compliance. As a result, the ECI has gradually
wrested the power of executing the code from political parties, drawing implicitly upon its constitutional power of superintendence of
elections. The judiciary has affirmed this claim in specific cases as

---

the play violated the MCC laid down by the ECI. The administration barred
the play specifically on the ground that 'no police permission was sought'
for staging it. The incident shows that the MCC could be used as a substitute for state power (see Shyamal Sarkar. 2011. 'Orwellian Drama in Marxist
Domain,' *The Editstreet*, 21 March).

falling within the purview of the ECI's responsibility towards conducting 'fair and free election'.

At the same time, however, the ECI has been wary of substituting statutory law for the MCC through which it currently wields such considerable power over the political executive during election time. While a statutory model code would take it from the domain of supplementary legality to explicit legality, if such a law were to be passed, it would likely constrain the ECI's powers, in particular limiting its ability to take immediate action against violators. The idea of supplementary legality draws from the notion of necessity, which should remain uncovered by law, so as to sustain as a source of electoral regulation, but outside the regime of electoral law. The purpose, ostensibly, is to produce conditions for an electoral trial, which is founded neither in the adversarial nor the inquisitorial mode, but in providing conditions of fair choice for the voter. The extent to which these conditions are conducive to facilitating choice, and do not by themselves create conditions in which free speech and expression is thwarted in a burgeoning regime of surveillance, is a matter open to debate, where the sides arrayed in the debate remain equivocal.

ೕ

4

Creating Spaces for Democracy

The trajectory of electoral democracy in India would show that much has changed since the country first went to the polls in 1951–2. The holding of elections and the act of voting had enormous immediate significance for a society that had broken free from colonial subjection. The demonstration of a capacity for self-determination expressed individually and collectively as a people was embodied in the constituent moment of the Republic. Yet the expression of popular sovereignty was to take shape in the procedural domain of electoral democracy, which required the laying down of precise templates of laws, rules, and institutional arrangements to facilitate the choice of representatives by the voter-citizen. These procedures, it was hoped, would sustain the electoral system amidst the flux in socio-economic and political processes and, at the same time, remain dynamic enough to respond to these changes so that elections would continue to retain their significance as an expression of the sovereign will of the people.

The discussions in the previous chapters have shown that the ECI is a constitutional body entrusted with the responsibility of conducting elections in India. While making the ECI pre-eminent in the domain of superintendence, direction, and control of elections, the Constitution has simultaneously invested Parliament with the power to make laws to regulate all aspects of the conduct of elections. When Parliament is not forthcoming in the exercise of this power, the ECI has been seen as invested with residuary powers. This effectively means that unless Parliament explicitly exercises its legislative powers in matters pertaining to the conduct of elections, and restricts or regulates the scope of its administrative powers, the ECI possesses an enormous repository of powers mandated by the Constitution to administer elections. The discussions in the earlier chapters on the electoral roll and the MCC showed the expansion of the executive powers of the ECI in areas that are not covered by electoral law. The unfolding of electoral governance over the past decades has shown that the powers of Parliament and the ECI remain overlapping and therefore contested, owing to the ambivalence regarding their relative powers in the Constitution itself. While the Constitution gives Parliament the power to make the laws that provide the statutory framework for elections through Articles 325–9, this power collides with the functional autonomy given to the ECI in the conduct, supervision, and superintendence of elections in Article 324. The precise areas of uncertainty and dispute appear around the competing claims of Parliament and the ECI over the *power* to govern and the *responsibility* to govern, respectively. While these contending claims apparently relate to the first level of electoral governance, that is, the level of rule-making, since this is the level where Parliament is pre-eminent, the tension over unclaimed power and the scope of executive authority and administrative responsibility, manifests itself mostly at the second and third levels of electoral governance, that is, at the levels of rule application and rule adjudication. These areas of tension in electoral governance are important for understanding how the statutory and institutional practices of electoral governance unfold within specific socio-economic and political contexts.

Making the Electoral Process 'Fair, Transparent, and Equitable' and the Question of Trust

The 16th Lok Sabha elections in India were spread over 9 days, from 7 April to 12 May 2014, in what was the highest number of polling days for any election in India so far. The total electorate was more than 814 million (814,591,184), with 426 million (426,615,513) male voters, 387 million (387,911,330) women voters, and 28,341 who identified themselves as others. About 2.8 per cent of the total electorate, that is, close to 23 million (23,161,296) were first-time voters, that is, those who had turned 18 after the last election in 2009. Votes were cast in 930,000 polling stations, where 8 million civilians and 3 million security personnel were deployed. The option NOTA (None of the Above) was used for the first time in these elections. The EVMs were used for the first time on an experimental basis in India in 1989 in the state assembly elections, and again in 1998, with progressively widening usage in subsequent elections. For the first time in the history of election in India, in 2014, the EVMs were used in all polling stations replacing the ballot papers totally. The 2014 elections saw the highest ever voter turnout at 66.40 per cent (see Table 4.1) and the most number of political parties to contest an election (Table 4.2).[1]

Table 4.1 Voter Turnout and Male and Female Voter Percentages

General Election Year	Male (%)	Female (%)	Total (%)
First 1951–2	Not available	Not available	61.16
Second 1957	Not available	Not available	63.73
Third 1962	60.02	46.63	55.42
Fourth 1967	66.73	55.48	61.33
Fifth 1971	60.09	49.11	55.27
Sixth 1977	65.63	54.91	60.49
Seventh 1980	62.16	51.22	56.92
Eighth 1984–5	61.2	58.6	64.01
Ninth 1989	66.13	57.32	61.95
Tenth 1991–2	61.58	51.35	55.88
Eleventh 1996	62.06	53.41	57.94
Twelfth 1998	65.72	57.88	61.57
Thirteenth 1999	63.97	55.64	59.99
Fourteenth 2004	61.66	53.3	58.07
Fifteenth 2009	60.14	55.82	58.21
Sixteenth 2014	67.09	65.30	66.40

Source: Election Commission of India. 2014. 'General Elections 2014: Highest Ever Voter Turn-Out'. Available at http://pib.nic.in/newsite/PrintRelease.aspx?relid=105118; accessed on 24 February 2017.

[1] See the official website of the ECI (www.eci.nic.in), the Press Bureau of India, and 'General Elections 2014: Highest Ever Voter Turn-Out,' print release, 21 May 2014, Press Information Bureau, Government of India,

Table 4.2   Party Types

Year	Party Type	Registered
2004	1. National Parties	6
	2. State Parties	56
	3. Unrecognised Parties	702
	Total Registered	**764**
2009	1. National Parties	7
	2. State Parties	39
	3. Unrecognised Parties	1,014
	Total Registered	**1,060**
2014	1. National Parties	6
	2. State Parties	47
	3. Unrecognised Parties	1,634
	Total Registered	**1,687**

Source: Election Commission of India. 2014. '464 Political Parties Participated in General Elections 2014'. Available at http://pib.nic.in/ newsite/archiveReleases.aspx; accessed on 24 February 2017.

The increase in voter turnout in successive elections, the manifold increase in the size of the electorate, and the plurality of electoral competition with the increase in the number of political parties is generally seen as an aspect of the consolidation of electoral democracy. In the Indian context, the phenomenon of increase has also been explained in terms of a 'democratic upsurge', referring thereby, not only to the processes of democratic consolidation but also to the new churnings that have emerged as an outcome of this consolidation. Both the processes—that of democratic consolidation and of democratic upsurge—are, at a fundamental level, reflective of people's faith in the electoral system to provide the space through which the citizen-voters can register their consent or dissent regarding the existing political structure/formation.

The electoral process involves much more than periodic acts of voting and competition among political parties for forming the government. It also involves some enduring rules and structures that must

New Delhi. Available at http://pib.nic.in/newsite/PrintRelease.aspx?relid =105118; accessed on 24 February 2017.

ensure procedural certainty. Procedural certainty may be regarded the principal task of electoral governance, helping to ensure the democratic principle of uncertainty of electoral outcome. Thus, electoral governance, comprising a set of related activities including the making, implementation, and adjudication of rules that determine the framework within which the uncertainties of electoral outcomes unfold, forms an important aspect of understanding and comparing principles of equality and democratic participation in different political and socio-historical contexts.

Procedural certainty, by itself, would remain inadequate for assuring both democratic uncertainty and deliberative properties of elections, unless the procedures conform to the standards of electoral integrity. The literature on electoral integrity proposes that all EMBs responsible for the conduct of elections aim to ensure that the rules of conduct of elections satisfy the standards of independence, impartiality and fairness, integrity and honesty, and transparency and openness. All of these build trust and confidence in the electoral process, legitimacy for public and political institutions, and satisfaction with the performance of democracy. According to Pippa Norris, the standards of fairness and transparency are constitutive of electoral integrity. When these standards are adequately met, there is heightened civic engagement and civic activism, and a corresponding weakening of public protest. Simultaneously, there is an entrenchment of political representation, electoral accountability, responsiveness of elected officials to public concerns, accommodation of diversity, reducing grievances, minimising the risks of violence and civil war, and the acceleration of the democratisation process by facilitating regime transitions, consolidating democratic norms, and reducing pressures for institutional reforms.[2]

The Indian context, however, presents a strange paradox. The electoral domain has seen increased participation since the 1990s and also a corresponding decline in trust in political institutions. This paradox of increased participation and a simultaneous distrust of political institutions, 'the simultaneity of involvement and alienation', manifests the disconnect that exists between the tendencies towards democratisation of the electoral space and its institutionalisation in

---

[2] Pippa Norris, 'Challenges of Electoral Integrity,' Election Integrity Project. Available at www.electionintegrityproject.com; accessed on 22 January 2017.

the political space (Yadav 2010). At a deeper level, however, the para-dox embodies a question that has constantly troubled students and scholars of Indian politics. This question pertains to why people vote for persons who they know to be unworthy of their trust. The litera-ture on political socialisation in India tells us that the introduction of adult franchise in India at Independence was done with the expec-tation that the expansion of franchise would make the government accountable. The increase in political participation and a commensu-rate diminishing of trust in political institutions, as surveys indicate, seem to suggest that trust in political authority can be only 'effective' and not 'absolute'. People are likely to defer to authority structures, in response to the patronage and protection they offer, and get their work done in return for money and also loyalty.[3] The effectiveness and responsiveness of local institutional regimes matter to people, and those at the national scale may have only symbolic relevance. It is to the local structures of authority—political and bureaucratic—that people turn to, because of their capacity to 'facilitate' things. In such a context, trust becomes 'effective', even in the absence of the components that make authority 'trustworthy'.

[3] Surveys conducted by the CSDS with Azim Premji University in 2017, for example, have shown that people's trust in political authority varies. Generic offices of political authority like the executive (the office of the prime minister, if not the man/woman) are considered trustworthy. Yet, it is the army that is rated the highest in terms of 'effective trust' or being trusted absolutely by the people. The higher rating of a non-political body is because it is seen as selfless, distinct from the selfishness and corruption that marks the political class. This trust is also reflective of how, in the recent past, the army has become part of the political discourse of nationalism. Significantly, institutions of political participation and representation at the local level—the gram panchayats and the *nagar palikas*—enjoy higher levels of trust than Parliament and state assemblies. The lowest levels of trust are seen for the police, government officials, and political parties. Yet, the district commis-sioner and the tehsildar enjoy greater trust. Trust in the entire court system from the Supreme Court to the district courts persists. See key findings of CSDS and APU study: CSDS & APU, *Society and Politics between Elections* (2017). Available at http://www.lokniti.org/pol-pdf/KeyFindingsoftheReport. pdf; accessed on 1 December 2017. A detailed report of the study was published in 2018 (see Azim Premji University and CSDS-Lokniti 2018).

Indeed, absolute trust in political authority seems to have diminished, as the power money and muscle have in politics has become a publicly acknowledged fact. In his comprehensive study of criminalisation of politics in India, Milan Vaishnav makes an important argument about the reasons why 'crime pays' in politics. Just as markets favour intermediaries who help to match buyers and sellers, political parties, argues Vaishnav, have welcomed to the party, politicians with dubious backgrounds:

> Election costs in India have risen considerably over the years as the size of the population has ballooned and the competitiveness of elections has grown. This resource crunch has compelled all political parties to innovate in their desperate search for financial 'rents'. While these campaign funds are raised to cover the exorbitant costs of elections, undoubtedly some of these resources end up lining the pockets of party leaders. In parties' struggles to identify reliable sources of funding—a partial reflection of the decline in their organizational strength—they have increasingly placed a premium on candidates who can bring resources into the party and will not drain party coffers. (Vaishnav 2017: 19)

It is publicly acknowledged that money and muscle manipulate the composition and functioning of political power. Indeed, it is not just that 'crime pays' in politics—political office has itself become a source for amassing wealth. Innumerable reports have shown how incomes of politicians or their family members have grown, in some cases exponentially, after they assumed office. The increase in trust in a body such as the ECI is largely construed as recognition of the fact that the ECI does what it is expected to do, that is, conduct elections in a free and fair manner. The steps towards making the electoral procedure more credible and the electoral outcome democratic came from the ECI, sometimes on the orders of the Supreme Court and the high courts in response to public interest litigations, but often on its own initiative. It may be said that in a political culture where rigging, booth capturing, and violence in elections were not uncommon, the ECI has, over the years, been able to affirm the autonomy that the Constitution had conferred on it. To an extent, the affirmation of its powers of regulating the electoral space has progressed alongside a sustained reticence and reluctance on the part of the legislators who have been empowered by the Constitution to enact laws to curtail electoral malpractices or to introduce changes, which would address the challenges of democratic deficit. At the most, committees have been instituted periodically to suggest electoral reforms, which have recommended substantial changes, but the efforts to convert the recommendations into laws have been desultory. More often than not, bills drawn up to make specific reform suggestions effective have either been attempts to consolidate the position of the party in power or, as in the case of the Electoral Reform Bill introduced in Parliament in July–August 2002, a desperate attempt to reclaim the grounds lost by Parliament and the political class to the ECI.

Among the initial attempts towards electoral reforms was the setting up, in 1971, of a joint parliamentary committee of the two Houses of Parliament under the chairpersonship of Jagannath Rao. The Jagannath Rao Committee submitted two reports to Parliament in the months of January and March 1972, suggesting amendments to the RPAs. A Bill was subsequently introduced in the Lok Sabha in 1973 taking on board some of these suggestions, including contentious ones like electoral offences and election finance. Some of the important provisions in the Bill were: (*a*) specifying four qualifying dates in a year instead of one for the qualification of voters, (*b*) prohibiting capricious transfers of election staff on the eve of elections, (*c*) disqualification of persons with contracts with the government or any public-sector undertaking, from contesting elections, (*d*) counting of election expenses from the date of the notification calling for election instead of the date of nomination, (*e*) enhanced punishments for certain election-related offences, and so on. In the absence of a political will to pass the Bill expeditiously, the Bill lapsed in 1975 with the dissolution of the Lok Sabha and the truncation of its powers during the Emergency. Some amendments relating to election expenses were brought about in 1974–7, and were generally seen as favouring the ruling party. Contrary to the recommendations of the Jagannath Rao Committee, the new amendment favoured the counting of election expenses from the date of nomination and not from the date of notification. Election expenses by political parties or individuals other than the candidate or his agent were not to be taken into account. Expenditure by a government servant during the course of his duty was to be excluded.[4]

---

[4] Act No. 40 of 1975 and No. 58 of 1974.

Subsequent attempt at electoral reforms by a committee chaired by Justice Tarkunde set up by the Janata Party government (1977–9) proved futile since the Janata government was dislodged from power rather quickly. But the recommendations of the committee relating to adequate modes of representation, and control of party finances continued to be significant.[5] In the 1980s, significant changes were introduced in the electoral system through constitutional amendments, in place of changes in the electoral law. The 52nd amendment in 1985 inserted the 10th schedule in the Constitution, which laid down 'defection' as a ground of disqualification for MPs,[6] the use of EVMs,[7]

[5] The short tenure of the government and internal dissensions prevented the adoption of the report as a legal measure. Some of the more significant recommendations of the committee aiming towards loosening the influence that ruling parties may have over election outcomes, were: (a) introduction of a partially proportional representation system of election; (b) appointment of the CEC by the president in consultation with a committee consisting of the chief justice, the prime minister, and the leader of the opposition in the Lok Sabha (instead of consultation only with the prime minister); (c) the government in office should work only as a caretaker government during the election period; (d) prohibition of contributions by companies to political parties; (e) audit of account of candidates and parties; (f) some limited financial assistance to all parties by the state.

[6] The 10th Schedule of the Constitution added by the Constitution (Amendment) Act, 1985, was a subject of criticism both on political and legal grounds since its enactment. In *Kihota Hollohan v. Zachilhu* (AIR 1993 SC 412), the Supreme Court gave its final verdict on the validity of the 10th Schedule. For more details on the majority decision upholding the amendment and other legal aspects of the amendment (see K.C. Sunny 2000: 226–9).

[7] In May 1982, the ECI used EVMs for the first time in 50 polling stations of Parur assembly constituency in Kerala. The EVMs were produced by two central government undertakings, Electronics Corporation of India Limited, Hyderabad, and Bharat Electronic Limited, Bangalore. The following year, the EVMs were used in 10 other constituencies across India. In 1983, the Supreme Court put a halt to its use in an election petition (*A.C. Jose v. Sivan Pillai & Others*, AIR 1984 SC 921) holding that the action of the ECI in introducing EVMs was without jurisdiction, since at that time, there was no provision in the RPA empowering the ECI to conduct polls using a device other than ballot. *AIR* 1984 SC 921. On the recommendation of the ECI, in December 1988, the government inserted a new Section 61A in the

provision of registration for political parties,[8] and so on. The 61st constitutional amendment in 1988 brought down the minimum age of voting from 21 to 18 years. The Goswami Committee under law minister Dinesh Goswami, set up when V.P. Singh was the prime minister, made some significant recommendations in May 1990.[9] A bill to implement some of these recommendations, while excluding the two important suggestions pertaining to identity cards and ban on donations by companies, was introduced in the Rajya Sabha. In September 1998, the 170th Report of the Law Commission of India, which dealt specifically with electoral reforms, recommended limited state funding towards elections and a substantial increase in the deposits made by candidates to discourage non-serious candidates representing non-recognised political parties.

In order to make the Lok Sabha more representative, the Law Commission recommended the addition of 138 seats in the Lok Sabha and the substitution of the 'first past the post' method of election with a list system. To prevent the 'wastage' of a large number of votes that went 'unrepresented' under the first past the post system, the Law Commission suggested that 25 per cent of the seats be distributed on the basis of the proportion of votes polled by political

---

RPA, 1951, empowering the ECI to use voting machines. See also 'History of Electronic Voting Machines in India,' Foundation for Advanced Management of Elections. Available at http://fame-india.com/article_view_2.php?art_id=6; accessed on 23 December 2013.

[8] An association or body of individual citizens of India calling itself a political party and intending to avail itself of the provisions of Part-IV-A of the RPA, 1951, (relating to registration of political parties) is required to get itself registered with the ECI. The guidelines for registration are issued by the ECI from time to time.

[9] These recommendations pertained to making post offices the focal points for preparing electoral rolls, issuing identity cards to voters within a time-bound schedule, prohibiting persons from contesting election from more than one constituency, making specific provisions of the MCC statutory, banning donations by companies, providing financial assistance from the state to candidates of recognised parties, and amending the 10th schedule to the Constitution so that disqualification for defection be decided by the governor or the president and not by the speaker of the Lower House or the chairperson of the Upper House.

parties. To prevent 'criminalisation of politics', the Law Commission recommended the disqualification of those candidates against whom charges had been framed under any section of the IPC, Customs Act and Sections 10 to 12 of the Unlawful Activities (Prevention) Act, Section 7 of the 1988 Religious Institutions (Prevention of Misuse) Act, and the Protection of Civil Rights Act, 1955. Again, as far as the 10th Schedule was concerned, the Law Commission recommended the scrapping of the Anti-Defection Act to ensure that neither 'split' nor 'merger' be allowed, and once elected, a candidate would remain a member of that political party for the entire duration of the term. It also emphasised that political parties should be obliged to maintain accounts showing the details of amounts received and spent by them. On the basis of these recommendations, the draft 1998 Representation of People (Amendment) Bill was framed.[10] In 2001, the Election and Other Related Laws (Amendment) Bill 2001, based on the recommendations of a committee under the chairpersonship of Indrajit Gupta, proposed amendments in the RPA, 1951, to regulate fundraising by political parties in elections. For the ECI, cleaning up the electoral space of both 'criminalisation' and excessive spending, which were bred by and also reinforced corruption in politics, have remained the most pressing concerns. The ECI has addressed these through its regulatory powers which have been buttressed by judicial interventions.

'Criminalisation of Politics', the Right to Know, and the Citizen-Voter

In the run-up to the state assembly elections in Delhi, Rajasthan, Madhya Pradesh, Chhattisgarh, and Mizoram in December 2013, the *Indian Express* ran a series of columns titled 'I hereby declare'. The columns carried bulleted information on the personal assets declared

---

[10] Law Commission of India, *170th Report of the Law Commission on Electoral Reforms*. New Delhi: Government of India, 1999; and newspaper reports, 'Panel Proposes State Funding of Polls,' *The Statesman*, 19 September 1998; 'Law Panel Suggestions on Electoral Reforms,' *The Statesman*, 20 September 1998, 'Ban Splits, Bar those Charge-sheeted,' *The Indian Express*, 17 September 1998.

by candidates in their 'disclosure statements', that is, the affidavits which the candidates submitted at the time of filing their nomination papers. Among these was the truly bewildering disclosure of the wealth accumulated by the BJP candidate from Delhi, Sat Prakash Rana, in a span of five years of his election to the state assembly. Rana's disclosure in 2013 showed that the combined figures of his family's wealth (his and his wife's) had witnessed an exponential increase to 111.91 crores from the 6.37 crores that he had declared in the affidavit submitted with his nomination papers in the earlier state assembly election in 2008. While Rana's wealth showed the highest increase among the several candidates who were re-contesting the assembly elections in Delhi, Rana was not the wealthiest, and only one among the numerous *crorepati* (billionaire) candidates fielded by the leading political parties in the state, that is, the Congress and the BJP.[11]

The affidavits filed by the candidates contesting the state assembly election in Delhi in December 2013, as required under the RPA amended in 2003, were put up on the ECI's website for the information of the voters. An examination of these affidavits conducted by the Association for Democratic Reforms (ADR) and Delhi Election Watch (DEW), which have been monitoring the relationship between crime, wealth, and elections for several years, showed that the assets of the 66 members of legislative assemblies (MLAs) re-contesting the election in the state had increased substantially from the last election.[12]

---

[11] Rana had listed a commercial property worth 50 lakhs as a new acquisition, and the property that was the same as those declared in the 2008 affidavit was listed at the appreciated rate. Rana had two criminal cases against him pertaining to defacement of property in Delhi. From 'I Hereby Declare,' *The Indian Express*, 4 December 2013, p. 4. Manjinder Singh Sirsa, Shiromani Akali Dal candidate from Rajouri Garden constituency, had declared the highest assets at Rs 235.51 crore, followed by Sushil Gupta, Congress candidate from Moti Nagar, with declared assets of Rs 164.44 crore. Ashok Kumar Jain of Congress from Delhi Cantt constituency had declared assets of Rs 143.69 crore. ('Number of Candidates with Criminal Cases Up in Delhi,' *The Indian Express*, 8 December 2013.)

[12] The ADR and DEW analysed affidavits of 796 of 810 candidates contesting the Delhi assembly polls, which were held on 4 December 2013. ('Number of Candidates with Criminal Cases up in Delhi,' *The Indian Express*.) The

Even if one were to attribute some of the increase to the appreciation in the value of their previously existing assets, which would be true for persons in any other profession, the study concluded that for those in politics, the growth in assets was substantially and often extraordinarily more rapid.[13]

The number of candidates with criminal records had also gone up in Delhi from 111 out of 790 (14 per cent) in 2008 to 129 out of 796 (16 per cent) in 2013. Out of these 129 candidates, 93 (72 per cent) had declared serious charges, including murder, dacoity, and crimes against women, which had been made against them.[14] Among the

---

National Election Watch by the ADR has a portal 'myneta.info' carrying the tabulated information on all MPs and the state legislative assemblies. A Facebook service 'know your candidate' is also made available by ADR.

[13] The study said that 265 of 796 candidates (33 per cent) were crorepatis. In 2008, this number was 180 out of 790 (23 per cent). The average assets per candidate in 2008 was Rs 1.77 crore which went up to Rs 3.43 crore in 2013. Among the major parties, the average asset per candidate for Congress was Rs 14.25 crore, BJP candidates had average assets of Rs 8.16 crore, and for AAP, the figure was Rs 2.51 crores ('Number of Candidates with Criminal Cases up in Delhi,' *The Indian Express*).

[14] Educated up to class 10, with 16 cases registered against him for offences as serious as trafficking, murder, promoting enmity between communities, and committing acts prejudicial to the maintenance of harmony, the RJD candidate Asif Mohammed Khan, who won the by-election from Okhla in September 2009, ending the 15-year Congress reign in the constituency, topped the list of candidates with a criminal background in Delhi. The charges against Khan were as follows: two charges related to promoting enmity between different groups on grounds of religion, race, place of birth, residence, language, and so on, and doing acts prejudicial to maintenance of harmony (IPC Section-153A), one charge related to 'buying minor for purposes of prostitution, etc'. (IPC Section-373), one charge related to theft (IPC Section-379), four charges related to obstructing public servant in discharge of public functions (IPC Section-186), three charges related to acts done by several persons in furtherance of common intention (IPC Section-34), three charges related to assault or criminal force to deter public servant from discharge of his duty (IPC Section-353), two charges related to rioting (IPC Section-147), two charges related to rioting, armed with deadly weapon (IPC Section-148), two charges related to criminal intimidation (IPC Section-506), one charge related to rioting (IPC Section-146), one charge related to criminal

political parties, the BJP led the list with 31 of its 68 candidates having criminal charges against them, followed by the Congress, which had 15 such candidates out of the 70 candidates it had fielded, the BSP which had 12 out of 67, and the AAP with 5 out of 70 candidates with

---

trespass (IPC Section-447), one charge related to statements conducing to public mischief (IPC Section-505). The details of charges along with the FIR numbers of cases lodged in different police stations are available on the National Election Watch website of the ADR. Available at http://myneta.info/ dl2008/candidate.php?candidate_id=44&print=true; accessed 21 December 2013. Khan was followed by an independent MLA Bharat Singh, who made headlines last year after being shot at by four gunmen in Najafgarh, his constituency. A former municipal councillor, he has three registered cases of murder and attempted murder against him. His brother Kishen Pehalwan is among Delhi's most wanted criminals with multiple murder cases registered against him. BJP's Kulwant Rana, from Rithala constituency in Delhi, was arrested by the Delhi Police in April after being chargesheeted for offences under the Scheduled Castes and Tribes (Prevention of Atrocities) Act. According to the Delhi police, Rana is a 'habitual offender with no respect for law', who is also involved in criminal cases for obstructing public servants, unlawful assembly, and assault. When he got elected in 2008, Rana had two cases against him for kidnapping, unlawful confinement, and using criminal force to deter a public servant from discharging his duty, as per ADR's analysis of his affidavit. The other three MLAs accused of serious crimes include Devendar Yadav of the Congress, MLA from Badli, who faces charges that include theft and criminal intimidation; BJP's Naresh Gaur from Babarpur who is accused in three cases for offences that include obstructing public servants from discharging their duties, voluntarily causing hurt and theft; Neeraj Basoya, Congress MLA from Kasturba Nagar and an advocate by profession, who is accused of using dangerous weapons to cause hurt, criminal intimidation, and wrongful restraint. The lone convicted MLA in the Delhi Assembly as per ADR's report is Mohan Singh Bisht. A BJP MLA from Karawal Nagar, Bisht was convicted in 1995 of causing voluntary hurt and of wrongful confinement. He had appealed against the verdict. Bisht is accused in four other criminal cases for rioting armed with deadly weapon (punishable with up to three years), using criminal force to deter public servant from discharging his duties and voluntarily causing hurt and insulting the modesty of a woman, among other offences. From ADRs analysis, 'Delhi Polls 2013: From Murder to Kidnapping, Know Your MLA's Crimes,' *Firstpost*, 13 October 2013.

charge sheets against them. The other 64 candidates who declared criminal charges against them were from smaller parties or were independent candidates.[15]

The December 2013 state assembly elections in Delhi were remarkable in several ways, not the least because the AAP—a debutant political party—emerged as a political game changer. In these elections, the AAP reduced the Congress party, which had been in power in the state for the past 15 years to a meagre tally of 8 seats, and the BJP to a position where although it gained the highest number of seats, it could not muster the required majority to form the government.[16] More significant perhaps was the AAP's foregrounding of 'elimination of corruption' as its main political plank, following which it made 'transparency' integral to its electoral campaign, and indeed, its modus operandi. Not only did the AAP make public on its website all the donations it received and the expenses it incurred, it also ran the most inexpensive election campaign for a political party in recent

[15] Eight Congress candidates (11 per cent) had serious criminal cases against them, while the figure was 22 (32 per cent) for the BJP, 12 (18 per cent) for the BSP, and five (7 per cent) for the AAP. For the Congress, the number of candidates with criminal cases had come down from 30 per cent in the 2008 assembly elections to 21 per cent in the 2013 polls. For the BJP, the corresponding figure went up from 35 per cent to 46 per cent ('Number of Candidates with Criminal Cases Goes up in Delhi,' *Business Standard*, 26 November 2013. Available at https://www.business-standard.com/article/news-ians/number-of-candidates-with-criminal-cases-goes-up-in-delhi-113112600882_1.html; accessed on 8 December 2013). See also a survey by ADR and National Election Watch of the crime and money in politics, in a 12-page press release issued by them for the information of the press. ADR, 'Ten Years of Election Watch: Comprehensive Reports on Elections, Crime and Money,' press release, 29 July 2013. Available at http://online.wsj.com/public/resources/documents/Election.pdf; accessed on 8 December 2013.

[16] Of the 70 Assembly seats in Delhi, the BJP got the highest at 31 seats, the AAP followed with 28 seats, the Indian National Congress with 8 seats, the JDU and Shiromani Akali Dal with 1 seat each, and an independent candidate with 1 seat. The AAP formed the government with the Congress providing it support from outside the government. See the Election Commission website. Available at http://eciresults.ap.nic.in/; accessed on 25 December 2013.

times in India, making it possible as it were, for an *aam aadmi* (common man) to contest an election.[17] Its campaign also showed that a political party could voluntarily open itself to public scrutiny instead of being forced to submit to one by law.

The desirability of opening the electoral space to scrutiny on behalf of the voter had been recommended by the Law Commission in its 170th report. This became possible only after a protracted contest between the members of Parliament, who preferred selective disclo-'sure of information, and the Election Commission and the judiciary, which favoured extensive disclosure of information to the voter.

The process of eliciting disclosure began with the municipal corporation elections in Chandigarh and Delhi in February–March 2002, when the state election commission made it mandatory for all candidates to file an affidavit stating whether or not they had faced trial and conviction in the past three years.[18] In the absence of a clear law enabling the ECI to issue instructions for eliciting and disseminating information on the antecedents of the candidates contesting elections, these instructions were issued under the provisions of Article 243V of the Constitution, which specifies that a member would be disqualified from seeking election to the municipality 'if he is so disqualified by or under any law for the time being in force for purposes of elections to the Legislature of the State concerned', and Section 8 of the RPA, 1951, which spells out the disqualifications. The ECI was further buttressed by the judgment of the Delhi High Court instructing the ECI to carry out the recommendations of the Law Commission of India. The returning officers were issued directions on 22 February 2002 by the joint election commissioner, under the

---

[17] See http://www.aamaadmiparty.org/donation-list; accessed on 21 December 2013.

[18] The unprecedented measure taken under Section 8 of the RPA, 1951—for those contesting parliamentary and assembly elections—was implemented for the first time during the Chandigarh Municipal Corporation polls. The returning officers were issued a special set of directions under the subject: 'Criminalisation of politics—participation of criminals in electoral processes as candidates—disqualification on conviction for offences—effect of appeal and bail' ('Criminals at Bay,' *The Hindu*, 24 February 2002).

specific subject heading, 'Criminalisation of politics—participation of criminals in electoral process as candidates—disqualification on conviction for offences—effect of appeal and bail'. The directions noted that 'criminal elements [had] taken to politics in a big way and the country [was] facing the serious problem of criminalisation of politics'. They also reminded the officers of the Delhi High Court's ruling, which had taken the view that release on bail did not 'wipe off' the 'disqualification' spelt out under Section 8(1) of the RPA, 1951. A proforma issued to the candidates, which was to be submitted along with the affidavit, explained that information was being sought under specific legal provisions and listed the various heads under which it was being sought, including information regarding conviction in cases, and cases pending before courts.[19]

It is to be noted that the ECI attempted to filter out only those candidates who had a 'proven criminal record', which was a dilution of the recommendation of the Law Commission that considered the framing of charges by the court sufficient ground for disqualification. The Delhi High Court's judgment of 2 November 2001 directed the ECI to seek information on the background of candidates contesting elections, which included their criminal record (if any), educational qualifications and assets, to evaluate their capability to become MLAs or MPs. The high court judgment came in response to a petition filed by the ADR for directions to implement the recommendations made by the Law Commission in its 170th report and to make changes in the conduct of election rules. The 170th report of the Law Commission was an outcome of a comprehensive study undertaken by it, acting upon a mandate by the government to suggest measures required to expedite hearing of election petitions, and a thorough review of the RPA, 1951. The review of the RPA, 1951, was to be done with the objective of making 'the electoral process more fair, transparent and equitable and to reduce the distortions and evils that [had] crept into the Indian electoral system and to identify the areas where the legal provisions required strengthening

[19] Directions, No. SEC/MCD/15/2002, issued by the State Election Commission to Returning Officers of Delhi Municipal Wards, 22 February 2002.

and improvement'.[20] While the high court in its order of 2 November 2001 held that it was Parliament and not the high court that could make the necessary amendments in the law, it upheld the validity of the petition. It stressed that in order to make the right choice, the voter needed to know whether the candidate was worthy of the vote, and directed the ECI to 'secure to voters', the following information relating to each candidate:

1. Whether the candidate was accused of any offence punishable with imprisonment, with its details.
2. Assets possessed by the candidate, his/her spouse, or dependent relations.
3. Facts giving insight into the candidate's competence, capacity, and suitability for acting as a parliamentarian or a legislator including his/her educational qualifications.
4. Information which the ECI of India considers necessary for judging the capacity and capability of the political parties of the candidates seeking election for Parliament or state legislature.[21]

The ECI was empowered by the high court to issue directions to the agencies of the central and state governments, including the Intelligence Bureau, to assist it in gathering the relevant information, and the authority approached by the ECI for assistance was 'duty bound to provide the same'. Non-compliance with the directions

[20] As expressed by Justice Jeevan Reddy, in his forwarding letter No. 6(3)(35)/95-LC(LS), dated 29 May 1999 to Ram Jethmalani, minister of Law, Justice and Company Affairs. Available at http://www.lawcommissionofindia. nic.in/lc170.htm#LAW%20COMMISSION%20OF%20INDIA; accessed on 29 December 2013. It may be noted that the Law Commission recommended that a candidate be debarred from contesting elections even if charges have been framed against him by a Court in respect of certain offences and asked that a candidate should necessarily furnish details regarding criminal cases pending against him. It also suggested that true and correct statement of assets owned by the candidate, his/her spouse, and dependent relations should also be disclosed.

[21] Affidavit on behalf of Respondent No. 2 (Election Commission of India) in the Supreme Court of India in the Special Leave Petition (Civil) No. 737 of 2001, *Union of India v. Association for Democratic Reforms and Another.*

issued by the ECI 'in conformity with the directions of the High Court' could 'entail consequences according to law'.[22]

An appeal against the high court judgment was made to the Supreme Court by the BJP-led NDA government, joined through an intervention by the Indian National Congress. In their appeal, the government and both political parties contended that the high court should have addressed Parliament to make the necessary amendments in law instead of approaching the ECI to implement the changes recommended by the Law Commission. The appellants also argued that the order was irrelevant since the necessary disqualifications for specific electoral offences and corrupt practices were already listed in the RPA and elaborate procedures for presenting valid nomination papers were already in place. They, moreover, pleaded that 'non-disclosure' of assets or pending charges was not a disqualification under the Act. The ECI's directions, they believed, did not have the support of law, were indeed contrary to the law, and should not, therefore, have been issued.

On the point of law regarding whether or not the ECI was empowered to issue directions as ordered by the high court, the Supreme Court reiterated the position previously established in *Vineet Narain and Others* v. *Union of India* (1998).[23] The Court affirmed that it had the power to issue directions to the ECI to step in to fill a legal vacuum, till a suitable law was enacted. Evidently, the question of inconsonance with law did not arise, since the courts and the ECI were plugging a gap in the existing law. Describing Article 324(1) of the Constitution as a 'reservoir of power', the Supreme Court averred that the Article gave scope for the exercise of 'residuary power' by the ECI in an infinite variety of situations that may emerge from time to time.[24] Even though, as the government pleaded, the disqualifications pertaining to corruption and criminal offences were already listed in

[22] Affidavit on behalf of Respondent No. 2 (Election Commission of India) in the Supreme Court of India in the Special Leave Petition (Civil) No. 737 of 2001, *Union of India* v. *Association for Democratic Reforms and Another.*

[23] *Vineet Narain and Others* v. *Union of India and Another*, 1998: SCC 226.

[24] The Court was making reference here to the judgment delivered by the constitution bench of the Court in *Mohinder Singh Gill* v. *The Chief Election Commissioner*, New Delhi, 1978: SCC 405.

law, the court orders made 'disclosure' of facts binding on candidates. Underlying both the high court and Supreme Court judgments was the belief that the courts were ultimately safeguarding the fundamental rights of the people and facilitating the meaningful exercise of political rights in a democracy. Democracy, the judges asserted, could not survive 'without free and fair elections, without free and fairly informed voters' and votes cast by 'uninformed voters' would be 'meaningless'. The significance of the judgment, moreover, lay in the manner in which the Supreme Court's verdict enhanced the scope of the fundamental rights of citizens to freedom of speech and expression (Article 19[1]). The exercise of franchise was for the Court a 'form of speech and expression': 'the voter speaks out ... by casting the vote'.[25] The casting of vote as a form of speech and expression required, as any fundamental right in the Constitution, the conditions conducive for its exercise. Conducive conditions would not merely mean non-discrimination and equality enabling all eligible citizens to vote, but in addition, also ensuring that the act of voting would be meaningful and fulfilling for both the voter and the political community of which the citizen-voter was a part. The latter was an important democratic principle, necessary to make electoral democracy substantive. Information about the candidate to be selected, would, the judges felt, enable and also compel the voter—the 'little man'—'to think over before making his choice of electing law-breakers as lawmakers'.

The Court considered the fundamental freedom of speech and expression to be commensurate with the right of citizens to know. In the process of emphasising this, the Supreme Court also widened the scope of the ECI's constitutional powers to superintend and conduct elections. By binding the ECI to the duty of ensuring that the voters are informed of the antecedents of their candidates, their abilities and competence, and the possibilities of their disqualification after they have been elected, the Supreme Court made it necessary for the ECI to publicise the details of the candidates among the voters.[26] The widening of the scope of ECI's powers under Article 324 of the Constitution also meant that the ECI now had the authority to make

[25] *Union of India* v. *Association for Democratic Reforms & Another* (SC 249/2002).

[26] All affidavits are put on the ECI's website, and reports on candidates' backgrounds are widely reported in newspapers and by civil society groups.

rules in this area rather than wait for Parliament to legislate. They also expanded the scope of Article 324 as not merely vesting all residuary powers in the ECI, but also envisaging it as a 'reservoir of powers', 'where law [was] silent'.[27]

In a rare show of consensus, the political parties reacted to the Supreme Court's judgment by rejecting the ECI's directive giving effect to the Court's orders making it mandatory for candidates contesting Parliament and state legislative assembly elections to furnish affidavits that gave details of their assets, conviction for any criminal offence, and liability to a public financial institution. The law ministry rejected the ECI's directive that nomination papers must be suitably modified to elicit the required information from the candidate, and set out to make changes in the law itself.[28] In a collective show of strength, the parliamentarians sought to retrieve and hold on to their claim of representing the political domain and accused the judiciary of encroaching into it.[29] In an attempt to 'neutralise' the Supreme Court's order and the ECI directives, Parliament promulgated the Representation of the People (Amendment) Ordinance on 24 August 2002, replaced later by the Representation of the People (Third) Amendment Act in December 2002.[30]

---

[27] For details and context of the Supreme Court judgment, see *Union of India* v. *Association for Democratic Reforms & Another* (SC 249/2002) and newspaper reports: 'The Voter's Right to Know,' *The Hindu*, 4 May 2002; 'Voters Have the Right to Know Candidate's Antecedent: SC,' *The Hindu*, 3 May 2002; 'SC Order for Cleaner Pools,' *Hindustan Times*, 3 May 2002.

[28] 'Govt. to Consult Parties on Court Fiat to EC,' *The Hindu*, 19 June 2002.

[29] Despite rejection by the parties, the order of the Court and the directive issued by the EC under it is legally binding. The government had reportedly asked the EC to approach the SC to extend the time limit from 2 July.

[30] The Bill made no reference to the disclosure of a candidate's financial assets and liabilities, which was central to the Supreme Court's judgment on the citizen's right to know. The proposed legislation also did not say anything about disclosing the educational background of candidates, which was a relatively minor element among the three main constituents of the judgment. As far as acquainting the voter with the candidate's criminal past was concerned, the draft Bill required all those accused of offences punishable with a sentence of two years to furnish the required details (see 'Neutralising the Court,' *The Hindu*, 20 July 2002).

The ordinance and the act that replaced it amended the RPA, 1951, by inserting new Sections 33A, 33B, 75A, 125A, and 169A, pertaining to 'right to information', 'declaration of assets and liabilities', and 'penalties for filing false affidavit etc'.[31] A comparative chart given in Table 4.3 shows how the provisions under the new Act diluted the Supreme Court order of 2 May 2002.

Table 4.3 makes it amply clear that under the Amendment Act, a candidate contesting election was not required to disclose: the cases in which he or she was acquitted or discharged of criminal offence(s), his or her assets and liabilities, and educational qualification. The assets of candidates were to be disclosed to the Speaker of the Lok Sabha, *after* the candidate had been elected to Parliament. The RPA thus seemed to suggest that once a person was acquitted or discharged of any criminal offence, there was no necessity of disclosing the same to the voters. Moreover, information pertaining to the assets

---

[31] The Representation of the People (Amendment) Ordinance, Ministry of Law and Justice, 24 August 2002. On 30 July 2004, the ECI submitted to the prime minister a set of proposals for electoral reforms. Among these was a proposal outlining a simplified procedure for disqualification of a person found guilty of corrupt practice. This proposal had been among those submitted on 15 July 1998 by the CEC to the law minister and reiterated in the letter dated 22 November 1999 addressed to the prime minister. The current procedure for disqualification of a person found guilty of corrupt practice was that after a high court pronounced its judgment in an election petition, finding a person guilty of corrupt practice, the case of every such person had to go to the president of India under Section 8A(1), through the concerned state legislature secretary or the secretary general of Lok Sabha or Rajya Sabha as the case may be. Thereafter, under Section 8A(3), it came from the president to the ECI, where a judicial hearing was given to the affected party and the period of disqualification judged by the ECI and communicated to the president, who then decided the period of disqualification on the basis of the opinion given to him. Since the elements that went into what could be construed as a corrupt practice under the RPA, 1951, were numerous, the ECI's proposals did not prefer a uniform automatic disqualification for six years for all those found guilty of corrupt practices, as was being advocated in some quarters. While suggesting that the existing system, which allows flexibility be retained, the ECI recommended that decisions on questions of disqualification be taken expeditiously, which at present were delayed inordinately (See Election Commission of India 2004).

Table 4.3   Supreme Court Judgment and the Ordinance Compared

Subject	Supreme Court Judgment (2 May 2002)	Provisions under the Ordinance/Act August/December 2002
Past Criminal Record	*Para 48(1) of the judgment:* All past convictions/acquittals/discharges, whether punished with imprisonment or fine to be disclosed.	*Section 33A(1)(ii):* Conviction of any offence (except Section 8 offence) and sentenced to imprisonment of one year or more to be disclosed.
Pending Criminal Cases	*Para 48(2):* Prior to six months of filing of nomination whether the candidate has been accused of any criminal offence punishable with imprisonment of two years or more, and charge framed or cognizance taken.	*Section 33A(1)(i):* Any case in which the candidate has been accused of any criminal offence punishable with imprisonment of two years or more, and charge framed.
Assets and Liabilities	*Para 48(3):* Assets of candidate (contesting the elections), spouse, and dependents.	*Section 75A:* No such declaration by a candidate who is contesting elections. After election, elected candidate is required to furnish information relating to him as well as his spouse and dependent children's assets to the speaker of the House of People.
	Para 48(4): Liabilities, particularly to government and public financial institutions.	No provision is made for the candidate contesting elections. However, after election, Section 75A(1)(ii)(iii) provides for elected candidate.

(Cont'd)

Table 4.3 (Cont'd)

Subject	Supreme Court Judgment (2 May 2002)	Provisions under the Ordinance/Act August/ December 2002
Educational Qualifications	*Para 48(5):* To be declared.	No provision.
Breach of Provisions	No direction regarding consequences of noncompliance.	*Section 125A:* Creates an offence punishable by imprisonment for six months or fine for failure to furnish affidavit in accordance with Section 33A, as well as for falsity or concealment in affidavit or nomination paper. *Section 75(A):* Wilful contravention of rules regarding asset disclosure may be treated as breach of the House.

Source: Supreme Court Judgment in People's Union for Civil Liberties (PUCL) & Another v. Union of India and Another, Judgements Today, 2(10), 20 March 2003, SC.541–542.

of the candidate was not considered important for disclosure at the time of contesting the election. While the spirit of the Supreme Court judgment had been to equip the voter with maximum information so as to enable the voter to exercise the right to vote judiciously, the Act preferred to inform the voter only selectively at the time of election. Thus, information pertaining to (*a*) convictions and sentence under one year, (*b*) acquittals and discharge, (*c*) accusation of a criminal offence punishable with two years, and (*d*) educational qualifications were to be screened off entirely from the public domain, while those pertaining to (*i*) assets of candidate, spouse, and dependents and (*ii*) liabilities were to brought onto the public domain *after* the election process had ended, for the elected candidates only. Further, Section 33B rolled back the Supreme Court judgment and directives of the ECI, which it explicitly stated were supplanted by the new law.[32]

The Representation of the People (Third) Amendment Act, 2002, was subsequently challenged in the Supreme Court by the People's Union for Civil Liberties (PUCL), Lok Satta, and ADR. In its judgment delivered on 13 March 2003, the Supreme Court declared the Act null and void and asked the ECI to issue revised instructions to ensure implementation of Section 33A in accordance with the Court's judgment. In the process of delivering the judgment, the Supreme Court revisited the relative powers of the ECI and Parliament, examined the scope of the legislative powers that Parliament claimed through Article 33B in the amended Act, and reaffirmed the right to information as an integral part of a citizen's constitutional right to vote.

The 2 May 2002 judgment of the Supreme Court in the case *Union of India* v. *Association for Democratic Reforms* had shown, as has been discussed earlier, that Article 324 was envisaged by the Court as a 'reservoir of powers' giving the ECI 'residuary powers', 'where law [was] silent'. In its subsequent judgment of 13 March 2003 in the case *People's Union for Civil Liberties and Another* v. *Union of India and*

---

[32] Section 33B inserted in the amended act lay down 'Notwithstanding anything contained in any judgment, decree or order of any court or any direction, order or any other instruction issued by the Election Commission, no candidate shall be liable to disclose or furnish any such information, in respect of his election which is not required to be disclosed or furnished under this Act or the rules made thereunder'.

Another, the Court conceded that the directives given by the Court to the ECI in its judgment could operate only till there was a legislative vacuum in the matter. Once a law was made, the directives would cease to have effect. But the law, when made (in this case the Representation of the People (Third) Amendment Act), was subject to the Supreme Court's 'independent assessment' and evaluation for appropriateness. The standard of evaluation sustained from its earlier judgment, which was, 'whether the items of information statutorily ordained are reasonably adequate to secure the right to information available to the voter/citizen'. In other words, it was for the Supreme Court to decide whether the amendments brought in through the new law secured to the citizen-voter the information that made possible a substantive exercise of the right to vote. The judges found the information falling short of what could be termed adequate.

The judgment, moreover, specifically struck down Article 33B as invalid, on the additional ground that the 'legislature could remove the basis of a decision rendered by a competent court by rendering it ineffective, but it could not direct the instrumentalities of the state to disobey or disregard the decisions given by the court'. Section 33B, as mentioned earlier, laid down that any judgment or order of any court or a direction, order or any other instruction issued by the ECI, could not compel a candidate to disclose or furnish any such information, with respect to his election, which is not required to be disclosed or furnished under the amended Act of Parliament. The judgment thus reaffirmed the premises of the earlier judgment holding that the voter's fundamental right to know the antecedents of a candidate was a fundamental right, which existed 'independent of statutory rights under the election law': 'The attempt of courts should be to expand the reach and ambit of the fundamental rights by a process of judicial interpretation. There cannot be any distinction between the fundamental rights mentioned in Chapter III of the Constitution and the declaration of such rights on the basis of the judgments rendered by the Supreme Court'.[33]

Following the Supreme Court judgment, the ECI issued revised instructions to ensure the implementation of Section 33A, which

---

[33] *People's Union for Civil Liberties (PUCL) & Another v. Union of India and Another, Judgements Today*, 2(10), 20 March 2003, SC 529–533.

required disclosure of those cases in which charges had been framed and a court had taken cognisance. The ECI proposed that with the Supreme Court striking down 33B of the RPA, the direction of the Supreme Court in its 13 March 2003 order had become the law of the land in terms of Article 141 of the Constitution. To facilitate the implementation of the Supreme Court's order, the ECI recommended that there should be a single form of affidavit containing all vital information as required under Section 33A, and Form 26 may be amended so as to include in it all the items mentioned in the format of affidavit prescribed by the ECI.[34] In addition, the ECI recommended that a candidate had to file another affidavit in pursuance of the Supreme Court's order of 13 December 2003. In this affidavit, the candidate had to give information relating to: all pending cases in which cognisance had been taken by a court, his or her assets and liabilities, and educational qualifications. The affidavit was to be duly sworn before a magistrate of the first class or a notary public or a commissioner of oaths appointed by the high court of the state concerned. Non-furnishing of the affidavit was to be considered a violation of the order of the Supreme Court, leading to rejection of the nomination of the candidate by the returning officer at the time of scrutiny. The information furnished by each candidate in the affidavit was to be disseminated by the respective returning officers by displaying a copy of the affidavit on the notice board of his/her office and also by making the copies of the affidavit available 'freely and liberally' to all other candidates and the representatives of the print and electronic media. Moreover, if any rival candidate furnished information to the

[34] Through its order dated 27 March 2003, the ECI proposed the following changes in the affidavits to be filed by candidates on criminal antecedents, assets, and the like: (a) In terms of Section 33A of the RPA, 1951, read with Rule 4A of Conduct of Election Rules, 1961, each candidate had to file an affidavit in Form 26 appended to the Conduct of Election Rules, 1961, giving information on the following: (i) Cases, if any, in which the candidate has been accused of any offence punishable with imprisonment for two years or more in a pending case in which charges have been framed by the court. (ii) Cases of conviction for an offence other than any of the offences mentioned in Section 8 of the RPA, 1951, and sentenced to imprisonment for one year or more.

contrary, by means of a duly sworn affidavit, then such affidavit of the rival candidate was to be disseminated along with the affidavit of the candidate concerned in the same manner.[35]

In its subsequent proposals for reforms, the ECI pointed out that in the past few elections, the candidates have had the tendency of leaving a few columns blank or giving grossly undervalued information about their assets. While Section 125A provides for punishment of imprisonment for a term of up to six months with or without fine for furnishing wrong information or concealing any information in Form 26, the ECI felt that this punishment was inadequate considering the salience given by the Supreme Court to the right of the citizen to information. The ECI proposed that in order to protect the right to information of the electors in the spirit of the judgment of the Supreme Court, the punishment should be made more stringent by providing for imprisonment of a minimum term of two years and doing away with the alternative clause of fine. In addition, it suggested that the conviction for offences under Section 125A should be made part of Section 8(1)(i) of the RPA, 1951, which deals with disqualification on the ground of conviction for certain offences. Such a provision, the ECI felt, could reduce instances of candidates wilfully concealing information or furnishing wrong information. While agreeing that it was reasonable to keep a person accused of serious criminal charges out of the electoral arena, as a precaution against 'motivated cases by the ruling party', the ECI proposed that only those cases which were filed prior to six months before an election would lead to disqualification. It also proposed that persons found guilty by a commission of enquiry should also stand disqualified from contesting elections (Election Commission of India 2004: 1–4). In the same set of proposals, the ECI reiterated the proposal made earlier in July 1998 by M.S. Gill, then CEC, to the law minister, suggesting that any false declaration before the ECI, CEO, DEO, presiding officer, or any authority appointed under the RPA, 1951, in connection with any electoral matter, should be made an electoral offence under the Act. This was in line with Section 31 of the RPA, 1950, under which any false declaration or statement in connection with the preparation/revision of electoral rolls or inclusion/exclusion of any name in/from the

---

[35] Order No. 3/ER/2003/JS-II issued by the ECI on 27 March 2003.

electoral roll constituted an electoral offence (Election Commission of India 2004: 24).

Despite the suggestion by the ECI that misinformation or deception could constitute an electoral offence, in the absence of a law backing this, there has not been much that the ECI has been able to do to enforce them. Disclosure has, therefore, remained limited to dissemination of information. Interestingly, not only were candidates under-reporting their wealth in their disclosure statement, officials of the state election commission pointed out that the initial scrutiny of the nomination papers showed that most affidavits had the signature of the same public notary, the oath commissioner, or a first-class magistrate. In a number of cases, the affidavits were without the signatures of the candidates.[36] Moreover, even when affidavits were in order, it was extremely difficult to validate the information provided in the affidavits.[37] Thus, while equipping the voter with information about the candidate, the affidavits do not by themselves give the ECI any power to disqualify a candidate either for furnishing wrong information or for any disproportionate increase in wealth after becoming a representative of the people. It would appear that the power to 'punish' criminal and corrupt candidates was solely by 'rejection', and left entirely to the wisdom of the voter.

Yet, in a later judgment in the case *Resurgence India* v. *the Election Commission of India* (Writ Petition (Civil) No. 121 of 2008, delivered by Chief Justice of India P. Sathasivam on 13 September 2013), the Supreme Court reiterated the binding nature of its earlier judgments in *Union of India* v. *Association for Democratic Reforms and Another* (2002) and directed the ECI to make it compulsory for the returning officers to ensure that the affidavits filed by the contestants were complete in all respects and reject the affidavits having blank particulars. In this case, the petitioner, a non-governmental organisation (NGO) called Resurgence India, undertook what it called the Punjab Election Watch and scrutinised the affidavits of candidates of the major political parties contesting assembly elections in 2007, in order to verify

---

[36] See 'Candidates Make a Mockery of Poll Panel's Revision,' *The Hindu*, 6 March 2002.

[37] Interview with Mr Khaneta, joint state election commissioner, on 16 May 2002.

that they were complete. The organisation made a representation to the ECI of India and reported a large number of non-disclosures or affidavits accompanied by forms with blank or incomplete entries, and incompetent and inaccurate scrutiny by the returning officers.

Through a letter dated 20 February 2007, the ECI expressed to Resurgence India its inability to reject the nomination papers of the candidates on grounds that incomplete or false information was furnished by the candidate. This was because of an interpretation emerging from the Supreme Court's decision in *People's Union for Civil Liberties (PUCL) and Another* v. *Union of India and Another* (2003), which in the ECI's opinion did not empower the returning officer to reject a nomination paper solely on the basis of incomplete information or blank spaces in the affidavit.[38] The NGO subsequently petitioned the Supreme Court requesting it to issue a writ of mandamus to make it compulsory for the returning officers to ensure that the affidavits filed by the contestants were complete in all respects and reject those that did not comply with this requirement. Failure on the part of the returning officer to ensure compliance would invite punishment. In its response to the Supreme Court, the ECI sought clarification on the matter from the Supreme Court itself, by pleading that the ECI too favoured the rejection of incomplete nomination papers, but felt constrained by the judgment of the Court in PUCL (2003). The Union of India sought a clarification of a different nature. It questioned the justification for accepting a nomination paper with a signed affidavit, which gave false information, while rejecting another, which was merely incomplete. It pleaded that both blank and false information should be treated at par for rejection. Based on this premise of parity, the Government of India, unlike the ECI, did not seek just the rejection of the nomination paper of the candidate who failed to furnish complete facts in the affidavit. The government asked that such a candidate be prosecuted under Section 125A of the RPA, 1950.[39]

[38] *People's Union for Civil Liberties (PUCL) and Another* v. *Union of India and Another*, 5 SCC 294.

[39] Under Section 125A of the RPA, 1950, the penalty for filing false affidavit, and the like, a candidate who himself or through his proposer, with intent to be elected in an election: (*a*) fails to furnish information relating to

Arguing along lines similar to its earlier judgment affirming the right to know of the citizen-voter, the Court yet again asserted that the right to know is a natural right, and integral to democratic rights of citizens flowing from Article 19(1)(a) of the Constitution. The filing of nomination papers along with the affidavits under the guidelines framed by the Supreme Court and the RPA was a procedural requirement essential for making this right effective. It was the duty of the returning officer, therefore, to ensure and even 'compel' adherence to the procedures, which were vital for the consummation of this right. At the same time, the Court emphasised that the (power to) reject the nomination papers must be exercised 'very sparingly' and the 'bar should not be laid so high that the [sic] justice itself is prejudiced'. The Court also laid down that a certified copy of an entry in the electoral roll, for the time being in force in a constituency, shall be conclusive evidence of the fact that the person referred to in that entry is an elector for that constituency, unless it is proved that he is subject to a disqualification mentioned in Section 16 of the RPA, 1950 (43 of 1950). The Court went into the objectives of filling the proforma, which it construed as 'necessary and relevant information' pertaining to the candidate under Section 8 of the RPA. The returning officer was entitled to satisfy himself as to whether or not the candidate was qualified to contest. The returning officer was authorised, therefore, to seek the required information at the time of or before scrutiny. If the candidate did not furnish the required information or stayed away at the time of scrutiny, then such absence would be construed as 'avoiding a statutory inquiry' being conducted by the returning officer under Section 36(2) of the RPA to confirm his eligibility under Section 8 of the Act. The court construed that the returning officer had the power to reject the nomination papers on the ground that the contents to be filled in the affidavits were 'essential to effectuate the

---

sub-section (1) of Section 33A; or (*b*) gives false information which he knows or has reason to believe to be false; or (*c*) conceals any information, in his nomination paper delivered under sub-section (1) of Section 33 or in his affidavit which is required to be delivered under sub-section (2) of Section 33A, as the case may be, shall, notwithstanding anything contained in any other law for the time being in force, be punishable with imprisonment for a term which may extend to six months, or with fine, or with both.

intent of the provisions of the RP Act'. Leaving it blank or incomplete would prevent the returning officer from verifying whether the candidate was indeed qualified to contest or needed to be disqualified on the grounds that were not revealed by the candidate.[40]

Yet, even as the Supreme Court made it clear that the returning officer had the power to reject those nomination papers that were accompanied with incomplete affidavits, it did not address the concerns raised by the government regarding those affidavits which although complete, furnished false information. Significantly, the ECI, which had favoured the right to know of the citizen-voter and was arrayed against the parliamentarians when the right was being contested by them in the Delhi High Court and the Supreme Court of India, considered itself inadequately equipped to make the right effective in substantive terms, that is, in terms of procuring complete information and also confirming that the information was correct. In an interview given to a newspaper before the Delhi Assembly elections of December 2013, CEC V.S. Sampath pointed out that there was no provision in the RPA for disqualification on the ground of submitting wrong information. In the absence of explicit and adequate provisions in the RPA or in the Conduct of Election Rules, the ECI was not empowered to scrutinise the information submitted by candidates. In its own reforms proposals, the ECI asked for laws to provide for disqualification and imprisonment up to two years in case a candidate filed a false affidavit. The CEC felt, however, that since

[40] Decision in the case *Resurgence India* v. *Election Commission of India* reached on 13 September 2013, in the writ petition (Civil) No. 121 of 2008. Available at http://indiankanoon.org/doc/77678068/; accessed on 21 December 2013. A public interest litigation disputed the election of the then Gujarat Chief Minister Narendra Modi, from Maninagar constituency in 2012, for giving incomplete information in the affidavit. The petitioner claimed that since Modi put a dash in front of the column indicating his marital status, the affidavit must be treated as incomplete and was in defiance of the Supreme Court order in the *Resurgence India* case. The Supreme Court, however, dismissed the PIL, stating that the 'defects' in the affidavit had been explained by the candidate to the CEO. The Supreme Court, while rejecting the PIL, affirmed that reasoning of the election officer in not rejecting the affidavit, was sufficient ('SC Dismisses PIL Disputing Modi's Election Over "Incomplete" Affidavit,' *The Indian Express*, 23 November 2013).

the information was put on the website of the ECI, it was open to public scrutiny. Any individual could lodge a complaint under Section 125A of the RPA, 1951, if the information was not correct. Indeed, the ECI asked the Central Board for Direct Taxes (CBDT)[41] and Financial Intelligence Unity (FIU)[42] to download the affidavits and take necessary actions under their laws pertaining to suspect financial transactions or evasion of taxes. Moreover, even though the income tax laws prohibit disclosure of income tax returns to the public, and candidates may not therefore be asked to attach a copy of their income tax returns with their affidavits, they are required to disclose their PAN and income shown in the last return.[43] Moreover, while the candidates are required to furnish the details of the actual (initial) cost of immovable property, any investment made on it, and current market value, there is no provision in the law to get the property evaluated by an approved evaluator before the affidavit is filed. Yet, this lacuna could be overcome since the current market value can be computed on the basis of the location details.[44] The ECI has, however, consistently sought

[41] The CBDT is part of the revenue department of the Ministry of Finance and is responsible for making policy and administering the direct taxes through the Income Tax Department. See the website of the CBDT. Available at http://incometaxindia.gov.in/ccit/CBDT.asp; accessed on 1 February 2014.

[42] Financial Intelligence Unit-India (FIU-IND) was set by an order of the government on 18 November 2004. As an independent body reporting directly to the Economic Intelligence Council (EIC) headed by the finance minister, the FIU was envisaged as the central national agency responsible for receiving and processing information relating to suspect financial transactions. The FIU was also seen as an investigating and coordinating agency in the global efforts against money laundering and related crimes. See the website of the FIU. Available at http://fiuindia.gov.in/about-overview.htm, accessed on 1 February 2014.

[43] 'People Can Go to Court against Candidates Filing False Affidavits,' *The Indian Express*, 6 December 2013 (interview of CEC V.S. Sampath with Shyam Lal Yadav).

[44] Similarly, even though candidates were likely to undervalue their gold and jewellery, their value could be gauged reasonably accurately by their weight, which the candidates are required to give. ('People Can Go to Court against Candidates Filing False Affidavits,' *The Indian Express*, 6 December 2013 [interview of CEC V.S. Sampath with Shyam Lal Yadav]).

to make information available to the voter in more substantial and accessible forms. In the 2013 elections, for example, it required that the affidavits filed by the candidates also carry their photographs, so that the voters could identify their candidates. It also lay down that apart from the details of their property, the candidates also give information about their liabilities, along with their email addresses and their serial number on the electoral rolls.[45]

On 16 February 2018, in a significant judgment in a writ petition filed by the NGO Lok Prahari, a bench of the Supreme Court decided that the affidavits of disclosure filed by candidates should also give additional information regarding their sources of income, along with those of their spouse and dependents. The petition was filed by the NGO with reference to the alleged substantial increase in the assets of 26 Lok Sabha and 11 Rajya Sabha members and 257 MLAs. The judges agreed with the petitioners that any increase in the assets of a candidate that do not correspond to their known sources of income can only be logically explained as 'abuse of the legislator's constitutional office'. In line with the earlier Supreme Court judgments that affirmed that the citizen-voter had the right to know, the judges stated

---

[45] Candidates in Parliament and assembly elections, henceforth, were required to give additional information about themselves and attach their photographs while submitting affidavits on their criminal background, assets, liabilities, and education qualification with their nomination papers. These details were to be provided on a single format, unlike two separate affidavits on criminal background and assets and liabilities. This was done on a proposal moved by the ECI for amalgamating the two affidavits into one format, following which the Government of India amended Form 26 so as to include in it all the information that was sought in the two separate affidavits from the candidates. The candidates would give additional details, including part and serial number of their name in the electoral roll, phone number, email address, details of liabilities, which are in dispute, and also mention the amount involved and the authority before which it is pending. One such case was reported in Uttar Pradesh in April when the ECI received a complaint against Peace Party President Mohammad Ayub from the State Bank of India, that he had hidden details of two loans, totalling Rs 10 crore, in the affidavit of assets and liabilities he submitted with his nomination papers in the Assembly polls. ('Centre Revises Affidavit Format to Get More Data on Poll Candidates,' *The Indian Express*, 30 August 2012).

that the purity of electoral process was fundamental to the survival of a healthy democracy. There was need, therefore, they argued, for appropriate prescriptions for carrying out the purpose of the RPA, 1951, and a mechanism to 'continuously' monitor the assets and sources of income of legislators and their associates.[46] In the course of making the argument, the judges sought to reinforce the normative value of socialism enshrined in the Preamble of the Constitution, and in Articles 38 and 39 of the Constitution, which declared that the 'State shall direct its policy towards securing that the ownership and control of material resources of the community are distributed so as to best serve the common good and guaranteeing that the economic system does not result in the concentration of wealth and means of production to the common detriment'.[47] Indeed, in a context when the relevance of socialism as an ideal in the Constitution was being questioned (along with secularism) by the ruling regime, the argument that accumulation of wealth by legislators disproportionate to their known sources went against the 'spirit' of the Constitution is a powerful reminder of the democratic imaginary that the electoral process was expected to achieve.

The Disqualification Debate

The delay by Parliament in putting together a viable legal framework to put into effect the Law Commission's recommendations to address the concerns around criminalisation of politics and the difficulties which the ECI encountered in implementing changes in the municipal elections in Delhi and Chandigarh, were projected onto the larger political theatre of state politics in the assembly elections in Bihar in October–November 2005. In an attempt to pre-empt the possibility of criminals contesting elections, the ECI

[46] 'SC Raises Poll Disclosure Bar: Candidates Must Reveal Their, Kin's Income Source,' *Financial Express*, 17 February 2018.

[47] The Supreme Court bench of Justice J. Chelameswar and Justice Abdul Nazeer delivered the judgment on 16 February 2018, in the case *Lok Prahari* v. *Union of India* (writ petition(C) No. 784 of 2015. Available at http://www.live-law.in/landmark-judgment-electoral-reforms-lok-prahari-vs-uoi-explainer/; accessed on 17 February 2018.

sought to delete the names of 'absconders' from the electoral rolls. The 'absconders' were persons against whom non-bailable warrants (NBWs) had been issued for over six months, and who had not been arrested so far. The ECI sought information from the government of the state of Bihar about the 23,000 NBWs issued by various courts in the state, which had remained unexecuted. In addition, it asked the DGP of the state to give the CEOs a complete list of absconders with the details of their residential addresses. Noting that several proclaimed offenders/absconders had been evading arrest and contesting elections by getting their nominations filed by their proposers, the ECI directed the CEOs to delete their names from the electoral rolls before the poll.[48]

In a note issued by the ECI in August 2005, the ECI widened the scope of its directive, issuing general instructions to EROs in the entire country to delete from the voter's list the names of those against whom NBWs were pending for over six months.[49] The directive worked on the principle that the non-execution of an NBW on the ground that the person against whom the warrant had been issued was not available at the address given in the warrant, despite repeated visits by the police, made the person an absconder under Sections 82 and 83 of the CrPC. An absconder, it could be assumed, was not 'ordinarily resident' at the address provided by him. An essential qualification for contesting an election to Parliament or the state legislatures is that the person aspiring to be a candidate must be registered as an elector in a constituency (under Sections 3–6 of the RPA, 1951). An essential condition to be eligible for enrolment as an elector in any constituency is that a person must be 'ordinarily resident' in that constituency (Section 19(b) of the RPA, 1950). A person who is absent from his or her given address for long periods and is not available to or traceable by the police authorities and the agencies entrusted with the task of executing NBW against him could, as a logical consequence, be presumed to be not ordinarily

[48] 'EC Deletes 20 Lakh Names from Rolls,' *The Indian Express*, 22 September 2005.

[49] Press note by the Election Commission of India, No. ECI/PN/33/2005, on the subject, deletion of names of electors declared as absconders, etc, 5 August 2005.

resident at that address.[50] The name of a person who has ceased to be 'ordinarily resident in the constituency' could be deleted by the ERO under Section 22 of the RPA, 1950, at any time before the last date for the nomination of candidates at an election from the constituency.[51] Deletion of name from the voter's list was intended to be a step towards disqualification from the electoral arena. The directives of the ECI, while intending to deter those with a criminal record from contesting elections, quite like the disclosure affidavits, could be rendered ineffective. In the case of Bihar, which was going to the polls in October–November 2005, the only effect the directives might have had was to compel persons who figured in the list of absconders to surrender before the courts and get bail. Even when imprisoned, the candidates were eligible to contest from prison and become MPs or members of the state legislature.

In the meantime, however, before the 2004 Lok Sabha election, in an order dated 30 April 2004, the Patna High Court ruled that since a person convicted of an offence and imprisoned is not allowed to vote, and under the Indian constitution, only an 'elector' can be a candidate for election, a person thus disqualified from franchise should also be barred from contesting elections. Arguing that the right to vote is a statutory right and subject to limits and restrictions that may be prescribed by law, the Patna High court ruled:

A right to vote is a statutory right, the Law gives it, the Law takes it away. Persons convicted of crime are kept away from elections to the Legislature, whether to State Legislature or Parliament, and all other public elections. The Court has no hesitation in interpreting the Constitution and the Laws framed under it, read together, that persons in the lawful custody of the Police also will not be voters, in which case, they will neither be electors. The Law temporarily takes away the

[50] Press note by the Election Commission of India, No. ECI/PN/33/2005, on the subject, deletion of names of electors declared as absconders, etc, 5 August 2005.

[51] This deletion of name under Section 22 could be done by the ERO even suo motu, after giving a reasonable opportunity to the person concerned, of being heard in respect of the action proposed to be taken in relation to him. Press note by the Election Commission of India, No. ECI/PN/33/2005, on the subject, deletion of names of electors declared as absconders, etc, 5 August 2005.

power of such persons to go anywhere near the election scene. To vote is a statutory right. It is privilege to vote, which privilege may be taken away. In that case, the elector would not be qualified, even if his name is on the electoral rolls. The name is not struck off, but the qualification to be an elector and the privilege to vote when in the lawful custody of the police is taken away.[52]

Indeed, Section 16 of the RPA, 1950, which lays down the disqualifications for registration in the electoral roll, specifies that if a person is not an Indian citizen, is of unsound mind, or has been disqualified from voting under the provisions of any law relating to corrupt practices and offences related to elections, he or she cannot be a voter. Section 62 of the RPA 1951, which details the conditions under which a right to vote may be exercised, lays down that a person who is 'confined in a prison, whether under a sentence of imprisonment or otherwise, or is in the lawful custody of the police' shall not be eligible to vote. This provision does not, however, apply to a person under preventive detention (Section 62(5) of the RPA, 1951). An appeal against the high court order was made in the Supreme Court in the case *Chief Election Commissioner v. Jan Chowkidar (People's Watch) and Others.* In its decision reached on 10 July 2013, the Supreme Court upheld the order of the Patna High Court. Justice A.K. Patnaik and Justice Sudhansu Jyoti Mukhopadhyay, who constituted the Supreme Court bench which heard the case, did not find any infirmity in the order passed by the Patna High Court that 'a person who has no right to vote by virtue of the provisions of sub-section (5) of Section 62 of the 1951 Act is not an elector and is therefore not qualified to contest the election to the House of the People or the Legislative Assembly of a State'.[53]

[52] Common Order No. 500/128/2004/vol.-II-RCC, dated 30 April 2004 by the Patna High Court in C.W.J.C. No. 4880 of 2004 and C.W.J.C. No. 4988 of 2004. Cited in circular dated 30 July 2013, by the secretary of the ECI, to the CEOs of all states and union territories, for further circulation to all returning officers and political parties 'for their information and necessary action'. The circular carried the operative parts of the Patna High Court and the Supreme Court orders.

[53] Common Order No. 500/128/2004/vol.-II-RCC, dated 30 April 2004 by the Patna High Court in C.W.J.C. No. 4880 of 2004 and C.W.J.C. No. 4988 of 2004.

Another judgment delivered the same day by the same bench of judges, in the cases *Lily Thomas v. Union of India and Others* (WP (Civil) No. 490 of 2005) and *Lokprahari v. Union of India and Others* (WP (Civil) No. 231 of 2005) had equally far-reaching ramifications. In this judgment, the Supreme Court declared sub-section (4) of Section 8 of the RPA, 1951, unconstitutional,[54] withdrawing thereby the protection against immediate disqualification from membership that was enjoyed by sitting members upon conviction and sentence to

[54] Section 8 of the RPA, 1951, and the exception provided by Sub-section 4 are as follows:

Section 8 lays down the disqualification on conviction for certain offences:

(3) A person convicted of any offence and sentenced to imprisonment for not less than two years [other than any offence referred to in Sub-section (1) or Sub-section (2)] shall be disqualified from the date of such conviction and shall continue to, be disqualified for a further period of six years since his release.

(4) Notwithstanding anything in Sub-section (1), Sub-section (2) of Sub-section (3) a disqualification under either sub-section shall not, in the case of a person who on the date of the conviction is a member of Parliament or the Legislature of a State, take effect until three months have elapsed from that date or, if within that period an appeal or application for revision is brought in respect of the conviction or the sentence, until that appeal or application is disposed of by the court. Grounds for declaring election to be void: (1) Subject to the provisions of Sub-section (2) if the High Court is of opinion—(a) that on the date of his election a returned candidate was not qualified, or was disqualified, to be chosen to fill the seat under the Constitution or this Act; or (b) that the result of the election, in so far as it concerns a returned candidate, has been materially affected—

  (i) by the improper acceptance or any nomination, or
 (ii) by any corrupt practice committed in the interests of the returned candidate by an agent other than his election agent, or
(iii) by the improper reception, refusal or rejection of any vote or the reception of any vote which is void, or
(iv) by any non-compliance with the provisions of the Constitution or of this Act or of any rules or orders made under this Act, the High Court shall declare the election of the returned candidate to be void.

imprisonment or fine for the offences mentioned in sub-sections (1) (2) and (3) of Section 8 of the Act.[55] Following the Supreme Court's verdict, the ECI sent a circular to all chief secretaries of the various states, with the request:

> to devise and provide for a fool-proof mechanism by involving the office of Advocate General/Directorate of Prosecution and other channels, if any, for tracking and promptly reporting to the Speaker/Chairman of the House concerned and the Commission cases of conviction of sitting MPs/MLAs/MLCs across Courts at all levels in the State. In order to ensure that cases do not go un-noticed, the Commission desires that the State Governments may send to the Commission a monthly report about cases of conviction, if any, of sitting members of Parliament or

---

[55] The judgment stated:

Sitting members of Parliament and State Legislatures who have already been convicted for any of the offences mentioned in sub-section (1), (2) and (3) of Section 8 of the Act and who have filed appeals or revisions which are pending and are accordingly saved from the disqualifications by virtue of sub-section (4) of Section 8 of the Act should not, in our considered opinion, be affected by the declaration now made by us in this judgment. This is because the knowledge that sitting members of Parliament or State Legislatures will no longer be protected by sub-section (4) of Section 8 of the Act will be acquired by all concerned only on the date this judgment is pronounced by this Court.... However, if any sitting member of Parliament or a State Legislature is convicted of any of the offences mentioned in sub-sections (1), (2) and (3) of Section 8 of the Act and by virtue of such conviction and/or sentence suffers the disqualifications mentioned in sub-sections (1), (2) and (3) of Section 8 of the Act after the pronouncement of this judgment, his membership of Parliament or the State Legislature, as the case may be, will not be saved by sub-section (4) of Section 8 of the Act which we have by this judgment declared as *ultra vires* the Constitution notwithstanding that he files the appeal or revision against the conviction and/or sentence.

Cited in circular No. 509/127 /2005/RCC, dated 7 August 2013 to the chief secretaries of all states and union territories by the principal secretary of the ECI, and CEO of all states, for the monitoring of cases of conviction among all sitting members and reporting to the speaker/chairperson of the houses concerned, and to the ECI.

State Legislature. The statement may be submitted to the Commission by 15th of every month through the Chief Electoral Officer of the State. For the sake of uniformity in reporting, a model format for the report is enclosed.[56]

As was the case in the right to know judgment, irrespective of their political affiliations, the parliamentarians rallied together to move the Supreme Court for a review of the 10 July 2013 judgment. In its review petition, the central government argued that the Supreme Court bench had overlooked the judgment given by the constitution bench judgment in *K. Prabhakaran* v. *P. Jayarajan* (2005), which had upheld the validity of Section 8(4) of the RPA that had been struck down in the present judgment. The judgment in *Prabhakaran* v. *Jayarajan* was a common judgment in two different cases of appeals[57] before the Supreme Court against the decisions of the high courts in election petitions asking for the disqualification of members elected in state legislative assemblies of Kerala and Haryana, respectively.

While examining the intention of Section 8 of the RPA, 1951, the judges in *Prabhakaran* v. *Jayarajan* agreed that the disqualifications enacted in Section 8(3) of the RPA, 1951, were to prevent criminalisation of politics: 'Those who break the law should not make the law' and must be prevented 'from entering into politics, and the House—a powerful wing of governance.... Thus, Section 8 seeks to promote freedom and fairness at elections, as also law and order being maintained while the elections are being held'.[58] Section 8(3) may not, however, the judges suggested, be read in isolation but along with sub-section

[56] The format included the name of the member, the name of the court that passed the conviction order, the sections under which conviction was made, its date, and the punishment (Circular No. 509/127 /2005/RCC, dated 7 August 2013 to the chief secretaries of all states and union territories by the principal secretary of the ECI, and CEO of all states, for the monitoring of cases of conviction among all sitting members and reporting to the speaker/chairperson of the houses concerned, and to the ECI).

[57] The second case was C.A.6691 of 2002, *Ramesh Singh Dalal* v. *Nafe Singh and Others.*

[58] *K. Prabhakaran* v. *P. Jayarajan*, Case No. Appeal (civil) 8213 of 2001, judgment delivered on 11 January 2005. Available at www.indiankanoon.org/doc/994167/; accessed on 15 July 2013.

8(4), which carved out an exception within Section 8. To the judges, a comparative reading of the sections showed that for the purpose of giving effect to the disqualification provisions, the law made a clear distinction between those who were at the time of conviction by the court, a member of parliament or state legislature, and those who were not. These two 'well defined and determinable groups' constituted two 'definite classes' based on what the judges thought was a reasonable and 'well laid down differentia' to serve 'a public purpose'.

The public purpose was not the individual right of a person to contest an election or to continue as a member of an elected House, but 'the very existence and continuity of a House democratically constituted'. If a member was compelled to forfeit his or her membership, it would lead to two consequences: the depletion of the strength of the House and also that of the political party to which the convicted member belonged. In a case where the member belonged to the ruling party, and the government constituted by the party was 'surviving on a razor edge thin majority', the disqualification would have a 'deleterious effect on the functioning of the government' or lead to the 'futile' exercise of holding a by-election, especially if a higher court subsequently acquitted the member of all the charges. The protection of sub-section 8(4) was therefore important and necessary since it exempted a sitting member from immediate disqualification, providing a three-month period of relief within which he or she could appeal to a higher court. The disqualification of the member would then stand deferred till the time the appeal was heard and decided by the court. The section was ultimately seen as a protection for the House rather than conferring an advantage to a person. It would cease to apply once the House was dissolved, bringing the convicted member at par with all others. No longer protected by Section 8(4), such a member will be back within the purview of Section 8(3) and disqualified from contesting elections from the date of conviction and for a further period of six years after release from prison.[59] According to the government, the Prabhakaran judgment confirmed that once

---

[59] K. Prabhakaran v. P. Jayarajan, Case no. Appeal (civil) 8213 of 2001. The judgment was delivered by a bench headed by the Chief Justice of India, R.C. Lahoti, and included the following other judges: Shivaraj V. Patil, K.G. Balakrishnan, B.N. Srikrishna, and G.P. Mathur.

the House had come into existence, and a member was convicted and sentenced, such a situation should be dealt with on a different footing, because the context was not about the privilege or right of a sitting member but of the existence of the House itself. Seeking an oral hearing (instead of being decided by the judges in the chambers), the government asserted that the issues raised were of paramount national interest, having constitutional ramifications.[60]

Simultaneously, the parliamentarians went ahead to expeditiously frame and pass a law that would amend the RPA, 1951, to give effect to the Supreme Court judgment in *Prabhakaran*. Effectively, the law intended to dilute and circumvent the Supreme Court judgments in *Lily Thomas* v. *Union of India* (2013) and *Lokprahari* v. *Union of India and Others* (2013). At an all-party meeting, the government received support for both the proposals, which were approved in the form of amendments to the RPA in two separate bills to be tabled in Parliament subsequently. According to one of the proposed amendments, an MP, MLA, or member of legislative council (MLC) could not be disqualified after conviction if he or she filed an appeal within 90 days from the date of conviction, and such conviction was stayed. A proviso was proposed to Section 8(4) of the RPA, which allowed a convicted member to continue to take part in the proceedings of Parliament or the legislature of a state, but withdrew the right to vote in Parliament and disallowed the payment of salary and allowances till the appeal or revision was finally decided by the court. Another amendment cleared by the Cabinet added a proviso to sub-section (2) of Section 62 of the RPA to state that a person cannot cease to be a voter while in detention as his or her right is only temporarily suspended. It further stated that as the name of a person in jail continues to be on the electoral roll, he or she also continues to be an elector and can file nomination for election.

The amendments to the RPA were expected to come into effect retrospectively from 10 July 2013, the day the Supreme Court delivered the two judgments providing for immediate disqualification of

[60] 'Centre Seeks Review of Ruling on Disqualification of Tainted MPs, MLAs,' *The Hindu*, 13 August 2013. Available at http://www.thehindu.com/news/national/centre-seeks-review-of-ruling-on-disqualification-of-tainted-mps-mlas/article5015991.ece; accessed on 26 August 2013.

convicted lawmakers and barring those in jail from contesting.[61] In September 2013, the government tried to push these amendments by promulgating an ordinance. A certain amount of drama ensued with (then) Congress vice president Rahul Gandhi tearing up the ordinance in a press conference, calling it complete nonsense, and the opposition criticising Rahul Gandhi's theatrics as Congress tactics. The bill and the ordinance, were, however, both withdrawn, and a number of prominent political leaders including Lalu Prasad Yadav of the RJD lost their seats soon afterwards, when they were found guilty by the courts in the cases pending against them.

Political Corruption and Electoral Reforms

Along with criminalisation of politics, discussed in the earlier section, political corruption has remained a festering issue in all considerations for electoral reforms. Both criminalisation and corruption constrain the autonomy of politics and dilute its ethical, dialogical, and deliberative character. As in the case of criminalisation of politics, concern for the stability of democracy is central to the debates around reforming the electoral space to free it from corruption. The concern for democracy stems not only from the effect political corruption has on people's faith in the government and the manner in which representatives are chosen, but also from the progressive distrust, indifference, or cynicism it breeds about the electoral process itself. The restoration of people's trust in the electoral process requires concerted and visible efforts on the part of the government to 'reform' political finance. E. Sridharan (2001a) points out that while election campaigns are the foremost 'visible' activity of political parties, there are a variety of activities for which political parties require funds. It is, however, election finance and expenditure incurred on campaigns that the reforms appear to focus on.

As required by Section 77 of the RPA, 1951, all candidates who contest elections must keep an account of their expenditure from

---

[61] 'Disqualification of Convicted MPs: Cabinet Okays Change in Law to Negate SC Ruling,' *The Times of India*, 22 August 2013. Available at http://articles.timesofindia.indiatimes.com/2013-08-22/india/41436859_1_convicted-mps-cabinet-okays-union-cabinet; accessed on 26 August 2013.

the date of nomination to the date of declaration of the result.[62] In 1996, in a decision in an appeal by Common Cause, an organisation that works, among other things, for transparency in the electoral process, the Supreme Court of India decided that the scope of the term 'conduct of election' in Article 324 of the Constitution of India was broad enough to give the ECI authority to issue directions for political parties to submit details of all election-related expenditures.[63]

[62] Sub-section (1) of Section 77 of the RPA, 1951, (43 of 1951) casts an obligation on every candidate at an election to the House of the People or a state legislative assembly to keep, either by himself/herself or by his/her election agent, a separate and correct account of all expenditure in connection with the election incurred or authorised by him/her or by the election agent between the date on which he/she has been nominated and the date of declaration of the result, both dates inclusive.

[63] In a public interest petition filed under Article 32 of the Constitution of India to 'bring transparency to the collection of money used by candidates in the process of election', Common Cause argued that Article 324 of Constitution of India coupled with the cumulative effect of three statutory provisions—Section 293A of the Companies Act 1956, Section 13A of the Income-tax Act 1961, and Section 77 of the RPA 1950—had the purpose of bringing transparency to the process of election funding. Without the imposition of transparency, 'those already in power were capable of collecting inordinate amounts of "black money"'. The political parties subject to the petition admitted that no tax filings or other election-related disclosures had been made, but argued that they did not have any income liable to be taxed. In its decision, the Court ruled that: (a) the political parties that had not been filing tax returns violated the provisions of the Income Tax Act and (b) the burden lies with the candidate to prove that expenditures were incurred by the party and not the candidate himself or herself. The Court then addressed the constitutional issue of the role of the ECI in bringing transparency to the process of election (pp. 10–13) and concluded that the ECI's constitutional authority includes issuing directions for political parties to submit, for its scrutiny, the details of all expenditures incurred or authorised by the parties in connection with the election of their respective candidates (p. 15). Thus, the Court ruled that the secretary, Ministry of Finance, Department of Revenue, and Government of India shall (a) appoint a body to inquire into why requirements under the Income Tax Act for the disclosure and filing of income tax by political parties were not being enforced by the tax authorities, and (b) investigate political parties that had failed to disclose and file income tax and

All candidates are required to submit their signed statements of election expenditure to the ECI, which are subsequently put up on the websites of the CEOs of states and the ECI of India. Interestingly, despite requests by political parties and candidates to enhance the cap on election expenditure that can be undertaken by individual candidates, no candidate reports having spent in excess of what is allowed by the ECI. There is no cap on the expenditure incurred by political parties, but all political parties are obliged to report their expenditure to the ECI within 75 days of the polls in the case of state assembly elections and 90 days in the case of Lok Sabha elections.

Writing about the exponential increase in the money spent by political parties in their electoral campaigns, Maitrayee Chaudhuri (2017) points at the unprecedented scale of money spent in the general elections of 2014, which was widely commented upon in international media (Sridharan and Vaishnav 2017). Reuters reported that Indian politicians were expected to spend around 5 billion dollars on campaigning for elections, which was 'a sum second only to the most expensive US presidential campaign of all time'.[64] This was the second record that the 2014 elections in India were expected to break, the first being the largest number of people who were entitled to vote in the election counting up to 814 million. Indeed, the data put up by the ECI on its website, on election spending by six recognised national parties shows that only three parties (the BSP, CPI(M), and the NCP)

---

initiate action, including any penal action against the defaulting political parties, in accordance with the Income Tax Act (p. 16) (see *Common Cause* v. *The Union of India* (1996), 1996 SCALE (3) 258; see also (1996) 2 SCC 752. Available at http://www.right2info.org/cases/r2i-common-cause-v.-union-of-india; accessed on 28 January 2017).

[64] Sruthi Gottipati and Rajesh Kumar Singh, 'India Set to Challenge U.S. For Election-Spending Record,' 9 March 2014. Available at http://in.reuters.com/article/india-election-spending-idINDEEA2804B20140309 (cited in Maitrayee Chaudhuri 2017: 264). The Centre for Media Studies too estimated a similar expenditure, making it the second most expensive elections of all times, behind only the 2012 US presidential campaign in which, according to the US presidential commission, 7 billion dollars were spent (see 'Election Watch: Indian General Election 2014.' Available at http://www.scoop.it/t/Indian-general-election-2014 [cited in Choudhury 2017: 261]).

submitted their statements of expenditure by the deadline. The ECI is authorised to derecognise a party if it fails to submit its statement of expenditure.[65] It should also be noted that since there is no cap on the election expenditure of political parties, a substantial percentage of the campaign expenditure incurred by candidates is put by them into the account of their party.

Data collated from the statement of expenditure filed by different political parties for the Lok Sabha elections of 2014 shows a significant trend. Table 4.4 shows the spending by major political parties in the election. It will be interesting to examine these figures in the context of the recent debate to hold simultaneous elections for the Lok Sabha and state legislative assemblies, generated by the BJP government's proposal, in order to evaluate the argument around mounting costs of elections.

How much does the government spend on conducting elections? The entire expenditure on actual conduct of elections to Lok Sabha is borne by the Government of India. But expenditure towards law and order maintenance is borne by the respective state governments. A Press Information Bureau (PIB), Government of India, release on 'election expenditure per elector', put up on the PIB website a couple of months before the 2014 general elections, compared the expenditure by the government from the first to the 2009 general elections. The release stated that the expenditure had gone up 20 times:

In the first general elections, the Government spent Rs. 0.60 on an elector whereas it went on spending Rs. 12 in 2009 General Elections. Considering expenditure in absolute terms, Rs. 10.45 Crore were spent in 1951–52 whereas Rs. 846.67 Crore was the amount the Government spent for 2009 General Elections. Cost wise 2004 General Elections was the heaviest on government exchequer with about Rs. 1114 Crore spent in the elections. This was the election when per elector cost was also the highest. Government spent Rs. 17 on an elector. Significantly, there was increase in the election cost by 17.53% vis-à-vis 1999 General

---

[65] See Election Commission of India. Available at https://www.eci.gov.in/candidate-political-parties/expenditure-reports/expenditure-reports/; accessed on 27 January 2018.

Table 4.4 Statement of Election Expenditure of Political Parties in the 2014 Lok Sabha Elections

S.N.	Name of the Party	Opening Balance (A)	Receipt of Funds from All Sources by Party (in Rupees) (B)	General Party Propaganda Expenses Authorised by Party Headquarters (in Rupees) (C)	Gross Expenditure Authorised by Party Headquarters for Candidates (in Rupees) (D)	Total Lump Sum Given by Party Central Headquarters to State Units of the Party for Election Expenses (in Rupees) (E)	Gross Expenditure by Party Headquarters for General Party (in Rupees) (C+D+E)
1.	Dravida Munnetra Kazhagam	1,582,623,180	36,663,736	220,133,918	195,000,000	Nil	415,133,918
2.	Indian National Congress (including legislative assemblies of Andhra Pradesh, Arunachal Pradesh, Odisha, and Sikkim)	3,425,331,844	1,721,810,901	3,696,072,829	16,376,830	515,965,980	4,228,415,639
3.	Communist Party of India (Marxist)	12,447,419.77	45,492,594	1,490,654	Nil	3,100,000	4,590,654

No.	Party						
4.	Bharatiya Janata Party	632,784,833	1,928,625,912	4,870,391,516	9,000,000	232,690,000	5,112,081,516
5.	Aam Aadmi Party	96,566,404.85	252,473,510.60	25,485,958.30	77,059,675	110,040,383	212,586,016.30
6.	Bahujan Samaj Party	3,452,794,516	772,600,000	300,584,822	Nil	Nil	300,584,822
7.	Nationalist Congress Party	13,316,734	155,500,000	163,785,734	13,000,000	146,500,000	323,285,734
8.	Samajwadi Party (including legislative assemblies of Andhra Pradesh, Odisha, and Sikkim)	42,200,192,980	868,437,522	641,158,351	52,017,250	Nil	693,175,601
9.	Communist Party of India (including Legislative Assembly elections in Andhra Pradesh and Odisha)	1,494,392	16,924,002	17,573,966	7,000,000	7,000,000	31,573,966

Note: The statement of expenditure covers the period between the date of announcement of the polls (5 March 2014) and the date of completion (16 May 2014).

Source: See https://www.eci.gov.in/candidate-political-parties/expenditure-reports/expenditure-reports/https://www.eci.gov.in/candidate-political-parties/expenditure-reports/expenditure-reports/;accessed on 26 January 2018.

Elections even when there was reduction in number of polling stations buy 11.26% [sic].[66]

The rapid increase in government expenditure per elector, as illustrated in Table 4.5, from the first six general elections' cost of less than a rupee per elector was attributed in the official press

Table 4.5   Election Expenditure by the Central Government for 15 Lok Sabha Elections

Year	Expenditure (in Crores of Rupees)	No. of Electors	Expenditure per Elector (in Rupees)	Polling Stations
1952	10.45	173,212,343	0.6	196,084
1957	5.9	193,652,179	0.3	220,478
1962	7.32	216,361,569	0.3	238,031
1967	10.8	250,207,401	0.4	243,693
1971	11.61	274,189,132	0.4	342,918
1977	23.04	321,174,327	0.7	373,910
1980	54.77	356,205,329	1.5	436,813
1984–5*	81.51	400,375,333	2	506,058
1989	154.22	498,906,129	3.1	580,798
1991–2**	359.1	511,533,598	7	591,020
1996	597.34	592,572,288	10	767,462
1998	666.22	605,880,192	11	773,494
1999	947.68	619,536,847	15	774,651
2004	1,113.88	671,487,930	17	687,402
2009	846.67	716,985,101	12	830,866

Note: According to the release, the figures excluded Jammu and Kashmir in 1991–2, 1989, elections were held separately for the states of Assam and Punjab in 1985, and for the state of Punjab in 1992.
Source: 'Election Expenditure per Elector up by Twenty Times in 2009 Compared to First General Elections', *Press Information Bureau*, Government of India, Election Commission, 11 March 2014.

[66] Press Information Bureau, Government of India, 'Election Expenditure per Elector Up by Twenty Times in 2009 Compared to First General Elections,' press release, Election Commission, 11 March 2014. See also http://pib.nic.in/newsite/PrintRelease.aspx?relid=104557; accessed on 27 January 2018.

release to the devaluation of money owing to inflation, and to the 'increased level of democratic activities'. The increase in democratic activities was a consequence of more political parties coming into existence, the participation of large numbers of independent candidates, 'voter-friendly initiatives' like voter awareness campaigns, and distribution of voter slip ahead of election date.[67]

The use of voter-verified paper audit trail (VVPAT), used on a smaller scale in 2014, to be made ubiquitous in 2019 following the Supreme Court's orders in 2013 and 2017, would increase the expenditure further. But these, the PIB citing the ECI said, were efforts 'focused at strengthening the very structure and values of democracy'. In 2013, in response to a petition by BJP MP Subramanian Swamy, the Supreme Court held that VVPATs were an indispensable part of 'fair and free' elections, necessary for restoring the confidence of voters in the electoral system.[68] The Supreme Court ordered a phased installation of VVPAT in the EVMs before the 2014 elections. In 2017, following a petition by the BSP joined by the Congress and the All India Trinamool Congress, the Supreme Court asked the Central government and the ECI why its 2013 orders were not complied with. Indeed, the 2017 order came amidst apprehensions of the possibility of hacking of the EVMs, which was disputed by the ECI, and appeal by many opposition parties including the BSP, Congress, and AAP, after elections to the state assemblies, to install VVPAT machines. A VVPAT machine allows the voter to see the vote cast by her/him, as recorded by the machine, for 7 seconds after the button on the EVM is pressed. A paper slip is generated, which drops into a box, is secured by the ECI for 45 days after the results, and can be presented in the court in case of an election dispute. Immediately after the reprimand by the Supreme Court in April 2017, the central government released the funds to the ECI for procuring 16.15 lakh VVPAT machines in preparation for the 2019 general election. The cost of the machines is estimated at

---

[67] Press Information Bureau, Government of India, 'Election Expenditure per Elector Up by Twenty Times in 2009 Compared to First General Elections'.

[68] Krishnadas Rajagopal. 2017. 'Why No EVMs with Paper Trails, SC Asks Centre,' *The Hindu*, 13 April.

Rs 3,173 crores, which the government split over two financial years, 2017–18 and 2018–19.[69]

While the details of the expenditure incurred by the government in holding the 2014 Lok Sabha elections is not available, and is likely to come before the next general election, studies done prior to the elections projected that the combined spending by the government, political parties, and candidates was likely to be a 'whopping' Rs 30,000 crores, making it the most expensive electoral exercise in Indian history, and second only to 42,000 crores (7 billion dollars) spent by candidates and political parties in the 2012 presidential election in the United States of America. The study, done by the Centre for Media Studies, found that out of the estimated 30,000 crores, the government was likely to spend Rs 7,000–8,000 crores and the rest would be spent by the political parties. One of the reasons for the increase in expenditure was the lifting of the cap on spending by individual candidates to Rs 70 lakhs. In case all candidates spent the maximum they were permitted, and political parties continued the earlier trend, the expenditure by political parties per candidate, the study concluded, would be close to Rs 500 per voter.[70] A large proportion of this money was 'unaccounted money' pumped in by 'crorepati candidates, corporates and contractors'.[71]

In 2012, then CEC S.Y. Quraishi responded as follows to a question on what steps the ECI had taken to curb 'black money' during polls:

The commission has taken a series of measures to prevent the flow of illegal money during polls. These include opening of separate bank accounts for campaign expenditure for easy monitoring, restriction on cash movements without proper documents, deployment of

[69] 'Cabinet Approves Funds to Procure VVPAT Units for 2019,' *The Times of India*, 19 April 2017. The EVMs and VVPATs are manufactured by Bharat Electronics Limited (BEL) and Electronics Corporation of India Limited (ECIL). The design has been approved by a Technical Experts Committee.

[70] 'Rs. 30,000 Crore to be Spent on Lok Sabha Polls: Study,' *NDTV*. Available at https://www.ndtv.com/elections-news/rs-30-000-crore-to-be-spent-on-lok-sabha-polls-study-554110; accessed on 20 January 2018.

[71] 'Rs. 30,000 Crore to be Spent on Lok Sabha Polls: Study,' *NDTV*. Available at https://www.ndtv.com/elections-news/rs-30-000-crore-to-be-spent-on-lok-sabha-polls-study-554110; accessed on 20 January 2018.

surveillance squads at strategic points, 24×7 vigilance and maintenance of a shadow expenditure register for each candidate to prevent
under-reporting. A large amount of cash has already been seized. As
of today, it is 360 million rupees ($7.0 million). Expenditure observers
combined with teams of revenue and police officials are keeping a
hawk-eye on illegal money.[72]

Yet, the 'hawk-eye' on illegal money cannot be a substitute for
an appropriate system of 'regulating political finance' to curb its
entry effectively at the threshold itself. Kapur and Vaishnav (2018:
7–8) point out that a host of reasons have contributed to the 'influx'
of money in Indian elections. These include: the opening of the
economy in 1991 and the resultant increase in the size of the
economy, combined with the increase in the size of the electorate,
the increased competitiveness of the elections and the dip in the
margin of victories, diminishing of the organisational strength of
parties, which are steadily being replaced by charismatic and often
dynastic leaders 'increasingly reliant on private funds as opposed to
party coffers', and finally the increase in the number of elections,
if one were to include all the tiers down to the *panchayati* raj elections, increasing the stakes of winning elections. The institutional
mechanisms for regulating political finance have, however, 'strug-
gled' to keep up with this influx. As a result, India has figured low
on global indicators on effective regulation and enforcement of
political finance.[73]

[72] Vibhuti Agarwal. 2012. 'Q&A: India's Chief Election Commissioner
S.Y. Quraishi,' *Wall Street Journal*, 17 January. Available at https://blogs.wsj.
com/indiarealtime/2012/01/17/qa-indias-chief-election-commissioner-s-y-
quraishi/; accessed on 27 January 2018.

[73] In the Money, Politics and Transparency Campaign Finance Indicators
project, which works with inputs from political finance experts across the
world, India received a score of 31 per cent, which placed it 12th from
the bottom among 54 countries. See Money, Politics and Transparency.
Available at https://data.moneypoliticstransparency.org/. In another study on
'Perceptions of Electoral Integrity' by Pippa Norris and others, the ECI scored
high on overall electoral management, but was placed 'middling' on its performance in relation to political finance at a rank of 51 out of 125 countries.
Both studies cited in Kapur and Vaishnav (2018: 8).

Election spending is the most evident and tangible aspect of corrupt practices in election, and political finance has remained at the centre of suggestions for electoral reforms for a long period. In a comprehensive analysis of the trajectory of attempts at reforming political finance, E. Sridharan (2001a) has pointed out that there are several arrangements that determine and frame political finance, of which election finance is one, albeit the most visible and integral part. All political parties require a steadily increasing amount of money for expenditure during election campaigns, and for sustenance beyond elections, and during electoral interregnums (Sridharan 2001a).[74] Indeed, over the years, elections have become exponentially expensive, and corporate funds and money from big businesses have become inextricably entrenched in politics. The dependence of political parties on corporate finance, coupled with the lack of transparency in transactions and exchanges between political parties and business houses, including the pressures and promises extracted and offered, have become rampant.

Suggestions for reforms in the domain of political corruption have, however, not focused on putting in place an effective and empowered oversight regime steered by the ECI. Even as the powers of the ECI to elicit information through disclosures have enhanced, the absence of corresponding enforcement powers have made the ECI ineffective in these matters. The suggestions for reforms that have come over the years have focused on transparency and disclosure of sources of funding on the one hand, and on the other hand, they have concerned themselves with curbing excessive spending. The four areas in which they have sought reforms are limits on contributions, limits on expenditure, public funding of elections, and the need for disclosure (Sridharan and Vaishnav 2018: 19). Following Sridharan (2001a)

---

[74] Sridharan (2001a) points out that political parties need funds for three activities: election campaigns, inter-election maintenance of campaigns, inter-election maintenance of their organisations and political activities, and support of research and information infrastructure of the parties. The origins of election finance reform have roots in corruption scandals (for example, the hawala scandal of payoffs to politicians of most major parties via illegal foreign exchange transactions that surfaced in January 1996), rising campaign costs, and public concern for equal opportunity for political participation.

and Gowda and Sridharan (2012), the trajectory of reforms in India may be seen to have unfolded along three distinct phases: (*a*) the 1970s and 1980s, which was the period when legal limits on electoral finance and electoral expenditure were being sought; (*b*) the 1990s, when these limits were being seen as unrealistic; (*c*) the 2000s, when suggestions for reforms were guided by concerns for democracy. To Sridharan and Vaishnav (2018: 18–19), these three phases correspond to three broad periods in the evolution of political finance regime in India: the first period ending around 1990 was characterised by 'the emergence and consolidation of a corrupt, opaque equilibrium'; the second, beginning in 1990 and ending with 2003, saw the 'early beginnings of reform'; and the third, ending with 2017, saw a combination of greater transparency with frugal structural changes. To these three phases, Sridharan and Vaishnav add a fourth period, which they see emerging with the changes brought in by demonetisation and the introduction of electoral bonds, by the Narendra Modi-led NDA government, marked by 'curbing the use of cash at the expense of transparency'.

The 'corrupt equilibrium' (Sridharan and Vaishnav 2018) between 1947 and 1990—generated by the relationship between a political regime dominated by a single political party and the strict regulatory control of private business by the political regime, and characterised by tax evasion by business and donation of 'black money' to political parties—formed the context in which suggestions for limiting electoral reforms were made. In 1969, private funding of elections, which had hitherto been the main source of funding for political parties, was banned. The ban followed the concerns raised by the Santhanam Committee on Prevention of Corruption (1964) and the Wanchoo Direct Taxes Enquiry Committee (1971) on 'black money' being siphoned into the political system, particularly through political fundraising, in order to influence policies to favour big businesses (Gowda and Sridharan 2012). It was largely believed that the ban came in the wake of the dwindling electoral fortunes of the Congress party led by Indira Gandhi and the challenge mounted to its ascendancy by the pro-business Swantantra Party and the Hindu nationalist party Jan Sangh, both of which attracted corporate donations (Sridharan and Vaishnav 2018). No alternative provisions for state funding were instituted. In 1985, an amendment in the Companies Act (Section

239A) allowed company donations to political parties and individuals under certain conditions.[75]

The RPA, 1951, which provides the statutory framework for regulating the finances and expenditure of political parties, was amended in 1975 to invalidate the judgment of the Supreme Court in the *Kanwar Lal Gupta* v. *Amar Nath Chawla* case (1974). In the judgment in *Kanwar Lal Gupta* case, the Supreme Court had laid down that party spending *on behalf* of a candidate should also be included in the election expenses of a political party.[76] The 1975 amendment to the RPA, 1951, added Explanation 1 to Section 77(1) of the Act stating that party and supporter expenditure not authorised by the candidate did not count in election expenses, and all such extra expenditure would not be counted for the enforcement of expenditure ceiling.[77]

In 1990, a committee to suggest electoral reforms was set up under the chairpersonship of Dinesh Goswami who was the law minister in V.P. Singh's National Front government. This committee looked into the question of election funding, advocated a ban on company donations to political parties, and suggested state funding, but for specified

---

[75] A substantial percentage of contributions was/is, however, made through the black money route, since utilising the provision meant revealing party identification and possible problems with shareholders (Sridharan and Vaishnav 2018).

[76] *Kanwar Lal Gupta* v. *Amar Nath Chawla & Ors*, decided on 3 October 1974, 1975 AIR 308.

[77] The National Commission for the Reform of the Constitution set up in 2000, to review the working of the Constitution and suggest reforms, identified Explanation 1 to Section 77(1) of the RPA, 1951, as a significant loophole, suggesting that under such an Explanation, there could never be any violation of expenditure limits. The appointment of a Constitution (review or reforms) commission was part of the BJP's election manifesto for the 12th general election. The commission could not be appointed as the BJP-led NDA government headed by Atal Bihari Vajpayee resigned and the 13th general elections were held. The NDA issued a National Agenda for Good Governance, which also included the promise of appointing a constitution review commission that would examine the more than 50 years of the working of the Constitution of India and make suitable recommendations for change. The Commission was finally set up in February 2002 (see Kashyap, Khanna, and Kueck 2000).

and limited logistical purposes, such as vehicle fuel, hiring charges for microphones, issue of voter identity slips, and additional copies of the electoral rolls. It did not, therefore, address fully the question of party finance, in which the ambivalences of the 1970s persisted. This ambivalence resonated in the consultation paper on electoral reforms by the National Commission to Review the Working of the Constitution (NCRWC 2000). The National Commission expressed the question of electoral finance as a conundrum:

> The question is how do we go about reducing the role that money can play? The answer to this is not easy. The fact is that political parties need tons of funds for political activity, which includes campaigning for elections. Political parties should have legitimate sources of these funds. If they don't have these funds legitimately and then if (and this is the critical part) the system permits them to do so, they will find illegitimate funds. This is what has been happening in India and with illegitimate funding the spending has also been comparatively limitless. One party started it but others soon caught on. However, it is only true that if the system did not permit the kind of spending that is happening, the various candidates would have found their equilibrium at a much lower level. (NCRWC 2000: 42)

The NCRWC went into the 'problem of party funding', 'regulating political contributions', 'controlling electoral expenditure', and 'monitoring electoral expenditure' (NCRWC 2000). In its consultation paper presented for public debate, the Commission made several recommendations, which included reforming Explanation 1 to Section 77, the question of state funding, and issues concerning transparency and information that needed to be made available to voters.[78]

---

[78] These recommendations were: Explanation 1 to Section 77 of the RPA, 1951, under which the amounts spent by persons other than the candidate and his agent could not be counted in the candidate's election expenses, which effectively meant that there could never be any violation of the expenditure limit. This needed to be rectified and all expenditure made by or on behalf of the candidate needed to be included in the calculation of expenditure for the purpose of assessing the expenditure limit; political parties as well as individual candidates should be subject to proper statutory audit for the amount they spend; partial state funding of elections; continuation of time provided on national media for campaign activities of recognised parties; proposed state

Indeed, as Sridharan (2001a) has shown, the 1990s was a period in which the conundrum expressed by the NCRWC in 2000 was made manifest in the initiatives by institutions like the Confederation of Indian Industry (CII) on the one hand, and the Supreme Court on the other, which devised ways (in the case of the CII) and issued instructions (in the case of the Supreme Court) for making election funding more transparent. In 1993, a task force set up by the CII recommended state funding of elections, resources for which were to be raised through tax or alternatively through contribution by the industry to a state-managed pool of election fund.[79] In January 1996, the

---

funding to be linked to legal regulation of political parties and to create a foolproof mechanism for the strict implementation of financial limits to deter expenditure violations; bring in transparency into all political funding; permit corporate donations within prescribed limits and keep them transparent; make all legal and transparent donations tax exempt and treat this tax loss to the state as its contribution to state funding of elections; all political party accounts, much like the accounts of a public company, should be published yearly with complete disclosure under predetermined account heads. The ECI should have these accounts audited; the campaign expense accounts—both receipts and expenses—of all candidates to be made public in their constituencies; there should be a serious attempt at reducing election expenses which could be done by changing the ground rules for electoral campaigns—partly by encouraging the use of electronic and digital technology to campaign at state cost and simultaneously by totally and effectively banning other overt and wasteful *tamashas* of campaigning; reasonable restrictions must be placed on the following: wall writings, display of cut-outs, hoardings, and banners, hoisting of flags (except party offices, public meetings, and other specified places), use of more than a specified number of vehicles for election campaign and for processions, announcements or publicity by more than a specified number of moving vehicles, holding of public meetings beyond the specified hours, and display of posters at places other than those specified by the district/ electoral authorities. Election rallies only under covered roofs should be allowed. No outdoor public rallies should be permitted; create an effective mechanism to implement these rules and create an effective deterrence against violations (NCRWC 2000: 83–4).

[79] The task force set up by the CII also recommended that corporate contributions be made tax-deductible and that board decisions should be

Supreme Court issued notices to political parties, to file their income tax and wealth tax returns, in order to enforce transparency. In July 1996, another step towards constraining election expenditure was taken through an amendment in the RPA by the United Front government. The amendment reduced the period of election campaign by a week, that is, from 21 days to 14 days, with the intention of reducing the cost of election. Simultaneously, on 31 December 1997, the expenditure limit was raised to Rs 15 lakhs for major states.[80] The next initiative came when the Indrajit Gupta Committee on State Funding of Elections, recommended at least a partial though non-cash state funding for election. On the basis of the recommendations of the Indrajit Gupta Committee, the Law Commission of India submitted a draft bill, the Representation of People (Amendment) Bill, 1998, to the Ministry of Home Affairs and the ECI.[81] Another bill, the Election and Other Related Laws (Amendment) Bill, 2001, was initiated in December 2001. While framing the draft bill, the Law Commission made three proposals pertaining to: (a) receipts and expenditure of political parties; (b) audit of accounts of political parties; and (c) state funding. The Law Commission proposed curtailing the expenditure on elections, and regulating the receipts and expenditure by the political parties. The issue of state funding was also considered in this

---

required to be confirmed by shareholders. Indeed, prior to the 1998 elections, in a significant development, election-funding trusts were set up by some large business houses. In 1997, the TATA group, followed in 1998 by the A.V. Birla and Mahindra and Mahindra groups, set up an election fund pool from which it could make contributions to all political parties, without getting politically identified with any party due to the fact that allocations to parties were to be based on a specified formula (see Sridharan 2001a).

[80] The expenditure limit, which was Rs 1.5 lakhs for Lok Sabha and Rs 50,000 for state assembly constituencies was revised in 1994 to Rs 4.5 lakhs and 1.5 lakhs, respectively. This was the limit in the 1996 elections (see Sridharan 2001a).

[81] See Law Commission of India, *170th Report of the Law Commission on Electoral Reforms*; 'Panel Proposes State Funding of Polls,' *The Statesman*, 19 September 1998; 'Law Panel Suggestions on Electoral Reforms,' *The Statesman*, 20 September 1998, 'Ban Splits, Bar Those Chargesheeted,' *The Indian Express*, 17 September 1998.

context and the first proposal in this behalf was to delete Explanation 1 to Section 77 of the RPA, 1951, because of the abuse inherent in the said Explanation. It proposed introducing provisions to make it obligatory upon political parties to maintain regular accounts clearly and fully recording all amounts received by them and all expenditure incurred. It was further suggested that these accounts should be duly audited at the end of each year and the audited accounts should be submitted to the ECI before a prescribed date every year. The ECI was required to publish the said accounts for public information. The Law Commission followed the provisions contained in the Bill prepared by then law minister, Dinesh Goswami in 1990, which proposed limited state funding.[82]

The Election and Other Related Laws (Amendment) Act, passed subsequently in 2003 by the BJP-led NDA government, marked the beginning of a period that Sridharan and Vaishnav (2018) call 'greater but limited transparency'. By making corporate and individual donations to political parties, 100 per cent tax-deductible under the Income Tax Act, the 2003 law paved the way towards transparency by encouraging people to donate to party funds through cheques. Under Section 29C of the RPA, it became compulsory for political parties to inform the ECI on a yearly basis of all donations above Rs 20,000 received by them, disclosing the names of donors and the amount received. While this was a move towards transparency, it was still limited, since donations below the specified amount could remain undisclosed, and parties could receive multiple donations below that amount to avoid full disclosure. An important measure introduced by the Act, by way of addressing the space for non-disclosure provided by Explanation 1 of Section 77, was to make it mandatory for candidates to report expenditure made on their behalf by political parties, which would be counted as expenditure within the specified limit for individual candidates. Sridharan and Vaishnav (2018: 25) point out, however, that there was enough 'fine print', which allowed circumvention and undercutting, through exemptions of various kinds.

---

[82] Law Commission of India, *170th Report of the Law Commission on Electoral Reforms.*

In its proposals for electoral reforms submitted to the prime minister in 2004, the ECI favoured compulsory maintenance of accounts by political parties and its audit by agencies specified by the ECI. It considered that the political parties had a responsibility to maintain proper accounts of their income and expenditure and to get them audited annually by agencies specified by the ECI. While making the same proposal in 1998, the ECI had mentioned that there was a strong need for transparency in the manner in which election funds were being spent by political parties. The ECI felt that the amendment made through the Election and Other Related Laws (Amendment) Act, 2003, which provided for the preparation of a report of contributions in excess of Rs 20,000 received by political parties, was not 'sufficient' for ensuring transparency and accountability in the financial management of political parties. It recommended, therefore, that 'political parties must be required to publish their accounts (at least abridged versions) annually for information and scrutiny of the general public and all concerned, for which purpose the maintenance of such accounts and their auditing to ensure their accuracy is a pre-requisite' (Election Commission of India (2004: 11). The ECI reiterated the proposal, with the modification 'that the auditing may be done by any firm of auditors approved by the Comptroller and Auditor General. The audited accounts should be available for information to the public' (Election Commission of India 2004: 11).

The ADR requested the Central Information Commission (CIC) to make the income tax returns filed by political parties public under the provisions of the RTI, 2005. The CIC conceded to the request in 2008, despite strong opposition by political parties. While the CIC did not provide for an independent third-party audit of party finances, as recommended by the ECI, in 2014, the ECI issued its own transparency guidelines. Under these guidelines, all political parties were expected to disclose the donations received by them, along with the identity of the donor and the amount received (Sridharan and Vaishnav 2018: 26).

As things stand now, corporate donations constitute the bulk of the funds received by political parties. As mentioned earlier, the statements of expenditure of all parties are put up on the ECI website with the break-up of the spending of political parties under various heads including propaganda and the amount authorised to candidates or state party units for campaigning during the period between announcement of election dates and its completion. On 1 February 2017, the Ministry for Finance announced that in the interest of transparency, political parties could not receive donation in cash above Rs 2,000 from any individual. But they were entitled to receiving donations by cheque or in digital mode from donors and had to file income tax returns within a specified period. In addition, the finance minister proposed an amendment to the Reserve Bank of India Act to enable specific banks to issue anonymous electoral bonds, triggering a debate on transparency in electoral funding.[83] Under the proposed scheme, a donor could purchase an electoral bond from an authorised bank by making a payment by cheque or through digital transaction. A registered party could receive these bonds and redeem them in its designated account, within a prescribed time limit. Such a step, according to the finance minister, would curtail anonymous donations in cash, which was the way most donations were hitherto being made, with only a slight improvement in transparency—achieved by the requirement that all parties maintain a list of donors who had contributed more than Rs 20,000.[84]

Almost a year later, the scheme was made effective with the finance minister announcing that bonds of the values of 1,000, 10,000, 100,000, 1,000,000, or 10,000,000 could be bought by an Indian citizen or an Indian corporate body from specified branches of the State Bank of India. The electoral bonds would be valid only for 15 days after the date of their purchase and the donor's name would remain a secret. The details of the donor, as the purchaser of a bond will, however, exist in the records of the bank issuing the bond since the sale of the bonds could be authorised only after the credentials of the 'customer' was

[83] For the details of the announcement made by the finance minister while making his budget speech on 1 February 2017, see Press Information Bureau, Ministry of Finance, Government of India, 'Political Parties Cannot Receive Donation above Rs. 2000 in Cash,' press release, 1 February 2017.

[84] Press Information Bureau, Ministry of Finance, Government of India, 'Political Parties Cannot Receive Donation above Rs. 2000 in Cash,' press release, 1 February 2017.

approved.[85] The relationship between anonymity of the donor and transparency is not clear, however. In May 2017, the ECI of India in its submission to a parliamentary committee on law and personnel had dismissed the scheme of anonymous electoral bonds as 'retrograde', saying that it would compromise transparency in political funding. Eight months later, in January 2018, it changed its position to say that it hoped that electoral bonds were a step in the right direction, even though they could not solve all problems pertaining to transparency in political funding.[86] Political analysts and scholars have expressed concerns around the reinforcement of opacity through electoral bonds and the loss of oversight and accountability, which may in future become 'the very wellspring of institutionalised corruption'.[87] Indeed, while reforms since the 1970s had concerned themselves with the problem of private funding of elections, the introduction of electoral bonds seemed to veer towards the 'aim of reducing unaccounted cash in the electoral process and not the corporate control of politics'.[88] As argued by Zoya Hasan:

> Sure enough, the bonds scheme imposes no restrictions on the quantum of corporate donations. Consequently electoral bonds cannot address the problems that arise from the corporate control over politics and corporate capture of government policy and decisions. Rather electoral bonds will result in unlimited and undeclared funds going to certain political parties which will be shielded from public scrutiny as

[85] The donations could be made only to parties registered under Section 29A of the RPA, 1951 (43 of 1951) and which secured not less than one per cent of the votes polled in the last general election to the House of the People or a legislative assembly. The bonds are available for purchase for 10 days each in the months of January, April, July, and October. The window would be for an additional 30 days in the year of general election ('Poll Bonds Life 15 Days, Donor Name Secret but KYC Must,' *The Indian Express*, 3 January 2018).

[86] 'Election Commission Hopes Electoral Bonds Are Step in 'Right Direction,' *New Indian Express*, 18 January 2018. Available at commission-hopes-electoral-bonds-are-step-in-right-direction-1757733.html; accessed on 26 January 2018.

[87] Zoya Hasan. 2018. 'A Vote for State Funding,' *The Hindu*, 29 January.

[88] Zoya Hasan, 'A Vote for State Funding.'

the balance sheets will not show which party has been the beneficiary of this largess.[89]

Seen in conjunction with the lifting of the maximum limit of 7.5 per cent on the proportion of profits that a company can donate to a political party, anonymous electoral bonds raise the possibilities of shell companies being set up with the purpose of funding political parties.

In an interview with the *Indian Express*, O.P. Rawat, who was the CEC for almost a year from January to December 2018, said that both these concerns—regarding opacity in political funding and loss-making companies donating money to political parties—were raised with the government when electoral bonds were brought into effect through the Finance Bill of 2017.[90] In a letter dated 26 May 2017, the ECI had objected strongly to the provisions of the Finance Bill 2017, rejecting the amendments it proposed in the Income Tax Act, the RPA, 1951, and the Companies Act, 2013. All these amendments, the ECI argued, would have 'serious impact on transparency aspect of political finance/funding of political parties'.[91] The amendment in Section 29C of the RPA, 1951, excluded political donations made through electoral bonds, from the requirement of disclosure to the ECI through the Contribution Report as prescribed under Section 29 C of the RPA, 1951. The ECI considered this amendment 'retrograde' as far as 'transparency' of donations was concerned. The amendment, it argued, was in violation of Section 29B of the RPA, 1951, which prohibited political parties from taking donations from government companies and foreign sources. The ECI also objected to the amendment

[89] Zoya Hasan, 'A Vote for State Funding.'

[90] 'O P Rawat: Note Ban had Absolutely No Impact on Black Money,' *The Indian Express*, 16 December 2018.

[91] Letter No. 56/PPEMS/Transparency/2017, to the Secretary, Legislative Department, Ministry of Law and Justice, dated 26 May 2017. The letter acquired under RTI application by RTI activist Vihar Durve seeking the ECI's correspondence on the electoral bonds, has been uploaded by the *Quint* and is available at 'Election Commission's Letter to the Law Ministry Regarding the Electoral Bonds'. Available at https://www.scribd.com/document/377475157/Election-Commission-s-letter-to-the-Law-Ministry-regarding-the-electoral-bonds; accessed on 10 December 2018.

of Section 182 of the Companies Act, 2013, which removed the limit of 7.5 per cent of net profit in the preceding three financial years for companies to be able to donate to political parties, and the provision that firms must declare their 'political contributions' in their profit and loss statements. These changes, the ECI argued, made companies free to donate to political parties and even 'exist for the sole purpose of making donations', facilitating the pumping of black money into the system through electoral bonds, which demonetisation had claimed to erase. The amendment in Section 182(3) abolishing the provision that firms must declare their political contributions in their profit and loss statements, the ECI stated, similarly compromised transparency and encouraged use of black money for political funding.[92] In his interview to the *Indian Express*, O.P. Rawat, former CEC, reiterated the ECI's discomfort with the amendments, and also claimed that demonetisation, the other reform brought by the NDA government, had 'absolutely' no impact on 'money power' in elections. Indeed, the ECI, he said, had 'seized a record amount of money during elections' including the assembly elections in five states, which concluded in December 2018, where close to Rs 200 crores in cash was seized by the ECI.[93]

Instead of transparency, the reforms have led to opacity as far as public scrutiny of political finance is concerned, which is likely to favour the political party and regime in power. The BJP's annual income tax and audit report for 2017–18 submitted to the ECI show that it received 95 per cent of the electoral bonds worth 210 crores.[94]

---

[92] 'Election Commission's Letter to the Law Ministry Regarding the Electoral Bonds'. Available at https://www.scribd.com/document/377475157/Election-Commission-s-letter-to-the-Law-Ministry-regarding-the-electoral-bonds; accessed on 10 December 2018.

[93] 'O.P. Rawat: Note Ban had Absolutely No Impact on Black Money,' *The Indian Express*, 16 December 2018.

[94] The Congress had not submitted its report till the end of November 2018. Since the 2017–18 report carries income and expenditure details till 31 March, it covers the details of the first cycle of the electoral bonds scheme that was open from 1 to 10 March 2018. As per the information given by the government to the Lok Sabha, electoral bonds of Rs 222 crores were issued during this opening span. Information obtained under RTI from the State Bank of India revealed that bonds over Rs. 600 crores

In addition, despite the claims that the donor would remain anonymous, the government can extract the information from the issuing bank. Political parties have been steadfast in their refusal to come under the RTI Act despite the decision taken by the full bench of the CIC on 3 June 2013 that political parties were public authorities within the purview of the RTI Act. As such the donations received by them and the names of the donors would come under public scrutiny through their right to be informed.[95] The ADR has shown that 70 per cent of party funding has come from sources that are unknown and therefore cannot be disclosed. Anonymous bonds may only exacerbate the problem while claiming to alleviate it. Voluntary disclosure of the kind attempted by the AAP could be one response, but no other party has shown the inclination to follow it. Seen in the context of the total income declared by political parties in their declaration of annual accounts, the absence of transparency becomes a matter of concern. An analysis of the income and expenditure of national political parties for the year 2016–17 undertaken by the ADR based on the annual audited accounts of political parties filed in their income tax returns, shows that the seven national parties declared a total income of Rs 1,559.17 crores. Of this, the BJP claimed 66 per cent share, with an income of Rs 1,034.27 crores, followed at a distance by the Indian National Congress with 225.36 crores and 14.45 per cent of the total income. The report showed that between 2015–16 and 2016–17, the income of the BJP increased

---

were issued by the bank between 31 March and October 2018 ('Electoral Bonds: Ruling BJP Bags 95% of Funds,' *Economic Times*, 29 November 2018).

[95] The decision of the CIC came in the wake of an application in 2010 by the ADR to all national political parties, asking them information under the RTI Act regarding 10 maximum voluntary contributions received by them. While the BJP did not respond, the INC replied to say that it did not fall under the purview of the RTI Act, prompting the ADR to file a petition with the CIC. The parties have not complied with the order, leading to a non-compliance hearing against them. So far, the parties have continued to boycott the hearings ('Political Parties under RTI Act,' ADR India. Available at https://adrindia.org/sites/default/files/Political%20Parties%20under%20RTI%20Act.pdf; accessed on 3 February 2018).

by 81.18 per cent, while that of the Congress decreased by 14 per cent from Rs 261.56 crores to Rs 225.36 crores. Both the BJP and the Congress declared donations, grants, and contributions as their chief sources of income. Both the parties spent the maximum proportion of their income on election propaganda—Rs 606.64 crores in the case of the BJP and 69.78 crores in the case of the Congress.[96] The income and audit report of the BJP for the year 2017–18 shows that it raised Rs 1,027 crores and sustained its previous year's record of breaching the Rs 1000-crore mark. Of this, Rs 989 crores came from voluntary contributions, of which 52.8 per cent came from anonymous sources.[97]

* * *

Over the past years, specific issues pertaining to the micro-management of the electoral space have assumed importance. Most of these issues have emerged out of concerns for the normative frameworks of democracy. The ECI has over the years sought to make the electoral space democratic by laying down rules, which assure procedural certainty. Whether the rules concern themselves with the purging of the electoral space of corruption and criminality, or with providing a level playing field, they ultimately aim at affirming the normative principle of free and fair electoral competition, by providing procedural certainties. At the same time, the rules for the conduct of elections evolved by the ECI have generated tensions between the political class and the bureaucratic machinery of the ECI. Some of these areas of tension pertain to the 'right of the citizen to know' in order to cast an informed vote, the debate over disqualification of a candidate on conviction, and political finance and the question of transparency and accountability. While all these questions pertain to the integrity of the electoral system, at a deeper level, they are grounded in questions of appropriate and effective

[96] 'At Rs. 1,034 Crore, BJP Richest National Party in FY17: ADR Report,' *The Wire*, 10 April 2018.

[97] 'Electoral Bonds: Ruling BJP Bags 95% of Funds,' *Economic Times*, 29 November 2018.

representation and substantive democracy. It is, however, in the domain of political finance that the ECI remains ineffective and insufficiently empowered. Political corruption and the role money has come to play in electoral competition, which has become a high stakes game, has eroded the fairness of elections and distorted the procedural and normative bases of democratic representation.

ℯℵℴ

Conclusion

Institutions are integral to modern democracies. They give form and structure to the state, provide frameworks for the dispersal and democratisation of power, and give effect to the legitimation practices of the state. Debates on what constitutes the merely procedural aspects of democracy and their subsidiarity in relation to what are considered the higher-order components of substantive democracy are by now fairly well-rehearsed. Democratisation is largely seen as a process in which free, fair, competitive elections, an independent press, and the rule of law comprise the threshold that must be crossed before the normative ideals of democracy—freedom and equality—can be achieved. A 'good' democracy is seen as one which has graduated from being merely procedural, even though rules and procedures are vital for democracy, to one that is constitutive of enduring institutional structures capable of assuring equality to its citizens through legitimate modes of functioning.

Modern democracies are, however, located in complex societies. They are expected to perform a range of functions, and have to evolve appropriate institutional structures in order to do so. The institutional architecture is expected to buttress democracies against destabilisation and also secure the normative and functional existence of constitutional democracies. Most democracies may develop a 'thick institutional web' of 'a broad and deep matrix of relatively autonomous public institution', which may perform a variety of functions—'of restraint, regulation, coordination, and adjudication'—to manage 'risks' and maximise 'returns' (Kapur 2005: 30). The focus on institutional architecture and political stability, construed narrowly as peaceful regime change and the degree of stateness that a democracy may be said to possess, is, however, inadequate for understanding complex democracies. Democracies endure and create a normative lifeworld through diverse modes. To understand why democracies endure in diverse contexts and the institutional structures and normative frameworks they evolve to make it possible, it is important to study the specific historical trajectories they display and the transformations they bring about in the power relations in society.

While these concerns are pertinent for all democracies, they become all the more important for 'new' democracies, which have to constantly grapple with the anxieties of emulating the preferred institutional forms of the 'old', entrenched, and embedded democracies. Democratic regimes take different forms as they 'improvise' with their 'institutional tools' to address their historical problems. Democracies have, therefore, historically displayed 'a process of differentiation rather than singularity of form' (deSouza 2000: 204–5; Kaviraj 2000: 89–90). When concerns around institutional design and performance; their inadequacy, decay, and deficiency; and a corresponding pre-occupation with institutional building assume primacy, fundamental questions, emanating from the historically emergent relationship between democracies and state formation, the political culture which provides the ethical norms for institutions, and the social classes and relations which set the limits for institutional performance and institutional change, get occluded.

In the literature on democracy in India, an influential strand locates it in idealism and humanitarian sentiments, in the vows and promises of the national movement, and the mass mobilisation against colonial rule which generated an influential 'logic of democracy' (Austin 1966; Baxi 2002, 2008a; Kaviraj 2003). Indeed, the significance of the nationalist project has been seen to lie in the generation of a republican–democratic project, the choice of a parliamentary democracy, and the recourse to universal adult franchise, which embodied the goals of national and social revolution—transformative change, in other words, that had been denied to a colonised country. Yet, the establishment of a parliamentary democracy, which drew its legitimacy from a republican constitution to constitute the sovereign collective 'we' of democratic citizenship, had to contend with hierarchies and inequalities spelt by a strongly entrenched caste-differentiated society, coincident with social differentiation reinforced by economic and political power.

The unfolding of democratic politics in post-colonial India would show that in the process of articulation with modern democratic politics, the specific contours of Indian modernity took shape alongside processes that made modern democratic politics part of Indian political tradition (Kothari 1970: 21–2). It was in the domain of electoral politics that this transformation made itself most visible. The adoption of universal adult franchise as the basis of the camaraderie of equal citizenship was a triumphal moment in Indian constitutionalism. When the country went to polls in 1951–2, the electorate constituted through universal adult franchise was largely illiterate. The upper-caste elite, although politically and economically dominant, was numerically much smaller. Yet, the 'conflict over representation' and an upheaval in the existing caste-based power structures were deferred owing to the 'traditional habits of deference' towards the dominant social and political elite (Kaviraj 2003). The low levels of participation in the electoral arena gave rise to the impression of contest-free, stable institutions and, by implication, a durable democracy (Kaviraj 2003). This legitimation of political institutions emerging out of the deference to traditional authority, and the complacency of popular consensus it generated was, however, defied and eroded by the *political* logic of democracy.

The logic of democracy pushes the questions, who votes and who represents whom, both of which are politically fraught. The questions are also significant, not only for understanding electoral democracy, but also democracy as a value system with equality and freedom as its foundational principles. In this context, the phenomenon of the 'second democratic upsurge' (Yadav 1997, 1999) has become a significant counterpoint to the deference legitimation of the years immediately after Independence. The significance of the democratic upsurge lies in the possibilities of participation that the electoral process offers, irrespective and independent of the design of the electoral system. It draws attention to the processes whereby the democratic will of the people is *able* to make itself manifest effectively, breaking free from the historically entrenched hierarchies that inhibited political participation by large sections of people. The democratic upsurge of the 1990s has been attributed to the significant structural changes in the period—the change in the nature of political competition owing to the demise of the Congress system and the opening up of a range of radical possibilities in democratic politics. These created the enabling conditions for generating a political field in which institutions like the ECI and the judiciary asserted themselves.

Thus, if one were to examine the relationship between elections and democracy, it may be proposed that the contest over democracy has largely been the struggle to conform to the evaluative standards of equality and freedom in substantive terms. While elections are a necessary condition for democracy, they are not by themselves sufficient for democracy. Yet democratic elections have led to both the consolidation of the electoral system and also a churning within society, which has generated radical uncertainties within electoral democracies. Importantly, democracies are deeply imbricated in the imaginaries of the political community, the state and its institutional forms, in particular the manner in which it distributes and decentres power, constitutes identities of belonging, and the mechanisms through which it makes citizens legible.

In this context, the putting in place of institutions of electoral governance has been an important mechanism, which allows for a democratic consensus over the manner in which power is exercised. The debates around elections and electoral governance are pronounced with questions around issues of equality in representation, and devising statutory frameworks and institutional structures of electoral governance, which may enable the crafting of democratic politics as a continuum between representation and participation. Thus, even though elections do not exhaust the possibilities of democracy, in the lives of democracies, elections are times when political energies are grouped and expressed in plural ways. From the perspective of those who administer the institutional apparatus of electoral governance, elections are extraordinary times requiring efficiency in 'rule implementation'. Players in the election game—the political parties and the political class in general—are placed under regulatory control as political power is deferred until affirmed again by passing through an 'electoral trial'. The voter—the 'little-man', in the words of the Supreme Court of India—is the common man aggrieved by misrule, but also someone sufficiently empowered to change the course of the electoral game.

As the trajectory of the unfolding of electoral democracy in India would show, much has changed since the country first went to the polls in 1951–2. The first general election held on the basis of universal franchise was a transformative moment in a society making the transition from colonial subjection to republican government. The emphatic expression of popular sovereignty was to be demonstrated in the domain of electoral democracy. The capacity to self-govern had to be reiterated periodically as a statement against prophecies of doom that abounded at the time India became independent. The periodic renewal and affirmation of electoral democracy required laying down precise templates of laws and rules and institutional arrangements to facilitate the choice of representatives by the voter-citizen.

Indeed, as the Constituent Assembly debates around the need for setting up an ECI have shown, the Constituent Assembly had envisaged the ECI as an institution that would capture the essence of the transition from colonial subjecthood to sovereignty. The ECI, as the constitutional body responsible for conducting elections, has since emerged as a significant public institution within the shared political space of democracy in India. When the framers of the Constitution provided for the ECI to superintend, direct, and control the conduct of elections, they had envisaged a body which would be sufficiently empowered to discharge the responsibility of making the exercise of franchise fair and free, making it fundamental to a just and democratic society. Freedom from control by the Executive was, therefore, considered crucial, leading to the insertion of Article 324. Over the years, Article 324 has become a reservoir of powers for the ECI, and also a terrain of contest between the ECI and Parliament. The unfolding of electoral governance has shown that the powers of Parliament and those of the ECI remain overlapping and therefore contested. This has largely been due to the ambivalence induced in the Constitution by the coexistence of Articles 324 and 327, which make the ECI the primary body responsible for the conduct of elections, while simultaneously giving Parliament the power to make the laws to regulate the electoral domain. The precise areas of uncertainty and dispute, therefore, appear around the competing claims of Parliament and the ECI over the *power* to govern and the *responsibility* to govern the electoral domain, respectively.

The broad institutional framework within which voting and electoral competition take place operates on three levels: rule-making, rule implementation, and rule adjudication. The principal task of electoral governance, that is, 'organising democratic uncertainty by providing procedural and institutional certainty' (Mozaffar and Schedler 2002), must unfold at all three aforementioned levels of electoral governance. It is at the level of rule-making that the institutionalisation of democratic uncertainties takes place, through the establishment of procedural certainty. It is only through rules and procedures that ensure substantive uncertainty that elections can claim legitimacy as a means of eliciting popular participation and consent. The contending claims of Parliament and the ECI apparently relate to the first level of electoral governance, that is, the level of law-making, since this is the level where Parliament is pre-eminent. The tension over unclaimed power and the subsequent opening up of the scope of executive authority and administrative responsibility manifests itself mostly at the second and third levels of electoral governance, that is, at the levels of rule application and rule adjudication. Unless Parliament explicitly claims its legislative powers in matters pertaining to the conduct of elections and circumscribes thereby the ECI's powers of superintending elections, the ECI possesses an enormous repository of powers mandated by the Constitution. Over the years, this has led to expansion of the executive powers of the ECI in areas that are not covered by electoral law. The conflict between the ECI and political parties over the MCC is an illustration of the contest over limits to the ECI's powers of conducting elections.

A question that is integral to electoral governance, however, is the extent to which it has enabled the strengthening of democratic institutions. In other words, does the consolidation and strengthening of the electoral system through rules and procedures of governance, which facilitate participation, have longer-term impact of strengthening democratic government? While the efficient administration of the electoral domain has led to new mobilisations, they have affected institutions unevenly. This is manifest in the contemporary moment in the biography of Indian democracy, which presents the paradox of the deepening of democracy occurring alongside declining trust in political institutions. On the other hand, the consolidation of the electoral domain has had ramifications for the deliberative and substantive dimensions of democracy in India.

A regulatory regime of electoral governance has entrenched itself in the past decades, with specific issues pertaining to the micromanagement of the electoral space assuming importance. The modalities through which the ECI functions are largely geared towards bureaucratic efficiency and innovations in electoral governance. In the literature on electoral integrity, electoral governance is seen as a management enterprise undertaken by EMBs, which are bureaucratic apparatuses having the expertise for the efficient conduct of elections. An efficient model of electoral governance is expected to satisfy the standards of legitimacy, independence, impartiality and fairness, integrity and honesty, transparency, and effective professionalism. A study of EMBs in different contexts may, however, show distinct models and trajectories, with diverse interpretations of what constitutes electoral governance. Thus, while talking about the importance of 'scalability' in electoral management (Quraishi 2014: 77), referring to the enormity of the task of managing elections, former CEC S.Y. Quraishi speaks of the ECI as a 'self-effacing organization' (Quraishi 2014: xviii), of which people know fairly little.

Electoral management is not only about putting in place rules and procedures; it is also concerned with democratic outcomes, which would affirm popular sovereignty through an electoral morality different from everyday politics. Yet, like all institutions, the ECI is located in a political field that is constitutive of contests over political power. Ultimately, the ECI functions in a social context. When universal adult franchise was instituted in India, the vote was expected to foreground and, indeed, 'celebrate' the *legal* status of the *individual* as a 'universal vessel of free will and legal rights' (Gilmartin 2007: 56). Gilmartin argues that the figuration of the 'official, legally recognized voter' as a rational, autonomous actor was the 'conceit' that was expected to justify government by consent and define 'the people'. The voter was protected from 'undue' social influences by the electoral laws, which banned any 'systematic appeal to vote or refrain from voting on grounds of caste, race, community or religion or the use of, or appeal to, religious and national symbols, such as the national flag and the national emblem, for the furtherance of the prospects of a candidate's election' (Gilmartin 2007: 75).

The mounting influence of money and other appeals to religion and caste have, however, shown that the relationship between the citizen-voter and democratic representation is not one of a social contract; it is rather the outcome of a 'dense network of socio-material relations' (Bjorkman and Witsoe 2018: 154). Discussing the role played by money in this network, Bjorkman and Witsoe (2018) argue that the stricter enforcement of the secret ballot has resulted in the 'vertical ties and patronage politics' of the 'vote bank' losing much of its 'coercive character'. But institutional reforms in electoral governance have not succeeded in producing an electorate of 'autonomously reasoning voters', freed from 'undue influence' of community and society. According to Hansen, the liberation from 'vertical ties of patronage' has been followed by the transition from 'maabaapism to dadaism' (cited in Bjorkman and Witsoe 2018: 160). Guha (2008) argues that by obscuring the relationship between gifts and votes, electoral reforms have reversed 'the direction of vote-bank influence transferring the moral hazard from voter to party, which is left with little assurance that material inducements will actually secure the sought after votes of a particular group' (Bjorkman and Witsoe 2018: 160).

The citizen-voter is not part of a *camaraderie* of equals, and the right to vote may not be available equally to all. A large number of the rural and urban poor, migrants, people in conflict areas, or people displaced from their homes owing to ethnic conflict or economic reasons may not be able to participate in the political process. The question that one must address while exploring electoral governance, therefore, is the long term and systemic exclusion of large numbers of people. In this context, the political marginalisation of groups that are forced to remain outside the electoral system, that is, groups whose livelihood patterns do not coincide with the cycles of electoral democracy in India, becomes important. The example of registering as voters certain groups of people, for example, women, migrant labour, and communities, which are unlikely to be fully documented and often do not have fixed residences, is relevant in this context. A primary requirement for inclusion on an electoral roll is residence within the relevant jurisdiction, which implies that the citizen-voter must have a stable address. But this is not the reality for many people, mostly the rural poor, whose movement is motivated by the search for livelihood and economic opportunities. During the 1990s, for example, there was an exponential increase in distress migrations—something approaching an exodus—owing to a complete breakdown of rural economies. Many migrants are concentrated in clusters of villages within certain districts, so that certain seats and regions are most likely to be affected by the migration pattern. The end result is that large numbers of rural poor are excluded from the electoral process due to migration, and there are some periods in the cycle of migration when people are most likely to be away from their villages. For example, the months of April and May, when general elections have taken place, are ironically the months when absences from villages were at their peak. In this context, it is paradoxical, therefore, that the option of 'proxy' voting has been considered feasible and is being facilitated by the government for only one class of migrants—NRIs—in dilution of the principle of relationship between the voter-citizen and territorial constituencies.

In almost seven decades of its life as an institution administering elections in India, all political parties and ruling regimes have submitted to election outcomes. Yet, the ECI has often found itself in the middle of controversies, for example, the dispute over electoral rolls in Assam, the conduct of elections in conflict areas, the implementation of the MCC, political corruption and election funding, paid news, and more recently the debate over the EVMs. Indeed, a fundamental feature of all these controversies is the challenge to the ECI's capacity to function autonomously. In elections in conflict areas (for example, West Bengal in the 1970s, Assam in the 1980s, Punjab in the 1980s and 1990s, and Jammu and Kashmir in the 1990s), allegations of the ECI not being able to check the process of 'falsification of electoral verdict' were made (Roy 1975: 53). The large-scale election violence of the past, booth capturing, and charges of 'rigging' (*Economic and Political Weekly* 1971)[1] have receded with the securitisation, increased

---

[1] The then CEC S.P. Sen declared after a tour of the state that the elections in West Bengal were 'undoubtedly fair', although he also admitted that 'there are pockets of dissidence where normal campaign has been somewhat circumscribed'. Also see Roy Choudhury (1984: 135).

surveillance, and digitisation of electoral governance. The contest over identifying citizens and sifting out foreigners and illegal migrants from the electoral rolls presented a challenge that was acknowledged by the then CEC, S.L. Shakdher, in 1978. The 1983 election, which was perhaps the bloodiest in the history of electoral processes in India, marred by violent conflict along ethnic lines, seriously tested the election machinery. In the context of ethnic strife, elections were conducted in an extraordinary situation, where amidst a general opposition to the holding of election and the reluctance of the ECI to hold it, the central and state governments insisted on going ahead with it (Rao 1983).[2] A similar scenario emerged in Punjab in 1992, following repeated extension of president's rule in the state, and deferred elections—to which the ECI complied. Elections to the Punjab Legislative Assembly were held amidst the biggest ever anti-militancy operations, boycott of elections by Sikh leaders, low and unevenly distributed voter turnout, and victory for the Congress (Singh 2000).

The question whether, in conflict situations, the 'fairness' of elections can at all be assured is pertinent, given that significant political actors choose to abstain from the political process, and the ones that remain are often those who wield coercive power in the region. While the ECI officials are quite firm on the question that even if a state assembly is dissolved or comes to the end of its term, the time of the polls can only be decided by the ECI,[3] in situations of long-drawn conflict, the credibility of electoral governance and primarily the ECI may be put to test. In such a context, rather than an

[2] Parts of Assam, especially areas in Sibasagar district, were declared 'disturbed areas', many activists of AASU and All Assam Gana Sangram Parishad (AAGSP) were detained under NSA, a blanket ban under Assam Special Powers (Press) Act, 1960, was imposed for two months against six publications, and paramilitary forces were deployed all through the state. Also see *Economic and Political Weekly* (1983).

[3] Commenting on the speculation that the government may hold elections in Gujarat, the former CEC, C.V.G. Krishanmurthy, emphasised that it was not for the prime minister or the chief minister to announce elections, but the prerogative of the ECI. The ECI decides the time of the polls only after taking stock of the ground reality and whether or not they are conducive to free and fair elections (see 'Polls in Gujarat are for the EC to Announce,' *Hindustan Times*, 19 April 2002).

autonomous body entrusted with 'enabling' the people to exercise an informed choice, the ECI may come to be seen as representing and furthering the hegemonic interests of the state, opposed to the democratic aspirations of the people. The assembly elections in Jammu and Kashmir (September 2002), for example, opened up a debate on the credibility of an election process in conditions that were not conducive to a free, fair, and, importantly, *fearless* exercise of franchise. The All India Hurriyat Conference's announcement of a 'poll panel' in the elections, as an alternative ECI, may be seen as a manifestation of distrust of the election process in the prevailing circumstances.[4] James Lyngdoh (2004: vii), too, alludes to this distrust and the subsequent contradiction in the role of the ECI in Jammu and Kashmir: 'The Election Commission had been inseparably bound to elections in the state.... But I soon ran into the reality of the contradiction of an Election Commission otherwise held in high regard but seen in Jammu and Kashmir only as a tool of the Government of India.'

Successive elections in Jammu and Kashmir have elicited allegations of 'rigging', 'concoction', and 'irregularities'. In February 2001, the BJP had alleged 'gross irregularities' in the by-election to the Lok Sabha. In July 1996, Farooq Abdullah asserted that the 1996 Lok Sabha elections were a 'rigged and concocted exercise'. The same was said about the 1996 assembly elections that made Abdullah the chief minister. In the 1999 Lok Sabha elections, Abdullah's assembly constituency Ganderbal registered only 10 per cent voting, with 11 per cent in the parliamentary constituency of Srinagar, compelling the then CEC, M.S. Gill, to call it a 'democratic comment', and ask Parliament to take note of it.[5] Moreover, the renegade Ikhwan, the Rashtriya Rifles of the army, the CRPF, and the BSF were witnessed

---

[4] In February 2002, the Hurriyat Conference announced its poll panel with Tapan Kumar Bose of the Kathmandu-based South Asian Human Rights Centre and Sajjad Ali Shah as its two co-chairpersons. The Hurriyat hopes that this alternate commission will help choose 'the true representatives of the people of Jammu and Kashmir', in both Jammu and Kashmir and PoK, who would discuss the future of the people in tripartite talks (see 'Hurriyat Forms Poll Panel,' *The Hindu*, 13 February 2002).

[5] A.G. Noorani. 2002. 'One-Horse Race,' *Hindustan Times*, 28 May.

and reported by Indian correspondents 'sending people out like cattle from the narrow lanes of Srinagar', forcing them to vote.[6] Since 1995, the ECI held several elections in the region, including Lok Sabha and assembly elections, under the full sway of the armed 'counter-insurgency' groups. This is in marked contrast to the ECI's stance elsewhere where the presence of police in large numbers had provoked it to declare the elections null and void.[7] It is significant how in the absence of a political process and alienation of the people from the state, the conditions in which any election holds meaning in a democracy were not considered relevant. Instead, it became important for the ECI to emphasise the fairness and efficiency of the election machinery, and that it should be seen as such by people outside the state, the international community in particular.[8] In a comparable situation in Mizoram, it was only when a political process was set in motion with the Mizoram Accord of 30 June 1986, conferring statehood and a special status to Mizoram, that 'conditions were seen as conducive for holding free and fair elections', and the process of elections to the assembly initiated.[9]

The Supreme Court of India has considered 'free and fair' elections a basic feature of the Indian Constitution. This means that no part of the Indian Constitution can be amended by Parliament to dilute the provisions that secure democratic elections. The conduct of free and fair elections in situations of long-drawn conflict has presented challenges before the ECI. In terms of the logistics, these challenges concern the efficient conduct of elections, especially to make the polling process accessible to people. The substantive questions pertain, however, to democratic processes and the inclusion of those sections which have been rendered vulnerable by conflict. Election officers

[6] Noorani, 'One-Horse Race'.

[7] In June 1981, the CEC declared the by-election in two Garhwal constituencies to be null and void because of the reports it received from its team and officers of the large presence of Haryana police in the area (Noorani, 'One-Horse Race.').

[8] A.G. Noorani. 2002. 'Polls Apart,' *Hindustan Times*, 9 July; 'EC Passes for Foreign Diplomats to Witness Polls,' *The Hindu*, 14 September.

[9] Noorani, 'One-Horse Race'.

conducting elections in conflict areas have evolved 'best practices' premised on the understanding that the electoral process is an alternative to violence as it is a means of achieving governance. It is assumed that once elections are successfully conducted, violence will cease and will be substituted by 'good' governance. These measures of efficient conduct of elections may be seen as pitted against the distrust of elections by insurgent groups in the absence of a political accord, and their calls for boycott of election, which may have widespread or limited support among the local people.

Elections have been conducted in areas of conflict in India following a political accord between the insurgent groups and the government, for example, Mizoram and Assam in the 1980s, marking the onset of democratic electoral politics. In some context, however, elections have been conducted amidst conflict (for example, Jammu and Kashmir) in the hope that the electoral process would outpace and replace the politics of armed insurgency. The 'best practice' innovations in areas with what is called left-wing extremism (LWE), which are large tracts of forest land stretching contiguously across several states inhabited by the Adivasi (tribal) people, where armed Maoist groups have been active, take recourse to 'security management' of elections. Accordingly, they have devised a series of measures to secure elections in order to ensure 'area domination' through surveillance, gathering intelligence, and deployment of paramilitary forces in large numbers in sensitive areas—in other words, through the activation of 'law and order' apparatus of the state. The measures adopted by the electoral officers as a standard policy of electoral management in such areas raise questions pertaining specifically to the ramification of securing elections on the modes of representation and resolution of conflicts in general. Often 'electoral security' measures are adopted in contexts where the CPI (M) would have given a call of poll boycott, which follows from their critique of elections as an undemocratic exercise held under semi-feudal conditions to sustain misrule and corruption. It has also often been the case that the Maoists have gone beyond a mere 'call' for boycott to also 'ensuring' that voting did not take place in booths in areas under their control. An editorial in *Economic and Political Weekly* (2009: 6) points out that the Maoists have 'cynically used violence against the most undefended and weak links in the electoral system: the government servant going to a remote polling station, the constable guarding a polling booth, and roads and bridges bringing people from far-off areas to the booths—to drive fear in the minds of people and prevent them from exercising their right to vote'.[10] It argued that such strategies disenfrachise and disempower the poor, in a context where the records of voter turnout in elections show that it is the poor and the vulnerable who exercise their franchise in large numbers.

Electoral governance does not take place in a vacuum and unfolds in a political field that is structured in a way that produces vulnerabilities and participation and representation deficits. The ECI may be able to address them only in limited ways while conducting elections. The enrolment of voters, preparation of electoral rolls, ensuring a level playing field, and purity of elections by eliminating crime and money from influencing the electoral domain have presented challenges before the ECI. More recently, especially after the state assembly elections in Uttar Pradesh in 2017, which saw the BJP win by a huge margin, the controversy over the possibility of EVMs being susceptible to hacking erupted with renewed vigour.[11] The EVM imbroglio has made the machine itself suspect, diminishing reliability and transparency, which are integral to building trust in the electoral system and are

[10] In the first phase of polling for elections 2009 conducted on 16 April, Maoists attacked the polling process at 15 places, killing 18 people, including 5 election staff. There were similar attacks in the second round of polling on 23 April when five policemen escorting voting machines were killed in a landmine blast in Bihar (*Economic and Political Weekly* 2009: 6).

[11] EVMs manufactured in 1989–90 were used on experimental basis for the first time in 16 assembly constituencies in the states of Madhya Pradesh (5), Rajasthan (5), and NCT of Delhi (6) at the general elections to the respective legislative assemblies held in November 1998 (see Election Commission of India. Available at http://eci.nic.in/eci_main1/evm.aspx; accessed on 16 February 2018). The ECI has been using EVMs since then. The EVMs are manufactured by the Electronics Corporation of India, Ltd. (ECIL) and Bharat Electronics, Ltd. (BEL), which are public-sector units under the Department of Atomic Energy and the Ministry of Defence, respectively. The components of each EVM are sourced from companies in Japan and the United States of America. The ECI has claimed that this is done without compromising the EVMs in any way. Each EVM has a life of 15 years (see Vasudevan Mukunth. 2017. 'Ten Questions Worth Asking About EVMs,' *The Wire*, 10 May). The ECI

important ingredients of electoral integrity. The introduction of the VVPAT, insisted upon by the Supreme Court of India in its orders in 2013 and 2017, is likely to alleviate some of the doubts regarding the trustworthiness of the machine. Indeed, in an attempt to instil trust in the EVMs as the most appropriate mode of recording the vote, the ECI ran full page 'advertisements' in leading newspapers of the country to inform the voters of the reliability and efficiency of the system. Reminding the voters that the EVMs had 'ended the days of booth capturing and the delays and errors in counting ballot papers', the ECI added that the VVPATs were manufactured only at two public-sector units under the expertise of an 'independent Technical Expert Committee' and supervision of the ECI itself. It tabulated the details of the EVMs used in past elections going back to 2000 in different states and the efficacy of EVMs enhanced by VVPATs, which gave the voter the chance (for 7 seconds only after the vote had been recorded in the EVM) to verify if the vote had been recorded correctly.[12] Table C.1 gives the details of the years of elections and the number of polling stations in which the EVMs were used.

In the state assembly elections that concluded in December 2018, concerns were raised regarding the security of EVMs and VVPATs in the intervening period between the polling day, which was spread over the last week of November and first week of December, and 11 December, which was the day the votes cast in all five states were counted. Madhya Pradesh went to the polls on 28 November.

---

has sought to address these concerns by introducing a VVPAT system, which issues a paper slip of the vote cast, which can be used to later verify the data of votes cast in each EVM. The VVPAT was used for the first time in 2013 in Noksen Assembly Constituency in Nagaland. In its order delivered in October 2013 in a PIL filed by Subramanian Swamy, the Supreme Court of India instructed the ECI to use VVPAT along with EVMs in a phased manner so that all elections could be conducted with the EVMs and VVPAT by 2019.

[12] The ECI stated that VVPATs had been used in 933 state assembly constituencies and 18 parliamentary constituencies. In the 2017–18 assembly elections in seven states—Goa, Himachal Pradesh, Gujarat, Meghalaya, Nagaland, Tripura, and Karnataka—VVPATs had been used in all the polling stations in the assembly constituencies. (The advertisement carried by newspapers on 6 October 2018 is available at http://ceodelhi.gov.in/pdffolder/2018/Know-your-EVM-VVPAT-Engish.pdf; accessed on 8 October 2018.)

Table C.1   Use of EVM (2000–18)

State/Union Territory	Year of Election in which EVMs were Used	No. of Polling Stations
Andhra Pradesh	2004, 2009, 2014	43,129
Arunachal Pradesh	2004, 2009, 2014	2,191
Assam	2001, 2006, 2011, 2016	27,267
Bihar	2000, 2005, 2010, 2015	62,780
Chhattisgarh	2000, 2003, 2008, 2013	23,411
Goa	2002, 2007, 2012, 2017	1,642
Gujarat	2002, 2007, 2012, 2017	50,264
Haryana	2000, 2005, 2009, 2014	17,046
Himachal Pradesh	2003, 2007, 2012, 2017	4,749
Jammu & Kashmir	2000, 2004, 2009, 2014	10,641
Jharkhand	2000, 2005, 2010, 2014	29,424
Karnataka	2004, 2008, 2013, 2018	56,696
Kerala	2001, 2006, 2011, 2016	24,460
Madhya Pradesh	2003, 2008, 2013	65,200
Maharashtra	2004, 2009, 2014	91,451
Manipur	2002, 2007, 2012, 2017	2,817
Meghalaya	2003, 2008, 2013, 2018	3,082
Mizoram	2003, 2008, 2013	1,148
Nagaland	2003, 2008, 2013, 2018	2,194
Orissa	2000, 2004, 2009, 2014	35,896
Punjab	2002, 2007, 2012, 2017	23,089
Rajasthan	2003, 2008, 2013	51,227
Sikkim	2004, 2009, 2014	549
Tamil Nadu	2001, 2006, 2011, 2016	65,972
Tripura	2003, 2008, 2013, 2018	3,214
Uttar Pradesh	2002, 2007, 2012, 2017	15,9,957
Uttarakhand	2002, 2007, 2012, 2017	10,870
West Bengal	2001, 2006, 2011, 2017	77,354
Delhi	2003, 2006, 2011, 2017	13,418
Puducherry	2001, 2006, 2011, 2016	913

Source: 'Know Your EVM & VVPAT'. Available at http://ceodelhi.gov.in/pdffolder/2018/Know-your-EVM-VVPAT-Engish.pdf; accessed on 8 October 2018.

A petition in the high court of Madhya Pradesh by a Congress leader raised concern over what he believed was inadequate security of polled and unused EVMs and VVPATs in some districts of the state.

Dismissing the petition, the high court expressed its satisfaction with the details of security provided by the ECI—that 'the strong room with polled EVMs/VVPATs were sealed immediately after poll to be opened on the day of counting i.e. on 11.12.2018', and that the strong rooms were 'under the security of Central Armed Paramilitary Forces with a triple cordon of security'.[13]

An additional concern regarding the *secrecy* of the vote, which is seen as compromised by the manner in which votes recorded by the EVM are counted, presents a problem of a different order. Before the EVMs came to be used, the counting of votes cast through the ballot paper was done as per Rule 56B of the Conduct of Election Rules (1961). According to this rule, the ballot papers in the ballot boxes of more than one polling station in a constituency were taken out and mixed together, and then arranged in convenient bundles to be scrutinised for counting. With the introduction of the EVMs, however, the counting is done polling station-wise, except for those constituencies that are specially notified by the ECI under Rule 59A of the Conduct of Election Rules as those in which the ECI fears intimidation of voters. In such cases, the result from each EVM is fed into a master counting machine, so that only the total result of an assembly constituency is known and not the result in each individual polling station.[14]

The concern that the secrecy of the vote is likely to be compromised for all other polling stations, irrespective of whether or not they are vulnerable (as defined in Rule 59A), has remained. Considering that each polling booth caters to around 1500 voters or less, it is not farfetched to assume that in case a political party is able to access the information of how votes were cast in each polling station—an information which is stored in the EVMs—the political inclination of a locality and the likelihood of 'knowing' who voted for which party will be high. Indeed, it was in November 2008 that the ECI

---

[13] Ashok Kini. 2018. 'Madhya Pradesh HC Rejects Plea Alleging Lack of Sufficient Security to EVMs,' *LiveLaw*, 10 December. Available at https://www.livelaw.in/madhya-pradesh-hc-rejects-plea-alleging-lack-of-sufficient-security-to-evms-read-order/; accessed on 18 December 2018.

[14] See 'Section 59A of The Conduct of Election Rules 1961'. Available at https://indiankanoon.org/doc/61000643/; accessed on 17 May 2019.

had proposed that a 'totaliser machine' that could mix the votes cast in a number of polling booths through the EVM be used for counting the votes. It was expected that the use of such a machine would prevent disclosure of voting patterns across polling stations during counting, and alleviate fears of pre-poll intimidation or post-poll victimisation by candidates. The proposal was entrusted for the consideration of a standing committee of Parliament in 2009. In 2015, the Law Commission endorsed the use of such a machine. Six national parties, including the Congress, the BSP, and the NCP, have supported the machine, with the CPI(M) agreeing with it in principle but preferring a careful and phased introduction. In 2016, nudged by the Supreme Court, the BJP-led NDA government constituted a ministerial team consisting of Rajnath Singh, Arun Jaitley, Manohar Parrikar, Nitin Gadkari, and Ravi Shankar Prasad to give its recommendations to frame a response to the ECI's proposal.[15] By January 2018, the lines between the ECI and the central government for and against totalising the votes was clearly drawn with the government taking a position against the machine in its affidavit to the Supreme Court. The government argued that booth-wise information of votes cast was beneficial 'since it would facilitate the candidates and the parties to find out the areas where they have shown better results and area where they have not shown good results so as to work more for that area by bringing development activities to improve their performance in future elections'.[16]

The conundrum over the use of EVMs and the desirability of totalising votes remains unresolved so far, and so do a range of concerns that have evolved over a period of time in the different domains of electoral governance, most of which have implications for the way in which the sanctity of elections is maintained in India. Yet, these questions are not solely about electoral democracy and its procedural contours; they are inextricably associated with substantive democracy and how questions germane to democratic citizenship are contested and resolved in the public domain.

[15] 'Centre Moves on Vote Totalising Machine,' *The Hindu*, 17 October 2016.

[16] 'AG, EC Oppose Centre's Stand against Totalising of Votes,' *The Times of India*, 15 January 2018.

The institutional matrix in which the ECI is located is asymmetrical and uneven. The resistance by the parliamentarians to disclosure and the citizen's right to know was checked by the Supreme Court in its adherence to the principle that the right to know was integral to the fundamental right to speech, as well as in its decisions to disqualify MPs convicted of a crime, from both contesting and sitting in Parliament. Yet, in 2015, in the case *Rajbala* v. *State of Haryana*, the Supreme Court upheld the constitutional validity of the Haryana Panchayati Raj (Amendment) Act, 2015, rejecting the petitioner's plea that it violated the fundamental right to equality. The judgment upheld the five additional disqualifications laid down by the Act to exclude those who had criminal charges framed against them, were without a specified minimum educational qualification, in debt, did not have a functional toilet in their homes, and had arrears of electricity bills from contesting the elections to the Panchayati Raj. The burden of argument in the judgment was to establish that franchise as a constitutional right is a lesser right, which is to say, it was not a fundamental right and, therefore, not entitled to the same protection as a fundamental right. The judgment effectively created two classes of citizens: one which could vote but not govern and the other which could do both, reducing franchise to a mere statutory privilege, which could be subject to the whims of those who hold political power. Indeed, the political excision of the socio-economically disadvantaged was a betrayal of the promise of equal citizenship and transformative constitutionalism, which requires that everyone, especially those who are in power, live the ethic of transformation. While deciding the eligibility criteria for election to political office is the prerogative of the legislature, the amendment effectively converted a political right into a privilege, taking citizenship back to its association with status that was enjoyed by the propertied elite.

In January 2017, in a landmark judgment, the constitution bench of the Supreme Court interpreted Section 123(3) of the RPA to mean that seeking votes in the name of religion, caste, or community amounted to corrupt practice and the election of a candidate could be set aside on that ground.[17] The judgment, however, was not

---

[17] The appeal was filed in 1992 by Abhiram Singh of the BJP, whose election to Maharashtra Assembly in 1990 was set aside in 1991 by the Bombay High Court on the ground that he made an appeal to the voters as a Hindu.

unanimous. While the majority decision of four judges argued that elections were a secular exercise and the relationship between 'man and God' was an individual choice, the three dissenting judges felt that such a judgment would amount to judicial interference in the domain of law-making, which must be left to the Legislature. Moreover, they argued, issues affecting voters needed to be expressed and discussed in the public domain in elections, and excising issues affecting voters from elections would reduce democracy to an abstraction. To make the conduct of elections, 'its superintendence, direction and control' fair, as mandated by the Constitution of India, is a tall order, which the ECI cannot deliver in isolation.

Yet, what is it that makes the ECI a trusted institution, seen as a body that performs its functions more effectively than other institutions of the state—both political and bureaucratic? In an interesting formulation, Lant Pritchett asks the question, whether India is a 'flailing state', to explain the dissonance between the 'strong' 'head' of the state referring to the strength of the higher bureaucracy in drafting programmes and policy and its weakness in implementing them. Pritchett refers in particular to the domains of 'police, tax collection, education, health, power, water supply'—all the routine services, where 'rampant absenteeism, indifference, incompetence, and corruption' have led to the co-existence in India of elite institutions and chaotic conditions in service production:

> I argue that India is today a flailing state—a nation-state in which the head, that is the elite institutions at the national (and in some states) level remain sound and functional but that this head is no longer reliably connected via nerves and sinews to its own limbs. (Pritchett 2009: 3–4)

Peter Evans too has puzzled over the nature of the bureaucratic state apparatus in India, placing it in a typology where the state appears as a rational bureaucratic apparatus, but is not embedded

---

Judgment delivered on 2 January 2017 in Civil Appeal No. 37/1992, *Abhiram Singh v. C.D. Commachan (dead)*. Available at http://www.livelaw.in/seeking-votes-name-religion-corrupt-practice-sc-constitution-bench/; accessed on 20 January 2018.

enough to have strong networks in civil society and the dominant classes (Evans 1995). Evans presents the framework of 'embedded autonomy' to explain the different development trajectories that states take by linking state capacity and functions with class forces in civil society. The ECI can be seen, however, as an example of a centralised bureaucratic apparatus which has sustained itself as an institution where the head is as robust as its limbs in the states and districts. The manner in which it has evolved as an institution over the years gives a vantage point to examine the ways in which democracy itself has fared in India, which has often been chequered, but also persistent and resilient. The robustness of the institution and its ability to renew itself, despite flaws in its design, has largely emerged, quite like the Supreme Court of India, from its ability to enhance its powers inscribed in the Constitution itself. Both these factors—the inherent powers of self-regulation and the tendency over the years to consolidate and enhance them—have contributed to making the ECI a relatively autonomous institution, with a distinctive identity deriving from the democratic logic of the state.

ॐ

Select Bibliography

Abrams, Philip. 1988. 'Notes on the Difficulties of Studying the State (1977).' *Journal of Historical Sociology* 1(1): 58–89.

Agamben, Giorgio. 2005. *The State of Exception*, translated by Kevin Attell. Chicago and London: University of Chicago Press.

Austin, Granville. 1966. *The Indian Constitution: Cornerstone of a Nation*. New Delhi: Oxford University Press.

Azim Premji University and CSDS-Lokniti. 2018. *Society and Politics between Elections*. Azim Premji University, Bengaluru. Available at https://azim-premjiuniversity.edu.in/SitePages/pdf/Azim_Premji_Univ_PSBE_2018.pdf; accessed on 17 May 2019.

Barpujari, Indrani. 2006. *Illegal Migrants (Determination by Tribunals) Act 1983, Promulgation and Repeal: A Contextual Analysis*. Guwahati: Omeo Kumar Das Institute of Social Change and Development.

Baruah, Sanjib. 1986. 'Immigration, Ethnic Conflict, and Political Turmoil: Assam, 1979–1985.' *Asian Survey* 26(11): 1184–206.

———. 2011. 'The Partition's Long Shadow: The Ambiguities of Citizenship in Assam, India.' *Citizenship Studies* 13(6): 593–606.

Basu, D.D. 1996. *Shorter Constitution of India*. New Delhi: Prentice Hall of India.

Baxi, Upendra. 2002. 'The (Im)possibility of Constitutional Justice.' In *India's Living Constitution*, edited by Zoya Hasan, E. Sridharan, and R. Sudarshan. New Delhi: Permanent Black, pp. 31–63.

———. 2008a. 'Outline of a "Theory of Practice" of Indian Constitutionalism.' In *Politics and Ethics of the Indian Constitution*, edited by Rajeev Bhargava. New Delhi: Oxford University Press.

————. 2008b. 'Preliminary Notes on Transformative Constitutionalism.' BISA Conference on Courting Justice, Delhi, 27–9 April.

Birch, Sarah. 2011. *Electoral Malpractice*. Series: Comparative Politics. Oxford: Oxford University Press.

Bjorkman, Lisa and Jeffrey Witsoe. 2018. 'Money and Votes: Following Flows through Mumbai and Bihar.' In *Costs of Democracy: Political Finance in India*, edited by Devesh Kapur and Milan Vaishnav. New Delhi: Oxford University Press.

Brewin, Mark W. 2008. *Celebrating Democracy: The Mass-Mediated Ritual of Election Day*. New York: Peter Lang.

Chambers Jr., Henry L. 2016. 'State and Local Officials and Voter ID.' *Election Law Journal* 15(3): 234–46.

Chatterjee, Partha. 2004. *The Politics of the Governed*. New Delhi: Permanent Black.

Chaube, Shibanikinkar. 1973. *Constituent Assembly of India: Springboard of Revolution*. New Delhi: People's Publishing House.

Chaudhury, Maitrayee. 2017. *Refashioning India: Gender, Media, and a Transformed Public Discourse*. New Delhi: Orient Blackswan.

Choudhury, Profulla Roy. 1984. *Left Experiment in West Bengal*. New Delhi: Patriot Publishers.

Citrin, Jack, Donald P. Green, and Morris Levy. 2014. 'The Effects of Voter ID Notification on Voter Turnout: Results from a Large-Scale Field Experiment.' *Election Law Journal* 13(2): 228–42.

Constituent Assembly Debates. 2003 (first published in 1950). Vol I–XII, Lok Sabha Secretariat, New Delhi.

deSouza, Peter Ronald. 1998. 'The Election Commission and Electoral Reforms in India.' In *Democracy, Diversity, Stability*, edited by D.D. Khanna, L.L. Mehrotra, and Gert W. Kueck. New Delhi: Macmillan.

————. 2000. 'Election, Parties and Democracy in India.' In *Contemporary India: Transitions*, edited by Peter Ronald de Souza. New Delhi: SAGE.

Devi, V.S. Rama and S.K. Mendiratta. 2006. *How India Votes: Election Laws, Practice and Procedure*. New Delhi: LexisNexis/Butterworths.

Dunn, John. 1993. *Western Political Theory in the Face of the Future*. Cambridge: Cambridge University Press.

Dworkin, Ronald M. 1967. 'The Model of Rules.' *Faculty Scholarship Series*. Paper 3609, Yale Law School Legal Scholarship Repository. Available at http://digitalcommons.law.yale.edu/fss_papers/3609; accessed on 12 April 2012.

Economic and Political Weekly. 1971. 'West Bengal: Behind the Violence.' 6(3, 4, & 5): 193.

————. 2009. 'When the Maoists Disempower the Poor.' Editorial. 44(17): 5–6.

————. 2010. 'The Right to Vote.' Editorial. 45(4): 6.

————. 1983. Cover Page, 'Assam: What Kind of Election?' 53(3): 42–3.

Election Commission of India. 1979. 'Proceedings of the Commission's Meeting with Political Parties.' *Documentation Monthly*, July–September.

————. 1982a. 'Sunday, February 21–27, 1982.' *Documentation Monthly*, January–April: 88–90.

————. 1982b. 'The Statesman, January 8, 1982.' *Documentation Monthly*, January–April: 101–2.

————. 1984. 'First Annual Report, 1983', New Delhi April.

————. 1991. *Model Code of Conduct for the Guidance of Political Parties and Candidates*. New Delhi: Election Commission of India.

————. 1999. *Landmark Judgements on Election Law*. New Delhi: Election Commission of India.

————. 2004. *Proposed Electoral Reforms*. New Delhi: Election Commission of India. Available at http://eci.nic.in/eci_main/PROPOSED_ELECTORAL_REFORMS.pdf; accessed on 2 July 2012.

————. 2006. *Compendium of Instruction on Electoral Rolls, EPIC, SLAs and Computerisation*. Up to December 2005. New Delhi: Election Commission of India, Nirvachan Sadan. Available at http://www.eci.gov.in; accessed on 13 July 2011.

————. 2009a. *Compendium of Instructions*. Vol. 3, Model Code of Conduct. New Delhi: Election Commission of India.

————. 2009b. *Model Code of Conduct, LS Elections 2009 (for Political Parties and Candidates)*. New Delhi: Election Commission of India.

————. 2011. *Handbook for Booth Level Officers*. New Delhi: Election Commission of India.

————. 2013. *Systematic Voters' Education and Electoral Participation (SVEEP), Compendium of Instructions*. New Delhi: Election Commission of India.

————. 2016. *Manual on Vulnerability Mapping*. New Delhi, Document 5, Edition 1. Available at https://www.eci.gov.in/files/file/6911-manual-on-vulnerability-mapping-2016/; accessed on 4 July 2017.

Enskat, Mike, Subrata K. Mitra, and Vijay Bahadur Singh. 2001. 'India.' In *Elections in Asia and the Pacific*, edited by Dictor Nohlen, Florian Grots, and Christaf Hartmann. Oxford: Oxford University Press.

Evans, Peter B. 1995. *Embedded Autonomy: States and Industrial Transformation*. Princeton: Princeton University Press.

Foley, Edward B. 2008. 'U.S. Supreme Court Case Preview *Crawford v. Marion County Election Board*: Voter ID, 5–4? If So, So What?' *Election Law Journal* 7(1): 63–83.

Gadkari, S.S. 1996. *Electoral Reforms in India*. New Delhi: Wheeler Publishing.

Gilmartin, David. 2007. 'Election Law and the "People" in Colonial and Postcolonial India.' In *From the Colonial to the Postcolonial: India and Pakistan in Transition*, edited by Dipesh Chakrabarty, Rochona Mujumdar, and Andrew Sartori. New Delhi: Oxford University Press.

———. 2009. 'One Day's Sultan: T. N. Seshan and Indian Democracy.' *Contributions to Indian Sociology* 43(2): 247–84.

Gowda, M.V. Rajeev and E. Sridharan. 2012. 'Reforming India's Party Financing and Election Expenditure Laws.' *Election Law Journal: Rules, Politics, and Policy* 11(2): 226–40.

Guha, Ramchandra. 2002. 'The Biggest Gamble in History.' *The Hindu Magazine*, 27 January.

———. 2008. 'The Career of a Concept', *The Hindu*, 1 January.

Hansen, Thomas Blom. 2000. *Wages of Violence: Naming and Identity in Postcolonial Bombay*. Princeton: Princeton University Press.

Hauser, Walter and Wendy Singer. 1986. 'The Democratic Rite: Celebration and Participation in the Indian Elections.' *Asian Survey* 26(9): 941–58.

Hussain, Monirul. 1993. *The Assam Movement: Class, Ideology and Identity*. New Delhi: Manak Publications.

International Institute for Democracy and Electoral Assistance (IDEA). 1999. *Code of Conduct for Political Parties: Campaigning in Democratic Elections*. Stockholm: International IDEA.

Jauregui, Beatrice. 2017. *Provisional Authority: Police, Order and Security in India*. Ranikhet: Permanent Black.

Jorgen, Elklit and Andrew Reynolds. 2005. 'A Framework for the Systematic Study of Election Quality.' *Democratization* 12(2): 147–62.

Kapur, Devesh. 2005. 'Explaining Democratic Durability and Economic Performance.' In *Political Institutions in India: Performance and Design*, edited by Devesh Kapur and Pratap Bhanu Mehta. New Delhi: Oxford University Press.

Kapur, Devesh and Milan Vaishnav, eds. 2018. *Costs of Democracy: Political Finance in India*. New Delhi: Oxford University Press.

Kapur, Devesh and Pratap Bhanu Mehta, eds. 2005. *Political Institutions in India: Performance and Design*. New Delhi: Oxford University Press.

———. 2007. *Public Institutions in India: Performance and Design*. Oxford India Paperbacks. New Delhi: Oxford University Press.

Karp, Jeffrey, Alessandro Nai, Miguel Angel Lara Otaola, and Pippa Norris. 2017. *Professional Electoral Management: Building Capacity*. The Electoral Integrity Project, University of Sydney.

Kashyap, Subhash. 2000. 'Need to Review the Working of the Constitution.' In *Reviewing the Constitution?*, edited by Subhash Kashyap, D.D. Khanna, and Gert W. Kueck. New Delhi: Shipra Publications.

Katju, Manjari. 2009. 'Election Commission and Changing Contours of Politics.' *Economic and Political Weekly* 44(16): 8–12.

Kaur, Rajkumari Amrit. n.d. 'Women under the New Constitution.' In *Our Cause*, edited by Shyam Kumari Nehru. Allahabad: Kitabistan.

Kaviraj, Sudipta. 2000. 'Democracy and Social Inequality.' In *Transforming India*, edited by Francine Frankel, Zoya Hasan, Rajeev Bhargava, and Balveer Arora. New Delhi: Oxford University Press.

———. 2003. 'A State of Contradictions: The Post-Colonial State in India.' In *State and Citizens: History, Theory, Prospects*, edited by Quentin Skinner and Bo Strath. Cambridge: Cambridge University Press, pp. 144–63.

Kelly, Judith G. 2012. *Monitoring Democracy: When International Election Observation Works, and Why It Often Fails*. Princeton: Princeton University Press.

Khilnani, Sunil. 2004. *The Idea of India*. New Delhi: Penguin Books.

Kothari, Rajni, 1970. *Politics in India*. New Delhi: Orient Longman.

———. 1989a. *Politics and the People: In search of a Humane India*. Vol. II. New Delhi: Ajanta Prakashan.

———. 1989b. *State against Democracy: In Search of Humane Governance*. New Delhi: Ajanta Publications.

Kymlicka, Will. 1996. *Multicultural Citizenship: A Liberal Theory of Minority Rights*. Oxford: Clarendon Press.

Laperruque, Jake, 'Voter Access, Not Voter Fraud, Is a Pressing National Security Issue', *Just Security*, 13 July 2017 at 2:56 PM. Available at https://www.justsecurity.org/43062/voter-access-voter-fraud-pressing-national-security-issue/; accessed on 7 December 2017.

Lyngdoh, James Michael. 2004. *Chronicle of an Impossible Election*. New Delhi: Penguin.

McMillan, Alistair. 2010. 'The Election Commission.' In *The Oxford Companion to Politics in India*, edited by Niraja Gopal Jayal and Pratap Bhanu Mehta. New Delhi: Oxford University Press.

———. 2012. 'The Election Commission of India and the Regulation and Administration of Electoral Politics.' *Election Law Journal* 11(2): 187–201.

Mehta, Pratap Bhanu. 2003. *The Burden of Democracy*. New Delhi: Penguin.

———. 2010. 'What Is Constitutional Morality?' *Seminar* 615: 17–22.

Mehta, Uday. 2010. 'Constitutionalism.' In *The Companion Volume to Politics in India*, edited by Niraja Gopal Jayal and Pratap Bhanu Mehta. New Delhi: Oxford University Press.

Mohanty, Manoranjan, ed. 2004. 'Social Movements in a Creative Society.' In *Caste, Class, Gender*. New Delhi: SAGE.

Mozaffar, Shaheen and Andreas Schedler. 2002. 'The Comparative Study of Electoral Governance—Introduction.' *International Political Science Review* 23(1): 5–27.

Narayan, R.K. 2000. *The Story Teller's World: Essays, Sketches, Stories*. New Delhi: Penguin.

National Commission to Review the Working of the Constitution (NCRWC). 2000. 'Review of Election Law, Processes and Reform Options.' Consultation paper, National Commission to Review the Working of the Constitution, New Delhi.

Norris, Pippa. 2004. *Electoral Engineering: Voting Rules and Political Behavior*. New York: Cambridge University Press.

———. 2014. *Why Electoral Integrity Matters*. New York: Cambridge University Press.

———. 2015. *Why Elections Fail*. New York: Cambridge University Press.

———. 2017. *Strengthening Electoral Integrity*. New York: Cambridge University Press.

Norris, Pippa, Ferran Martinez i Coma, Alessandro Nai, and Max Gromping. 2010. 'Perceptions of Electoral Integrity, (PEI-4.5)', Harvard Dataverse, V2, UNF:6:dYcaQxA/dze+6Q4cMRMv1w== [fileUNF], 18 August. Available at https://doi.org/10.7910/DVN/LYO57K; accessed on 10 December 2018.

Norris, Pippa, Richard Frank, and Ferran Martinez I Coma. 2014. 'Measuring the Quality of Elections: A New Dataset.' *PS: Political Science and Politics* 47(4): 789–98.

Pillai, K. Shankar. *Don't Spare me Shankar', Cartoons from Shankar's Weekly*. New Delhi: CBT.

Plotke, David. 1997. 'Representation Is Democracy.' *Constellations* 4(1): 19–34.

Pritchett, Lant. 2009. 'Is India a Flailing State? Detours on the Four Lane Highway to Modernization.' HKS Faculty Research Working Paper Series RWP09-013, John F. Kennedy School of Government: Harvard University.

Quraishi, S.Y. 2014. *An Undocumented Wonder: The Making of the Great Indian Election*. New Delhi: Rupa Publications.

Rangarajan, Mahesh. 2001. 'Electoral Democracy and Social Aspirations in India.' Paper presented at the international symposium on Global Dimension of Electoral Democracy, Election Commission of India Golden Jubilee Celebrations, New Delhi, 18 January.

Rao, Amiya. 1983. 'Violence and Elections: Flexible Conscience.' *Economic and Political Weekly* 53(26): 1142.

Roy, Ajit. 1975. *Political Power in India: Nature and Trends*. Calcutta: Noya Prokash.

Roy, Anupama. 2005. *Gendered Citizenship: Historical and Conceptual Explorations*. New Delhi: Orient Longman.

———. 2010. *Mapping Citizenship in India*. New Delhi: Oxford University Press.

Roy, Profulla. 1984. *Left Experiment in West Bengal*. New Delhi: Patriot Publishers.

Rao, Ritu. 2004. 'Assessing the Electoral System: A Positive Verdict.' *Economic and Political Weekly* 39(51): 5437–40.

Rudolph, Lloyd I. and Susanne Hoeber Rudolph. 2001. 'Redoing the Constitutional Design: From an Interventionist to a Regulatory State.' In *The Success of India's Democracy*, edited by Atul Kohli. Cambridge: Cambridge University Press, pp. 127–62.

———. 2008. 'Redoing the Constitutional Design: From an Interventionist to a Regulatory State.' In *Explaining Indian Democracy: A Fifty-Year Perspective, 1956–2006, Vol. II: The Realm of Institutions: State Formation and Institutional Change*, edited by Lloyd I. Rudolph and Susanne Hoeber Rudolph. Oxford Collected Essays. New Delhi: Oxford University Press.

Rudolph, Susanne Hoeber and Lloyd I. Rudolph. 1987. *In Pursuit of Lakshmi*. New Delhi: Orient Longman.

Sadiq, Kamal. 2009. *Paper Citizens: How Illegal Migrants Acquire Citizenship in Developing Countries*. New York: Oxford University Press.

Schedler, Andreas. 2006. *Electoral Authoritarianism: The Dynamics of Unfree Competition*. Boulder and London: Lynne Rienner.

Scott, David. 1995. 'Colonial Governmentality.' *Social Text* 43: 191–220.

SDSA. 2008. *State of Democracy in South Asia: A Report*. New Delhi: Oxford University Press.

Shani, Ornit. 2018. *How India Became Democratic: Citizenship and Making of the Universal Franchise*. Gurugram: Penguin/Viking.

Shiva Rao, B., ed. 1968. *The Framing of India's Constitution: Select Documents*. Vol. I–VI. New Delhi: Indian Institute of Public Administration.

———. 1968. *The Framing of India's Constitution: Select Documents*. Vol. IV. New Delhi: Indian Institute of Public Administration.

Singh, Gurharpal. 2000. *Ethnic Conflict in India: A Case Study of Punjab*. London: Macmillan Press.

Singh, Ujjwal Kumar. 2004. *Institutions and Democratic Governance: A Study of the Election Commission and Electoral Governance in India*. NMML Monograph No. 9. New Delhi: Nehru Memorial Museum and Library.

Singer, Wendy. 2007. *A Constituency Suitable for Ladies*. New Delhi: Oxford University Press.

Sridharan, E. 2001a. 'Reforming Political Finance.' *Seminar* 506. Available at https://www.india-seminar.com/2001/506/506%20e.%2sridharan.htm; accessed on 20 April 2017.

———. 2001b. 'The Global Spread of Democracy—Reflections at the Beginning of the Twenty-First Century.' Paper presented at the international symposium on Global Dimension of Electoral Democracy, Election Commission of India Golden Jubilee Celebrations, New Delhi, 18 January.

Sridharan E. and Milan Vaishnav. 2017. 'Election Commission of India.' In *Rethinking Public Institutions in India*, edited by Devesh Kapur and Pratap Bhanu Mehta. New Delhi: Oxford University Press.

————. 2018. 'Political Finance in a Developing Democracy.' In *Costs of Democracy: Political Finance in India*, edited by Devesh Kapur and Milan Vaishnav. New Delhi: Oxford University Press.

Sunny, K.C. 2000. 'Election Laws.' In *Fifty Years of the Supreme Court of India*, edited by S.K. Verma and Kusum Kumar. New Delhi: Oxford University Press.

Swami, Praveen. 2001. 'Through the Pir Panjal Range.' *Frontline* 18(14). Available at https://frontline.thehindu.com/static/html/fl1814/18140650.htm; accessed on 20 April 2017.

Thiruvengadam, Arun K. 2017. *The Constitution of India: A Contextual Analysis*. New Delhi: Bloomsbury.

Thompson, Dennis F. 2004. 'Election Time: Normative Implications of Temporal Properties of the Electoral Process in the United States.' *American Political Science Review* 98(1): 51–64.

Urbinati, Nadia. 2000. 'Representation as Advocacy: A Study of Democratic Deliberation.' *Political Theory* 28(6): 758–86.

Vaishnav, Milan. 2017. *When Crime Pays: Money and Muscle in Indian Politics*. Noida: Harper Collins.

Venkatesan, V. 2002. 'Identity Questions', *Frontline* 19(5). Available at https://frontline.thehindu.com/static/html/fl1905/19050250.htm; accessed 12 April 2017.

Weiner, Myron. 1965. 'India: Two Political Cultures.' In *Political Culture and Political Development*, edited by Lucian Pye and Sydney Verba. Princeton: Princeton University Press.

————. 1977. 'The Indian Election—A Diary.' Centre for International Studies, MIT, Cambridge, Massachusetts, pp. 1–53. Available at https://dspace.mit.edu/bitstream/handle/1721.1/81918/03064421.pdf; 10 February 2016.

————. 1978. *India Votes 1977*. Washington: American Enterprise Institute for Public Policy Research.

————. 1983. 'The Political Demography of Assam's Anti-Immigrant Movement.' *Population and Development Review* 9(2): 279–92.

Yadav, Yogendra. 1997. 'Reconfiguration in Indian Politics: State Assembly Elections 1993–1995.' In *State and Politics in India*, edited by Partha Chatterjee. New Delhi: Oxford University Press, pp. 177–207.

————. 1999. 'Electoral Politics in the Time of Change: India's Third Electoral System, 1989–99.' *Economic and Political Weekly* 34(34/35): 2393–9.

————. 2000. 'Which Reforms? Whose Democracy? A Plea for a Democratic Agenda of Electoral Reforms.' In *Reviewing the Constitution?*, edited by Subhash Kashyap, D.D. Khanna, and Gert W. Kueck. New Delhi: Shipra Publications.

————. 2010. 'Representation.' In *The Oxford Companion to Politics in India*, edited by Niraja Gopal Jayal and Pratap Bhanu Mehta. New Delhi: Oxford University Press.

Young, Iris Marion. 1989. 'Polity and Group Difference: A Critique of the Idea of Universal Citizenship.' *Ethics* 99(2): 250–74.

————. 1997. 'Deferring Group Representation.' In *Ethnicity and Group Rights*, edited by Ian Shapiro and Will Kymlicka. New York: New York University Press.

ळ૦

Index

☙

About the Authors

Ujjwal Kumar Singh is professor at the Department of Political Science, University of Delhi, India. He has been writing on a range of themes including democracy and social movements, law and democracy, and political institutions in India. He is the author of *Political Prisoners in India* (1998) and *The State, Democracy and Anti-Terror Laws in India* (2007). He has also co-edited *Towards Legal Literacy: An Introduction to Law in India* (2008) and *Human Rights and Peace: Ideas, Laws, Institutions and Movements* (2009). His articles have appeared in several national and international journals. He has been a visiting fellow at universities in India, Australia, China, and Germany. He was the ICCR Rajeev Gandhi Visiting Chair Professor in Contemporary Indian Studies at University of Technology, Sydney, Australia, in 2012.

Anupama Roy is professor at the Centre for Political Studies, Jawaharlal Nehru University, New Delhi, India. Her research interests straddle legal studies, political anthropology of political institutions, political ideas, and gender studies. She is the author of *Gendered Citizenship: Historical and Conceptual Explorations* (2005), *Citizenship in India* (2016), and *Mapping Citizenship in India* (2010). She has also co-edited *Poverty, Gender and Migration in South Asia*

(2006). Her research articles have been published in national and international journals, and she has been a visiting scholar in universities in United Kingdom, Australia, and Germany.

൶